Ethnic Group Politics

Merrill Political Science Series

Under the editorship of

John C. Wahlke

Department of Political Science
The University of Iowa

Ethnic Group Politics

EDITED BY

Harry A. Bailey, Jr.
Ellis Katz

Temple University

CHARLES E. MERRILL PUBLISHING COMPANY
A Bell & Howell Company
Columbus, Ohio

Standard Book Number: 675-09436-4

Library of Congress Card Catalog Number: 73-85819

1 2 3 4 5 6 7 8 9 10 − 73 72 71 70 69

Printed in the United States of America

TO MARY BAILEY AND BARBARA KATZ

Preface

Given the tremendous heterogeneity of Americans, it is not surprising that social scientists have developed a voluminous literature on ethnic groups. However, it is unfortunate that the best of this literature has not been readily available to undergraduate students. Indeed, in political science, there has been a curious reluctance to give the politics of ethnic groups more than fleeting concern in the classroom. One partial explanation for this is that Americans generally have been loath to admit that ethnic loyalties could exert any influence on the making of American public policy. While we have recognized the legitimacy of political interests based upon geography, occupation, and even income, we have conceived of political interest based upon ethnicity as "un-American" and have often sought to stamp out such influences. Yet, as Moses Rischin has succinctly put it: "Political accommodation to the multi-ethnic character of American society has a long history, and the balanced ticket has become an axiom of American party politics, a normal expression of the American system."[1] In recent years, possibly because of an aroused interest in Negroes and civil rights and the election of a Catholic as President in 1960, political scientists have given more attention to the various political behaviors that characterize distinct ethnic groups.

We have brought together what we consider to be the best available literature in the social sciences on the ubiquity of ethnic group behavior and influence in American politics. Before we proceed, however, it is important to spell out what we mean when we speak of ethnic groups. First, men are separated from each other by

---

[1]Moses Rischin, *Our Own Kind: Voting by Race, Creed or National Origins* (Santa Barbara, California: Center for the Study of Democratic Institutions, 1960), p. 5.

differences which are racial, religious or national in character as well as by real or assumed physiological and cultural traits.[2] The result of these differences is the continuity of groups whose members are seen as sharing a unique social and cultural heritage. In this book, then, ethnic group is used as the generic term to cover racial, religious, or nationality groups in the United States who are assumed to possess certain traits, real or affective, distinctive from those of the larger population.[3] Nationality groups falling into this category usually, but not always, have their origins in other than Anglo-Saxon countries.[4]

It is not enough, however, for us to say that men are separated from each other solely because they are different racially, religiously, or nationally. A much more fundamental question is: do so-called ethnic group members identify along the lines which allegedly separate them? In short, is there such a thing as ethnic identification? The answer is an emphatic *yes*. There is substantial evidence that large numbers of people exhibit a propensity to use racial, religious or national affiliation to identify themselves and thereby to relate themselves to others. Indeed, studies of Negro children of nursery and primary school age, for example, indicate that identification on the basis of racial differences begins at that early age.[5] Jewish children of the same age group are known also to identify in religious terms.[6]

That ethnic group identification is real can be seen in many additional forms. Numerous agencies in the United States are organized by nationality groups[7] as well as by racial and religious

[2]See Peter I. Rose, *They and We: Racial and Ethnic Relations in the United States* (New York: Random House, 1964), p. 11; and Marian D. Irish and James W. Prothro, *The Politics of American Democracy* (Fourth edition; Englewood Cliffs, N. J.: Prentice-Hall, Inc., 1968), p. 194.

[3]Our view coincides with that of E. K. Francis. See his "The Nature of the Ethnic Group," *American Journal of Sociology,* LII (March, 1947), 393-400. See also Daniel Glazer, "Dynamics of Ethnic Identification," *American Sociological Review,* Vol. 23 (February, 1958), 31; and Emmett S. Redford, *et al., Politics and Government in the United States* (Second National Edition; New York: Harcourt, Brace, and World, Inc., 1965), p. 250.

[4]The Irish-Americans who were considered "ethnics" in an earlier day are a case in point.

[5]Mary E. Goodman, *Race Awareness in Young Children* (Reading, Mass.: Addison-Wesley Publishing Co., Inc., 1952), *passim.*

[6]Marian Radke Yarrow, "Personality Development and Minority Group Membership," in Marshall Sklare, ed., *The Jews* (New York: The Free Press of Glencoe, Inc., 1958), p. 455.

[7]Y. J. Chyz and R. Lewis, "Agencies Organized by Nationality Groups in the United States," *The Annals of the American Academy of Political and Social Sciences,* 262 (March, 1949), 148-158.

groups. Second, the existence of ethnic group identification can be
seen in the large numbers of foreign language publications in the
United States estimated to have a circulation of over ten million.[8]
Third, ethnic groups carry on a great many "separate" social activities. As Michael Parenti has said, "in a single weekend in New
York separate dances for persons of Hungarian, Irish, Italian, German,
and Polish extractions are advertised in the neighborhood newspapers
and the foreign language press.[9] Finally, as we intend to show,
ethnic groups behave in distinctive ways in the American political
system.

The articles brought together and presented here are based on the
thesis that ethnic identifications do exist and that one cannot really
understand the American political process without giving special
attention to racial, religious and national minorities. More important, we assume that the American scheme provides an ample
framework through which these ethnic minorities can conflict and
compromise their differences both among the separate ethnic groups
and the larger polity. Our final judgment is, despite the movement
of the country toward what some social scientists term "the mass
society," racial, religious and nationality identifications continue to
be powerful influences on political behavior.

It is difficult to determine precisely what should be included in a
"frontier" book of readings. In the final analysis our own understand-
ings regarding the subject matter and considerations of representativeness of the materials and space determined the articles presented.
While there are other examples of ethnic groups on the American
scene, some of which are included in the book, it is our assumption
that domestically, Negroes, Jews and Catholics are the most significant in American politics and thus of greater consequence for our
purposes. The bulk of our effort is devoted to these groups.

The book is divided into four parts. Introductions are provided
for each part to place the readings in meaningful perspective.
Part 1 deals with the historical dimensions of the categories and
identification of race, religion and nationality background. Part 2 is
concerned with social and psychological forces at work which lead
people of different ethnic groups to different patterns of political
behavior and seeks to document the differential political behavior
by the standard of voting in national elections. Part 3 is an effort to

---

[8]Louis Gerson, *The Hyphenate in Recent American Politics and Diplomacy*
(Lawrence: The University of Kansas Press, 1964), p. 23.

[9]Michael Parenti, "Ethnic Politics and the Persistence of Ethnic Identification," *American Political Science Review,* LXI (September, 1967), 719n.

determine to what extent people of different ethnic groups have been assimilated into the political process in the urban local framework. Finally, Part 4 deals with the extent to which ethnicity will continue to be an important variable in the explanation of political behavior.

For both of us, this was our first joint venture. As such it was remarkably free of conflict and frustration. Our names appear in alphabetical order, but the book is in every way a joint enterprise; a product of our common effort. Generally, both of us found ourselves in close agreement on theoretical positions and substantive concerns. The comments of the reviewers of the manuscript, Brett Hawkins, Matthew Holden, Jr., Maurice Klain, Allan P. Sindler, and John Wahlke, were very useful in our determination of the final product, but we are solely responsible for all errors of fact or interpretation that may appear in the book.

We wish to acknowledge the aid of Miss Linda Scherr for typing assistance and Mr. Hershel Kozlov and Misses Judith Ann Cole, Sarah Elpern, and Mary-Jane Roth who aided in the collection of material.

Harry A. Bailey, Jr. and
Ellis Katz

Temple University
Philadelphia, Pennsylvania
July, 1969

Contributors

ANGUS CAMPBELL, Director of the Survey Research Center at the University of Michigan, is interested in political psychology and is the co-author of *The American Voter* and *Elections and the Political Order.*

STOKELY CARMICHAEL is a well-known advocate of black power and is the former chairman of the Student Non-Violent Coordinating Committee. He is the co-author of the recent best-seller, *Black Power: The Politics of Liberation in America.*

PHILIP E. CONVERSE, Professor of Political Science and Sociology and Program Director of the Survey Research Center at the University of Michigan, is mainly interested in voting behavior. He is co-author of *The American Voter, Social Psychology: The Study of Human Interaction,* and *Elections and the Political Order.* In addition, his articles have appeared in such journals as the *American Political Science Review* and *Public Opinion Quarterly.*

ELMER E. CORNWELL, JR., Professor and Chairman of the Department of Political Science at Brown University, is interested in American government and politics and has authored or co-authored several books, including *Presidential Leadership of Public Opinion, The New Deal Mosaic,* and *The American Presidency: Vital Center.*

ROBERT A. DAHL is Sterling Professor of Political Science at Yale University and is well known for all his work in American political theory and community politics. His books include *Congress and Foreign Policy, A Preface to Democratic Theory,* and *Who Governs.*

E. U. ESSIEN-UDOM, Professor of Political Science, University of Ibadan, Ibadan, Nigeria, is known for his work on the American

Negro. He is the author of *Black Nationalism,* an analysis of the Black Muslim Movement in America.

JOHN HOPE FRANKLIN, Professor and Chairman of the Department of History at the University of Chicago, is a well known scholar in the field of Negro History. His most recent writings appeared in the *Journal of Southern History,* the *Journal of Negro History,* and *Daedalus.* His books include *From Slavery to Freedom: A History of American Negroes* and *Reconstruction After the Civil War.*

LAWRENCE H. FUCHS, Professor of American Civilization and Politics at Brandeis University, is interested in culture and personality, ethnicity and politics, and American values and character. His books include *The Political Behavior of American Jews* and *American Ethnic Politics.*

OSCAR GLANTZ, Associate Professor of Sociology at Brooklyn College, has done work in the field of political sociology. His articles have appeared in such journals as the *American Sociological Review, Western Political Quarterly, Journal of Negro History,* and *Public Opinion Quarterly.*

NATHAN GLAZER, Professor of Sociology at the University of California at Berkeley, is interested in urban problems and social policy. He is the author of several books, including *American Judaism, The Social Basis of American Judaism,* and *Beyond the Melting Pot* (with Daniel P. Moynihan).

SCOTT GREER, Professor of Sociology and Political Science at Northwestern University, is interested in social organization, urban sociology and political sociology. He is the author of several books including *Metropolitics: A Study of Political Culture* (with Norton Long), and *Urban-Renewal and American Cities.*

CHARLES HAMILTON is Professor and Chairman of the Department of Political Science at Roosevelt University. He is known for his work in urban affairs and Negro politics and his articles have appeared in such journals as the *Wisconsin Law Review, The Journal of Negro Education,* and the *Journal of Human Relations.*

OSCAR HANDLIN is the Director of the Charles Warren Center for Studies in American History at Harvard University and is well known for his work on the history of American ethnic groups. He has written numerous books, including *Immigrations as a*

Factor in American History, The Americans, and *The Newcomers: Negroes and Puerto Ricans in a Changing Metropolis.*

WILL HERBERG is at Drew University and is well known for his work on American religion. Among his books are *Judaism and Modern Man, Protestant-Catholic-Jew,* and *Community, State, and Church.*

ROBERT E. LANE, Professor of Political Science at Yale University, is interested in political thinking, ideology formation, and political behavior. He is the author of many articles and books, including *Political Life* and *Political Ideology.*

DWAINE MARVICK, Professor of Political Science at the University of California at Los Angeles, is interested in the areas of political recruitment, party organizational structure and political communications. He is the author or co-author of *Political Decision Makers: Recruitment and Performance* and *Competitive Pressure and Democratic Consent,* as well as numerous articles.

WARREN E. MILLER is the Program Director of the Political Behavior Project at the Survey Research Center at the University of Michigan. He is interested in electoral behavior and is the co-author of *The Voter Decides, The American Voter,* and *Elections and the Political Order.* His articles have been published in such journals as the *American Political Science Review, Journal of Politics* and *Public Opinion Quarterly.*

DANIEL P. MOYNIHAN is Assistant to the President for Urban Affairs. He has served on many governmental commissions dealing with civil rights and Negro politics and his books include *Beyond the Melting Pot* (with Nathan Glazer), *Poverty in America* (with Margaret S. Gordon and others), and *The Negro Challenge to the Business Community* (with Eli Ginzberg and others).

MICHAEL J. PARENTI is in the Department of Political Science at Sarah Lawrence College and is interested in the areas of American politics, ethnic politics, and political sociology. He is the author of *The Anti-Communist Impulse* and *Power and the Powerless* as well as articles which appeared in *Social Research, Journal for the Scientific Study of Religion,* and the *American Political Science Review.*

DONALD E. STOKES, Professor of Political Science and Program Director of the Survey Research Center at the University of Michigan, is doing work on the comparative study of elites. He is the co-author of *The American Voter* and *Elections and the Political Order,* as well as numerous articles.

JAMES Q. WILSON, Professor of Government at Harvard University, has written a number of articles in the fields of minority group problems, police behavior, voting, and urban issues. His books include *Negro Politics, The Amateur Democrat* and *City Politics* (with Edward Banfield).

Contents

Part 3   Ethnic Groups and Urban Politics

Part 4   The Persistence of Ethnic Group Politics

Ethnic Group Politics

Part 1

Nationality, Religious and Racial Divisions in American Society

The view that politics involves the "authoritative allocation of values"[1] involves the notion that there is conflict in the society over which values should be allocated. In the American political system this notion of conflict is well accepted, and one recognizes the legitimacy of individuals organizing into groups to defend and promote their interests. One question of major importance is, around what interests are individuals likely to organize for political action? Or, stated somewhat more broadly, what characteristics of individuals are likely to be perceived as relevant bases for political activity?

Karl Marx saw all politics as class struggle. For him, the only meaningful division in industrial society was between the owners of the means of production and those who labored at the machines. Thus, for Marx, the only valid basis for political activity was an

---

[1]The phrase is David Easton's. See his *The Political System: An Inquiry Into the State of Political Science* (New York: Alfred A. Knopf, Inc., 1963), pp. 129-135.

1

individual's relationship to the means of production; he was either a member of the bourgeoisie or of the proletariat. Other characteristics of individuals—such as race, nationality, etc.—were false bases of organization which hindered the polarization of society along class lines. In other words, for Marx, and probably for many others, class politics were normal; any other kind of politics were abnormal.[2]

While Marxian analysis has certainly never been widely accepted in the United States, many social philosophers do seem to make a similar assumption concerning the "normalcy" of class politics. For example, James Madison (who wrote almost sixty-five years before Marx) seemed to consider the economic division in society as the most important. In the *Federalist No. 10*, where he developed his notion of "factions" most explicitly, he wrote that ". . . the most common and durable source of factions has been the various and unequal distribution of property. Those who hold and those who are without property have ever formed distinct interests in society."[3] For Madison, politics was the process by which these two basic factions conflicted and compromised their differences.

The reported findings of modern political scientists would seem to support both Marx and Madison. For example, it is often noted that in any given election, a majority of those high on the socio-economic scale support one candidate while those on the bottom of the scale tend to support the other.[4] Thus, elections in the United States tend to reflect a basic economic division in society.

However, while an election might tend to reflect economic divisions in society, it is by no means a mirror image. After all, *all* businessmen do not vote Republican and *all* labor union members do not vote Democrat. In fact, one often finds large blocs of high income people voting Democrat and large blocs of low income people voting Republican.[5] Crude economic determinism, which maintains that one's economic situation is the only causal factor relating to political behavior is not able to capture the complexity and subtlety of American politics. To fully understand the American political system, one must turn to *non-economic* divisions in the society, which might themselves be independent variables in the explanation of political behavior.

James Madison was not a crude economic determinist. While he did not deny the primacy of economics, he did recognize the existence of

[2]See, for example, Seymour Martin Lipset, *Political Man: The Social Bases of Politics* (Garden City: Doubleday & Co., Inc., 1963), pp. 270-278; and Hugh Bone and Austin Ranney, *Politics and Voters* (New York: McGraw-Hill Book Company, 1963), p. 32.

[3]Edward Mead Earle (ed.), *The Federalist* (New York: Random House, Inc., 1937), p. 56.

[4]Bone and Ranney, *op. cit.*, p. 25.

[5]*Ibid.*

other schisms in society that would lead to the creation of factions. Again in the *Federalist No. 10,* he wrote:

> The latent causes of faction are thus sown into the nature of man; and we see them everywhere brought into different degrees of activity, according to the different circumstances of civil society. A zeal for different opinions concerning religion, concerning government, and many other points, as well of speculation as of practice; an attachment to different leaders ambitiously contending for pre-eminence and power; or to persons of other descriptions whose fortunes have been interesting to the human passions, have, in turn, divided mankind into different parties, inflamed them with mutual animosity, and then rendered them much more disposed to vex and oppress each other than to co-operate for their common good.[6]

Thus, Madison's concept of politics was actually broader than mere class conflict. For him, politics could be understood as the constant and normal conflict that took place among all the major factions that made up society.

Madison suggests that while "the latent causes of faction are sown into the nature of man," they may or may not be relevant to political activity "according to the different circumstances of civil society." In other words, at different times, and under different conditions, different characteristics of individuals will become relevant for political activity. In the United States, three such characteristics have proven to be of great importance. National origin, religion and race continue to provide categorizations of major significance as characteristics that influence much of American politics.

Taken together, the concepts of nationality, religion and race form what is generally conceived of as ethnicity. Thus broadly conceived, there can be little doubt that ethnic groups constitute a shaping force for both the historical development and contemporary processes of American society and politics.

This broad concept of ethnic groups, which includes classifications based upon nationality, religion and race, is considerably more useful than one which would include only nationality groupings. Not only is this broader notion more in keeping with contemporary usage, but it also provides one with a framework to compare the experiences of different types of groups. For example, one question of great contemporary significance is the extent to which the situation of Negro-Americans can be compared with the experiences of other ethnic groups in an earlier day. The readings in this section, and throughout

---

[6]Earle, *op. cit.,* pp. 55-56.

the book, are designed to point out similarities and differences between the two situations.

The reasons why ethnicity has been, and continues to be, an important factor by which people locate and identify themselves in American society are explored and documented in the readings in this section. However, one reason of paramount importance has been the attitude of the majority toward the new ethnic group at any given time. Generally speaking, the existing majority has not been very tolerant of the newer immigrants. For example, religious dissenters were regularly exiled (and even worse) from the Massachusetts Bay Colony during the 1600's. The attitude of the Puritan majority toward such dissenters is perhaps best expressed by the following statement:

> I dare take it upon me to be the Herald of New England so far as to proclaim to all the world in the name of our colony that all Familists, Antinomians, Anabaptists, and other Enthusiasts shall have free liberty to keep away from us and such as will come be gone as fast as they can, the sooner the better. . . .[7]

Later, in the 1800's, Protestants unified and turned their joint effort to discriminating against the newer Catholic immigrants. Throughout the nineteenth century, and into the twentieth, Catholics were not only barred from various forms of political participation, but were often set upon and beaten by members of the Protestant community.[8] Starting in the 1880's, when mass immigration from Eastern Europe began, the American society created a whole complex of discriminatory practices which effectively prevented the new immigrants from full participation in the mainstream of American society. This reached a peak during and after the First World War when much of the drive to purify America was based upon society's unwillingness and inability to accept people of foreign birth.[9] Finally, Negro-Americans face a similar and much intensified pattern of discrimination today.[10]

---

[7]Nathaniel Ward, "The Simple Cobbler of Aggawam" as quoted in Donald E. Boles, *The Bible, Religion and the Public Schools* (Ames, Iowa: Iowa University Press, 1961), p. 14.

[8]For a fascinating chronicle of this, see Ray Billington, *The Protestant Crusade* (Chicago: Quadrangle Books, Inc., 1964).

[9]For an interesting study of the interaction between political dissent and ethnic background during this period, see Charles Lam Markmann, *The Noblest Cry: A History of the American Civil Liberties Union* (New York: St. Martin's Press, Inc., 1965), pp. 1-132, *passim*.

[10]The literature on American race relations is voluminous, but see Charles Silberman, *Crisis in Black and White* (New York: Random House, Inc., 1964).

There is a curious paradox in American attitudes toward ethnic groups. On the one hand, Americans have always expected the newer arrivals to become "American"—that is to say, to become like them. At the same time, however, Americans have consistently discriminated against immigrant groups and have sought to prevent them from becoming full American citizens. Thus there has never really been a "melting pot" in America: rather, there has been constant tension and struggle between the existing majority and the newer immigrants until such time as the immigrant group became powerful enough to gain some degree of acceptance and participation.

The response of the ethnic group to the discriminatory practices of the majority usually has been the development of an "in-group" feeling and the formation of voluntary associations based upon ethnicity. This is not to say that the only force leading to the development and persistence of ethnic loyalties has been the discriminatory practices of the majority, but its importance should not be underestimated. Nor does the formation of such ethnic associations mean that the members of the ethnic group have abandoned hope for integration into the larger society. As Oscar Handlin points out, the formation resulted in an understandable ambivalence on the part of the members of the minority group which advocated both integration and group solidarity at the same time. The current split between the "integrationists" and the advocates of black separatism is a contemporary example of this ambivalence.

The articles in this section are concerned with the reasons and implications of societal schisms based on national origin, religion, and race. Oscar Handlin, in the first article, traces the development and primacy of nationality identifications in American society. Will Herberg carries the Handlin analysis a step further, and suggests that traditional nationality classifications have been replaced by broader religious ones. Finally, the last article, by John Hope Franklin, is concerned with some of the reasons and consequences of the polarization of society according to race. Franklin's article should be read with great care since it points out many of the similarities and differences between the historical experiences of Negro-Americans and members of other ethnic groups.

Historical Perspectives on the American Ethnic Group

Oscar Handlin

It is a commonplace of both scholarly and popular comment that American society is pluralistic in its organization. The immense size of the country, its marked regional differences and diversity of antecedents have sustained complex patterns of association and behavior and have inhibited tendencies toward uniformity. Social action in the United States, therefore, is presumed to come not within large unitary forms but within a mosaic of autonomous groupings, reflecting the underlying dissimilarities in the population.

Yet it is significant that serious attention to the operations of these groups has focused primarily upon the pathology of their relations with one another. Discrimination and prejudice, tension and conflict have provided students with their primary subject matter, perhaps because these produced the problems of greatest contemporary urgency, perhaps because they produced the most visible and most dramatic manifestations. For whatever reason, the normal functioning of American pluralism has been relatively neglected.

The result has been a serious deficiency in the understanding of the past development and present structure of American society. Viewed

Reprinted from *Daedalus,* Vol. 90, No. 1 (Winter 1961), 220-232, with permission of the publisher. Copyright 1961 by the American Academy of Arts and Sciences.

only at the points of breakdown, its healthy operations have remained shadowy and obscure; and without a clear comprehension of how the system worked, it has been difficult to explain the causes of its occasional failures.

This paper deals with one important type of American group, that in which membership tended to be transmitted by birth from generation to generation. An individual generally identified himself as an Odd Fellow or a Californian, as a member of the American Medical Association of the United Mine Workers, through decisions he made in the course of his own lifetime. He was usually, although not always, a Jew or a Negro, a Yankee or an Irish-American, through forces which existed from the moment of his birth and over which he had relatively little control. Ethnic ties frequently influenced the broader range of associations in which any given person participated, but they form a discreet subject of investigation which had peculiar importance in the United States. The analysis which follows aims at providing an account of the historic reasons why that was so.

It was the conscious desire of those who planted the colonies that would later become the United States to reproduce the social order they had left in Europe, entire or in an improved form. Once it became clear that these were not simply to be provisional trading stations but permanent settlements, the residents attempted to re-create the unitary communities they had known at home. That effort would be repeated in the eighteenth and nineteenth centuries by each succeeding group of arrivals.

In each case it failed. The communities the emigrants left had been whole and integrated, and had comprehended the total life of their members. There was one church, as there was one state, one hierarchy of occupations and status, a fixed pattern of roles and expectations, and the individual was therefore located in a precise place that defined the whole range of his associations.

Cracks in the solidarity and homogeneity of these communities had already begun to appear in seventeenth-century Europe. They would widen and deepen as time went on. Moreover, the men and women who went to America were peculiarly those least fixed in their places—religious dissenters, servants with no masters, uprooted peasants, captives by force of arms, and the victims of economic disaster. Their intentions remained attached to the norms of the society that had cast them out, but their lives were unsettled from the moment of their departure, and could rarely be restored to the old grooves after the shattering experiences of migration.

Moreover, all the conditions of the New World were uncongenial to the reestablishment of the old community. Even as coherent a group as the Massachusetts Bay Puritans found it difficult to exclude the disruptive influences of the unfamiliar environment. The terms of life of the wilderness, the dispersal of settlements over great distances, the inability to maintain discipline or to create distinct lines of authority— all these vitiated every effort to restore the traditional whole community. These hostile elements were even more powerful to the southward of New England, where settlement was less purposefully directed and where it lacked the leadership of an elite inspired by religious zeal and armed with sacerdotal sanctions.

The American setting remained unfriendly to efforts to unify communal life in succeeding centuries. In the eighteenth and nineteenth centuries, uninterrupted territorial expansion was the most consequential element in the situation. The constant penetration of one frontier after another, each with its own challenge of an altered physical environment, was repeatedly unsettling to the men who advanced into them and to the societies they abandoned. Almost everywhere the concomitant was a spatial and social mobility that exerted a continued strain upon existing organizations and habitual modes of behavior. And, before the effects of that form of expansion had played themselves out, industrialization and urbanization created new sources of communal disorder. The results were unqualifiedly destructive of every effort to reconstitute whole communities that bore some resemblance to the transplanted or inherited images derived from European antecedents.

These tendencies received additional force from the heterogeneity of the American population, already notable in the seventeenth century and destined to be immensely increased thereafter. Diversity of sources ruled out the possibility that some myth of common origin might supply a basis for creating communal order; it juxtaposed different and sometimes contradictory ideals of what that order should be like; and it left prominently embedded in society conflicting interests and values. Furthermore, since the various elements stood in no clearly delineated relation of superiority and inferiority to one another, except in so far as slavery depressed the Negro, none could impose its own conceptions upon the rest. In a country in which Quakers and Presbyterians, Anglicans and Catholics, Jews and Baptists all coexisted and all had access to power, it was impossible to think of one state, one church. In towns where Yankees and Germans, Irishmen and Italians lived together, no single set of institutions could serve the social and cultural needs of the entire body of residents. Given these differences, American communitites could only be fragmented rather than whole, partial rather than inclusive.

The looseness of political institutions furthered the same results. Not through design but through the unanticipated circumstances of colonial settlement, authority was long only tentatively exercised and the state was long too weak to serve fully the functions expected of it. The resultant vacuum nurtured habits of spontaneous, voluntary action on the part of the citizens. Through disuse, some powers of government atrophied, and the spheres in which they had been applied came to be occupied by associations which operated, not with political sanctions, but with the unconstrained support of their members. A pervasive ideology that interpreted every relation between the individual and the larger groups to which he belonged as contractual and dependent upon his free acquiescence set these practices within a context of respected rights that were not readily to be violated. The end result was hostility toward large overarching organizations remote from their membership, and the encouragement of smaller bodies deriving their competence to act from the consent of their participants.

The fluidity of American society, the diversity of its population, and the looseness of its institutional forms interacted upon and stimulated one another. The results therefore were cumulative in the extent to which they inhibited the appearance of a unitary community, the various arms of which were organically articulated with one another. Despite frequent conscious efforts to guide developments in that direction, the people of the United States did not become homogeneous, nor were their modes of action integrated into common over-all forms.

The only exceptions appeared in pockets of population which, for one reason or another, became isolated from the dominant currents of American life. Relatively small groups—the Pennsylvania Amish, the Southern mountaineers, the farmers of Northern New England, for example—were able to achieve a solidarity and continuity of experience that elicited the admiration of romantic observers who set a high premium upon stability and tradition. But the price was social stagnation and detachment from the forces which shaped the rest of the nation. Indeed, the contrast offered by these aberrations is a measure of the extent to which the main lines of social organization led away from the unitary community.

The result was neither anarchy nor the casting adrift of the individual left to his own resources. Rather, the failure to create a single integrated community led to the appearance of numerous smaller bodies which operated within fragmented sectors of society. Their character can best be understood in terms of the forces that brought them into being.

Men no longer embraced within the sheltering fold of a whole community felt the pressure of two types of needs they could not satisfy alone. Important functions in their lives could only be executed in groups; and, in addition, deep-rooted emotional desires for personal association also called for common action.

The American who had left or had never been part of a community that by tradition and habit satisfied all his needs quickly became sensitive to his inability to deal with problems that extended beyond his own person. The round of ritual and the patterns of reaffirmed beliefs of which the church had been custodian lost their potency when performed or held in isolation. It was essential to create the communion that would make them effective even without the aid of the state and at no matter what cost.

The crises of death, disease, and poverty produced a dependency that was intolerable in isolation. The necessities of these situations were twofold, bearing both upon the victim and the witness of man's helplessness. The dread of improper burial after death, of wasting illness, and of want troubled everyone conscious that he might himself be stricken down; and the worry haunted Americans more than it did other peoples who could anticipate such crises as expected incidents within a familiar setting. Equally as important, the obligation to dispose of the corpse, to succor the ill and to aid the indigent (all of which often bore a religious connotation) troubled everyone who could foresee such challenges to his conscience. It was imperative therefore that these functions should be performed in a group and with a propriety that would console both the victim and the witness. Again, in the absence of a community that did so, it was necessary to bring into being the organized means for performing these functions.

An analogous need arose out of the disruption of communications that was a consequence of the breakdown of the old community. The culture which expressed men's attitudes and which provided them with emotional and esthetic satisfaction had been wrenched away from its traditional media. The threatened deprivation of a heritage that gave life meaning hastened Americans toward contriving new forms through which they could speak and listen to one another.

Yet in the process of creating the vast array of churches, philanthropic societies, and cultural institutions that became characteristic of the United States, the participants were moved not only by the importance of the functions to be served. They were influenced also by the personal need to belong to a group, whatever function it served. As individuals, they sought a sense of anchorage through identification with some larger entity, hoping thus to offset the effects of the unsettling elements of life in and on the way to America. The achievement of such an identification would provide some compensation, furthermore, for the psychological loss of the unitary community.

The distinctive qualities of family life in the United States made the need for anchorage to a group particularly acute there. Whether in the seventeenth century or the nineteenth, the extended family quickly shrank after immigration to the conjugal pair and its offspring. Detached from the community and often physically and socially isolated, the American family was thrown back upon its own resources; and uncertainty as to the roles of its members frequently produced severe internal tensions. Such conditions increased the desire for identification with a group that would provide the family with roots in the past, locate it in the larger society, and supply it both with a pattern of approved standards of behavior and with the moral sanctions to aid in maintaining internal discipline.

The wish to belong for the sake of identification and the wish to belong out of the need for some functional service coincided most nearly when it came to subjects about which men had inherited firmly implanted beliefs and attitudes. In satisfying the need for religious worship and ritual and in arming themselves against the contingencies of dependency, they were likely to use forms that would draw together people of a common heritage and thus also satisfy the need for a sense of belonging.

Within the complex pattern of American associational life, therefore, clusters of organizations which served discreet ends but which were linked by derivation from a common pool of membership appeared. That pool constituted the ethnic group. A shared heritage, presumed or actual, formed the matrix within which the group organized its communal life. That heritage, in the United States, was sometimes associated with descent from common national or regional origins, sometimes with color, and sometimes with religion. Some groups were already aware of their identity at arrival, as were the Jews of the seventeenth and eighteenth centuries; others, like the nineteenth-century Italians, only developed theirs through the experience of life in the New World. In either case, these were not monolithic entities but aggregates of individuals, often internally divided and sometimes unclear about the boundaries to which their membership extended.

The ethnic group by no means preempted the total social experience of Americans. Other associations drew their participants from sources only slightly delimited by considerations of antecedents. But ethnic groups were peculiarly important by virtue of their durability, which extended them across the generations, and by virtue also of the critical segments of personal life that they organized.

Not every individual, of course, fitted neatly into one ethnic box or another. Many, particularly in the large cities of the nineteenth and twentieth centuries, remained unaffiliated and unattached and drifted into the disorganization resulting from their lack of a fixed place. Others were torn by multiple identifications, which were the product either of mixed antecedents or of the incompatibility of individual interests and intentions with the norms of the group. Still others permitted themselves only a limited and partial affiliation, participating in some activities on some occasions and refraining from taking a part in others. But it was precisely in such flexibility that the strength of the ethnic group lay. By permitting men to organize their lives on their own terms, without compulsion and with a wide latitude of choice, the ethnic group provided them with the means of acting cooperatively in those sectors of life in which they felt the need to do so, and yet it refrained from imposing irksome restraints upon them. It thus supplanted the totally organized, integrated community with a fluid pattern of association, that left the individual as unconfined as he wished to be.

The American ethnic groups maintained their fluidity through a delicate balance between the forces that detached and those that connected their members to the society outside their boundaries. They were able to preserve their identity without becoming segregated or isolated enclaves in the total society. Functioning effectively over long periods, they nevertheless were inhibited from acquiring attributes that would have permanently and decisively set apart the individuals affiliated with them. That balance left room for wide areas of personal choice on the part of the members, to whose interests and ideas the group was necessarily sensitive.

The internal dynamics of many groups led them, at the same time, to seek to preserve their own identity and yet to reach out to influence and even absorb outsiders. These contradictory impulses were particularly characteristic, although by no means confined to groups of English descent, who felt a special compulsion to make their limits coextensive with the whole nation.

By the eighteenth century, a missionary spirit had dissolved the earlier exclusive sense of election that had formerly separated one element from another. The desire to bar outsiders gave way to an urge to assimilate them; and a variety of groups came to consider themselves in competition for new adherents. The rivalry for the loyalty of new members was stimulated thereafter by the constant appearance of new religious sects which conducted unremitting raids upon the unaffiliated or the loosely affiliated.

Yet the ability to make converts, either in the religious or social sense, demanded some accommodation to the tastes, interests, and ideas of those who were to be persuaded. No group could attract outsiders by stressing the unique qualities of its own antecedents. A subtle process of adjustment, therefore, found each drifting away from the particularities of its heritage and reaching out toward a more general view of itself that would confirm and strengthen its place in the whole society. Through the eighteenth and nineteenth centuries a gradual softening of exclusionary doctrines and practices and a general accommodation to a shared pattern of beliefs and behavior that might be termed "American" were manifestations of this process.

The desire to assimilate outsiders altered many ethnic organizations as these widened the scope of their endeavors. Quaker efforts at benevolence, for instance, originally directed within the group, acquired a universal character when the group recognized its obligations to the whole society. Institutions like those for higher education, which were established to serve a specific ethnic group, also changed as they expanded their appeal. The early sectarian colleges were thus driven toward a steady broadening of their social bases. The whole process of extending the boundaries of the group tended to dilute its ethnic character.

The competition for the loyalty of their members also affected those groups which had no clear missionary intentions. The Jews and Italians of 1900, for instance, aimed not at drawing other Americans within their folds, but simply at preserving their hold over their own adherents. But to do so, they had to offset the attractions of potential rivals by establishing their own images as fully American and by emphasizing the depth of their own roots in the country. That involved a sacrifice of their own particularity. To the extent that they celebrated Haym Solomon or Christopher Columbus, they drew attention to elements that made them similar to rather than different from other Americans. They could develop a capacity for resisting the incursions of other groups only by diminishing the range of differences that set them apart. The necessities of a situation in which a multitude of ethnic groups coexisted in an open society prevented any one of them from erecting walls about itself unless it wished to become completely isolated.

The situation remained open because some contact among the members of various groups was inescapable in important sectors of social action. The organization of American economic, political, and cultural life compelled individuals often to disregard ethnic lines.

There were significant degrees of concentration in the distribution of occupations by ethnic groups. That situation was in part a product of their members' common experience and common preparation for the job market. Irishmen who came to New York City in 1850 lacked the skill or capital for anything but unskilled labor; Yankee newcomers to the same city had the education and resources to go into trade or take places as clerks. Furthermore, ties of kinship, country of origin, and religion sometimes significantly affected the conduct of business and the access to opportunity. It was advantageous to be a Scotsman in mid-nineteenth-century Pittsburgh, as Andrew Carnegie discovered. Conversely, prejudice and discrimination barred the way to desirable situations. Young women who were colored or foreign in appearance were not likely to become secretaries to executives, no matter how competent they were.

Nevertheless, the American productive system did not tolerate the development of caste-like groupings. Individuals always found it possible to move upward. In the swiftly expanding, competitive order of American enterprise, in which success held a preeminent value and in which the dangers of catastrophic failure were always imminent, men could not afford to subordinate the calculations of the market place to noneconomic considerations. The entrepreneur, aware of his own interests, hired the most efficient hand, bought from the cheapest seller, sold to the highest bidder, or suffered in consequence. That course built into the economic system the necessity for cooperation across ethnic lines, and this grew steadily more compelling as business became less personal and more closely oriented to considerations of price and cost. Business, professional, and labor organizations, which often had a distinct ethnic character to begin with, felt a steady pressure, therefore, to make room for qualified outsiders.

So too, ethnic groups often formed significant voting blocs. Party allegiances, thus engaged, enjoyed considerable continuity over time and occasionally outweighed other considerations in determining the outcome of political contests. But no group formed a majority secure enough to hold power, except on a very local level; those who sought office or advantages through politics quickly recognized the necessity for developing alliances that transcended ethnic divisions. The machines of Boston and New York in 1910 were Irish, but they depended upon working arrangements with Germans, Jews, and Italians. As in the economy, the imperatives of politics in an open society prevented any group from maintaining exclusiveness for very long.

Out of the conditions of these and other contacts there grew a vast array of media for general communication. The newspapers, the public schools, television—all addressed individuals rather than the members of groups. Even when they began with a specific ethnic orientation, the advantages of reaching out for the largest possible audience transformed those which survived and expanded. In the long run, the more general the medium, the more powerful it became. Its influence, therefore, tended to break down group exclusiveness.

As a result, a given American at any moment located himself in society by a complex of reference points. He was a German, but also a Lutheran, a Republican, a farmer, a Midwesterner, a reader of the *Volkszeitung* and the *Tribune*, a Mason, and a member of the Turnverein. Not all these affiliations were purely ethnic, although there was an ethnic element in most of them; and not all had equal weight in his existence. Which were salient and which subordinate depended upon the particular configuration that established the individual's identity. The ethnic factor was important by virtue of its connections with the past, with the family, and with the most impressionable years in the development of the personality. But it receded in importance if it were isolated, if the man's German affiliations appeared only on infrequent occasions, while his primary associations as a citizen, a resident, and a producer had other contexts.

The fluidity of the social system increased the necessities for contact and added to the variety of individual configurations. A rough correlation was always discernible between social status and ethnic membership. While the pattern was certainly not consistent at every time and place, social and ethnic groupings tended to coincide. Recent immigrants generally entered the labor market at the bottom, a place commensurate with their want of skill, capital, and prestige. That circumstance established the low social character of the group. Italian peasants who migrated to the United States at the end of the nineteenth century were prepared only for unskilled labor; Italians therefore were identified as among the lowest social groups. But in turn, by association, any kind of work that Italians did was imputed to be inferior. In actuality, the group's experience and the reputation it acquired thus reinforced one another.

Nevertheless, the actuality was never as restrictive as the reputation. Occasionally individuals did succeed in rising in the social and occupational hierarchy; Giannini and Bellanca were not permanently held down by their antecedents. Social mobility was a genuine, although as yet unmeasured, feature of American life.

Some men who moved up passed out of the group of their origin and entered another more compatible with their new positions; social and religious conversion remained significant throughout American history. But whether such individuals altered their identification or not, social mobility opened important avenues of contact with other groups. The exceptional men who remained within the group of their birth played a significant mediating role. Their rise in status brought with it the eminence of outside recognition and of leadership within the group, and it also broadened their contacts with the rest of society, which treated them as spokesmen for the group. They were thus marginal, influenced by a variety of contacts, and subject to a multiplicity of expectations.

Within the groups that were the product of immigration, the rate of upward mobility seems certainly to have increased in the second and subsequent generations. The children of those who had moved were even more marginal than their parents; born within a group, they passed significant parts of their youth and adolescence outside it. They too became channels for contacts across ethnic lines that occurred with increasing frequency and intensity, for the group could survive only by adjusting to their changing interests.

Conversely, the range of contacts narrowed when a group was excluded permanently or temporarily from the opportunities of American society. The prejudice that depressed the Negroes, the discrimination that sometimes held back Jews and Caholics, not only turned these people defensively inward but also reduced the possibilities for mediation and for mutual interaction between them and others. The abatement of prejudice and discrimination therefore was almost an essential precondition for opening the group to the influence of the broader society.

Underlying all these relationships and further militating against the solidarity of the group was a spirit for which no better term is available than individualism. In the eighteenth century, and even more intensely in the nineteenth, the assumption had formed that every man was to be judged and treated as an individual, without consideration of his group affiliations. His place in society, by the American creed, was to be the product of his own efforts, independent of antecedents or inheritance or identification. There were certainly great deviations in actuality from this ideal, but it nevertheless remained a vital element in American thought.

Above all, this assumption implied that group interests were invariably to be subordinated to individual ones. The consequences were nowhere more clearly illustrated than in relationship to intermarriage. The defined posture of every ethnic group was a hostility to marriages that crossed its own lines; only through endogamy could the group perpetuate itself across the generations and secure its survival. Yet, while the statistics are notoriously inaccurate, there is no doubt that unions across group lines were frequent, barred neither by legal impediments nor by social disapproval except where color was involved.

Marriage in America was not a means of securing the continuity of the group but of satisfying the desire of the individual for fulfillment as a personality, apart from any social considerations. The theme of romantic love grew steadily in importance; and it emphasized the capacity of the individual to surmount the barriers of ethnic difference, as also those of class. It was symptomatic of the conviction that the values associated with the individual invariably took precedence over those of the group. It existed to serve him, not he, it.

Thus, the very provisions of American society that permitted the ethnic group to exist freely also permitted its members to adjust their identification to the needs of their own personalities. The strength of these groups, derived from the voluntary accession of their participants, could not be used to isolate or segregate them.

It is against this background that one can best understand the points of breakdown at which conflicts among ethnic groups have appeared. A variety of such groups coexisted without difficulty so long as a fluid social order maximized their members' freedom of association. That is why the periods of greatest immigration and greatest expansion were usually free of tension.

Conflicts appeared rather as the result of efforts to introduce rigidity into the system, most often when one group sought to assert its own preeminence and to impose its own standards upon the others. Nativism, for example, was not simply a battle of "Americans" against immigrants. It was, rather, the effort of particular ethnic groups, whose position was challenged by events over which they had little control, to maintain their earlier dominance under cover of a fixed conception of Americanism.

The extreme of conflict appeared when the terms of ethnic affiliation were so defined as to eliminate all fluidity and to separate unalterably one group from another. The racist ideology of the latter half of the nineteenth century thus categorized individuals by heredity and treated their identifications as genetically fixed. It threatened therefore to eliminate the possibilities for contact and free movement that had theretofore been the essential conditions of group life in the United States. The Negro, who was most clearly identified, most decisively isolated, and burdened with the imputation of inferiority from his past as a slave, was the most seriously threatened by these views. But the danger to other groups—like the Jews and the Italians—was also serious, only slightly less so than that to the Negroes.

In the last two decades, the dissolution of racist ideas has ended that threat to the fluid social order of the United States, at least for groups not stigmatized by color. And there is the promise that the extension of the same degree of equality to Negroes will relax the most important tensions in their relations with other Americans and provide them with the basis for a sound group life of their own.

From time to time, efforts at voluntary segregation have also posed a threat to the free functioning of the ethnic group in American society. It is certainly possible such tendencies may gain force in the coming years. The spread of suburban life, which reduces the anonymity of the individual, the desire for stability and security in personal relationships, the drive for conformity in patterns of behavior, and the pressure to belong to some group—no matter which—are all evidence of developments in this direction. Whether they will be able to counteract the forces that continue to encourage mobility and fluidity remains to be seen.

In any case, the ultimate measure of their effect upon the ethnic group will be the latitude left to the individual in choosing the associations within which he conducts his life. In a period in which the isolated individual must confront the immense powers of the state and of the other massive organizations of the naked society, mediating institutions, such as those provided by the ethnic group, can still serve important functions. They can provide him with legitimate means, by which he can assert his distinctive individuality if he wishes to do so. On the other hand, if these groups become rigid and fall into place among the other instruments by which the individual is controlled and regulated, then they become assimilated to the other massive organizations that crush rather than liberate him.

Religious Group Conflict in America

Will Herberg

Religious group conflict in contemporary America reflects the changing shape of American pluralism; and this pluralism is today essentially religious.

I The Shape of American Pluralism

In some sense, all societies, even the most monolithic, have been
pluralistic, for there has never been a society without a wide diversity
of interest, opinions, and conditions of life.

Yet, when we speak of a pluralistic society, we mean something
more. We mean a society in which diversities not only exist as a
matter of fact, but are recognized, accepted, perhaps even institution-
alized into the structure and functioning of the social order. In this
sense, American society is thoroughly pluralistic, but pluralistic in a
very special way, with its own characteristic freedoms and restrictions. The shape of American pluralism helps define the underlying
pattern of American life, within which emerge the so-called "intergroup" problems that confront us today in such a variety of shapes
and forms.

Reprinted with permission of Oxford University Press from Robert Lee and
Martin Marty (eds.) *Religion and Social Conflict*, pp. 143-158. Copyright 1964
by Oxford University Press.

The pluralism of American society is the product of its history, and therefore reflects its inmost being, for the inmost being of men and their societies is essentially historical. From the very beginning, America has been a land of diversity striving for unity. And from the very beginning, too, the diversities have been racial, ethnic, cultural, and religious, whereas the unity striven for has been that of a new "way of life" reflecting the "new order of the ages" established in the New World (*novus ordo seclorum,* the motto on the reverse of the Great Seal of the United States).

This was the vision that fired the imagination of Hector de Crèvecoeur, the author of the celebrated "letters from an American Farmer," who was so eager to interpret the new American reality to the New and Old World alike. "Here," Crèvecoeur proclaimed proudly in 1782, "individuals of all nations are melted into a new race of men, whose labors and posterity will one day cause great changes in the world." Thus early was the "melting pot" philosophy explicitly formulated, and thus early did the problem of unity amidst diversity, and diversity amidst unity, emerge as the perennial problem of American life.

The conception implied in the image of the "melting pot" (or the "transmuting pot," as George H. Stewart prefers to call it)[1] has always been subject to a misunderstanding that is itself not without significance. When, at least until recently, Americans spoke of the "melting pot" (the term as such did not come into use until the first decade of this century), they generally had in mind a process by which foreign "peculiarities" of language and culture which immigrants brought with them from the old country would be sloughed off in the course of Americanization, and a new homogeneous, undifferentiated type of American would come into being.

Against this, the apostles of "cultural pluralism" protested; they stressed the richness of the immigrant cultures, deplored their threatening dissolution, and advocated a multicultural, even a multinational society, along familiar European lines. Both groups—the theorists of the "melting pot" and the "cultural pluralists"—gravely misunderstood the emerging patterns of American pluralism.

American pluralism, through all its changes and mutations, has remained characteristically American, quite unlike the pluralistic patterns prevailing in other parts of the world. The sources of diversity have been different, and the expressions of it even more so. By and

---

[1]George R. Stewart, *American Ways of Life* (New York: Doubleday, 1954).

large, we may say that, since the latter part of the nineteenth century, the sources of American pluralism have been mainly race, ethnicity, and religion, with sectionalism or regionalism playing a diminishing, though in some cases still not insignificant, role. It is in terms of these that Americans have tended, and still tend, to define their identities amidst the totality of American life.

The process of enculturation perpetuates the pattern. When asked the simple question, "What are you?", Gordon W. Allport has noted, referring to certain recent researches, only 10 per cent of four-year-olds answer in terms of racial, ethnic, or religious membership, whereas 75 per cent of nine-year-olds do so. "Race" in America today means color, white versus non-white; and racial stigmatization has introduced an element of caste-like stratification into American life.

For white Americans, ethnicity and religion have been, and still remain, the major source of pluralistic diversity, although the relation between them has changed drastically in the course of the past generation. It is this change that provides a clue to an understanding of the shape of present-day American pluralism, and of the nature and sources of religious group conflict in present-day America.

As long as large-scale immigration continued, and America was predominantly a land of immigrants, in the days when "the immigrants *were* American history," as Oscar Handlin puts it, the dominant form of self-identification, and therefore the dominant form of pluralistic diversity, was immigrant ethnicity. Religion was felt to be part of the ethnic heritage, recent or remote. The enthusiasts of the "melting pot" were eager to eliminate this diversity as quickly as possible; the "cultural pluralists" were determined to perpetuate it; but both alike moved within a framework of a pluralism based substantially on ethnicity, ethnic culture, and ethnic religion.

Within the past generation, the picture has changed radically. The stoppage of mass immigration during World War I, followed by the anti-immigration legislation of the 1920's, undermined the foundations of the immigrant ethnic group with amazing rapidity. What it did was to facilitate the emergence of the third and post-third American generations, with their characteristic responses and attitudes, as a decisive influence in American life, no longer threatened with submergence by the next wave of immigration. This far-reaching structural change has, of course, been reflected in the shape and form of American pluralism.

Specifically, within the threefold American scheme of race, ethnicity, and religion, a shift has taken place from ethnicity to religion as the dominant form of self-identification, and therefore also in the dominant form of pluralistic diversity.[2] Ethnic identifications and traditions have not altogether disappeared. On the contrary, with the third generation, as Marcus Lee Hanson has cogently shown, they enjoy a lively popularity as symbols of "heritage."

But the relation of ethnicity and religion has been reversed: religion is no longer taken as an aspect of ethnicity; it is ethnicity, or rather what remains of it, that is taken up, redefined, and expressed through religious identifications and institutions. Religion—or, at least, the tripartite differentiation of Protestant, Catholic, Jew—has (aside from race) become the characteristic form of pluralistic diversity in American life. American pluralism is today (again aside from race) characteristically *religious* pluralism, and all problems of American unity and diversity, cooperation and conflict, have to be interpreted in the light of this great fact.

This shift from ethnicity to religion is well documented in the recent and most impressive of community surveys particularly concerned with religion—the Detroit metropolitan area survey of 1958, reported and interpreted by Gerhard Lenski in *The Religious Factor:*

> Among the possible trends cited above [Lenski states in his concluding chapter], one deserves special comment both because of its far-reaching implications and because many of these implications have received so little attention from the general public. This is the possible trend toward increased socio-religious communalism. As we noted, . . . communalism along socio-religious group lines seems to have been gaining in strength in recent years, and promises to continue to gain in the foreseeable future.
>
> This development is one which has been greatly hastened by the rapid decline of the older ethnic subcommunities in recent years. . . . Until about a generation ago, the American population was sharply divided into a rather large number of relatively small ethnic subcommunities. . . . These groups, however, were unable to preserve their organizational integrity in the face of the powerful and pervasive pressures to Americanize the immigrant, and intermarriage across ethnic group lines has now become quite common. . . . *The successor of the ethnic subcommunity is the socio-religious subcommunity. . . . There seems to be little doubt that socio-religious groups are rapidly replacing ethnic groups as the basic units in the system of status groups in American society.*[3]

---

[2]For a fuller discussion, see my *Protestant, Catholic, Jew* (New York: Doubleday-Anchor Books, 1955).

[3]Gerhard Lenski, *The Religious Factor* (New York: Doubleday, 1961), pp. 326-7 (emphasis mine).

Such is the emerging shape of American pluralism, within which intergroup conflicts today arise and take their course: it is a religious pluralism, a pluralism defined in terms of religious identification and belonging.

But American pluralism, it has often been noted, is not simply plurality; it is also unity: it is, in fact, best designated by the term *pluriunity*—a unity in plurality as well as a plurality in unity. *E pluribus unum:* this phrase, which was originally employed to celebrate the unification of thirteen colonies into the new nation, serves very well as the formula for American pluralism as that has developed through the decades since the Civil War.

What is this unity that supplies the centripetal force in American life, or (to change the image) the common framework within which the pluralistic allegiances find both their freedom and their limits? This unity is the unity of the *American way of life.*

It is not easy to put into words just what the American way of life is, or how it functions to provide the over-all unity for the pluralistic diversity of American society. Perhaps the most important thing to say about it is that, for the American, the American way of life is that by virtue of which he is an American. Americans, with their incredible diversity of race, culture, and national origin, find their unity, their common "Americanness," in their adherence to, and participation in, the American way of life. This provides them their common allegiance and their common faith: it provides them, to use the words of the sociologist Robin M. Williams, Jr., with "the common set of ideas, rituals and symbols" by which an "overarching sense of unity" is achieved amidst diversity and conflict. If the pluralism of contemporary American society is primarily a religious pluralism, the unity within which this pluralism is expressed and contained is a unity of the American way of life. Religious group conflict in contemporary America is conflict within this overarching unity.

II Protestant-Catholic Tensions: Some Facts and Factors

Because American pluralism today is basically a religious pluralism, the tensions that affect the religious communities would seem to be of special importance for the future of America and the unity of its people. It is these tensions I should like to discuss—particularly, the Protestant-Catholic tensions, which concern us most immediately; but also Jewish-gentile tensions, which, though at the moment not very prominent, we cannot altogether ignore.

When I say I am going to discuss Protestant-Catholic tensions, I do not mean that I am going to take up all the various matters that are alleged to be at issue between Protestants and Catholics in this country. Not that these matters are not real and important; they are. But there are two considerations we should bear in mind.

1. These questions at issue, however real and important, do not seem to me to be so much the cause of the tensions as their expression. They are not merely questions under discussion; they are what we call issues. They become issues precisely because they arise in an already established context of tension, and become vehicles of this tension and conflict.

2. These controverted questions, even though they become issues between Protestants and Catholics, and Jews too for that matter, are rarely if ever questions on which one group is aligned all on one side and the other group all on the other. On the contrary, on every one of these questions, there are differences and divisions in each of the three religious communities, with sizable minorities in each group crossing the lines. Only in a very limited sense can it be said that the three religious groups have their special social and cultural outlooks, conflict over which is engendering the group tensions we are concerned with.

The real sources of religious group tensions in the America of today seem to me to be emphatically pre-ideological, although no doubt they are quickly rationalized and ideologized. The tensions we are concerned with, particularly the Protestant-Catholic tensions, seem to me to emerge from a number of closely related social changes under way in this country today, with far-reaching repercussions upon the religious situation.

The first of these basic social changes directly affecting religious group relations is the transformation of America, within this present generation, from a "Protestant nation" to a "three-religion country."

Writing just about thirty-five years ago, André Siegfried, the French observer, described Protestantism as America's "national religion," and he was largely right despite the ban on religious establishment in the Constitution. Normally, to be born an American in those days meant to be a Protestant; this was the religious identification that quite naturally and appropriately went along with being an American. Non-Protestants felt the force of this conviction almost as strongly as did the Protestants; Catholics and Jews, despite their greatly increasing numbers, experienced their non-Protestant religion as a problem, even as an obstacle to their becoming full-fledged Americans: it was a mark of their foreignness. Protestantism—not any of the multiplying denominations, but Protestantism as a whole—was America's "established church"; the others, the non-Protestants, were to some degree, and in varying measure, outsiders. America was a Protestant nation.

This is no longer the case. Today, unlike fifty years ago, the natural and appropriate religious belonging that goes along with being an American is not simply being a Protestant; it is (as the evidence amply shows) being a Protestant, being a Catholic, or being a Jew. These have become the three ways of being an American. Today, Catholics and Jews, as well as Protestants, feel themselves to be Americans not apart from, or in spite of, their religion, but because of it.

If America today prossesses an "established church" in Siegfried's sense, it is the emerging tripartite system of Protestant-Catholic-Jew. Whereas Justice Sutherland, in the 1920's, could still speak of America as a "Christian nation," Justice Douglas, in the 1950's, spoke of Americans as a "religious people, whose institutions presuppose a Supreme Being." From a Protestant nation, we have become a three-religion country. This transformation is the consequence not of any marked increase of Catholics or Jews in the population, but an accompaniment of the shift we have been discussing in the pattern of self-identification, and therefore also in the source of pluralistic diversity, from ethnicity to religion.

The second factor I should like to mention is closely related to the first. It is the transformation of American Catholics, again largely within our generation, from a peripheral, foreign, lower-class group into a nuclear, middle-class American community.

The remarkable upward mobility of the Catholic groups in the course of the past generation has been well presented and documented in Father Andrew M. Greeley's report to the International Conference of Religious Sociology, held in Brussels.

Now what have been, what are, the consequences of these two inter-connected processes for the religious situation, especially in terms of Protestant-Catholic tensions? I think it must be said that these two major social developments are having a discernible double effect, making at one and the same time for an exacerbation and a mitigation of these tensions, though at different range. In brief, it seems to me that their effect has been, in the short run, to aggravate the tensions, but, in the long run, to reduce and alleviate them.

Let us consider the latter effect first. Through the concomitant operation of both of the tendencies I have mentioned, Catholicism has become a legitimate part of American religion, one of the "three great faiths," with an assured place in the American scheme of things; and Catholics have become—perhaps I should say, are becoming—

middle-class Americans, a recognized part of the American people. To increasing numbers of Protestants, especially younger Protestants, Catholics have become, are becoming, "our kind of people," embraced in that potent formula of American comprehension: "After all, we're all Americans!" I shall have occasion to develop this point a little later; for the present, it is enough to bring it to the fore, and to emphasize how strongly it makes for the mitigation of Protestant-Catholic strains and tensions in the long run.

But the very same process that promises, in the long run, to mitigate these strains and tensions, would seem very much to exacerbate them in the short run. Why this double and contradictory effect?

Consider the position of the Protestant, particularly of the middle-aged or older Protestant, in present-day America. His whole outlook was shaped, his mind was formed, his feelings were articulated, in an America that was a Protestant nation; and he was America. Now he finds himself propelled into a post-Protestant America, into a three-religion country, where he is not the nation, but merely one of three.

Suddenly he finds himself faced with the threat of a loss of accustomed status; a privileged status long enjoyed and taken for granted is being subverted before his very eyes. He feels himself dispossessed; the Catholics—and Jews too—have moved in on him, and taken over what was once his. He feels himself threatened: Catholics are multiplying prodigiously, and are about to take over the country!

This nightmare of "Catholic domination" is not in the least warranted by the facts, but it has its own significant logic. Whereas Roman Catholic growth in the country as a whole has been relatively moderate, what one may call the Roman Catholic "presence" has grown prodigiously. There was a time when the mass of Catholics were of the lower classes, at the margin of society—laborers and servant girls, hewers of wood and drawers of water. The middle-class Protestant, resting securely in a middle-class Protestant nation, did not, generally, see them as a threat; indeed, in good times, he hardly noticed their existence, for they were not present in the nuclear institutions of the community.

Within the past generation, however, the extraordinary upward mobility of American Catholics have converted large numbers of these Catholics into solid middle-class Americans, and have brought them in mounting proportions into these very nuclear institutions. No wonder the old-line Protestant, with his older attitudes, feels himself surrounded and threatened: wherever he turns, in those very places he had been accustomed to regard as his own—the nuclear middle-class institutions and organizations of the community—he finds more and more of these Catholics, who, for him, remember, are still outsiders and interlopers. No wonder he finds himself terrified at the specter of "Catholic domination"!

He also resents what he thinks of as Catholic "divisiveness." As a minority group, Catholics were early constrained to build up separate Catholic community organizations to protect themselves and to advance their interests in the fierce group competition always so characteristic of American life. And so we have the vast proliferation of Catholic "separatist" organizations from the early Irish-Catholic Protective Society to the associations of Catholic lawyers and firemen and policemen and veterans and educators, and so on and on, today.

In this respect, Catholics have behaved very much as did the other minority groups in this country——Jews, Negroes (after emancipation), and first- and second-generation immigrants, who all felt the need for separate community organizations and quickly developed them. But, of course, in the older days, Protestants felt no such need, and took no such action. Until well into this generation, the general community institutions and organizations were, in fact, Protestant institutions and organizations, because this was a Protestant nation and a Protestant culture.

In the course of the past generation, the situation has been changing drastically: this is no longer a Protestant nation, and Protestants are today only one of three. Protestants can no longer count on the general community institutions and organizations as theirs; so that, in effect, they find themselves organizationally and institutionally disarmed in the face of the tightening Jewish and Catholic communities. The natural, one might almost say the normal, response of most Protestants has been to denounce the whole system of separate community institutions as "divisive" and "un-American," despite the fact that it fits in very well with the emerging pattern of American religious communalism, and actually operates as an integrative factor in American life. A growing number of Protestants, however, are coming to recognize the hard facts of the situation, and are proceeding, though haltingly, to build up their own Protestant communal institutions in the new three-religion America. In this, they are being prompted by the Negro Protestants, who, though Protestants, have never had America as their own, and have therefore been forced from the very beginning to elaborate a system of separate Negro institutions and organizations.

It is not necessary to extend this argument. It seems to me very clear that the rapid shift in social structure involved in the emergence of a three-religion America has imposed heavy strains on the Protestant mind and on Protestant attitudes, and has resulted—among large numbers of the older Protestants—in a feverish anti-Catholicism. This has been clearly recognized by many Protestant leaders themselves.

Some years ago, the editor of the *Christian Century* referred to this problem in a powerful editorial entitled, "Protestant, Be Yourself" in which he characterized this frenetic attitude as "Protestant paranoia."[4] Lest this characterization seem to be outrageously extreme, permit me to quote a passage in an editorial from the very same *Christian Century* three years before when the publication was under different editorship. "The worst mistake the new [Eisenhower] administration could make, short of plunging the world into atomic war," the *Christian Century* pronounced editorially, "would be to attempt to send an ambassador to the Vatican."[5] When sending an ambassador to the Vatican can be regarded as the Number Two Calamity to the Universe, it would seem that "Protestant paranoia" is not too strong a term.

But if we can speak of "Protestant paranoia," we must not forget the corresponding affliction of Catholics, which the *Christian Century* editorialist very aptly calls "Catholic claustrophobia." If many Protestants reveal the effects of a desperate anxiety over a threat of loss to their accustomed status, Catholics are status-anxious in another sense, in the sense of being anxious over the preservation of their newly acquired status.

They feel hampered, closed in; they are suspicious and touchy, discovering everywhere evidence that their highly prized, newly achieved status is not being properly or adequately acknowledged by the "others"; in this, curiously enough, they are very much like the famous "Texas millionaires," who too feel that their newly achieved status is not being adequately recognized by "intellectuals" and "society snobs." Catholics still uneasy in the new tripartite scheme of American life are easily tempted to self-assertiveness and to assuming postures of uneasy superiority. All along the line, they tend to overcompensate.

Here again it is not necessary to extend the argument. If we take these phrases, "Protestant paranoia" and "Catholic claustrophobia," as no more than figures of speech, we must recognize how apt they are in describing the attitudes of large numbers of Protestants and Catholics in the present changing religio-social situation. It is out of these

---

[4]Editorial, *The Christian Century* (October 19, 1955).
[5]Editorial, *The Christian Century* (December 31, 1952).

attitudes that the strains and tensions emerge which characterize religious group relations in this country today. In this supercharged emotional atmosphere, almost any question of social policy may easily become a matter of bitter conflict and hostility.

But within this situation of strain and tension, there are profound differences of attitude, almost as profound as the over-all situation itself. The first, and perhaps the most significant, kind of difference is the difference of generation. It is widely known that the younger people of all religious groups show a far less hostile attitude, a far less rigid attitude, than do the older people of their communities. This is often set down to their youth, which is supposed to keep the young people more "flexible," or to their education, which is supposed to render them more "tolerant." Whatever truth there may be in these allegations, they cannot point to the main factor. For if it were only youth, there would be no long-range shift, what with the younger people becoming older and therefore allegedly assuming less "flexible" attitudes; but there definitely is a long-range shift. Nor, if it were simply education, would there be any difference between the younger people and their elders of the same educational background; but there is a difference. The explanation must be sought somewhat deeper.

Every election year since 1940 (as well as at points in between), the American Institute of Public Opinion (Gallup Poll) has asked the same question: "If your party nominated a qualified man for the presidency this year, and he happened to be a Catholic, would you vote for him?" Here is a breakdown by age groups of the 1956 returns:

	21–29	*30–49*	*50 and over*
Yes	83	79	62
No	14	17	31
No opinion	3	4	7

At the same time, let us examine the long-range trend:

	1940	*1956*
Yes	62	73
No	31	22
No opinion	7	5

Anti-Catholic bias has been, and is, considerably lower in the youngest age group than in the oldest. At the same time, too, such anti-Catholic bias was considerably lower among the people as a whole in 1956 than it was in 1940. And, in 1960, a Catholic President was elected, for the first time in our history.

It seems to me evident that the younger people see these things in a rather different way from the older; and this less biased attitude, if we can call it that, persists after they become older. It appears to be not so much a matter of age as of the religio-social climate of opinion in which the mind had been formed: the older generation came out of a Protestant America, where Catholics were largely regarded as foreigners and outsiders; the younger people have come out of a three-religion America, where Catholics are "our kind of people" and are Americans like us.

On the issue of federal aid to parochial schools, a Gallup poll conducted in 1949 indicated that "the greatest acceptance of the Catholic argument ... was to be found among young voters of all religions." Very much the same was revealed in a survey (as yet unpublished) of public opinion in a New England town, which had become more than half Catholic in the course of less than thirty years. There was a great hue and cry about the "Catholic menace" in that town, but the survey indicated that it was largely limited to Protestants, and Jews, over 45 years of age. Very few of the younger people saw any menace; they were well aware that Catholics were multiplying in the town, but they refused to be thrown into a panic by that. Their characteristic response was: "So what? we're all Americans, aren't we?"

Martin Marty found something very similar among Lutheran groups in the Midwest. Here is how he is quoted in *The New York Times:*

> The Rev. Dr. Martin Marty, a noted Lutheran pastor, author, and editor, made an observation that had cropped up in other interviews in the south and midwest in the last month. It was that in the churches themselves, it was primarily the older generation of Protestants who were raising cries against a Catholic for President. The younger generation, he said, is not so dead set on preserving the old Protestant domination. . . .[6]

In other words, the older Protestant America is passing; but it is naturally only the younger generation which is having much success in adjusting itself to a post-Protestant three-religion country. This is one of the chief reasons for the present exacerbation of tensions; but it is also a very good reason for expecting a considerable alleviation of these tensions in the coming years. For, as the younger generation,

---

[6] *The New York Times* (September 19, 1960).

formed in a three-religion America, comes to constitute the mass of the nation, those attitudes that are now the special attitudes of the younger generation are bound to become the dominant attitudes of the American people. In this lies our best hope; but it is still a hope for the future.

Generational differences are not the only differences worth noting. It is a familiar fact that Protestant-Catholic relations are best and most amicable on the highest theological levels, where a genuine religious dialogue is beginning to emerge. Anti-Catholic bias among Protestants, and anti-Protestant bias among Catholics, would seem to be worst among those whose religious life is most primitive, and is most indiscriminately identified with the local culture. Or perhaps a qualification ought to be made; the most virulent anti-Catholicism is to be found among secularistic-minded "liberals," for whom Catholicism still represents Voltaire's l'Infâme, the quintessence of "dogmatic," "institutional" religion to be fought in the name of Enlightenment.

As Peter Viereck has well put it "Catholic-baiting is the antisemitism of the liberals." The Kennedy campaign, for a time, disrupted this syndrome; but recently it has been showing signs of recovering its old vigor, easily fusing with the more common anti-Catholicism long endemic in this country.

III Jewish-gentile Relations

A word now about Jewish-gentile relations, before I attempt to bring these various threads together to a conclusion. Although there are a number of communities, particularly in suburbia, where gentile-Jewish relations exhibit the same kinds of tensions as characterize Protestant-Catholic relations elsewhere, it seems to be generally agreed that what is usually, though I think inaccurately, called "anti-Semitism" is today at the lowest ebb in our history. It is hard to explain just why this should be so, but I will venture a guess or two.

It seems to me that something happened during the last World War that produced a sharp change in the American mind. In that war, we faced Hitler not only as the national enemy, but as the incarnation of evil, and the name of that evil was "anti-Semitism" or "racialism." Since the war, Americans, especially younger Americans, have been very uneasy about anything that smacks of race or ethnicity; gone is the minstrel show that had become so much a part of American entertainment; gone, too, are the lusty old ethnic jokes—what survives, at least in public, is a pale and genteel imitation of the genuine article.

Anti-Semitism has come to be regarded not merely as unenlightened, but as positively indecent, and, what is more, un-American, as well. Even those who harbor anti-Semitic feelings—and there are, of course, many millions of such people in our country—find it difficult to acknowledge it even to themselves, let alone to others. As I say, anti-Semitism—at least, overt anti-Semitism—has become un-American. This development has been considerably aided by the fact that, in the course of the past generation American Jews, even more than Catholics, have, in increasing numbers, become solid, well-educated, American-minded Americans.

Jews, on their part, especially the older generation, still retain something of the older attitudes, expressed in an almost neurotic defensiveness. Jews still see themselves, in fact, most threatened by Roman Catholics, though recent political and social causes have thrown them together quite closely. And Jews, particularly the spokesmen of Jewish institutions and organizations, seem to insist on thoroughgoing separation of church and state, that is, on the thoroughgoing secularization of public life. This attitude is shared even by Jews who are themselves deeply religious in their private lives.

This curious duality, which has brought Jewish organizations in repeated conflict with Roman Catholic and much of the Protestant opinion, seems to be due to the conviction, widely held though not often articulated, that because the western Jew achieved emancipation with the secularization of society, he can preserve his free and equal status only so long as culture and society remain thoroughly secular. It is easy to understand these fears; and it is easy to see how they engender that curious "Jewish schizophrenia," which has puzzled many observers—Jews, religious, even orthodox in their private life, yet radically secularistic in their public activity. This duality is bound to become more and more difficult to maintain in present-day America, with its very high valuation of religion; indeed, considerable sections of the newer generation of American Jews are beginning to find the negativism of this attitude unreasonable and unviable, and are searching for new approaches that will bring them closer to the main body of the other two religious communities in the United States.

I have said that anti-Semitism, at least overt anti-Semitism, is today at an all-time low; and that perhaps the major factor in bringing this about is the deep moral impact of the war against Hitler. However much we may welcome this development, there is one aspect that might give us pause. The extraordinary prudishness of Americans today on matters of race and ethnicity would suggest that there is involved a very considerable repression of quite contrary impulses. If such is the case, there may be storing up now great quantities of resentment, which, though for the time being repressed, may someday break through again in more virulent form. It might perhaps be better for the American Jew if all remarks about Jews were not so nervously taboo in decent American society. The repression is too close to the surface to be comfortable.

I know that these scattered remarks about Jewish-gentile tensions are inadequate; but actually we know very little about the situation, except one or two large-scale generalizations. In any case, I think it can be taken as a fact that when we speak of religious group conflict in this country today, we speak primarily of Protestant-Catholic conflict.

IV Some Conclusions

What do these remarks add up to? To me, it seems that they add up to the conclusion that sociologically what we have in this country today are really three religious minorities linked in a trifaith system. I know that, according to the 1957 Census survey, Protestants constitute over 66 per cent of the population, Catholics nearly 26 per cent, and Jews only 3.2 per cent; other estimates put the Protestant proportion even higher, nearly 70 per cent.

Yet, by and large, American Protestants feel and act as though they were a minority, just as Jews, with only 3.2 per cent, feel and act as though they were one of three. This formula, one of three, is precisely what I have in mind. When I say that all three are minority groups, despite statistics, I mean that all three—Protestants as well as Catholics and Jews—are coming to see themselves as involved in a continuing interplay of group interests, aspirations, and pressures in a situation where no single one of the groups can any longer hope to dominate the other two, and in which each group recognizes itself as inextricably linked with the others, for better or for worse.

Each group develops its characteristic form of minority-group defensiveness; each has its own image of itself, and correspondingly, its own stereotyped caricature of the others; each has its own notion of its particular virtues, and each has its own tale of grievances about bias and discrimination. Each sees itself as the best expression of American ideals and values, but each is ready to acknowledge the existence, and even the legitimacy, of the other two in the totality of American life.

The tensions and conflicts we are concerned with emerge out of this triple minority system, which falls in so well with the socio-religious communalism we have seen arising in this country today. In the context of a never sleeping minority-group defensiveness, every question of religious or social policy is transformed into an "issue" of group conflict, and thereby removed from the realm of serious, judicious discussion. Such is the case with the so-called "school question," with the birth-control question, with the question of the proper use of ecclesiastical power in politics, and with a score of other questions where religion so obviously impinges upon social policy.

It can only be hoped that the disturbing emotive factors, so powerful today, will diminish with the fuller development of current trends; and that a time will soon come when "Protestant paranoia," "Catholic claustrophobia," and "Jewish schizophrenia" will no longer be the apt characterizations of the minority-group attitudes they are now.

In that happy day, perhaps, the religious and social questions that now serve merely as battle-cries in religious group conflict, will receive the attention they deserve. For they *are* serious and important questions, touching on a variety of moral and social concerns and interests. They involve the religious communities, but do not necessarily set one against the other; in short, though they are religious questions, they do not necessarily have to become questions of religious conflict.

For, basically, the trifaith religious pluralism that characterizes mid-century America makes for national unity and cohesiveness rather than for division and disruption. All of the three groups are now American groups, committed to essentially the same American values, seeing things in essentially the same American way.

Group diversity and group interplay are of the very essence of our kind of democratic society, which (in principle, at least) abhors every form of uniformitarianism and totalitarianism. And it certainly augurs better for our national unity to have three American groups, all at the center of American life, than to have one group claiming to be the nation, with two other large groups relegated to an "outsider" position of foreignness and inferiority.

Despite the frequent bitterness and extravagance of our religious group conflict, it still remains a fact that the strength of our system resides in its pluriunity, in its capacity to comprehend diversity in unity, and to preserve unity in diversity. And in the America of today, this means a pluriunity of religious communities.

The Two Worlds of Race:
A Historical View

John Hope Franklin

I

Measured by universal standards the history of the United States is indeed brief. But during the brief span of three and one-half centuries of colonial and national history Americans developed traditions and prejudices which created the two worlds of race in modern America. From the time that Africans were brought as indentured servants to the mainland of English America in 1619, the enormous task of rationalizing and justifying the forced labor of peoples on the basis of racial differences was begun; and even after legal slavery was ended, the notion of racial differences persisted as a basis for maintaining segregation and discrimination. At the same time, the effort to establish a more healthy basis for the new world social order was begun, thus launching the continuing battle between the two worlds of race, on the one hand, and the world of equality and complete human fellowship, on the other.

For a century before the American Revolution the status of Negroes in the English colonies had become fixed at a low point that distinguished them from all other persons who had been held in temporary

Reprinted from *Daedalus*, Vol. 94, No. 5 (Fall, 1965), 899-920 with permission of the publisher. Copyright 1965 by the American Academy of Arts and Sciences.

bondage. By the middle of the eighteenth century, laws governing Negroes denied to them certain basic rights that were conceded to others. They were permitted no independence of thought, no opportunity to improve their minds or their talents or to worship freely, no right to marry and enjoy the conventional family relationships, no right to own or dispose of property, and no protection against miscarriages of justice or cruel and unreasonable punishments. They were outside the pale of the laws that protected ordinary humans. In most places they were to be governed, as the South Carolina code of 1712 expressed it, by special laws "as may restrain the disorders, rapines, and inhumanity to which they are naturally prone and inclined. . . ." A separate world for them had been established by law and custom. Its dimensions and the conduct of its inhabitants were determined by those living in a quite different world.

By the time that the colonists took up arms against their mother country in order to secure their independence, the world of Negro slavery had become deeply entrenched and the idea of Negro inferiority well established. But the dilemmas inherent in such a situation were a source of constant embarrassment. "It always appeared a most iniquitous scheme to me," Mrs. John Adams wrote her husband in 1774, "to fight ourselves for what we are daily robbing and plundering from those who have as good a right to freedom as we have." There were others who shared her views, but they were unable to wield much influence. When the fighting began General George Washington issued an order to recruiting officers that they were not to enlist "any deserter from the ministerial army, nor any stroller, negro, or vagabond, or person suspected of being an enemy to the liberty of America nor any under eighteen years of age." In classifying Negroes with the dregs of society, traitors, and children, Washington made it clear that Negroes, slave or free, were not to enjoy the high privilege of fighting for political independence. He would change that order later, but only after it became clear that Negroes were enlisting with the "ministerial army" in droves in order to secure their own freedom. In changing his policy if not his views, Washington availed himself of the services of more than 5,000 Negroes who took up arms against England.[1]

Many Americans besides Mrs. Adams were struck by the inconsistency of their stand during the War for Independence, and they were not averse to making moves to emancipate the slaves. Quakers and other religious groups organized antislavery societies, while numerous

---

[1] Benjamin Quarles, *The Negro in the American Revolution* (Chapel Hill, N. C., 1961), pp. 15-18.

individuals manumitted their slaves. In the years following the close of the war most of the states of the East made provisions for the gradual emancipation of slaves. In the South, meanwhile, the antislavery societies were unable to effect programs of state-wide emancipation. When the Southerners came to the Constitutional Convention in 1787 they succeeded in winning some representation on the basis of slavery, in securing federal support of the capture and rendition of fugitive slaves, and in preventing the closing of the slave trade before 1808.

Even where the sentiment favoring emancipation was pronounced, it was seldom accompanied by a view that Negroes were the equals of whites and should become a part of one family of Americans. Jefferson, for example, was opposed to slavery; and if he could have had his way, he would have condemned it in the Declaration of Independence. It did not follow, however, that he believed Negroes to be the equals of whites. He did not want to "degrade a whole race of men from the work in the scale of beings which their Creator may *perhaps* have given them. ... I advance it therefore, as a suspicion only, that the blacks, whether originally a distinct race, or made distinct by time and circumstance, are inferior to the whites in the endowment both of body and mind." It is entirely possible that Jefferson's later association with the extraordinarily able Negro astronomer and mathematician, Benjamin Banneker, resulted in some modification of his views. After reading a copy of Banneker's almanac, Jefferson told him that it was "a document to which your whole race had a right for its justifications against the doubts which have been entertained of them."[2]

In communities such as Philadelphia and New York, where the climate was more favorably disposed to the idea of Negro equality than in Jefferson's Virginia, few concessions were made, except by a limited number of Quakers and their associates. Indeed, the white citizens in the City of Brotherly Love contributed substantially to the perpetuation of two distinct worlds of race. In the 1780's, the white Methodists permitted Negroes to worship with them, provided the Negroes sat in a designated place in the balcony. On one occasion, when the Negro worshippers occupied the front rows of the balcony, from which they had been excluded, the officials pulled them from their knees during prayer and evicted them from the church. Thus, in the early days of the Republic and in the place where the Republic was founded, Negroes had a definite "place" in which they were expected at all times to remain. The white Methodists of New York

[2]John Hope Franklin, *From Slavery to Freedom: A History of American Negroes* (New York, 1956), pp. 156-157.

had much the same attitude toward their Negro fellows. Soon, there were separate Negro churches in these and other communities. Baptists were very much the same. In 1809 thirteen Negro members of a white Baptist church in Philadelphia were dismissed, and they formed a church of their own. Thus, the earliest Negro religious institutions emerged as the result of the rejection by white communicants of their darker fellow worshippers. Soon there would be other institutions—schools, newspapers, benevolent societies—to serve those who lived in a world apart.

Those Americans who conceded the importance of education for Negroes tended to favor some particular type of education that would be in keeping with their lowly station in life. In 1794, for example, the American Convention of Abolition Societies recommended that Negroes be instructed in "those mechanic arts which will keep them most constantly employed and, of course, which will less subject them to idleness and debauchery, and thus prepare them for becoming good citizens of the United States." When Anthony Benezet, a dedicated Pennsylvania abolitionist, died in 1784 his will provided that on the death of his wife the proceeds of his estate should be used to assist in the establishment of a school for Negroes. In 1787 the school of which Benezet had dreamed was opened in Philadelphia, where the pupils studied reading, writing, arithmetic, plain accounts, and sewing.

Americans who were at all interested in the education of Negroes regarded it as both natural and normal that Negroes should receive their training in separate schools. As early as 1773 Newport, Rhode Island, had a colored school, maintained by a society of benevolent clergymen of the Anglican Church. In 1798 a separate private school for Negro children was established in Boston; and two decades later the city opened its first public primary school for the education of Negro children. Meanwhile, New York had established separate schools, the first one opening its doors in 1790. By 1814 there were several such institutions that were generally designated as the New York African Free Schools.[3]

Thus, in the most liberal section of the country, the general view was that Negroes should be kept out of the main stream of American life. They were forced to establish and maintain their own religious institutions, which were frequently followed by the establishment of separate benevolent societies. Likewise, if Negroes were to receive any education, it should be special education provided in separate educational institutions. This principle prevailed in most places in the

---

[3]Carter G. Woodson, *The Education of the Negro Prior to 1861* (Washington, D. C., 1919), pp. 93-97.

North throughout the period before the Civil War. In some Massachusetts towns, however, Negroes gained admission to schools that had been maintained for whites. But the School Committee of Boston refused to admit Negroes, arguing that the natural distinction of the races, which "no legislature, no social customs, can efface renders a promiscuous intermingling in the public schools disadvantageous both to them and to the whites." Separate schools remained in Boston until the Massachusetts legislature in 1855 enacted a law providing that in determining the qualifications of students to be admitted to any public school no distinction should be made on account of the race, color, or religious opinion of the applicant.

Meanwhile, in the Southern states, where the vast majority of the Negroes lived, there were no concessions suggesting equal treatment, even among the most liberal elements. One group that would doubtless have regarded itself as liberal on the race question advocated the deportation of Negroes to Africa, especially those who had become free. Since free Negroes "neither enjoyed the immunities of freemen, nor were they subject to the incapacities of slaves," their condition and "unconquerable prejudices" prevented amalgamation with whites, one colonization leader argued. There was, therefore, a "peculiar moral fitness" in restoring them to "the land of their fathers." Men like Henry Clay, Judge Bushrod Washington, and President James Monroe thought that separation—expatriation—was the best thing for Negroes who were or who would become free.[4]

While the colonization scheme was primarily for Negroes who were already free, it won, for a time, a considerable number of sincere enemies of slavery. From the beginning Negroes were bitterly opposed to it, and only infrequently did certain Negro leaders, such as Dr. Martin Delany and the Reverend Henry M. Turner, support the idea. Colonization, however, retained considerable support in the most responsible quarters. As late as the Civil War, President Lincoln urged Congress to adopt a plan to colonize Negroes, as the only workable solution to the race problem in the United States. Whether the advocates of colonization wanted merely to prevent the contamination of slavery by free Negroes or whether they actually regarded it as the just and honorable thing to do, they represented an important element in the population that rejected the idea of the Negro's assimilation into the main stream of American life.

Thus, within fifty years after the Declaration of Independence was written, the institution of slavery, which received only a temporary

[4]P. J. Staudenraus, *The African Colonization Movement, 1816–1865* (New York, 1961), pp. 22-32.

reversal during the Revolutionary era, contributed greatly to the emergence of the two worlds of race in the United States. The natural rights philosophy appeared to have little effect on those who became committed, more and more, to seeking a rationalization for slavery. The search was apparently so successful that even in areas where slavery was declining, the support for maintaining two worlds of race was strong. Since the Negro church and school emerged in Northern communities where slavery was dying, it may be said that the free society believed almost as strongly in racial separation as it did in racial freedom.

II

The generation preceding the outbreak of the Civil War witnessed the development of a set of defenses of slavery that became the basis for much of the racist doctrine to which some Americans have subscribed from then to the present time. The idea of the inferiority of the Negro enjoyed wide acceptance among Southerners of all classes and among many Northerners. It was an important ingredient in the theory of society promulgated by Southern thinkers and leaders. It was organized into a body of systematic thought by the scientists and social scientists of the South, out of which emerged a doctrine of racial superiority that justified any kind of control over the slave. In 1826 Dr. Thomas Cooper said that he had not the slightest doubt that Negroes were an "inferior variety of the human species; and not capable of the same improvement as the whites." Dr. S. C. Cartwright of the University of Louisiana insisted that the capacities of the Negro adult for learning were equal to those of a white infant; and the Negro could properly perform certain physiological functions only when under the control of white men. Because of the Negro's inferiority, liberty and republican institutions were not only unsuited to his temperament, but actually inimical to his well-being and happiness.

Like racists in other parts of the world, Southerners sought support for their ideology by developing a common bond with the less privileged. The obvious basis was race; and outside the white race there was to be found no favor from God, no honor or respect from man. By the time that Europeans were reading Gobineau's *Inequality of Races*, Southerners were reading Cartwright's *Slavery in the Light of Ethnology*. In admitting all whites into the pseudonobility of race, Cartwright won their enthusiastic support in the struggle to preserve the integrity and honor of *the* race. Professor Thomas R. Dew of the College of William and Mary comforted the lower-class whites by indicating that they could identify with the most privileged and affluent of the community. In the South, he said, "no white man feels such inferiority of rank as to be unworthy of association with those around him. Color alone is here the badge of distinction, the true mark of aristocracy, and all who are white are equal in spite of the variety of occupation."[5]

Many Northerners were not without their own racist views and policies in the turbulent decades before the Civil War. Some, as Professor Louis Filler has observed, displayed a hatred of Negroes that gave them a sense of superiority and an outlet for their frustrations. Others cared nothing one way or the other about Negroes and demanded only that they be kept separate.[6] Even some of the abolitionists themselves were ambivalent on the question of Negro equality. More than one antislavery society was agitated by the suggestion that Negroes be invited to join. Some members thought it reasonable for them to attend, but not to be put on an "equality with ourselves." The New York abolitionist, Lewis Tappan, admitted "that when the subject of acting out our profound principles in treating men irrespective of color is discussed heat is always produced."[7]

In the final years before the beginning of the Civil War, the view that the Negro was different, even inferior, was widely held in the United States. Leaders in both major parties subscribed to the view, while the more extreme racists deplored any suggestion that the Negro could ever prosper as a free man. At Peoria, Illinois, in October 1854, Abraham Lincoln asked what stand the opponents of slavery should take regarding Negroes. "Free them, and make them politically and socially, our equals? My own feelings will not admit this; and if mine would, we well know that those of the great mass of white people will not. Whether this feeling accords with justice and sound judgment, is not the sole question, if indeed, it is any part of it. A universal feeling, whether well or ill founded, cannot be safely disregarded. We cannot, then, make them equals."

The Lincoln statement was forthright, and it doubtless represented the views of most Americans in the 1850's. Most of those who heard him or read his speech were of the same opinion as he. In later years, the Peoria pronouncement would be used by those who sought to

---

[5]John Hope Franklin, *The Militant South, 1800–1861* (Cambridge, Mass., 1956), pp. 83-86.

[6]Louis Filler, *The Crusade Against Slavery, 1830–1860* (New York, 1960), pp. 142-145.

[7]Leon F. Litwack, *North of Slavery; The Negro in the Free States, 1790–1860* (Chicago, 1961), pp. 216-217.

detract from Lincoln's reputation as a champion of the rights of the Negro. In 1964, the White Citizens' Councils reprinted portions of the speech in large advertisements in the daily press and insisted that Lincoln shared their views on the desirability of maintaining two distinct worlds of race.

Lincoln could not have overcome the nation's strong predisposition toward racial separation if he had tried. And he did not try very hard. When he called for the enlistment of Negro troops, after issuing the Emancipation Proclamation, he was content not only to set Negroes apart in a unit called "U. S. Colored Troops," but also to have Negro privates receive $10 per month including clothing, while whites of the same rank received $13 per month plus clothing. Only the stubborn refusal of many Negro troops to accept discriminatory pay finally forced Congress to equalize compensation for white and Negro soldiers.[8] The fight for union that became also a fight for freedom never became a fight for equality or for the creation of one racial world.

The Lincoln and Johnson plans for settling the problems of peace and freedom never seriously touched on the concomitant problem of equality. To be sure, in 1864 President Lincoln privately raised with the governor of Louisiana the question of the franchise for a limited number of Negroes, but when the governor ignored the question the President let the matter drop. Johnson raised a similar question in 1866, but he admitted that it was merely to frustrate the design of radical reformers who sought a wider franchise for Negroes. During the two years following Appomattox Southern leaders gave not the slightest consideration to permitting any Negroes, regardless of their service to the Union or their education or their property, to share in the political life of their communities. Not only did every Southern state refuse to permit Negroes to vote, but they also refused to provide Negroes with any of the educational opportunities that they were providing for the whites.

The early practice of political disfranchisement and of exclusion from public educational facilities helped to determine subsequent policies that the South adopted regarding Negroes. While a few leaders raised their voices against these policies and practices, it was Negroes themselves who made the most eloquent attacks on such discriminations. As early as May 1865, a group of North Carolina Negroes told President Johnson that some of them had been soldiers and were doing everything possible to learn how to discharge the

---

[8]Benjamin Quarles, *The Negro in the Civil War* (Boston, 1953), p. 200.

higher duties of citizenship. "It seems to us that men who are willing on the field of battle to carry the muskets of the Republic, in the days of peace ought to be permitted to carry the ballots; and certainly we cannot understand the justice of denying the elective franchise to men who have been fighting *for* the country, while it is freely given to men who have just returned from *four* years fighting against it." Such pleas fell on deaf ears, however; and it was not until 1867, when Congress was sufficiently outraged by the inhuman black codes, widespread discriminations in the South, and unspeakable forms of violence against Negroes, that new federal legislation sought to correct the evils of the first period of Reconstruction.

The period that we know as Radical Reconstruction had no significant or permanent effect on the status of the Negro in American life. For a period of time, varying from one year to fifteen or twenty years, some Negroes enjoyed the privileges of voting. They gained political ascendancy in a very few communities only temporarily, and they never even began to achieve the status of a ruling class. They made no meaningful steps toward economic independence or even stability; and in no time at all, because of the pressures of the local community and the neglect of the federal government, they were brought under the complete economic subservience of the old ruling class. Organizations such as the Ku Klux Klan were committed to violent action to keep Negroes "in their place" and, having gained respectability through sponsorship by Confederate generals and the like, they proceeded to wreak havoc in the name of white supremacy and protection of white womanhood.[9]

Meanwhile, various forms of segregation and discrimination, developed in the years before the Civil War in order to degrade the half million free Negroes in the United States, were now applied to the four million Negroes who had become free in 1865. Already the churches and the military were completely segregated. For the most part the schools, even in the North, were separate. In the South segregated schools persisted, even in the places where the radicals made a half-hearted attempt to desegregate them. In 1875 Congress enacted a Civil Rights Act to guarantee the enjoyment of equal rights in carriers and all places of public accommodation and amusement. Even before it became law Northern philanthropists succeeded in forcing the deletion of the provision calling for desegregated schools. Soon, because of the massive resistance in the North as well as in the

---

[9]John Hope Franklin, *Reconstruction After the Civil War* (Chicago, 1961), pp. 154-158.

South and the indifferent manner in which the federal government enforced the law, it soon became a dead letter everywhere. When it was declared unconstitutional by the Supreme Court in 1883, there was universal rejoicing, except among the Negroes, one of whom declared that they had been "baptized in ice water."

Neither the Civil War nor the era of Reconstruction made any significant step toward the permanent elimination of racial barriers. The radicals of the post-Civil War years came no closer to the creation of one racial world than the patriots of the Revolutionary years. When Negroes were, for the first time, enrolled in the standing army of the United States, they were placed in separate Negro units. Most of the liberals of the Reconstruction era called for and worked for separate schools for Negroes. Nowhere was there any extensive effort to involve Negroes in the churches and other social institutions of the dominant group. Whatever remained of the old abolitionist fervor, which can hardly be described as unequivocal on the question of true racial equality, was rapidly disappearing. In its place were the sentiments of the business men who wanted peace at any price. Those having common railroad interests or crop-marketing interests or investment interests could and did extend their hands across sectional lines and joined in the task of working together for the common good. In such an atmosphere the practice was to accept the realities of two separate worlds of race. Some even subscribed to the view that there were significant economic advantages in maintaining the two worlds of race.

III

The Post-Reconstruction years witnessed a steady deterioration in the status of Negro Americans. These were the years that Professor Rayford Logan has called the "nadir" of the Negro in American life and thought. They were the years when Americans, weary of the crusade that had, for the most part, ended with the outbreak of the Civil War, displayed almost no interest in helping the Negro to achieve equality. The social Darwinists decried the very notion of equality for Negroes, arguing that the lowly place they occupied was natural and normal. The leading literary journals vied with each other in describing Negroes as lazy, idle, improvident, immoral, and criminal.[10] Thomas Dixon's novels, *The Klansman* and *The Leopard's Spots,* and D. W. Griffith's motion picture, "The Birth of A Nation,"

---

[10]Rayford W. Logan, *The Negro in American Life and Thought: The Nadir, 1877–1901* (New York, 1954), pp. 239-274.

helped to give Americans a view of the Negro's role in American history that "proved" that he was unfit for citizenship, to say nothing of equality. The dictum of William Graham Sumner and his followers that "stateways cannot change folkways" convinced many Americans that legislating equality and creating one great society where race was irrelevant was out of the question.

But many Americans believed that they *could* legislate inequality; and they proceeded to do precisely that. Beginning in 1890, one Southern state after another revised the suffrage provisions of its constitution in a manner that made it virtually impossible for Negroes to qualify to vote. The new literacy and "understanding" provisions permitted local registrars to disqualify Negroes while permitting white citizens to qualify. Several states, including Louisiana, North Carolina and Oklahoma, inserted "grandfather clauses" in their constitutions in order to permit persons, who could not otherwise qualify, to vote if their fathers or grandfathers could vote in 1866. (This was such a flagrant discrimination against Negroes, whose ancestors could not vote in 1866, that the United States Supreme Court in 1915 declared the "grandfather clause" unconstitutional.) Then came the Democratic white primary in 1900 that made it impossible for Negroes to participate in local elections in the South, where, by this time, only the Democratic party had any appreciable strength. (After more than a generation of assaults on it, the white primary was finally declared unconstitutional in 1944).

Inequality was legislated in still another way. Beginning in the 1880's, many states, especially but not exclusively in the South, enacted statutes designed to separate the races. After the Civil Rights Act was declared unconstitutional in 1883 state legislatures were emboldened to enact numerous segregation statutes. When the United States Supreme Court, in the case of Plessy *v.* Ferguson, set forth the "separate but equal" doctrine in 1896, the decision provided a new stimulus for laws to separate the races and, of course, to discriminate against Negroes. In time, Negroes and whites were separated in the use of schools, churches, cemeteries, drinking fountains, restaurants, and all places of public accommodation and amusement. One state enacted a law providing for the separate warehousing of books used by white and Negro children. Another required the telephone company to provide separate telephone booths for white and Negro customers. In most communities housing was racially separated by law or practice.[11]

---

[11]John Hope Franklin, "History of Racial Segregation in the United States, *Annals of the Academy of Political and Social Science,* Vol. 304 (March 1956), pp. 1-9.

Where there was no legislation requiring segregation, local practices filled the void. Contradictions and inconsistencies seemed not to disturb those who sought to maintain racial distinctions at all costs. It mattered not that one drive-in snack bar served Negroes only on the inside, while its competitor across the street served Negroes only on the outside. Both were committed to making racial distinctions; and in communities where practices and mores had the force of law, the distinction was everything. Such practices were greatly strengthened when, in 1913, the federal government adopted policies that segregated the races in its offices as well as in its eating and rest-room facilities.

By the time of World War I, Negroes and whites in the South and in parts of the North lived in separate worlds, and the apparatus for keeping the worlds separate was elaborate and complex. Negroes were segregated by law in the public schools of the Southern states, while those in the Northern ghettos were sent to predominantly Negro schools, except where their numbers were insufficient. Scores of Negro newspapers sprang up to provide news of Negroes that the white press consistently ignored. Negroes were as unwanted in the white churches as they had been in the late eighteenth century; and Negro churches of virtually every denomination were the answer for a people who had accepted the white man's religion even as the white man rejected his religious fellowship.

Taking note of the fact that they had been omitted from any serious consideration by the white historians, Negroes began in earnest to write the history of their own experiences as Americans. There had been Negro historians before the Civil War, but none of them had challenged the white historians' efforts to relegate Negroes to a separate, degraded world. In 1882, however, George Washington Williams published his *History of the Negro Race in America* in order to "give the world more correct ideas about the colored people." He wrote, he said, not "as a partisan apologist, but from a love for the truth of history."[12] Soon there were other historical works by Negroes describing their progress and their contributions and arguing that they deserved to be received into the full fellowship of American citizens.

It was in these post-Reconstruction years that some of the most vigorous efforts were made to destroy the two worlds of race. The desperate pleas of Negro historians were merely the more articulate attempts of Negroes to gain complete acceptance in American life. Scores of Negro organizations joined in the struggle to gain protection

---

[12]George W. Williams, *History of the Negro Race in America from 1619 to 1880* (New York, 1882), p. x.

and recognition of their rights and to eliminate the more sordid practices that characterized the treatment of the Negro world by the white world. Unhappily, the small number of whites who were committed to racial equality dwindled in the post-Reconstruction years, while government at every level showed no interest in eliminating racial separatism. It seemed that Negro voices were indeed crying in the wilderness, but they carried on their attempts to be heard. In 1890 Negroes from twenty-one states and the District of Columbia met in Chicago and organized the Afro-American League of the United States. They called for more equitable distribution of school funds, fair and impartial trial for accused Negroes, resistance "by all legal and reasonable means" to mob and lynch law, and enjoyment of the franchise by all qualified voters. When a group of young Negro intellectuals, led by W. E. B. Du Bois, met at Niagara Falls, Ontario, in 1905, they made a similar call as they launched their Niagara Movement.

However eloquent their pleas, Negroes alone could make no successful assault on the two worlds of race. They needed help—a great deal of help. It was the bloody race riots in the early years of the twentieth century that shocked civic minded and socially conscious whites into answering the Negro's pleas for support. Some whites began to take the view that the existence of two societies whose distinction was based solely on race was inimical to the best interests of the entire nation. Soon, they were taking the initiative and in 1909 organized the National Association for the Advancement of Colored People. They assisted the following year in establishing the National Urban League. White attorneys began to stand with Negroes before the United States Supreme Court to challenge the "grandfather clause," local segregation ordinances, and flagrant miscarriages of justice in which Negroes were the victims. The patterns of attack developed during these years were to become invaluable later. Legal action was soon supplemented by picketing, demonstrating, and boycotting, with telling effect particularly in selected Northern communities.[13]

IV

The two world wars had a profound effect on the status of Negroes in the United States and did much to mount the attack on the two worlds of race. The decade of World War I witnessed a very significant migration of Negroes. They went in large numbers—perhaps a half million—from the rural areas of the South to the towns and cities

---

[13]Franklin, *From Slavery to Freedom*, pp. 437-443.

of the South and North. They were especially attracted to the industrial centers of the North. By the thousands they poured into Pittsburgh, Cleveland, and Chicago. Although many were unable to secure employment, others were successful and achieved a standard of living they could not have imagined only a few years earlier. Northern communities were not altogether friendly and hospitable to the newcomers, but the opportunities for education and the enjoyment of political self-respect were the greatest they had ever seen. Many of them felt that they were entirely justified in their renewed hope that the war would bring about a complete merger of the two worlds of race.

Those who held such high hopes, however, were naive in the extreme. Already the Ku Klux Klan was being revived—this time in the North as well as in the South. Its leaders were determined to develop a broad program to unite "native-born white Christians for concerted action in the preservation of American institutions and the supremacy of the white race." By the time that the war was over, the Klan was in a position to make capital of the racial animosities that had developed during the conflict itself. Racial conflicts had broken out in many places during the war; and before the conference at Versailles was over race riots in the United States had brought about what can accurately be described as the "long hot summer" of 1919.

If anything, the military operations which aimed to save the world for democracy merely fixed more permanently the racial separation in the United States. Negro soldiers not only constituted entirely separate fighting units in the United States Army, but, once overseas, were assigned to fighting units with the French Army. Negroes who sought service with the United States Marines or the Air Force were rejected, while the Navy relegated them to menial duties. The reaction of many Negroes was bitter, but most of the leaders, including Du Bois, counseled patience and loyalty. They continued to hope that their show of patriotism would win for them a secure place of acceptance as Americans.

Few Negro Americans could have anticipated the wholesale rejection they experienced at the conclusion of World War I. Returning Negro soldiers were lynched by hanging and burning, even while still in their military uniforms. The Klan warned Negroes that they must respect the rights of the white race "in whose country they are permitted to reside." Racial conflicts swept the country, and neither federal nor state governments seemed interested in effective intervention. The worlds of race were growing further apart in the postwar decade. Nothing indicated this more clearly than the growth of the

Universal Negro Improvement Association, led by Marcus Garvey. From a mere handful of members at the end of the war, the Garvey movement rapidly became the largest secular Negro group ever organized in the United States. Although few Negroes were interested in settling in Africa—the expressed aim of Garvey—they joined the movement by the hundreds of thousands to indicate their resentment of the racial duality that seemed to them to be the central feature of the American social order.[14]

More realistic and hardheaded were the Negroes who were more determined than ever to engage in the most desperate fight of their lives to destroy racism in the United States. As the editor of the *Crisis* said in 1919, "We return from fighting. We return fighting. Make way for Democracy! We saved it in France, and by the Great Jehovah, we will save it in the U.S.A., or know the reason why." This was the spirit of what Alain Locke called "The New Negro." He fought the Democratic white primary, made war on the whites who consigned him to the ghetto, attacked racial discrimination in employment, and pressed for legislation to protect his rights. If he was seldom successful during the postwar decade and the depression, he made it quite clear that he was unalterably opposed to the un-American character of the two worlds of race.

Hope for a new assault on racism was kindled by some of the New Deal policies of Franklin D. Roosevelt. As members of the economically disadvantaged group, Negroes benefited from relief and recovery legislation. Most of it, however, recognized the existence of the two worlds of race and accommodated itself to it. Frequently bread lines and soup kitchens were separated on the basis of race. There was segregation in the employment services, while many new agencies recognized and bowed to Jim Crow. Whenever agencies, such as the Farm Security Administration, fought segregation and sought to deal with people on the basis of their needs rather than race they came under the withering fire of the racist critics and seldom escaped alive. Winds of change, however slight, were discernible, and nowhere was this in greater evidence than in the new labor unions. Groups like the Congress of Industrial Organizations, encouraged by the support of the Wagner Labor Relations Act, began to look at manpower resources as a whole and to attack the old racial policies that viewed labor in terms of race.

---

[14]Edmund David Cronon, *Black Moses, The Story of Marcus Garvey and the Universal Negro Improvement Association* (Madison, Wis., 1955), pp. 202-206.

As World War II approached, Negroes schooled in the experiences of the nineteen-twenties and thirties were unwilling to see the fight against Nazism carried on in the context of an American racist ideology. Some white Americans were likewise uncomfortable in the role of freeing Europe of a racism which still permeated the United States; but it was the Negroes who dramatized American inconsistency by demanding an end to discrimination in employment in defense industries. By threatening to march on Washington in 1941 they forced the President to issue an order forbidding such discrimination. The opposition was loud and strong. Some state governors denounced the order, and some manufacturers skillfully evaded it. But it was a significant step toward the elimination of the two worlds.

During World War II the assault on racism continued. Negroes, more than a million of whom were enlisted in the armed services, bitterly fought discrimination and segregation. The armed services were, for the most part, two quite distinct racial worlds. Some Negro units had white officers, and much of the officer training was desegregated. But it was not until the final months of the war that a deliberate experiment was undertaken to involve Negro and white enlisted men in the same fighting unit. With the success of the experiment and with the warm glow of victory over Nazism as a backdrop, there was greater inclination to recognize the absurdity of maintaining a racially separate military force to protect the freedoms of the country.[15]

During the war there began the greatest migration in the history of Negro Americans. Hundreds of thousands left the South for the industrial centers of the North and West. In those places they met hostility, but they also secured employment in aviation plants, automobile factories, steel mills, and numerous other industries. Their difficulties persisted as they faced problems of housing and adjustment. But they continued to move out of the South in such large numbers that by 1965 one third of the twenty million Negroes in the United States lived in twelve metropolitan centers of the North and West. The ramifications of such a large-scale migration were numerous. The concentration of Negroes in communities where they suffered no political disabilities placed in their hands an enormous amount of political power. Consequently, some of them went to the legislatures, to Congress, and to positions on the judiciary. In turn, this won for them political respect as well as legislation that greatly strengthened their position as citizens.

---

[15]Lee Nichols, *Breakthrough on the Color Front* (New York, 1954), pp. 221-226.

V

Following World War II there was a marked acceleration in the war against the two worlds of race in the United States. In 1944 the Supreme Court ruled against segregation in interstate transportation, and three years later it wrote the final chapter in the war against the Democratic white primary. In 1947 the President's Committee on Civil Rights called for the "elimination of segregation, based on race, color, creed, or national origin, from American life."[16] In the following year President Truman asked Congress to establish a permanent Fair Employment Practices Commission. At the same time he took steps to eliminate segregation in the armed services. These moves on the part of the judicial and executive branches of the federal government by no means destroyed the two worlds of race, but they created a more healthy climate in which the government and others could launch an attack on racial separatism.

The attack was greatly strengthened by the new position of world leadership that the United States assumed at the close of the war. Critics of the United States were quick to point to the inconsistencies of an American position that spoke against racism abroad and countenanced it at home. New nations, brown and black, seemed reluctant to follow the lead of a country that adhered to its policy of maintaining two worlds of race—the one identified with the old colonial ruling powers and the other with the colonies now emerging as independent nations. Responsible leaders in the United States saw the weakness of their position, and some of them made new moves to repair it.

Civic and religious groups, some labor organizations, and many individuals from the white community began to join in the effort to destroy segregation and discrimination in American life. There was no danger, after World War II, that Negroes would ever again stand alone in their fight. The older interracial organizations continued, but they were joined by new ones. In addition to the numerous groups that included racial equality in their over-all programs, there were others that made the creation of one racial world their principal objective. Among them were the Congress of Racial Equality, the Southern Christian Leadership Conference, and the Student Non-Violent Coordinating Committee. Those in existence in the 1950's supported the court action that brought about the decision against segregated schools. The more recent ones have taken the lead in

---

[16]*To Secure These Rights, The Report of the President's Committee on Civil Rights* (New York, 1947), p. 166.

pressing for new legislation and in developing new techniques to be used in the war on segregation.

VI

The most powerful direct force in the maintenance of the two worlds of race has been the state and its political subdivisions. In states and communities where racial separation and discrimination are basic to the way of life, the elected officials invariably pledge themselves to the perpetuation of the duality. Indeed, candidates frequently vie with one another in their effort to occupy the most extreme segregationist position possible on the race question. Appointed officials, including the constabulary and, not infrequently, the teachers and school administrators, become auxiliary guardians of the system of racial separation. In such communities Negroes occupy no policy-making positions, exercise no influence over the determination of policy, and are seldom even on the police force. State and local resources, including tax funds, are at the disposal of those who guard the system of segregation and discrimination; and such funds are used to enforce customs as well as laws and to disseminate information in support of the system.

The white community itself acts as a guardian of the segregated system. Schooled in the specious arguments that assert the supremacy of the white race and fearful that a destruction of the system would be harmful to their own position, they not only "go along" with it but, in many cases, enthusiastically support it. Community sanctions are so powerful, moreover, that the independent citizen who would defy the established order would find himself not only ostracized but, worse, the target of economic and political reprisals.

Within the community many self-appointed guardians of white supremacy have emerged at various times. After the Civil War and after World War I it was the Ku Klux Klan, which has shown surprising strength in recent years. After the desegregation decision of the Supreme Court in 1954 it was the White Citizens' Council, which one Southern editor has called the "uptown Ku Klux Klan." From time to time since 1865, it has been the political demagogue, who has not only made capital by urging his election as a sure way to maintain the system but has also encouraged the less responsible elements of the community to take the law into their own hands.

Violence, so much a part of American history and particularly of Southern history, has been an important factor in maintaining the two worlds of race. Intimidation, terror, lynchings, and riots have, in succession, been the handmaiden of political entities whose officials have been unwilling or unable to put an end to it. Violence drove Negroes from the polls in the 1870's and has kept them away in droves since that time. Lynchings, the spectacular rope and faggot kind or the quiet kind of merely "doing away" with some insubordinate Negro, have served their special purpose in terrorizing whole communities of Negroes. Riots, confined to no section of the country, have demonstrated how explosive the racial situation can be in urban communities burdened with the strain of racial strife.

The heavy hand of history has been a powerful force in the maintenance of a segregated society and, conversely, in the resistance to change. Americans, especially Southerners whose devotion to the past is unmatched by that of any others, have summoned history to support their arguments that age-old practices and institutions cannot be changed overnight, that social practices cannot be changed by legislation. Southerners have argued that desegregation would break down long-established customs and bring instability to a social order that, if left alone, would have no serious racial or social disorders. After all, Southern whites "know" Negroes; and their knowledge has come from many generations of intimate association and observation, they insist.

White Southerners have also summoned history to support them in their resistance to federal legislation designed to secure the civil rights of Negroes. At every level—in local groups, state governments, and in Congress—white Southerners have asserted that federal civil rights legislation is an attempt to turn back the clock to the Reconstruction era, when federal intervention, they claim, imposed a harsh and unjust peace.[17] To make effective their argument, they use such emotion-laden phrases as "military occupation," "Negro rule," and "black-out of honest government." Americans other than Southerners have been frightened by the Southerners' claim that civil rights for Negroes would cause a return to the "evils" of Reconstruction. Insecure in their own knowledge of history, they have accepted the erroneous assertions about the "disaster" of radical rule after the Civil War and the vengeful punishment meted out to the South by the Negro and his white allies. Regardless of the merits of these arguments that seem specious on the face of them—to say nothing of their historical inaccuracy—they have served as effective brakes on the drive to destroy the two worlds of race.

One suspects, however, that racial bigotry has become more expensive in recent years. It is not so easy now as it once was to make

---

[17]John Hope Franklin, "As For Our History," in Charles G. Sellers (ed.), *The Southerner as American* (Chapel Hill, N. C., 1960), pp. 1-18.

political capital out of the race problem, even in the deep South. Local citizens—farmers, laborers, manufacturers—have become a bit weary of the promises of the demagogue that he will preserve the integrity of the races if he is, at the same time, unable to persuade investors to build factories and bring capital to their communities. Some Southerners, dependent on tourists, are not certain that their vaunted racial pride is so dear, if it keeps visitors away and brings depression to their economy. The cities that see themselves bypassed by a prospective manufacturer because of their reputation in the field of race relations might have some sober second thoughts about the importance of maintaining their two worlds. In a word, the economics of segregation and discrimination is forcing, in some quarters, a reconsideration of the problem.

It must be added that the existence of the two worlds of race has created forces that cause some Negroes to seek its perpetuation. Some Negro institutions, the product of a dual society, have vested interests in the perpetuation of that society. And Negroes who fear the destruction of their own institutions by desegregation are encouraged by white racists to fight for their maintenance. Even where Negroes have a desire to maintain their institutions because of their honest commitment to the merits of cultural pluralism, the desire becomes a strident struggle for survival in the context of racist forces that seek with a vengeance to destroy such institutions. The firing of a few hundred Negro school teachers by a zealous, racially-oriented school board forces some second thoughts on the part of the Negroes regarding the merits of desegregation.

VII

The drive to destroy the two worlds of race has reached a new, dramatic, and somewhat explosive stage in recent years. The forces arrayed in behalf of maintaining these two worlds have been subjected to ceaseless and powerful attacks by the increasing numbers committed to the elimination of racism in American life. Through techniques of demonstrating, picketing, sitting-in, and boycotting they have not only harassed their foes but marshaled their forces. Realizing that another ingredient was needed, they have pressed for new and better laws and the active support of government. At the local and state levels they began to secure legislation in the 1940's to guarantee the civil rights of all, eliminate discrimination in employment, and achieve decent public and private housing for all.

While it is not possible to measure the influence of public opinion in the drive for equality, it can hardly be denied that over the past five or six years public opinion has shown a marked shift toward vigorous support of the civil rights movement. This can be seen in the manner in which the mass-circulation magazines as well as influential newspapers, even in the South, have stepped up their support of specific measures that have as their objective the elimination of at least the worst features of racism. The discussion of the problem of race over radio and television and the use of these media in reporting newsworthy and dramatic events in the world of race undoubtedly have had some impact. If such activities have not brought about the enactment of civil rights legislation, they have doubtless stimulated the public discussion that culminated in such legislation.

The models of city ordinances and state laws and the increased political influence of civil rights advocates stimulated new action on the federal level. Civil rights acts were passed in 1957, 1960, and 1964—after almost complete federal inactivity in this sphere for more than three quarters of a century. Strong leadership on the part of the executive and favorable judicial interpretations of old as well as new laws have made it clear that the war against the two worlds of race now enjoys the sanction of the law and its interpreters. In many respects this constitutes the most significant development in the struggle against racism in the present century.

The reading of American history over the past two centuries impresses one with the fact that ambivalence on the crucial question of equality has persisted almost from the beginning. If the term "equal rights for all" has not always meant what it appeared to mean, the inconsistencies and the paradoxes have become increasingly apparent. This is not to say that the view that "equal rights for some" has disappeared or has even ceased to be a threat to the concept of real equality. It is to say, however, that the voices supporting inequality, while no less strident, have been significantly weakened by the very force of the numbers and elements now seeking to eliminate the two worlds of race.

Part 2

Ethnic Groups and Political Behavior

The direction of an individual's political behavior will vary with such factors as his age, his social class, and his ethnic background. In some cases, the variation in political behavior among people of different social groupings is very significant. For example, in 1960 only forty-five per cent of those over age fifty favored the Democratic Party compared with fifty-eight per cent of those between the ages of twenty-one and twenty-nine; sixty-five per cent of the trade union members favored the Democrats compared with only forty-five per cent of the white collar workers; and eighty-one per cent of the Jews and seventy-three per cent of the Catholics favored the Democrats compared with less than forty per cent of the Protestants.[1] Furthermore, many of these variations hold true regardless of social class. For example,

---

[1] American Institute of Public Opinion release of October 11, 1960 as quoted in Hugh Bone and Austin Ranney, *Politics and Voters* (New York: McGraw-Hill Book Company, 1963), p. 25.

American Jews voted Democratic in every Presidential election since 1936 despite their high socio-economic level.[2]

To correlate group membership with political behavior is interesting, and it does provide us with a better profile of the American electorate. However, it lacks theoretical significance unless one also demonstrates precisely *how* these group memberships affect behavior. In other words, *why* are Jews more Democratic than non-Jews of the same social class; or *why* are New England Italian-Americans more prone to identify with the Republican Party than are their Irish-American counterparts?

Before dealing with this question directly it will be useful to differentiate among different types of social groupings according to the nature of the participation of the members. According to this criterion of participation, social scientists usually distinguish three types of social groups. They are the *categoric group*, the *secondary group*, and the *primary group*.[3]

The categoric group is hardly a group at all, but instead refers to a category of individuals who have some characteristic in common. All women, all Negroes, all people between the ages of twenty-one and twenty-nine, and all people having annual incomes of over $10,000 are examples of categoric groups. The essential quality of categoric groups is that the "members" do not interact with each other on the basis of the shared characteristic.

The term secondary group is used to refer to those large, often impersonal associations that an individual belongs to. Trade unions, professional associations, fraternal organizations, and civic groups are usually examples of secondary groups. Their important characteristic is that an individual participates in a rather narrow set of roles and that the relationship among the members tends to be impersonal and limited.

Primary groups involve intimate, face-to-face relationships that tend to involve the individual as a whole person. The family is the classic example of a primary group, but the notion would also include peer groups, play groups, work groups, and other small and personal relationships in which people are involved. Generally, behavioral scientists have found that primary groups exert the greatest influence on an individual's attitudes and behavior.

The fact that members of the same categoric group exhibit similar attitudes and behavioral patterns results from a shared characteristic

---

[2]See Lawrence H. Fuchs, "American Jews and the Presidential Vote," *American Political Science Review*, XLIX (June 1965), 385-401.

[3]See Bone and Ranney, *op. cit.*, pp. 23-39.

which places them in a special relationship to the rest of the society. For example, Negroes—as distinct from Whites—suffer a common pattern of discrimination at the hands of the rest of society. Consequently, they may develop similar patterns of reacting to the society. More specifically, they may develop certain political attitudes and behavioral patterns that would be shared by large numbers of Negroes.[4] To some extent, the Democratic bias of Negroes, Jews and Catholics may be explained by the fact that these groups often suffered political discrimination at the hands of the Republican Party's white Protestant leadership.[5] Secondly, members of the same ethnic group may share certain attitudes which are more compatible with the doctrines of one party than the other. For example, both Lawrence Fuchs[6] and Daniel Elazar[7] argue that there are certain theological aspects of Judaism that propel Jews to support the social welfare policies of the Democrats rather than the more individualistic philosophy of the Republican Party. In any event, the fact that members of the same categoric group exhibit similar behavioral patterns is to be explained in terms of the characteristic they share in common rather than in terms of any interaction among the members.

Membership in secondary groups tends to structure and reinforce attitudes and behavioral patterns associated with the shared characteristic.[8] In other words, social interaction on the basis of a shared attitude tends to strengthen that shared attitude. This suggests a certain dynamic quality between categoric groups and secondary groups which bears elaboration. Categoric groups are, in a sense, "potential groups."[9] That is to say, a categoric group may become a secondary group if the members of the categoric group organize and interact with each other on the basis of the shared charaacteristic. For example, in 1909, Negroes (a categoric group) organized the National Association for the Advancement of Colored People (a secondary group) in order to better promote and defend their shared racial

---

[4]Abram Kardiner and Lionel Ovesey, *The Mark of Oppression: A Psychological Study of the American Negro* (New York: W. W. Norton & Company, Inc., 1951).

[5]This is the thesis of E. Digby Baltzell in his *The Protestant Establishment: Aristocracy and Caste in America* (New York: Random House, Inc., 1954).

[6]Lawrence H. Fuchs, "Sources of Jewish Internationalism and Liberalism," in Marshall Sklare (ed.), *The Jews* (Glencoe: The Free Press, 1958), pp. 595-613.

[7]Daniel J. Elazar, "American Political Theory and the Political Notions of American Jews: Convergences and Contradictions," *Jewish Journal of Sociology*, IX (June 1967), 5-24.

[8]One of the best statements of this process is found in David B. Truman, *The Governmental Process* (New York: Alfred A. Knopf, Inc., 1951), pp. 23-33.

[9]*Ibid.*

interests.[10] Thus, according to this analysis, Negroes are still a categoric group which, in turn, is organized into a multitude of secondary
groups on the basis of the shared characteristic of race. Much of the
same thing would be true for Jews (organized into B'nai B'rith, the
American Jewish Congress, etc.), Italians (organized into Sons of
Italy Associations and other Italian-American groups), Irish (many
fraternal organizations based on ethnicity), and all other ethnic
groups. If the shared characteristic becomes salient for social or political activity, then individuals sharing it are likely to organize to better
protect and promote their common interest. In the context of ethnic
groups in America, the discriminatory practices of the majority of the
society have been important in making ethnicity politically salient and
in causing the formation of secondary groups based upon ethnicity.
Participation in such an organization then reinforces and structures
the shared attitudes.

Behavioral scientists have long recognized the importance of the
primary group in shaping attitudes and behavior. The influence of the
family is so strong[11] that approximately seventy per cent of children
maintain the same political party loyalty as their parents.[12] Furthermore, this partisan loyalty is likely to be retained even where the
socio-economic status of the children differs markedly from that of
their parents. This tendency goes far in explaining the fact that
middle class Catholics and Jews retain their less affluent parents'
loyalty to the Democratic Party.

The first three readings in this section describe and explain the
influence of ethnic groups—categoric, secondary and primary—on
their members. The readings by Angus Campbell and Robert Lane
elaborate on some of the concepts used in this introduction and
should serve as a theoretical basis for understanding how group memberships influence political behavior. Dwaine Marvick's reading is
addressed to both the role of the primary group in the socialization
process and the extent to which political values differ from one ethnic
group to another.

The distinctive political behavior of ethnic groups is best demonstrated by examining their differential patterns of voting behavior,
exemplified by the case of the Jews. The article by Lawrence Fuchs

---

[10]For a brief description, see W. Haywood Burns, *The Voices of Negro Protest
in America* (New York: Oxford University Press, 1963), pp. 18-36.

[11]See, for example, Herbert McClosky and Harold E. Dahlgren, "Primary
Group Influence and Party Loyalty," *American Political Science Review*, 53
(September 1959), 757-776.

[12]Angus Campbell, *et. al., The American Voter* (New York: John Wiley &
Sons, Inc., 1960), p. 147.

presents evidence to show that the pro-Democratic orientations of Jews show little if any variation with class or status. Indeed, there is ample evidence that wealthier and better educated Jews are more pro-Democratic than those who are lower-income and less educated.

Among American Negroes, as among Jews, social and economic status make little difference in their voting behavior. While Negroes are less pro-Democratic than are Jews, they tend to be more Democratic than whites on any given income level.[13] In the third reading, Oscar Glantz shows that, despite a sharp drop in distinctiveness in voting behavior between 1952 and 1956, Negroes have remained high on the Democratic side in all the presidential elections since 1936.

The degree of socio-economic assimilation of the Irish Catholic population in the American mainstream is well recognized[14] although Catholics follow Jews, Negroes and labor union members in the degree of their affinity for the Democratic party. Yet, "Catholics . . . tend to perceive members of their faith as more Democratic than Republican in their political allegiance."[15] However much this is true, a greater number of Catholics than Jews, Negroes and labor union members have been changing in a Republican direction. In the fourth reading, Scott Greer shows why this is so but also gives reasons to show why the cohesive force of ethnic affiliation should not be underestimated.

---

[13]Seymour Martin Lipset, *Political Man: The Social Bases of Politics* (Garden City, New York: Doubleday & Company, Inc. [Anchor Books], 1963), p. 261.

[14]Angus Campbell, *et. al., Elections and the Political Order* (New York: John Wiley & Sons, Inc., 1966), p. 103.

[15]Angus Campbell, *et. al., op. cit.,* p. 87.

Membership in Social Groupings

Angus Campbell
Philip Converse
Warren Miller
Donald Stokes

During each political campaign we hear comment about the "Catholic vote," the "Negro vote," the "labor vote," and so on. Unlike the political parties, these groups stand at one remove from the political order. Their reason for existence is not expressly political. The labor union exists to force management to provide more liberally for the worker; the Catholic church exists for religious worship. But members of these groups appear to think and behave politically in distinctive ways. We assume that these distinctive patterns are produced, in one fashion or another, by influence from the group.

The Problem of Group Influence

Groups have influence because we tend to think of them as wholes, and come to respond positively or negatively to them in that form. In this sense, even people who are not members of a group may be influenced by the position that a group takes in politics. Groups can become reference points for the formation of attitudes and decisions about behavior; we speak then of *positive* and *negative reference groups*. People who are actually members of the group are likely to have a more differentiated image of it. But there remains a sense of norms and values attributed to a generalized "group": these are the expectations concerning appropriate behavior for the "loyal" Catholic or union member. It is the group standards that are psychologically real and are responsible for influence when it occurs.

We are concerned with the apparent political influence exerted among major, nationwide groupings such as the labor unions, Negroes, Catholics, and Jews. This is not the only level at which political influence dependent on social contact may be examined. Much influence is exerted in smaller, face-to-face "primary" groups such as families, circles of friends, and the like. In fact, there is some evidence to suggest that when primary-group influences run counter to secondary-group political standards, the more intimate contacts may more often than not carry the day.[1] Nonetheless, although many of the mechanisms of influence may be the same in both cases, the study of secondary-group effects has its own unique fruits. It is probably accurate to assume that influence ramifies through primary groups at the grass roots of the nation in a manner fairly constant for both parties. The success or failure of influence at a face-to-face level is not likely to account for the gross trends of the sort constituted by secondary-group voting. If every man managed to influence his wife to vote as he does, we would have no more than a "multiplier" effect on both sides of the political fence. In contrast, successful influence by secondary groups can cause a large-scale, unidirectional shift in the partisan division of the national vote. We are interested in understanding the conditions under which these group pressures are more or less successful.

When we discussed the political parties, it seemed reasonable to speak in terms of a "psychological group," in part because the boundaries of the parties are so poorly delimited by the fact of official membership. In secondary membership groups like labor unions, these formal group boundaries are quite clear. We do not have to ask our informants whether they "consider" they belong to one or another groups; membership is a factual matter. But as we examine these groups more closely, it turns out that the concept of group identification and psychological membership remains extremely valuable. Individuals, all of whom are nominal group members, vary in *degree* of membership, in a psychological sense; and this variation provides us with an excellent tool for breaking apart a voting "bloc," like the American Negro community, in order to understand the workings of influence within the secondary group.

---

[1]Norman Kaplan, "Reference Group Theory and Voting Behavior," (unpublished doctoral dissertation, Columbia University, 1955).

The significance of group identification in all social groupings provides us with a foundation for a more general model of group influence in politics. The scheme would tell us what dimensions of the situation were important for measurement, and how these measures should be combined once they were taken. Appropriate measurements based on such a scheme would allow us to anticipate the direction and degree of the influence that the grouping would wield in the specific situation.

We treat membership in social groupings by sketching the outlines for a general model of this sort. The specific currents observed in the Negro vote in the 1956 election become, in this light, substance of a case study to lay against the more abstract elements called for by the scheme. Likewise, the distinctive behavior of union members toward the objects of politics becomes a special case of the broad phenomenon of group influence.

The Elements of the Model

A model for group influence should perform two distinct services:

1. Increase our understanding of deviation from group political standards by individual members. If the group exerts influence on its membership, and these individuals are members, how and why do they resist?

2. Increase our understanding of the waxing and waning of distinctive political behavior on the part of certain social groupings in the population. What specific conditions govern this variation in group political "strength"?

The same system of variables can handle both problems, for the problems are closely related. If we can specify the conditions under which an individual fails to be influenced by his group, then it is likely that the decline of group potency in politics will result from the extension of these conditions to an increasing proportion of the membership.

At the simplest level, there is a triangle of elements involved in the situation: (1) the individual, (2) the group, and (3) the world of political objects. This triangle suggests three different relationships among these elements: (a) the relationship of the individual to the group; (b) the relationship of the group to the political world; and (c) the relationship of the individual to the political world. These three relationships determine the types of variables that we take into account. A full model will call for measurements that adequately capture the important dimensions of each relationship, if we are to understand the way in which the individual will respond to politics *given the presence of a group that is real in the sense that it can exert a greater or lesser influence on his behavior.*

The relationship of the individual to the world of politics represents a combination of group and nongroup forces. The group forces in the field are predictable as a function of two "background" terms; the relationship of the individual to the group and the relationship of the group to the world of politics. The nongroup forces are, of course, independent of either of these terms. An analysis of the social origins of political motives therefore involves (1) the manner in which the two background terms interact to produce group forces; and (2) the manner in which group forces interact with other forces in the immediate field of political attitudes.

Two important implications are suggested by a logical exercise of this sort. On one hand, we must arrive at some means of sorting the group forces in which we are interested from nongroup forces, within the total field that characterizes the relationship of the individual to the world of politics. But if we pay little systematic attention to the total relationship of the individual to the political world in elaborating this portion of the model, we must not forget that these nongroup forces exist. In fact, this is a first-level answer to the problem of member deviation from group political standards. Group members do not make political decisions in a psychological field limited to group forces, any more than nonmembers make decisions in a vacuum. The current objects of orientation in the political world are available to everybody and, if perceived, have characteristics that can be distorted only within limits.

Our immediate concern lies with the strength of group-generated forces. We wish to understand the conditions under which that strength varies, over time, from individual to individual and from group to group. For this task we can conceptually ignore other forces in the field, which derive from the relation of the individual to politics, *group considerations aside.* But we must remember that these forces exist and contribute to the final attitudes and behavior.

Establishing the Fact of Group Influence

The immediate problem is to find ways to estimate the strength of group forces on the individual. With other forces present in the field, it is easy to mistake their effects for the effects of group influence.

First, it is important to think in terms of the *distinctiveness* of group behavior, rather than its absolute nature. For example, a majority of Catholics in our 1956 sample voted Republican. Traditionally, there has been a Democratic norm among Catholics. Does this finding mean that the norm has died away, or that the group now has new, pro-Republican standards? It means neither. The Catholic Republican vote moved only slightly above the 50 per cent mark, when the nation as a whole was voting 57 per cent Republican. The group force was weak and nongroup forces pushing toward a Republican vote were strong; the nongroup forces were dominant enough to pull a majority of Catholics into the Republican camp, but the presence of group forces in a Democratic direction remains detectible, *relative to the behavior of nongroup members.*

With vote distinctiveness as a criterion, Table 1 summarizes the behavior of several key secondary membership groups with traditional Democratic voting norms over a period of three presidental elections. Several aspects of the table are striking. First we find that there is considerable variation in *degree* of distinctiveness, from election to

TABLE 1

The Distinctiveness of Voting Behavior among Several Social Groupings with Democratic Norms, 1948–1956[a]

	1948	1952	1956
Members of union households[b]	+35.8	+19.8	+18.1
Union members	. . .[c]	+24.9	+21.4
Catholics	+16.2	+12.8	+7.1
Negroes	. . .[d]	+41.2	+24.7
Non-South	. . .[d]	+50.8	+33.1
South	. . .[d]	+17.6	−1.1
Jews	. . .[d]	+31.9	+40.8

[a] The entry in each cell represents the deviation in per cent Democratic of the two-party vote division from the comparable per cent among the residual, nonmember portion of the total sample. A positive deviation indicates that the group vote was more Democratic; a negative deviation indicates that the group was more Republican than the residual nongroup.

[b] "Members of union households" includes both union members, where interviews were conducted with the member himself, and other nonunion individuals living in a household that contained a union member. In most cases, the nonmember is the wife of a member.

[c] Members and nonmembers were not separated within our sample of union households in 1948.

[d] Due to the reduced size of the 1948 sample and the small proportion of Negroes and Jews in the parent population, insufficient cases are available for presentation.

election and from group to group. We also find that each group seems to vary within a characteristic range. Catholics tend to be least distinctive throughout; the labor unions fall in a middle range. Negroes, despite a sharp drop in distinctiveness between 1952 and 1956, remain on the high side along with Jewish voters.

Nevertheless, there is room for dissatisfaction with distinctiveness, cast in this form, as a working measure of influence. The fact of membership in secondary groupings of the type we are considering locates the person in a peculiar position in social structure, which *in itself* ensures a distinctive pattern of life experience. For example, Negroes have been kept in the lower levels of the nation's status structure; they tend to predominate in the least desirable occupations, receive the lowest pay, are least well educated, and so on. Their high birth rate means that young people are more numerous among Negroes than among other elements in the population. In the North, they tend to reside in metropolitan areas; in the South, in small towns and rural areas. All of these distinctive characteristics have a potential effect on their reactions to politics; and this would be true *even if the group did not exist as an entity cognized by its members*. Northern Negroes as a group made a massive shift of allegiance from the Republican to the Democratic Party during the 1930's. Was this group cohesiveness in response to an Administration interested in the welfare of the Negro community, or was it simply the independent reaction of a set of individuals to economic pressures, part and parcel of the nationwide establishment of Democratic dominance at the lower status levels? In the one case, we would speak of group influence; in the other, we would turn to considerations of social class and economic deprivation.

Of course, we cannot ignore the fact that group influence is in part contingent upon the life situations of the membership. But the important point remains that group influence *is* an additional element in the picture; shared membership provides a focus and direction for behavior that is lacking among nongroup members who happen to be placed in the same life situation. Therefore, it is important to distinguish between the patterns of behavior that develop from the life situations of group members, without reference to the group *qua* group, and the residual distinctiveness that may be traced directly to the fact of group membership.

Hence we must contrast behaviors of group members not simply with those of the remainder of the population, but with the restricted part of that population that shares the peculiar life situations of group members. We want to isolate a "control" group of nonmembers that matches the "test" group of members on all important aspects of life situation save the fact of membership.

With life situation controlled, our estimate of group distinctiveness should be materially improved. Table 2 summarizes this new estimate for groups in the context of the 1956 election. If we compare the figures for vote distinctiveness with those in Table 1, we find that much of the picture has remained the same. Catholic distinctiveness has almost disappeared, and the estimate of Jewish distinctiveness has risen slightly. But the major change has been a substantial reduction in the estimate of distinctiveness of the non-Southern Negro vote. This group remains significantly Democratic; but taking into account its extremely low status, its relative youth, and its Southern origins leaves it less Democratic than might appear at first glance.[2]

With such controls, we have more nearly reduced the relationship betweeen the individual and the world of politics to its group-relevant aspects. In effect, we have arrived at an improved estimate of the strength of group forces in the total field at the time of the voting act. The estimate is not perfect and depends on an aggregation of cases;

TABLE 2

Distinctiveness of Presidential Vote among Certain Groups,
with Life Situation Controlled, 1956[a]

	1956 Presidential Vote
Members of union households	+17.1
Union members	+20.4
Catholics	+2.9
Negroes	
Non-South	+11.6
South	+15.4
Jews	+45.4

[a] The entry in each cell represents a deviation in per cent Democratic of the two-party vote within the test group from a comparable per cent computed for control groups matched with the test groups for a variety of conditions of life situation.

---

[2] The application of the Southern-origin factor to Negroes represents one point at which we lack sufficient information to exercise controls prudently. As the matter stands, the distinctiveness of the Negro group may be underestimated in Table 2.

we cannot say that any specific group member is more swayed by the group than any other, although we get the clear impression that some groups exert more effective influence than others. We must now turn to other elements in the model to account for this variation in influence.

The Relationship of the Individual to the Group

The first variables to be considered must define the way in which the individual relates himself to the group. We would like to measure aspects of the individual-group relationship that are meaningful for the relationship of *any* individual to *any* group, whether or not that group ever expends effort in political affairs.

Let us think of the group as a psychological reality that exerts greater or lesser attractive force upon its members. Whatever the nominal membership status of the individual, there is room for a great deal of variation in the degree of psychological membership that characterizes the relationship. Just as party identification measures the sense of personal attachment to a political party, so a measure of group identification will indicate the closeness or "*we* feeling" that an individual senses with regard to his membership group.

We have measured group identification by asking members of various politically significant groups the following questions:

Would you say that you feel pretty close to (e.g.) Negroes in general or that you don't feel much closer to them than you do to other kinds of people?

How much interest would you say you have in how (e.g.) Negroes as a whole are getting along in this country? Do you have a good deal of interest in it, some interest, or not much interest at all?

From responses to these items an index of group identification was prepared. The first hypothesis that the model suggests is as follows: *the higher the identification of the individual with the group, the higher the probability that he will think and behave in ways which distinguish members of his group from nonmembers.*

Actually hypotheses much like this have found supporting evidence in other empirical work on voting behavior. Therefore, we are not surprised to find that if we take all members of groups that vote distinctively Democratic, the people who are highly identified with these groups vote even more distinctively Democratic than members who are less highly identified. The least identified third voted 43 per cent Democratic, a figure not very different from the vote proportion in the population as a whole. Medium identifiers, however, voted 56 per cent Democratic; and those most highly identified with these groups voted 69 per cent Democratic. In general, then, the hypothesis receives clear support, and strength of group identification deserves a place as a variable in our model.

Secondary groups that are not primarily political take little interest in some issues, and in these cases group members do not hold attitudes that differ significantly from those of nonmember control groups nor do high identifiers differ from more peripheral members. But as a general rule, whenever a group holds distinctive beliefs about some issue, then within the group a differentiation appears between members according to the strength of their group identification.

This combination of facts argues most conclusively that we are dealing here with a true group-influence phenomenon. To ascertain that influence exists is but a first step, however. We are also interested in assessing the relative strength of influence exerted by various groups and the conditions under which this strength increases or decreases. We find considerable variation in the degree of disparity in presidential vote between strong and weak identifiers within various groups. Table 3 summarizes this variation. If we compare these figures

TABLE 3

Vote Division Within Four Test Groups, According to Strength
of Group Identification, 1956[a]

	Highly Identified	Weakly Identified	Discrepancy
Members of union households	64	36	+28
Catholics	51	39	+11
Negroes			
Non-South	72	63	+9
South	...[b]	...[b]	...[b]
Jews	83	55	+28

[a] The entries in the first two columns represent the per cent Democratic of the two-party vote division. The final column summarizes the differences between percentages in the first two, a plus indicating that high identifiers in the group voted more strongly Democratic.

[b] Southern Negro voters in the sample are too few for further subdivision.

with those in Table 2, we find some interesting similarities in the rank ordering of the groups. Vote distinctiveness *within the group* bears some relation to distinctiveness between the group and a control group matched for life situation, as we would expect if both were taken to reflect strength of group political influence. But there are differences, also: high identifiers are more distinct in the union case and less distinct in the Negro case than Table 2 would lead us to expect. Most Negroes are highly identified with their group; therefore the total group is more clearly Democratic than it might appear if the proportion of high and low identifiers within the Negro group was closer to that found within the union group. But part of the discrepancy results from other factors to be added to the model shortly.

Group identifications help to answer the two primary questions with which a theory of group influence must deal. At the individual level, we may sort out a set of nominal members who are most likely to deviate from the group position under nongroup forces. They are the people who do not strongly identify with the group, who are psychologically peripheral to it.

A similar proposition can be formulated at the group level. Some groups boast memberships intensely loyal to group purposes and interests. Others have trouble maintaining member identifications. We shall call a group enjoying high member identification a *cohesive*

TABLE 4

Relation of Group Cohesiveness to Group Identification, 1956

Cohesiveness	Mean Identification Score[a]	Group
High	2.5	Southern Negro
	2.2	Non-Southern Negro
	2.2	Jewish
Low	1.8	Union Member
	1.6	Catholic
	1.6	Member, union household

[a] The response to the two identification questions are scored such that a maximum value on the index is 3.0, when the most positive response is made to both items. The corresponding minimum value is 0.0, when the most negative response is made to both items. About 61 per cent of Southern Negroes responded positively toward the group on both items; the corresponding proportion among Catholics was 28 per cent.

group.[3] Group cohesiveness is one determinant of the influence which a group can wield over its membership.

If a group has generated distinctive political attitudes and behavior among its members, this distinctiveness will fade if group cohesiveness is destroyed. Cohesiveness itself must depend on a number of factors according to the type of group and the setting involved. Within the large and far-flung social groupings under discussion in this chapter, a prime determinant may simply be the degree to which group members feel set apart from other people by virtue of social barriers. If we set up a mean identification score as a simple index of cohesiveness for each group, the resulting array (see Table 4) seems to support this hypothesis.

The Relationship of the Group to the World of Politics

If the relationship between individual and group is summarized by the concept of identification, attempts to deal with the relationship of the group to the world of politics focus upon a vaguer concept of *proximity*. All of our secondary membership groups except the political party have their basic existence outside of the political order. At this point it becomes important to specify this distance from the world of politics more precisely.

If we analyze our intuitions concerning proximity, we find that they depend upon the frequency with which we have seen the group *qua* group associated intimately with objects that are clearly political—issues, candidates, and parties. We would think, for example, of lobbying activity, political pronouncements, and candidates who publicize the fact of membership in that group. We would consider what we know of the primary goals of the group, and their apparent relevance to politics. The perceived relationship between the group and the world of politics has substantial grounding in objective events, constituted largely by the actions of group leaders. But we could not expect that all individuals, or even all group members, would perceive the relationship of the group to politics in precisely the same manner. Thus we shall think of proximity as a subjective dimension, a tendency to associate group and politics at a psychological level.

Where proximity has partisan significance we would hypothesize that: *as proximity between the group and the world of politics increases, the political distinctiveness of the group will increase.*

Or, at the individual level: *as perception of proximity between the*

---

[3]Dorwin P. Cartwright and Alvin Zander, *Group Dynamics: Research and Theory* (Row, Peterson and Co., Evanston, Ill., 1953), Part II, pp. 71-134.

group and the world of politics becomes clearer, the susceptibility of the individual member of group influence in political affairs increases.

The concept of proximity will have to undergo further refinement before these hypotheses have full meaning. We must specify a good deal more precisely the dimensions that are involved in our general sense of proximity, and attempt to measure them more objectively.

We have suggested that perceptions of proximity between one's group and the world of politics rest upon associations that have been built up between the group and the political objects. How do these links become established? In some cases, the associations are directly given, as when the political candidate is a highly visible member of the group. The link is, so to speak, "built into" the object of orientation itself. We shall discuss phenomena of this sort under the general heading of *group salience* in politics. More often, however, the establishment of associations between the group and politics depends on conscious effort by elements within the group to propagate certain standards of member behavior. This *transmission of standards* is a communication process, and its effectiveness depends on the clarity with which the standard is transmitted and the insistence that accompanies it.

But the perceived proximity of the group to the world of politics depends on more than the perception of a group standard at a point in time. While the successful transmission of a group standard in a particular situation may increase the member's sense of proximity, we would propose that the effect of any particular standard, once received, will vary according to the individual's generalized, preexisting sense of proximity between group and politics. In part, then, proximity is dependent upon reception of past standards; in part, too, it is dependent on the individual's sense of the *fitness* of group activity in politics. Underlying values that deny the group a legitimate role in the political world act as barriers to reduce the sense of proximity, however clearly standards may be received.

What we have roughly labeled proximity, then, has a number of dimensions that demand independent treatment, and we shall discuss several of these. Throughout, we encounter evidence that the perceived relationship of the group to politics, like the relationship of the individual to the group, bears directly upon the strength of group forces in the field at the time of political decision.

The Transmission of Group Political Standards

Whatever the process of communication that alerts the member to a partisan group standard, we can think of group norms as forces, having a given direction and varying degrees of strength. The standard prescribes support of one party, candidate, or issue position, and forbids support of the other. And these prescriptions are propagated with varying amounts of urgency or intensity.

There are two conditions in which group standards may lack sufficient clarity to permit influence. The end result of each is the same—a lack of distinctiveness in the aggregate group vote—but the differences are of considerable theoretical interest. In one case, the usual channel for communication of such norms is silent as to a particular standard, or emits it very weakly. For example, within international unions where standards were most clear according to the content analysis of preelection editions of official journals, the vote division among members in our sample was 67 per cent Democratic. This fell to 55 per cent, then to 51 per cent, and finally to 44 per cent where standards were least clear. These differences occurred even though the proportion of high identifiers from category to category varied over a range of only 3 per cent, so that we cannot explain the variation in vote by differences in group cohesiveness.

In the other case, conflicting standards are conveyed to the membership. When standards conflict, there are several possible outcomes. At one extreme, we might find that no single member became aware of the conflict in standards, but that various sets of members felt pressures in opposing directions. Here is the point at which analysis of influence at the individual level becomes more accurate than that at a group level. For in such a situation, even if every member responded to influence, the aggregate outcome might lead the observer to believe that no influence had occurred at all.

At the other extreme, all members may be aware of a conflict in standards. To some degree, the group force is cancelled out: even if the member is concerned with respectability in the eyes of the group, he can pick the standard that would best suit his desires independent of group considerations and act accordingly without feeling guilt. If, however, the situation is ripe for influence—if the individual is motivated to conform to the group—it is unlikely that events will work out in just this way. A conflict in group standards usually occurs as a result of decentralization of leadership. Few large and far-flung groups can long maintain a leadership with monolithic control over group standards. Among the secondary membership groups this is especially true. But if an unwieldly group tends to develop its subgroups with their conflicting standards, the general model still applies. Although awareness of different standards among other elements of the total group may relax group pressures to some degree, the individual is likely to feel most strongly the forces from the subgroup with which he is most strongly identified.

Conflicting Standards: A Case Study

We have found the Negro community to be the most cohesive of the groups we have surveyed. Furthermore, Negroes, as we shall see, are almost unanimous in their belief that the group has a right to further its ends by political activity. Several of the necessary conditions for influence are fulfilled. In 1952, there was a good deal of solidarity among Negro leaders in their endorsement of the Democratic presidential ticket. And the Negro vote itself in 1952 was very distinctively Democratic.

In 1956, however, Negro leaders were much less enthusiastic about the Democratic Party, owing in part to the role of Southern Democratic legislators in blocking civil rights legislation and in part to Republican sympathy with Negro aspirations. The National Association for Advancement of Colored People adopted a posture of watchful waiting, with occasional executive threats of a Republican endorsement. The two senior United States Congressmen from the Negro community gave clear public support to opposing candidates for the presidency: Adam Clayton Powell in New York City endorsed Eisenhower, whereas William L. Dawson of Chicago supported Stevenson.

This conflict in standards was reflected in the perceptions of Negroes in our sample. When asked how they thought Negroes around the country would vote in the 1956 election, responses had shifted sharply away from the near Democratic unanimity that the same question elicited in 1952. Furthermore, the conflict was most clearly perceived at the level of the leadership. Almost as many Negroes saw the leadership voting Republican as Democratic in 1956. The distinctiveness of the Negro vote fell off sharply.

We hypothesized that when a secondary group fragments into subgroups propagating standards that conflict, much the same influence process goes on, with identification focused on the appropriate subgroup rather than the total group. In Chicago, where Dawson had stood firm for the Democrats, there was an overall decline of 5 per cent in the Democratic presidential vote, by comparison with 1952. Within the city, three of the most clearly Negro wards declined 4 per cent, 4 per cent, and 9 per cent—close to the city average. In New York City, the picture was different. In the heavily colored New York

Assembly Districts 11 and 12, which included much of Powell's constituency, the Democratic presidential vote fell about 15 per cent. And this occurred despite a fraction of a per cent increase in the Stevenson vote in New York County as a whole. The effect of conflicting standards is to reduce the distinctiveness of the total group vote; but where we can isolate subgroups, we find evidence of influence.

The Political Salience of the Group

In some situations, the need for active propagation of group standards is at a minimum, because the standard is self-evident. This is the case when important political objects of orientation embody group cues, so that the course of behavior characteristic of a "good" group member cannot be held in doubt. Fundamentally, this situation is no more than a special case of the transmission of clear and strong standards. But it deserves separate treatment because it implies a simpler and less fallible communication process and because it involves a stratagem dear to the hearts of political tacticians. This dimension is one component of the model that is especially subject to short-term variation, since salience usually depends on the most transient objects of political orientation: the candidates and the issues.

Political salience of the group is high, for example, when a candidate for the election is recognized as a member of the group. Attracting the votes of members of a particular group by nominating a candidate who is a group member is, of course, a time-worn strategy in the art of political maneuver. Frequent executive appointment of group members to high posts is of the same order, although perhaps less potent in creating salience. It is our thesis that the success of the maneuver among group members depends upon the values of other variables in the total model. High salience alone does not create a unanimous group response.

The political salience of the group can also be increased by a coincidence between group goals and current political issues. The degree of salience that accrues with regard to issues in any particular situation is some joint function of the importance of the issue in the campaign and the importance of the goal to the group. One of the central issues of the 1948 campaign was the Taft-Hartley Act, which union leadership felt threatened vital aspects of the movement. To the degree that these elements communicated to the rank and file, the labor union ought to have been particularly salient for members voting in the election. Since that time, civil rights controversies have tended to increase the political salience of Negro membership.

Salience: A Case Study

The behavior of Catholic voters toward Catholic candidates for the United States Congress allows us to examine the salience phenomenon. We recall that in Table 2 the presidential vote among Catholics in 1956 was barely more Democratic than that among a Catholic control group (a margin of 3 per cent). We find a much more distinctive vote if we shift the scene to those congressional races in which a Catholic candidate was pitted against a non-Catholic (Table 5). Furthermore, Catholic voters are quite willing to cross party lines to support a candidate of the same creed. Thus if we decompose Table 5 we find that where the Catholic candidate is a Democrat, Catholics vote over 10 per cent more Democratic than their control group; but where the Catholic candidate is Republican, Catholics vote over 10 per cent more *Republican* than their controls.

TABLE 5

Political Salience: The Vote of Catholics for Catholic Congressional Candidates in Races Involving Non-Catholics, 1956[a]

	Catholic Identification		
	High	Low	Total Group
Catholic voters	63%	59%	61%
	(43)	(51)	(94)
Catholic control	...	...	49%
			(76)

[a] The per cent entry refers to the proportion of the indicated group voting for the Catholic candidate in the split-religion congressional race. The figure in parentheses indicates the number of cases involved in each proportion.

By sacrificing a large proportion of our cases, we can refine the data in a manner that sharpens these relationships further. Obviously, the theory underlying the salience hypotheses demands that the voter recognize the candidate as a group member if salience effects are to emerge. If we restrict our attention to those voters (one-third of the total) who can refer to their congressional choices by name after the election, we should clear away some individuals for whom we could little expect salience to be operative.

TABLE 6

Group Salience: The Vote of Catholics for Catholic Candidates
Whose Names Can Be Recalled, in Races Involving Non-Catholics, 1956[a]

	Catholic Identification		
	High	Low	Total Group
U. S. House of Representatives			
Catholic voters	85%	69%	77%
	(13)	(13)	(26)
Catholic control	. . .	. . .	51%
			(25)
U. S. Senate			
Catholic voters	86%	57%	70%
	(22)	(28)	(50)
Catholic control	. . .	. . .	49%
			(47)

[a] The per cent entry refers to the proportion of the indicated group who voted for the Catholic candidate in the split-religion congressional or senatorial race. The figure in each parenthesis indicates the number of cases involved in each proportion.

Although the cases for analysis are few, Table 6 shows a group vote much more distinctive yet than that in Table 5. And the inadequate number of cases is offset somewhat by the fact that similar results are to be found when we look for the same patterns within the 1956 U. S. senatorial races in which Catholics were involved. These similarities emerge even though the Catholic voters appearing in both segments of the table are few indeed.

There is, therefore, substantial evidence that the salience of a group membership, created by group cues in the political object, intensifies group forces in the member's psychological field at the time of the vote decision. On the other hand, we should note that the sharpening of findings from Table 5 to Table 6 indicates that lack of attention to candidates for House and Senate may make severe inroads upon the vote increment which the aspirant can reap from salience effects.

The Legitimacy of Group Political Activity

However strong the group identification, and however firm the association between group and political objects, the member may resist the intrusion of "non-political" groups upon the political scene. There are cultural values bound up with beliefs about democracy and the individual that inveigh against such activity. The sophisticated view of democracy as a competition between interest groups does not have great popular currency. Voting, whether at the mass or the legislative level, is morally a matter of individual judgment and conscience; recognition of group obligation and interests is thoroughly taboo to some Americans.

We asked members of various groups whether they felt it was "all right" for organizations representing the group to support legislative proposals and candidates for office. The responses to these questions showed a fairly strong relationship with the group identification variable. The more highly identified a group member, the more likely he was to grant the group a right to engage in political activity. Within each level of group identification, however, members of the two religious groups—Catholics and Jews—show much greater reluctance to accept the legitimacy statements than either of the two more secular groupings—Negroes and union members. Also, with identification controlled, there is somewhat less readiness to grant legitimacy among older people. This fact would conform with the impressions that popular values opposing frank interest-group politics represent an older America.

The Backgrounds of Group Identifications

We have indicated some of the sources of feelings about legitimacy. It is natural to inquire as well concerning the roots of group identification. Why do some group members identify with the group, whereas others fail to?

This is a difficult problem, and our evidence to date is fragmentary. But we can draw a few general conclusions about major determinants of identification. There are numerous groups, of course, that are created for the purpose of political and ideological persuasion, such as the National Economic Council or the American Civil Liberties Union. Members are recruited and come to identify with the group on the basis of pre-existing beliefs and sympathies. Here the case for influence is much less clear, except as group activity serves to reinforce and guide member efforts. But in most groups formed along occupational, ethnic, or religious lines membership is more likely to determine attitudes than are attitudes to determine membership.

There is little doubt of this fact in the groups we have watched most closely. Except in some semiorganized areas of the South, even membership in the labor union is effectively involuntary. If labor union members vote distinctively, we cannot say that only workers with certain attitudes join the union; rather, we must concede that influence exists. But if membership is involuntary, identification is not. How can we be sure that high union identification plays a formative role in the development of political attitudes?

There is a clear and substantial relationship between strength of union identification and length of membership in the union. The longer an individual has belonged to the union, the more likely he is to identify strongly with it, and we can find no other causative factors that begin to approach this relationship in strength. A relationship between age and union identification has been observed before, but it was never clear whether the relationship existed because of simple contact with the union over time, or because the unusual "barricades" generation of the 1930's would currently constitute the bulk of older union members. Our data show clearly that older men who have recently joined the union have weak identification with it, whereas younger men aged 25 and 30 who have belonged to the union for longer periods show stronger identifications with it. In fact, if we control length of union membership, we find that the relationship between age and union identification is somewhat negative. The later in life a person joins a union, the less completely he will be identified with it given any particular length of membership. His identification will still increase with length of membership, but the level will not be quite as strong as it would be for a person who had joined when younger.

This cluster of findings is of considerable theoretical significance. In the first place, it makes it difficult to maintain that identification with the union results as a rule from existing political attitudes similar to those represented by the union. Instead, we get a sense of an acculturation process—slow and cumulative influence over a period of time, with identification as the key intervening factor. It appears that a potent force in the growth of group identifications is simple contact and familiarity, just as an immigrant comes to identify with the new country and accept its customs as time passes. Furthermore, like the immigrant, identifications never become as strongly rooted if the initiate is no longer young.

These findings are important from another point of view as well. For the pattern of relationships between age, length of membership, and strength of identification is precisely the same as we found where the group involved is the political party. That is, party identification appears to grow stronger with age; but the critical variable, instead of being age, is length of psychological membership in the party. With length of membership controlled, age is negatively related to party identification, just as it is in the union case.

Those few persons who have been union members for long periods of time yet who have remained unidentified are less likely to vote Democratic than any of the other union subgroups isolated. Not only are they much more Republican in their vote than union members generally; they are even more Republican than the control group matched with union members on aspects of life situation (33 per cent Democratic vote among those who have been members 15 years or more, as opposed to 36 per cent for the control group). Thus lack of identification among long-standing members of the union may have actively negative implications not present among new members who are not yet strongly identified.

We find no such clear relation between age and group identification among Catholics, Negroes, or Jews. Age, in these groups, logically coincides with "length of membership." There is some faint increase in identification among older Catholics, and an equally faint decrease in identification among older Negroes. We would expect these differences to appear if Catholic cohesiveness is waning and if the current civil rights ferment is beginning to sharpen cohesiveness among Negroes. But these tendencies are very weak, and there is no trend visible at all in the Jewish situation. We must conclude that no reliable relationship is present.

The contrast in the development of identification between these groups and the union or party is sharp. We are led to consider differences in the characteristics of the several groups that might account for such variation. It is obvious that the individual takes on serious membership in a union or in the psychological group represented by a political party later in life than is the case with the other groups. The individual grows up within the atmosphere of a religious or ethnic group in a much more inclusive sense than with either the party or the union.

Thus, different patterns of identification may be traced to basic differences in types of groups. But it is possible to suggest a more general proposition to cover all cases: instead of considering age or even the absolute length of time of group membership as the proper independent variable, let us employ the *proportion of the individual's life* spent as a member. Recast in this fashion, the presence of the strong positive relationship between length of membership and identification, the negative relationship between age and identification with length of membership constant, and the fact that certain ascribed groups show no variation with age would all be predicted by a single independent variable. If there is no relationship between "length of membership" and identification among Catholics, Jews, and Negroes, it is because members of these groups have held membership for 100 per cent of their lives, and variation in their identification must be explained with other factors. We arrive at the general proposition that one fundamental determinant of group identifications is the proportion of one's life spent in close (psychological) contact with the group.

Secondary Groups, the Political Party, and the Influence Process

If the political party, and psychological membership in it, fit a more general model for social memberships and political influence, it is equally clear that the party has a peculiar location in the space that the model encompasses. We have laid out with some care what seem to be the components of the relationship between any group and the world of politics. This effort was necessary because the secondary groups with which we dealt were not at base political, and this fact turns out to be a crucial limitation in the political influence they can wield. Now if we were to fill in the values that the scheme requires for prediction, we would find that in the case of the party, proximity is at an upper limit, for the party has a central position in the world of politics. In all major elections, its salience is absolutely high: one candidate is always a group member, the prime group goal is political victory, and all controversial issues represent subordinate goals that the group has assumed. The legitimacy of its activity in politics goes without question, for the major parties at least, and the communication of their standards is perfect. Therefore, we would expect that the political influence of psychological membership in a party would be extremely potent, relative to other secondary memberships. If we take distinctiveness of political attitudes and behavior as a criterion, this proposition cannot be questioned.

We are most directly interested, at this point, in suggesting the processes by which nonpolitical membership groups come to have a certain amount of political influence. Thus far we have paid little attention to the fact that these processes have duration over time. The political influence of secondary memberships, as witnessed in the distinctiveness of a group vote, is not necessarily a product of the immediate situation. The labor union need not indoctrinate its mem-
1956, there is no need to presume that this distinctiveness represents
bership anew at each election. If the labor vote was distinctive in

only the political action of the union during the 1956 campaign. Influence, when successful, has enduring effects, and in this sense the distinctiveness of a group vote at any point in time represents cumulative influence. We hypothesize that the political party plays a crucial role in the durability of this influence.

When a political candidate is a member of one's group, or when the issues of politics bear directly upon goals important to the group, membership in that group becomes salient in the individual's orientation to politics. In these instances, the need for political translation, for communication of specific standards regarding proper group behavior, is slight. But under normal circumstances, when salience is not high, the group, if it is to have influence, must lend the observed world political meaning in terms relevant to the group.

Now issues and candidates are transient political objects; the entity that endures is the party. If group influence leads the identified member to take on identification with the party, then little renewal of influence is needed. The individual has, as it were, acceded to a self-steering mechanism, that will keep him politically "safe" from the point of view of group standards. He will respond to new stimuli as a party member and code them properly. As time passes, his identification with the party will increase of its own accord, because the individual will find that event after event demonstrates—in nongroup matters as well as group matters now—the rectitude of his own party and the obnoxiousness of its opponent.

If there were no parties, but only a flux of candidates and issues, it does not follow that there would be no political influence exerted by other membership groups. The psychological economy of the individual demands parties as an organizing principle, and if bereft of this, there might be much more straightforward dependence on other groups for guidance. In situations of this sort, secondary groups with quite apolitical origins have in fact come to function as political parties.[4] But where parties exist, influence from nonpolitical secondary groups is likely to have a good deal of continuity.

Given the flux of objects like candidates and issues, group influence is likely to be most effective when meaningful contact is established between the group and the party, for parties subsume candidates and issues and, more important, endure over time. However, this proposition is true only if we define influence in a very particular way, that is, as cumulative over time. An individual led to a Democratic orien-

---

[4]As an example, see Key's treatment of factionalism in the South. Secondary groups constitute one type of nucleus for the factions that compete for political power in a one-party system. V. O. Key, *Southern Politics in State and Nation* (Alfred Knopf, New York, 1950), pp. 52-57.

tation by a group membership in 1930 may still be registering a manifestation of that influence in 1956.

But for the practical politician who wants to know how many votes a group leader can "deliver" to one party or the other in a specific election, influence may have a rather different meaning. Here we encounter a paradox. If party identification is a trustworthy bridge from group identification to "proper" political behavior, it is also a structure which, once laid down, is not readily moved. Thus the mechanisms that are best calculated to build a reliably distinctive group vote are at the same time mechanisms that tend to undermine the maneuverability of the group in politics.

When political events cause a group leadership to switch official support to the opposing party, the strong party loyalties that it has helped to create and reinforce may be reversed only with great difficulty.[5] We can imagine that these loyalties, even when direct creations of group influence, gain some functional autonomy as they grow stronger. They come to have a force of their own, rather than remaining dependent on forces from the nonpolitical secondary group. And, since the political party can exert unusually intense influence on political motives, this force may turn out to be stronger than any counter-force that the nonpolitical group can bring to bear *in politics* at a later date. It would follow from the general outlines of our theory that when such reversals of group standards occur, the new influence will have most effect among the youngest group members.

The political party may be treated, then, as a special case of a more general group-influence phenomenon. The party may be located within our model, and values on appropriate dimensions may be calculated for the party member at any point in time. The nature of the group, so located, ensures the power of its influence within the world of politics. But of great significance also is the role of the party as a bridge between other social groupings and that political world. The influence of other secondary groups in politics comes to have more enduring effects as loyalties directed toward them may be transferred to abiding political loyalties.

---

[5]It is interesting to note that for large-scale, secondary groups at the national level, these switches are rare and tend to be limited to rebellious factions. Many aspects of political process seem to converge toward maintenance of these continuities. Factors such as the dependence of the party on group support and the loyalties and interpersonal commitments built up between group leaders and the party enhance the temptation to work for reform within the chosen party when things go awry. These facts make treatment of influence in its cumulative sense the more meaningful.

The Way of the Ethnic in Politics

Robert E. Lane

How do race, religion, immigrant status, and origins in other than Anglo-Saxon countries, a complex of factors which we refer to as "ethnic," affect political participation? Unlike subordinate class status, subordinate ethnic status is, in general, unlikely to depress political interests.[1] The most visible ethnic minority, the American Negro, is, it is true, systematically deprived of the right to participate in civic affairs in the South, but in the North he votes as frequently as the average—indeed, perhaps a little more frequently than is common among those of similar economic position. This is true in relatively small towns, such as Delaware, Ohio, and in the large cities of Detroit

---

Reprinted with permission of The Macmillan Company from *Political Life: Why People Get Involved in Politics* by Robert E. Lane. Copyright The Free Press, a corporation 1959.

[1]The general conclusions on ethnic voting are supported by evidence in the following: Charles E. Merriam and Harold F. Gosnell, *Non-Voting* (Chicago: University of Chicago Press, 1924); Harold F. Gosnell, *Getting Out the Vote* (Chicago: University of Chicago Press, 1927); Angus Campbell, Gerald Gurin and Warren E. Miller, *The Voter Decides* (Evanston, Ill.: Row, Peterson, 1954); Ben A. Arneson and William H. Eells, "Voting Behavior in 1948 as Compared With 1924 in a Typical Ohio Community," *American Political Science Review, 44* (1950), pp. 432-34; Louis Harris, *Is There a Republican Majority?* (New York: Harper, 1954); Edward H. Litchfield, *Voting Behavior in a Metropolitan Area* (Ann Arbor, Mich.: University of Michigan Press, 1941); Gerhart H. Saenger, "Social Status and Political Behavior," *American Journal of Sociology, 51* (1945), pp. 103-13; Alfred de Grazia, "The Limits of External Leadership over a Minority Electorate," *Public Opinion Quarterly, 20* (1956), pp. 113-28.

and Chicago, and "across the board" in the North.[2] And, like color, recency of immigration is not a systematic factor affecting rates of turnout.[3] Once the minimum legal period has been achieved and citizenship won, the immigrant votes now, as he did thirty years ago, fully as frequently as the non-immigrant. Nor does generation time in this country affect frequency of participation—at least not in any systematic way.[4]

On the whole, as might be expected, those nationality groups that settled in the cities (Irish, Italian, Polish) have somewhat higher rates of participation than those who have substantial proportions in rural areas (German, Scandinavian), and, it may be noted, each group has slightly higher rates than the natives in circumstances similar to its own. This is a change in the proportions which prevailed in the twenties, when nationality groups other than natives of "Yankee" origin tended to participate in politics much less than the average.[5]

As for religious differences in rates of participation, the rising standards of living and assimilation of Catholics and Jews, has now brought their rates of participation equal to or above the rates of similarly situated Protestants. Today, of all ethnic and religious groups, the Jews are the most frequent participants.[6] Among the various ethnic groups however, different patterns of participation sometimes emerge; Jews write more letters to their congressmen; Catholics are more likely to be members of political clubs; Negroes have a higher than average rate of formal group membership (perhaps chiefly focused upon church membership).[7]

Ethnic Stakes in Politics

Persons of ethnic background are interested in politics for the same reasons as the rest of the population: they have occupational interests

---

[2] On Negro voting, see also, Gunnar Myrdal, *An American Dilemma* (New York, Harper, 1944), Vol. I, pp. 474-504; V. O. Key, *Southern Politics in State and Nation* (New York: Knopf, 1949), pp. 517-22; Donald S. Strong, "The Rise of Negro Voting in Texas," *American Political Science Review*, 42 (1948), pp. 500-09; Paul Lewison, *Race, Class, and Party* (New York: Oxford, 1932); Harold Gosnell, *Negro Politicians* (Chicago: University of Chicago Press, 1935).

[3] H. F. Gosnell, *Getting Out the Vote*, p. 87.

[4] A. Campbell and associates, *op. cit.*, p. 78.

[5] B. A. Arneson and W. H. Eells, *op. cit.*, p. 433; E. H. Litchfield, *op. cit.*, p. 12; see also Hugo V. Mailey, *The Italian Vote in Philadelphia Between 1928 and 1946* (Philadelphia, Hugo V. Mailey, 1950).

[6] B. A. Arneson and W. H. Eells, *op. cit.*, p. 433; E. H. Litchfield, *op. cit.*, p. 18; A. Campbell and associates, *op. cit.*, p. 70. See also Lawrence H. Fuchs, *The Political Behavior of American Jews* (Glencoe, Ill.; Free Press, 1956).

[7] G. H. Saenger, *op. cit.*, pp. 105-06.

which may be affected by tariffs or regulation, they are subject to local and national taxation, they have personal preferences among candidates and parties. But there are additional reasons for ethnics to be concerned about political decisions. The first of these has to do with the ethnic rivalry or conflict which takes a variety of forms throughout the country. In "Eastern City" in the 1920's the dominant Irish group in certain wards heightened their activity to keep control from the invading Italians. But the Italians, partly through the use of "repeaters," gained control of a number of wards.[8] In New Haven, the Italian challengers, unable to win concessions from the Irish Democrats, organized their strength in the Republican party and the tensions between the two groups became politicized. Similarly, in the first decade of this century the Jews in Boston went to work for the Republicans because "wherever . . . they moved they found the Democratic organization tightly controlled by Irishmen."[9] In the same way the native white Protestant group may respond to ethnic challenge by political organization. In Jonesville, at the turn of the century, the native Protestants organized a branch of the anti-Catholic American Protective Association to stop the growing power of the Democratic Irish Catholic group originally brought in to work on a nearby canal.[10] In New York and Massachusetts the Yankees sought allies in the same basic struggle with the Irish: The "Republicans attempted to woo the Italians and Jews to break the hold of the Irish Democrats on the city vote."[11]

There are many areas of domestic policy which are of special concern to one ethnic group or another.[12] National policy dealing with immigration was a matter of considerable concern for Italian groups in the 1920's. The National Origins Act, limiting Italian immigration to 5,802, not only "made the Italians (in America) fully aware of their nationality," but was defended in terms which wounded their dignity and aroused a great wave of protest.[13] In 1948 the Citizens Committee on Displaced Persons had the largest single number of lobbyists of any group in Washington, a fact which reflects the Jewish demand for a more generous admission policy toward Nazi vic-

---

[8]William F. Whyte, *Street Corner Society* (Chicago: Chicago University Press, 1955), pp. 194-96.

[9]L. H. Fuchs, *op. cit.,* p. 56.

[10]W. Lloyd Warner, *Democracy in Jonesville* (New York: Harper, 1949), p. 215.

[11]Oscar Handlin, *The Uprooted* (Boston: Little, Brown, 1951), p. 216.

[12]For a discussion of the history of American suffrage for aliens and naturalized citizens see above pp. 13-14.

[13]H. V. Mailey, *op. cit.,* p. 82.

tims.[14] Efforts to pass the child labor amendment in New York produced a flood of postcards from Catholic communicants who were told by the Church leaders that this represented "youth control" contrary to Church policy.[15] It has been said that the Democratic bosses of certain Massachusetts cities, on occasion, have eagerly sought to have birth control referendum on the ballot in state elections because this enlisted the efforts of the Church in getting out the Catholic—and Democratic—vote. The March on Washington Committee of the mid-forties, organized by A. Phillip Randolph of the Brotherhood of Sleeping Car Porters, revealed the intensity of political feeling among a group of Northern Negroes once an ethnic issue of relevance to them had been developed.[16] The prohibition issue for Protestant Church members and for such immigrant groups as the Philadelphia Italians, the desegregation issue, the alien registration acts of the two world wars, grants in aid for education excluding private, i.e. parochial, schools, all reveal the fact that in large measure the national domestic issues which have excited the public are often not class issues but ethnic issues.

The interest which members of various ethnic groups take in foreign policy also leads these groups into the political arena. In explaining the relatively high rate of voting of Jews and Catholics in New York in the 1940's, Saenger says, "Jews and Catholics in New York City are first-, second-, or third-generation Americans. As such, they are more closely identified with the population of their home countries and may be more aware of the effect of recent political events abroad and at home."[17] In Albany (1948) more first- and second-generation citizens said that they are interested in foreign affairs than did third and fourth generation citizens.[18] The specific relation of religious, as contrasted to immigrant-based interest in foreign affairs, is revealed in the greater number of Catholics than Protestants who were aware of and excited about the imprisonment of Cardinal Mindszenty in Hungary.[19] Similarly, Jews, regardless of country of origin, have displayed concern about the status of co-religionists abroad.

---

[14]Robert E. Lane, "Notes on the Theory of the Lobby," *Western Political Quarterly*, 2 (1949), p. 157.

[15]Tom Ireland, *Child Labor as a Relic of the Dark Ages* (New York: Putnam, 1937), pp. 207-39.

[16]See Louis C. Kesselman, *The Social Politics of FEPC* (Chapel Hill, N. C.: University of North Carolina Press, 1948).

[17]G. H. Saenger, *op. cit.*, p. 104.

[18]Survey Research Center, *Interest, Information, and Attitudes in the Field of Foreign Affairs*, Ann Arbor, Mich., 1949, (mimeographed), p. 44.

[19]*Ibid.*, p. 10.

It is only natural that such an interest in foreign affairs should create pressure for changes in American foreign policy. Gradually "In the party platforms appeared planks that espoused the immigrant causes: Irish independence, Italian nationalism, Zionism."[20] The American commercial treaty with Russia in 1907, which permitted the Imperial Government to exclude American Jews from entry into Russia, aroused a wave of protest causing both parties to promise a revision in their 1908 platforms.[21] During the Italo-Ethiopian war, the American Italian Red Cross held a "monster rally" in Madison Square garden which, according to the *Progresso Italiano-Americano*, was "to show that 5,000,000 Italian Americans who live in the United States are ready to immolate themselves on the altar of the great motherland."[22] Republicans were quick to remind the Italians that the man responsible for sanctions against Italy was Franklin D. Roosevelt and to enlist their support on these grounds. In the Second World War (following Roosevelt's "stab in the back" speech when Italy invaded France, a speech which set off a great protest from the American Italians), the Democrats wooed the Italians by having Italy declared a co-belligerent against Germany and by publicizing the economic aid going to Italy.[23] After World War II the Polish-Americans came to believe that "the Democrats had sold their homeland down the river at Yalta and in the years that followed."[24] As a consequence, a solidly Democratic group moved dramatically toward the Republican camp in 1952. In these many ways ethnic groups with special interests in events abroad, identification with co-religionists or fellow-countrymen, and special stakes in American foreign policy, are politically activated by foreign policy issues.

But in a real sense, the seat of ethnic politics is the local community, not the national capitol. This is evidenced by the fact that although ethnic groups often vote no more frequently than native white Protestants in national elections (with the Jews excepted) and sometimes less frequently, they usually vote more frequently in local elections.[25] This means, among other things, that the difference in turnout between local and national elections is almost always substantial for non-ethnics, but is usually much smaller for ethnic groups.

There are many reasons for this greater interest in local politics. One of them, as Myrdal has pointed out, is the failure of American

---

[20]Oscar Handlin, *op. cit.*, p. 208.
[21]L. Fuchs, *op. cit.*, p. 53.
[22]H. Mailey, *op. cit.*, p. 95.
[23]*Ibid.*, p. 97.
[24]Louis Harris, *op. cit.*, pp. 100, 102.
[25]E. H. Litchfield, *op. cit.*, pp. 10, 24-25; H. Mailey, *op. cit.*, p. 33.

cities to develop an impartial non-political bureaucracy and local magistracy, attributable in part to a traditional fear of bureaucracy going back to revolutionary days.[26]

> . . . this means a mutually greater dependence of public officials on the voters and of the voters upon public officials. In this system it has become customary to distribute jobs, protection, and public service in some relation to the voting strength of the various regional, national and religious groups in the community.

This relationship between political strength and distribution of rewards becomes even more important if, as is usually the case, the ethnic groups live in physically segregated areas, for then street-paving, sewage disposal, street-lighting, school facilities and other municipal services become ethnically related matters.

A few instances of how local issues become ethnic issues will illustrate this aspect of the problem. In the twenties, in the Russian Jewish wards of New York still under the control of the Irish, peddlers without a license were often badly treated by the police, and, "in some places school children often received bad grades for being absent on Jewish holidays."[27] In an Italian district of Eastern City, political contacts could expedite a WPA job for a "deserving" voter in the thirties.[28] And "in Memphis, where Negro votes are an important support of the Crump machine, there are relatively few Negroes killed by the police."[29]

Some of the rewards and services of government, particularly local government, are termed patronage; ethnic politics breeds a kind of group patronage in which awarding jobs, contracts, or privileges to a member of the group, rather than to the individual, becomes important. Part of the Negro support for Huey Long in Louisiana in the thirties was based on the fact that "he put Negro nurses in the hospitals, Negro servants in the state Capitol."[30] When they came into power in 1953 the Democrats in New Haven sought to win back the Italian vote by retaining the very large number of Italians in the Department of Public Works placed there by the previous Italian Republican mayor.

Although at the lower levels of patronage economic motives are

---

[26]G. Myrdal, *op. cit.*, p. 435.
[27]L. Fuchs, *op. cit.*, p. 62.
[28]W. F. Whyte, *op. cit.*, p. 196-97.
[29]G. Myrdal, *op. cit.*, p. 499.
[30]*Idem.*

generally salient, when the positions at stake achieve visibility, prestige, and power a different range of motives comes into play. These include having a "friend at court," that is, a co-member of the ethnic group who can intercede on one's behalf, and more importantly, symbolic recognition of the group with implied estimation of its worth and dignity. Lubell labels the desire of the Rhode Island Italians to achieve political recognition of this kind a "passion," gratified when Salvatore Pastore was elected governor in 1946.[31] The *Jewish Day* held that the appointment of Jews to high office by Roosevelt and Wilson was "a high compliment unmatched by anything the Republicans had done."[32] Negro representation on a ballot has an even greater effect:[33]

> With the election of a Negro judge every colored person in the country felt that he was benefited in some way, however slight. Likewise, a Negro congressman, who sits in the national capitol and who is the sole representative of an entire racial group in the federal legislative process [in 1957 there were two Negroes in Congress], is in a position of great respect in the eyes of his racial kinsmen. . . . It is all part of the process of the emancipated group struggling for freedom in a larger field.

In 1956 the Republicans prepared for circulation in Negro districts and colleges some brochures listing the Negro appointments to important posts in the National government. Most of the row offices in both state and municipal elections represent a careful balance of the several important ethnic groups (although Negro representation in these administrative posts is rare).[34] One index of the strength of ethnic identification is the fact that voters tend to vote for candidates of the "opposite" party more often than they vote for candidates of a religion different from their own.[35]

In this connection, it may be noted that the short ballot tends to weaken ethnic involvement in political contests. This is also true of city-wide elections for city council, where the ethnic candidates stand less of a chance of getting on the ballot as ethnic group representa-

---

[31]Samuel Lubell, *The Future of American Politics* (New York: Harper, 1951), p. 67.

[32]L. Fuchs, *op. cit.*, p. 65.

[33]H. Gosnell, *Negro Politicians*, p. 92.

[34]*Ibid.*, p. 91.

[35]Madge M. McKinney, "Religion and Elections," *Public Opinion Quarterly*, 8 (1944), pp. 110-14.

tives. On the other hand, proportional representation gives ethnic voting an important means of expression.[36]

The ethnic, like others, is often drawn into the political arena because of his identification with a political leader. In Oscar Handlin's account of the way in which immigrants in mid-nineteenth century became politicized, he stresses the role of the ethnic "Boss Laborer" (shortened later to Boss) in mobilizing his ethnic following in politics.[37] Partly, this represented an exchange of votes for jobs, but partly it represented ethnic solidarity behind a leader of their own. This kind of identification is today apparent in ethnic responses to criticism of a leader drawn from their own ranks: Regardless of the nature of the criticism it is interpreted as a criticism of the ethnic group itself. In a mayoralty election in "Metropolis" a reform group found that "the exposé of criminal-political ties led directly to the Negro boss and other Negro politicians, among others; any attack on Negro leaders would be considered by many Negroes and white liberals as an attack upon the Negro people."[38] The bond between ethnic rank and file and leader is more than a functional relationship, it is a bond of common idenity. This does not always prevail, of course. Gosnell found that in the 1920's and early 1930's many of the Negro rank and file lacked confidence in their own leaders and trusted white leaders more.[39] But the closeness of the tie, particularly when the leader is challenged—as he is in politics—is usually stronger among ethnics than among non-ethnics.

At least in the past, members of most urban ethnic groups have had persistent trouble with the law, partly because they come from social strata where lawlessness is more common, partly because of the strains of assimilation and identification, partly because the laws have represented cultural norms which they do not share, and partly, according to Kardiner, because of the psychology of low self-esteem.[40]

---

[36]The change to city-wide elections in Chattanooga in 1920 reduced Negro representation on the board of aldermen. On the effect of proportional representation on ethnic voting, see Belle Zeller and Hugh A. Bone, "The Repeal of P.R. in New York City—Ten Years in Retrospect," *American Political Science Review*, 42 (1948), pp. 1127-48.

[37]O. Handlin, *op. cit.*, p. 210.

[38]A. de Grazia, *op. cit.*, p. 126.

[39]H. Gosnell, *Negro Publications*, p. 358.

[40]Crime statistics are notoriously difficult to interpret, but the evidence seems to show that Negroes have a higher than average rate of crime while the foreign born have a lower than average rate. Criminality among foreign nationality groups, then, is likely to be a second-generation problem more than an immigrant problem. See U.S. Department of Justice, Federal Bureau of Investigation, *Uuiform Crime Reports*, Washington, D. C., issued quarterly.

Politics, then, in many ethnic wards becomes affected by the necessity to secure protection from the police. The Italian politicians of "Eastern City" admit in private that they are dependent upon the racketeers for funds and organizational support.[41] The gambler must develop political strength to achieve police protection, but he does not find this difficult. Mailey explains it this way:[42]

> The gambler is worth at least five votes within his immediate family because of the proximity of relatives. Added to this number are the people who "play" with the [policy] writer. His plea to them is "if you don't help, you won't be able to play."

He quotes one Democratic legislator as saying:

> Why number writers mean more votes than jobs on election day. My ward is infested with them. They control my people.

And,

> There is a good deal of truth in the assertion that the main return for the Negro vote in the machine dominated cities is protection for the Negro underworld and minor administrative jobs for the petty Negro politicians who marshal the Negro vote.[43]

One reason for this is that in the Negro community, and also in other relatively impoverished ethnic groups,

> Of all the contestants, the gambling kings, the vice lords, and the liquor magnates were most likely to have political funds of their own which they could invest in politics.[44]

A party which achieves a reputation for friendship for one or another ethnic group on such grounds as those mentioned above survives for a time upon such traditional support. The party name itself becomes part of the ethnic "ethnocentric" pattern of identification. The authors of the Elmira study found that none of the old issues which tied the Catholics to the Democratic party were salient in 1948,

---

[41]"Let's not kid ourselves, Bill; when we want to win, we go to the racketeers—all of us," says an Eastern City politician to William F. Whyte. See his *Street-corner Society*, p. 205.

[42]H. Mailey, *op. cit.*, p. 105.

[43]G. Myrdal, *op. cit.*, p. 499.

[44]H. Gosnell, *Negro Politicians*, p. 361.

yet Catholic party loyalty persisted. "Here ... we find a condition not anticipated nor endorsed by classical political theorists: a non-political, associative factor with strong influence upon the electoral decision."[45] Is party loyalty stronger, or less strong, among ethnic groups? In 1903 it was said that "The Jews (of Boston) are not wedded to any party or faction, and the handling of their vote is a strain on the sagacity of even an Irish politician."[46] But in 1948 and 1952, Jews of all classes showed a party loyalty to the Democrats which resisted the tide of growing Republicanism.[47] The Italian loyalties, which had been predominantly Democratic in the thirties, switched to Republican because of the war, when other groups continued to be Democratic, but swung back again in 1948 and 1952.[48] Negroes switched from the Republican to the Democratic party in 1934 and 1936, stayed in the Democratic camp when other groups went Republican in 1952, and in 1956 tended to drift back to Republicanism—although they gave the Democrats a majority. It can only be concluded that ethnic political loyalties are no more stable than the political loyalties of other groups although, because of a more total and emotional involvement in politics, with some element of ethnic pride at stake in many elections, they may be more intense. Party loyalty for the ethnic is often a derived loyalty, receiving its emotional charge from the primary ethnic loyalty and dependent upon an ethnic-party identification for its direction.

In summary, then, we may generalize as follows:

> The greater the ethnic conflict in a community (where all may vote) the greater the rates of participation of the conflicting groups.
>
> Ethnic participation is increased by the ethnically (group) relevant nature of a wide range of national domestic issues as well as foreign policy. In the United States the more usual class-based issues are frequently subordinated to such ethnically-relevant national issues.
>
> The less impartial and "bureaucratized" the administration of justice and services, the more ethnic (and other socially identifiable groups) will be drawn into politics. The conduct of American municipal administration is unusually sensitive to the relative voting strength of ethnic groups.
>
> The more residentially segregated a group, the more municipal administration becomes politicized for that group.

---

[45]Bernard R. Berelson, Paul F. Lazarsfeld, and William N. McPhee, *Voting* (Chicago: University of Chicago Press, 1954), p. 66.
[46]L. Fuchs, *op. cit.*, p. 121.
[47]*Ibid.*, p. 81.
[48]H. Mailey, *op. cit.*, pp. 48-57.

The more self-conscious and status-conscious an ethnic group, the more the members of that group will be sensitive to the politics of "recognition," i.e., appointment to office and political candidacy of fellow ethnics. Sensitivity of this kind limits opposition criticism on ethnically irrelevant grounds.

Ethnic groups establish special needs for the protection of illegal activities (sometimes conducted with wide ethnic popular support); these activities create strong politicizing motives and the organizations to make them effective.

Ethnics usually participate more in local politics than non-ethnics (for the above reasons).

Party loyalty for ethnic groups is partially based upon an identification of the party with ethnic goals; this loyalty derives its emotional charge from ethnic feeling and, because it is derived, is often unstable.

Ethnic Beliefs and Social Patterns

The immigrant and the emancipated Negro enter the political scene with a heritage of belief and culture which influences their political activity in a variety of ways, not just for the first generation, but, in dwindling force, for subsequent generations, as well. A majority of immigrants were, in their old world status, peasants. Of the Polish peasant's attitude toward government in the old country, Thomas and Znaniecki say:[49]

The political order appears to a certain extent as an impersonal and a moral power, absolutely mysterious, whose manifestations can possibly be foreseen, but whose nature and laws cannot be changed by human interference. But this order has also another side, more comprehensible but more unforeseen, with some moral character, that is, capable of being just or unjust and of being influenced; in this respect it is the exact parallel of the divine world. . . . This whole system, this combination of impersonal power and half-religious hierarchy, evidently permits a certain explanation of everything, but excludes absolutely any idea of political activity.

Handlin agrees that for the immigrant generally, "In the business of ruling, he did not act, was only acted upon."[50] Nor was it different for the rural Negro emigrating North for many decades following the

---

[49]William I. Thomas and Florian Znaniecki, *The Polish Peasant in Europe and America* (Boston: Richard G. Badger, 1918), Vol. 1, p. 141.

[50]O. Handlin, *op. cit.*, p. 202.

Civil War.[51] Such, then, was the political frame of mind which encountered the institutions and demands of American democracy.

By 1924 the immigrants, in Chicago at least, and presumably elsewhere, were participating in political life as frequently as the native white, and the urban Negroes followed close behind.[52] What occasioned this change in political mentality? And what forces deterred it? For the most part, the immigrant came to America, not for political liberty, but for the economic opportunities said to exist here and because he was said to be welcome. Yet when he came, he entered a slum and found the living precarious and the welcome less than cordial. He was uprooted, and sought to protect himself by reinstituting the institutions and practices of the old country. He banded together in colonies of fellow-ethnics, sought to re-establish the Church as he knew it back home, and organized associations of fellow nationals who held the same loyalties and faced the same problems. He was pitifully conservative, seeking amidst so much change to maintain some traces of what he had known. Above all, he was religious.[53] What then, was the role that this religious revival played in his political transformation?

In the first instance, it retarded political development. Because there was no established church in the United States, there was no occasion for the ethnic churches to create strong political connections and no need to protest against governmental favoritism or official discrimination against church schools. The question of government aid to religious schools was to come later. Moreover to some extent, the focus upon religion served, as Marx said it would, as an "opiate" for the immigrant; his attention was diverted from the real world and what might be done about his troubles. God and Caesar were kept separate. Friction between nationality groups tended to fractionate the broader denominations, so that congregations, parishes, and synagogues tended to be organized on a nationality basis, reinforcing the inward-looking features of immigrant status. For some groups, like the Norwegian-Lutherans in the Middle West, the puritanical code of the religious group tended to prevent members from joining or mixing in the social events of other groups.[54] In the first instance, then,

---

[51]See G. Myrdal, op. cit., p. 758. Even today in parts of Harlem, David Riesman finds the same basic "tradition-directed" orientation toward politics. See his Faces in the Crowd (New Haven: Yale University Press, 1952), pp. 73-151.

[52]H. Gosnell, Getting Out the Vote, p. 87. Apparently the Negro rate of voting in Chicago increased markedly from 1924 to 1930. Compare Merriam and Gosnell, op. cit., p. 40 and Gosnell, Negro Politicians, p. 17.

[53]O. Handlin, op. cit., p. 110, 117.

[54]See W. L. Warner, op. cit., pp. 174-75.

religious influences led away from politics. And this was true of the Negro church, as well.

But today, the more highly organized religious groups, the Jews and Catholics, participate more than Protestants and the Protestants participate more than those with no acknowledged religion.[55] A number of complicated factors are at work. In the first place the mere fact of organized relationships tends to increase a sense of mutual interest and raise the salience of group membership. This influence is increased by the organized social life centering in the Church. In one study of twenty-three urban Southern Catholic parishes, it was found that each parish had an average of 13.2 church-associated societies for lay people designed to serve a variety of non-religious social needs.[56] The Protestant churches in Jonesville (rather more than the Catholic Church) also surround themselves with many allied societies. Yet the proportion of communicants who participate in their activities is not large: 3.6 per cent in the case of the Southern parishes. And the extra-curricular life of the church is divided by educational barriers and ethnic rivalries just as in the large society.[57] Church-related organizational life is important, then, but limited.

This interaction, where it exists, tends to reinforce the dominant interests of the group. As Myrdal says "the Negro church fundamentally is an expression of the Negro community itself."[58] And among Italians, "the priests did not lead the people to accept Roosevelt. They merely followed direction of the parish itself."[59] When, for other reasons, the community becomes interested in politics, the church tends to reflect and, to some extent reinforce this interest. This may not be the intention of the church leaders, who have other things on their mind, but the communal gathering of people with common interests will usually achieve this effect. The Negro church becomes politicized even though the leaders may drag their feet. While "the protest has been rising in the Negro community, the church has, on the whole, remained conservative and accommodating."[60]

But church leaders are not free of political pressures either. "The bosses of political machines frequently like to do 'favors for Father,'

---

[55]G. Saenger, *op. cit.*, p. 104. But care should be taken in interpreting figures on "agnostics" or people with "no religion." This group seems to be made up of a small well-educated participant group and a group of poorly educated disoriented individuals.

[56]Joseph H. Fichter, S. J., *Social Relations in the Urban Parish* (Chicago: University of Chicago Press, 1954), p. 157.

[57]*Ibid.*, pp. 49-50.

[58]G. Myrdal, *op. cit.*, p. 877.

[59]H. Mailey, *op. cit.*, p. 124.

[60]G. Myrdal, *op. cit.*, p. 876.

with more or less subtle expectations that Catholic votes will be thereby influenced."[61] And Negro ministers are often wooed by political leaders with the same expectations. If it is clear that one party is more sympathetic to the group than another, the priests, ministers, and rabbis will not remain indifferent.

Religion leads into politics through other channels. As we have noted many issues have religious or church relationships: Quakers and disarmament, Catholics and the struggle against "atheistic communism," Jews and Zionism. Thus a church may organize a political campaign for or against a policy. In New York State, when nine constitutional amendments of interests to unions, parties, and the Catholic Church were presented to the voters, analysis of the voting pattern revealed that the influence of religious leaders on the vote was greater than that of either party leaders or union leaders.[62] And at every class level, religious identification still influences the vote decision.

There is even some evidence that the Church can influence the vote without greatly affecting the political convictions of the communicants. In 1944 there was a disproportionate increase in the Catholic vote in New York at the same time that Catholics reported that they did not believe that the outcome of the election would make much difference to themselves or to the nation. It is certainly possible to believe with Saenger that this reflects the concern not of the "flock" but of the Church leaders about the rise in Communism in the world.[63] Pressure without much persuasion seems to be at work here.

There are indications that this force is waning. In younger age groups the religious differences in vote decision is less than in older groups. Moreover, the forces which are said to be generally weakening the hold of religion on the public also weaken the force of religious identification and church pressure on political participation. As one Italian priest said, "How could we influence their (parishioners') selection of candidates when we couldn't get them to come to

---

[61]J. Fichter, op. cit., p. 132.

[62]Madge M. McKinney, "Constitutional Amendment in New York State," Public Opinion Quarterly, 3 (1939), pp. 635-45. In this study, McKinney reports: "Repeatedly evidence was discovered which indicated that this endorsement of certain amendments by the Roman Catholic clergy had effect upon Catholic laymen. In contrast to this, no evidence was produced that the leaders of organized labor or that the leading gubernatorial candidates exerted great influence upon their followers in regard to the amendments," p. 636.

[63]G. Saenger, op. cit., p. 104.

church?"[64] But with the rise of church attendance, perhaps this too will change.

The role of the church in politics, is, in the United States, a matter on which parishioners do not agree. In a study of the attitudes of members of a large Protestant sect toward the proper role of the minister in politics and of the injection of the church in social and international issues, persons who wanted to keep church and politics separate were generally (a) those with less education, (b) those least informed and presumably, therefore, least interested in public issues, and (c) those whose organizational life was built more around church centered organizations (and who also attended church more regularly). In interpreting these findings the authors of this study suggest that the more traditionalistic group, those who seek to return to a closer tie between church and family, resist and resent the intrusion of the secular political world in this relationship.[65] Yet it is precisely this group that is most influenced by the political orientation of the clergy.[66] Vulnerable, they wish to avoid exposure.

The specific content of the religion, the religious teachings, seem to bear little relationship to the development of political interest. The alleged emphasis upon duty in the Protestant religion may be focused upon avoidance of liquor and the value of hard work just as much as upon civic duty. The focus upon this world and enjoyment thereof of the Jewish religion failed to bring the Jews into the political arena in the early years of their migration when religious influences were strongest.[67] Only a few of the Catholics who become interested in politics have ever heard of the Papal Bulls of Leo XIII.[68] The relationship between politics and religion is based on organizational

---

[64]H. Mailey, op. cit., p. 124. But Mailey says of the increased church attendance by Italian Catholics: "They will gradually be taught to listen to the dictates of the priest and exhibit the meekness that American prelates expect to find in other American Catholics" (p. 124).

[65]Benjamin J. Ringer and Charles Y. Glock, "The Political Role of the Church as Defined by its Parishioners," Public Opinion Quarterly, 18 (1954-55), pp. 337-47. There are broader forces involved in this question of church and politics: "To many, for the church to lobby for political measures weakens its spiritual position, for such actions violate the American tradition of separatism of church and state." W. Lloyd Warner and associates, Democracy in Jonesville, p. 149.

[66]B. Berelson and associates, op. cit., pp. 67-69.

[67]See L. Fuchs, op. cit., pp. 189-90. Fuchs takes the view that elements of the Jewish culture have a direct and important bearing on their "political style." This is probably true, but those elements of the culture which are found in the theology of Judaism probably have the most tenuous relationship to politics.

[68]O. Handlin, op. cit., p. 224.

pressure, group interaction and identity, and group interest, not theology.

The nationalist component of the rise of ethnic interests in politics came later than the initial turning to religion. It flowered into a mass of organizations such as the Sons of Italy or the Polish National Alliance. Like the churches, these organizations brought people together, but in these instances the focus of interest was political, though foreign. For the most part, the initial orientation was to "look homeward" to the old country, not toward the local issues of jobs, street-paving, and protection from the police. "The task of the Polish National Alliance, as conceived by its initiators, was thus to turn the Polish immigrants in this country into a strong and coherent part of the Polish nation."[69] Only the Negro "nationalist" organizations were primarily focused on the home scene, with the National Association of Colored People and the Urban League as the two principle enduring groups.

These organizations for nationality groups and Negro groups alike, served important political functions. They served as vehicles for political action, including lobbying. They were important means of communicating political messages. They increased the group's sense of power and importance. But perhaps even more important they provided first-hand experience in the ways of democracy. People with no intimate personal experience with democratic forms and usages cannot be expected to participate in democratic affairs on a national or even community scale.

It cannot be said, generally, that broad ideologies, such as socialism, anarchism, fascism, or communism, played much part in politicizing ethnic groups. Although there were some leaders, like Carl Schurz, who fled Europe for political reasons, and carried their convictions to America, these were in the minority. By and large the immigrants were conservative, turning for solace to religion rather than radicalism. And the radical's antipathy to religion served to alienate him from his fellow immigrants.[70]

Among the Poles, before the First World War, for example, the Alliance of Polish Socialists sought to ensure that Poland should be a socialist nation when it achieved nationhood. But the membership of this group was infinitesimal compared to the Polish National Alliance. And, in any event, even this small socialist group inevitably became fractionated and those interested in American socialism joined the

---

[69]W. I. Thomas and F. Znaniecki, *op. cit.*, Vol. 5, p. 113.
[70]O. Handlin, *op. cit.*, p. 192.

Polish section of the American Socialist Party.[71] Nor was the Negro drawn into politics through ideological or "radical" doorways. The efforts of the Communists to enlist Negroes ran into the frame of mind expressed in the statement: "It is bad enough being black, without being black and red."[72]

Only the Jews, with their European traditions of socialism, assumed an ideological posture. As one settlement worker in a Jewish district put it, "the real university of the East Side was Marx's *Capital*. . . . What the East Side was excited about was Socialism."[73] In part this was because of the internationalist character of socialism, and the Jews, because of their history, had long been internationalists. In part it might be said that it stemmed from elements of Jewish culture focused upon the concepts of *Torah* (learning) and *Zedekah* (charity).[74] But the important causes for this liberal-socialist ideal seem more likely to come from the fact that the Jews were an urban group with a long history of persecution which had prepared them for the general ethnic discrimination in America. They were ready when persecution came, so to speak, while others were not.[75]

Certain changes in perspectives on themselves also brought the ethnics into politics. At first the concepts of equality were as alien as they were in fact unreal. This doctrine of equality "did not square with their own deep-rooted ideas of status, with their own acceptance of differences of rank. . . . These people could find nothing in their life in the Old World or the New that would confirm the democratic hypothesis that they themselves could participate meaningfully in the exercise of power."[76] But their children learned in school that everyone was equal and that democracy was built on the principle "one man, one vote." At this point, the doctrine of equality became a powerful politicizing influence, not only were they equal in their electoral rights, but they might use this weapon to achieve status and equality in other areas of life. Moreover, they could feel, as the working classes never could, that their lack of status was due to discrimination. The American culture said that only an individual was

---

[71]W. I. Thomas and F. Znanieicki, *op. cit.*, p. 127.

[72]G. Myrdal, *op. cit.*, p. 509.

[73]L. Fuchs, *op. cit.*, p. 124.

[74]*Ibid.*, pp. 184-203.

[75]While ideological politics seems to have had a minimal appeal to the immigrant and Negro group (Jews excepted), reform politics up until the New Deal was no more attractive. The issues of the time: tariff, trust-busting, civil service, municipal corruption and reorganization did not strike home to this group, absorbed as they were in the immediate problems of earning a living and keeping out of trouble. See O. Handlin, *op. cit.*, pp. 218-23.

[76]O. Handlin, *op. cit.*, p. 206.

to blame for economic failure. For the ethnic failure to achieve status, one could blame a discriminatory society. In large part this explains why the ethnic underdog developed an active political life aimed at increasing status while the economic underdog ("proletariat") did not.

But the most important politicizing force for the ethnic was the political machine. This dealt with affairs of immediate and practical interest: jobs, protection, services. In politics the ethnic leader was able to convert his ethnicity into a positive advantage, whereas in other areas of life it served him ill. The ethnics had a marketable commodity: votes. They understood from the Old Country the utility of petitioning for favors and now they found that they could petition with sanctions behind them. As a consequence in Chicago, Elmira, Philadelphia, "Eastern City," and wherever ethnic politics has been studied, the rapport between ward leaders and constituencies has been a crucial force in mobilizing ethnic groups for political action. If a ward changed ethnic complexion and the old leader of a different ethnic group remained in office, the ward tended to become depoliticized.[77] And in Elmira it was found that the more self-contained and isolated the group, the more important is this ethnic political tie with the machine.[78] The assimilation into American life of the ethnic group is, indeed, one of the main reasons for the decline of the great political machine.

Ethnics are mobilized for political action by certain intermediary leaders, of whom the ward captains represent only one group. To some extent, these leadership patterns will be molded by the occupational choices and social organization of the group. For these reasons, Negro leadership comes on the one hand, from the Church, and to a lesser extent from fraternal organizations, rather than from lawyers and business men. On the other hand, many Negro politicians come from the leaders of the demi-monde, the gambling, vice, and racketeering elements.[79] The Jews, because of their concentration in the professions, have been fortunate in the availability of many lawyers, for whom politics is a congenial profession, and a large merchant class. Among the Italian group, the concentration of Italian leadership in building and construction, with its close political ties, has led to politics through this door, just as gambling and the connection with liquor established in Prohibition days opened a back door to Italian politicians. For the Italians (and for the Negroes also) the undertaker

---

[77]C. Merriam and H. Gosnell, *op. cit.*, pp. 210, 228.

[78]B. Berelson and associates, *op. cit.*, p. 165.

[79]G. Myrdal, *op. cit.*, pp. 730-33.

is often an important political person in the community, with leisure for politics and the incentives provided in operating a regulated trade.[80] Thus each ethnic group may have a specialized approach to politics reinforced by its occupational and leadership patterns.

The union in a trade where one ethnic group has a solid majority is a prime vehicle for ethnic political action. "To the immigrant Jews in New York, the two most important sources of political opinion were the trade unions and the Yiddish newspapers."[81] The intense political activity of both the International Ladies Garment Workers Union and the Amalgamated Clothing Workers Union is traceable, in large part, to their origins at predominantly Jewish unions. The leadership of the Brotherhood of Sleeping Car Porters formed the nucleus of the March on Washington Movement of the World War II years, continuing after the war as the Committee for a Permanent Fair Employment Practices Commission.[82] The Irish in the building trades unions, and the Italians in certain locals of the teamsters union, also tended to mix ethnic politics with union politics. And the close relations between the unions and the political machines tended to make complementary appeals for ethnic votes, although occasional trouble developed (as in Jersey City) when the machine leaders became jealous over union intrusion on their political power.

As indicated above, the foreign language or nationality press, or the Negro press, and, more recently, the nationality radio stations have given political indoctrination to the ethnic public. "The influence of a foreign language paper in the past has been so great crafty politicians conspired to buy the foreign vote through the newspaper."[83] The owners of such papers became important political magnates through such means. But today most of them have converted to the English language and are losing their clientele. The power of the Italian press and perhaps other nationality papers was temporarily sustained by the rise of ethno-nationalism during the war, but, at least in Philadelphia, both Democratic and Republic leaders agree that these papers today have very little influence.[84] This is not true of the Negro press

---

[80]Myrdal speaks of "burial societies" rather than professional undertakers. Whyte says "If he has an established funeral business, the undertaker will be well known and well supplied with personal contacts before he enters politics. He counts on his own kind as a nucleus for political support. . . . A political campaign advertises his funeral business, and the funeral business widens political contacts," *op. cit.*, p. 202.

[81]L. Fuchs, *op. cit.*, p. 125.

[82]See Louis Kesselman, *op. cit.*, pp. 13, 25-46.

[83]H. Mailey, *op. cit.*, p. 116.

[84]*Ibid.*, p. 118.

which, in 1942, included 210 weekly papers and 129 magazines of various kinds. Myrdal says: "The importance of the Negro press for the formation of Negro opinion, for the functioning of all other Negro institutions, for Negro leadership and concerted action generally, is enormous."[85] Although a relatively small percentage of the content of this press has to do directly with politics, by indirection—by the reporting of police treatment of Negroes, appointment of Negroes to office, and so forth—the political impact is substantial. Since this press "defines the Negro group to the Negroes themselves," the image in the press of the Negroes as politically active serves to politicize an entire group.

In review then, the following hypotheses may be set forth.

Political apathy is a function of peasant (or rural Southern) origin with its associated views of government as part of a natural order beyond control.

The early religious orientation of immigrant and Negro groups tended to reduce political interests because (a) the separation of church and state reduced the opportunity for political conflict, (b) religion offered an otherworldly solace for temporal ills, (c) church groups became fractionated and narrowly in-group oriented, (d) the reinforcement of some religious norms imposed barriers to broader social participation by communicants.

Religious interests and organization (at a later stage) increased political activity of communicants through (a) increasing the social interaction of communicants and increasing their perception of group stakes in political matters, (b) direct political pressures on clergymen, (c) development of church-related political issues, (d) providing an organ of political expression. Those who resist the intrusion of the church in politics are those most vulnerable to church influences. The theological content of the religion is only marginally important for politics.

Immigrant nationalism and nationalist groups served as a means of politicizing ethnics, but the program of nationalist groups failed to relate to the most urgent needs of the ethnic groups. (In this respect Negro organizations were an exception.) Nevertheless, they served as important politicizing agents, particularly as they trained groups and their leaders in the use of democratic processes.

Ethnic groups (with the exception of the Jews) failed to become politicized by broad ideological programs because of the interposition

---

[85]G. Myrdal, *op. cit.*, p. 923.

of other-worldly religious orientations, fear of further rejection by society, rural backgrounds and low education, and lack of preparation for their alienation in the New World.

The political machine with its ethnic ward connections was the chief instrument politicizing the ethnic group. Through this means the ethnic leader converted his ethnic membership from a liability to an advantage and the group could achieve group rewards through its local party connections.

Labor unions in trades where ethnics were concentrated politicized their members because of mutually reinforcing ethnic, occupational, and class interests. The nationality press and radio politicized ethnic groups, but due to waning language barriers and broadening ethnic interests the nationality media have lost much of their influence. In contrast, the Negro press has grown in political and social influence.

Ethnic Status and Political Attitudes

Membership in an ethnic group produces attitudes and, indeed, qualities of personality, which have a bearing on the social and political participation of the individual. Among these is the sense of subordinate status, the feeling that society undervalues the individual and his group, or at least the feeling that they are constantly on trial. Let us consider some of the implications of this attitude.

In the first place, as Kardiner and Ovesey points out in an analysis of the psychological effects of being a Negro, social evaluation may be accepted, or partially accepted, by the individual, and he comes to think of himself as a person of low worth and little consequence.[86] This, by itself, leads to apathy, hedonism, living for the moment, expectations of other worldly rewards, and low political participation. The Southern Negro and many Northern Negroes are said to embody this pattern. This is the basic, first-order response, one which explains in part why the most oppressed groups rarely revolt, or even take advantage of their democratic rights. Contrary to some statements on the subject, not low self-esteem but doubts about how to esteem oneself serve as the basis of many political drives.[87]

---

[86]Abram Kardiner and Lionel Ovesey, *The Mark of Oppression: A Psychosocial Study of the American Negro* (New York: Norton, 1951).

[87]Harold Lasswell is ambiguous on this theme, but in general he agrees. Thus: "The accentuation of power is to be understood as a compensatory reaction against low estimates of the self (*especially when coexisting with high self estimates*)." *Power and Personality* (New York: Norton, 1948), p. 53 (emphasis supplied).

But the ascription of low status to a group may produce other attitudes of political consequence. It may produce a withdrawal from contact with outside society and the Ghetto psychology which Lewin says produces a kind of personal security for the individual, counteracting the abrasive force of social undervaluation. Thus, until the 1930's, the Jews created politically withdrawn, but culturally rich and psychologically secure, ethnic communities which were isolated from the larger society.[88]

As contact with the larger society increases for groups losing their language and custom differences, the ethnic group looks outward and becomes an embattled social group, enormously sensitive to reflections on group status and eager to advance group interests by all available means. Under these circumstances, undervaluation by society produces, not acceptance of low esteem but doubts and anxiety about the self and the group, which may be resolved by individual or group achievement. It is said that this accounts for the restlessness of the Jews as the Ghettos disappear.[89] It produces the ethnic's "passion for respectability" to be won by political recognition. But, it also produces fear of personal participation in groups of higher status, for fear of slight or humiliation.[90]

This is the point at which many of the American ethnic groups have now arrived. Although they live in ethnic colonies, the borders are often vague, and outside culture contacts are, at least for the men, relatively frequent. Their ethnicity is important to them and leads to high participation in the more ethnically relevant local politics. To some extent their politics also reflects their alienation: for the Negro and the Italian social undervaluation and self-doubts combined with hostility lead to crime, rackets, and the political connections these imply; for the Jews, the alienation leads to radicalism and support of socially disapproved third parties.

The recent history of each group dictates a somewhat different political solution. The Negro in the North is emerging from acceptance of social undervaluation and low self-esteem and is becoming a politically embattled solidary ethnic group. From research data we can see the psychological change underlying this change in political status. In a national sample, including the South, Negroes indicated a

---

[88]See Kurt Lewin's discussion of "Psycho-Sociological Problems of a Minority Group," in his *Resolving Social Conflicts* (New York: Harper, 1948). See also Louis Wirth, *The Ghetto* (Chicago: University of Chicago Press, 1928), p. 279.

[89]K. Lewin, *loc. cit.*

[90]See Genevieve Knupfer's account of the way the underdog feels in PTA, or civic group meetings in the presence of persons of higher status; "Portrait of the Underdog," *Public Opinion Quarterly, 11* (1947), pp. 103-14.

very low sense of political effectiveness (I cannot influence authorities; they will not listen to me); but in a sample of Detroit union members, Negroes had a higher sense of political efficacy than did the whites.[91] Moreover, in the South, in addition to a low sense of political efficacy, the Negro must often overcome a "psychopathological form of apathy" brought about by the fear techniques of the ruling class.[92] For the Negro the time has not yet come for assimilationist politics. On the contrary, it is still true that the "Negro will be able to extract the maximum advantage by acting as a political unit."[93] In his situation ethnic salience must, for practical reasons, remain high.

The Jews, Italians, Poles, Greeks, Mexicans, and other ethnic groups, however, are in a somewhat different position. Both Jews and Italians are emerging from a period of reinforced ethnic solidarity occasioned by, in the one case, the rise of Naziism and the Zionist movement, and in the other, by the Second World War which pitted America against the Italian motherland. As a partial consequence, the Jews have moved from a relatively non-political group to "the most politicized group in the United States." The Italians generally have not been so politically aroused and have been much more divided in their political loyalties. After the war their relative rates of participation tended in some places to decline.[94]

What will assimilation do to the political participation of these ethnic groups? Mailey puts it this way:[95]

> Italian political recognition blossomed with Roosevelt and by the end of World War II Italians in Philadelphia were turning a deaf ear to ethnic solidarity. As one intelligent political leader put it, 'It lost its punch with the war.' Many Italians feel that the Italians would suffer in the long run if they continue to assert their background too long. . . . [In Philadelphia they] feel that this [ethnic] appeal can only be afforded by Italians who are a large part of the electorate as in New York. Otherwise, the Italians wish to assimilate quickly and make their demands for political rewards on another basis.

Politically speaking, assimilation means new motives for old. This means a shift in the psychological bases of participation but not necessarily an increase or a decrease in political salience. The more

---

[91]A. Campbell and associates, *op. cit.*, p. 191; Arthur Kornhauser, Albert J. Mayer, and Harold L. Sheppard, *When Labor Votes* (New York: University Books, 1956), p. 157.

[92]G. Myrdal, *op. cit.*, p. 490.

[93]*Ibid.*, pp. 505-06.

[94]L. Fuchs, *op. cit.*, p. 202; H. Mailey, *op. cit.*, p. 42.

[95]H. Mailey, *op. cit.*, p. 91.

assimilable immigrant groups, such as the Canadians or English, in Ann Arbor in the thirties, sometimes voted more and sometimes less than those with greater religious, language, or cultural barriers to overcome.[96] In depriving ethnic voters of one motive for an interest in politics, assimilation may make room for others. Loss of ethnic group identification may create personal restlessness and drives for *personal* achievement which find political expression. In this context it is probably true that moderate anxiety over group status represents one of the main drives for entering politics. Or assimilating ethnics may accept the dominant citizen duty norms of middle-class society and participate for these conventional reasons. Or they may develop stronger socio-economic class interests and place their political loyalties on this footing. Litchfield finds that "insofar as participation is concerned, there is greater solidarity among economic than ethnic and race groups," but a close examination of his figures shows that while this is true of native whites, it is only tenuously true for nationality groups.[97] The ambiguity of these data reflect the fact that the unassimilated ethnics are clinging to ethnic reference group criteria whereas the assimilating ethnics are free of the necessity to vote as an ethnic bloc and are developing other criteria for political preference.

But the assimilating ethnic with rising status runs certain risks. The ethnic politician who assimilates may lose his clientele. The rank and file ethnic may find himself caught between two worlds and withdraw into apathy, as Child says the second-generation Italian has often done.[98] Perhaps it is for this reason that in Philadelphia, although there was no consistent relationship between income and turnout in presidential elections, in local elections there was a tendency for lower income and presumably less assimilated Italians to participate to a greater extent than Italians with higher incomes.[99] One reason for this is that once homogeneous parish groups become divided along class lines they lose their cohesiveness.[100] Another reason is suggested by Frazier's view of middle-class Negroes who rise above their former working-class status and become members of the "bourgeoisie," says Frazier, suffer from "nothingness" and their lives generally lose both content and significance. In a state of "nothingness"

---

[96]See James K. Pollock, *Voting Behavior: A Case Study* (Ann Arbor, Mich.: University of Michigan Press, 1939), p. 28.

[97]E. H. Litchfield, *op. cit.*, pp. 25-26. On the intensity of ethnic identification and ethnic voting norms see B. Berelson and associates, *op. cit.*, p. 72; also see L. Fuchs, *op. cit.*, pp. 88-90.

[98]Irvin L. Child, *Italian or American? The Second Generation in Conflict* (New Haven: Yale University Press, 1943).

[99]H. Mailey, *op. cit.*, pp. 39-41.

[100]J. H. Fichter, *op. cit.*, p. 49.

politics can have little meaning.[101] In this connection it is worth noting that one study of Negro voting in Philadelphia finds that prosperous Negroes have lower rates of voting than the less prosperous Negroes.[102] Or these groups may take the view of the upper-class Jews who, caught between their class pressures and their ethnic identifications, express the opinion that "both parties are the same."[103] If they do not withdraw from the polling booth, they withdraw their affect from politics. This may account for the later vote decisions of those in both Erie County and Elmira who were caught between religious and class identifications of this kind.[104] In the kind of assimilation represented by the rise from working-class to middle-class status, the risks of depoliticization are substantial.

In reviewing these problems of ethnic status and approaches to politics, we may say:

> Ethnic groups (based on nationality, religions, recency of immigration, and race) are generally accorded lower than average status in the American society. Low political participation is a function of the acceptance and internalization of this social image of low status and worth by the members of an ethnic group.
>
> Social estimates of low status and worth of a group may turn a group inward so that they withdraw from social and political participation whether or not they accept these estimates.
>
> Social contact with the majority in the American (equalitarian) society weakens the acceptance of low status and worth and replaces it with doubts which encourage efforts to repudiate the "low worth" doctrine through political participation. Some of these efforts find outlet in alienated or anti-social politics but most remain in the main political stream.
>
> Progress in assimilation means a change in political motivation for members of ethnic groups. To the extent that citizen norms, economic interests, and pressure for individual (as contrasted to group) achievement can serve as substitutes, ethnic political participation will not suffer a relative decline.
>
> But assimilation tends to depoliticize groups when it breaks up the homogeneity of ethnic associational life, leads to lack of direction and "anomie," or creates cross pressures which weaken partisan political attachments.

---

[101]See E. Franklin Frazier, *Black Bourgeoisie* (Glencoe, Ill.: Free Press, 1957).

[102]J. Errol Miller, "Atypical Voting Behavior in Philadelphia," *Public Opinion Quarterly, 12* (1948), pp. 489-90.

[103]G. Saenger, *op. cit.,* p. 104-05.

[104]See Paul F. Lazarsfeld, Bernard B. Berelson, and Hazel Gaudet, *The People's Choice* (New York: Columbia University Press, 1948) pp. 58-59; B. Berelson and associates, *op. cit.,* p. 131.

The Political Socialization of the American Negro

Dwaine Marvick

In the middle of the twentieth century, the political socialization of the American Negro is rapidly and drastically changing. In part, the trends involve and reflect a massive migration from the rural South into Northern metropolitan slums. In part the trends are embodied in the perspectives of successive generations—those under forty today, whose awareness of American political life is therefore exclusively post-World War II, and their elders, who grew up in a prewar or wartime climate of opinion.

These key dimensions—migration and generation—will be repeatedly considered as we sift the findings available from recent research into how people are inducted into their political culture, which is what we mean by the phrase "political socialization." And because change is the outstanding feature in considering both dimensions, the findings raise questions about "resocialization" quite different from those involved in teaching civics to children or in other ways giving young people a "feel for politics." Protest, alienation, reconciliation, reintegration: these are all relevant terms when we examine how Negroes adjust to the rules and arrangements of American politics.

Political socialization refers to one's induction into a political culture, and perhaps one's capacity to change it. As a learning process, it

Reprinted from the *Annals*, Vol. 361 (September, 1965), 113-127, by permission of the author and publisher. Copyright 1965 by the American Academy of Political and Social Science.

needs to be seen as often painful, embarrassing, and even stultifying. It is a school of hard knocks for those on the receiving end as American Negroes are. It is not a pleasant academic routine of lessons learned and grades achieved in a civics class. It is the process by which adults come to learn what is expected of them as citizens and, perhaps, leaders.

Political socialization, then, is concerned with how a person "comes to terms" with the roles and norms of the concentric political worlds—local, regional, and national—into which he passes as he grows up. Necessarily it focuses on formative experiences—in the family, school, and primary group contexts of childhood—that shape ideals and give insight into political aspects of life. It requires consideration of a set of motivational factors—rooted in each individual's private problems of psychic management, including also the patterned goals and goads to which he responds with some regularity. Negro Americans in many ways are excluded from the dominant political culture of their community and nation, and are denied its rewards. Norms and roles for political performance are learned in a special Negro subculture, which is at present undergoing basic changes, creating for the next Negro generation new prototypes for political action, and creating also new tensions and new frustrations for the individual.

But the psychological transformation—the "internalized revolution"—in the way Negroes are being inducted into American political life still confronts the would-be "new Negro" with some practicalities that can make all the difference. The study of political socialization requires attention also to situational insights and beliefs—sets of ideological, group-oriented, or self-interested calculations made by a person which largely determine the level of his involvement and participation in any specific occasion or process. Attitudes of skepticism may be widely prevalent among Negro citizens, but they are surprisingly differentiated from person to person, and from situation to situation. And linked to these situational appraisals also is the question of what resources can be marshaled. A full analysis of the changes occurring in Negro political socialization would take into account a long list of capabilities—skills, knowledge, contacts, style, energy, strength, reputation, access, control of organizations—each of which is distributed unequally within the Negro population, and each of which implies control by an active intelligence to be effectively invoked.

Finally, political socialization is not simply the study of how people come to terms with the conventional practices and arrangements which are manifestly referred to as "political" or "governmental" in the institutional sense. It involves examination also of a set of functional equivalents, ways of doing indirectly what cannot be done directly. Because of the history of Negro exclusion—both nationally and in his residence localities—from active and accepted participation in the conventional processes of governance, it is especially relevant to look at his political education as it is functionally acquired, even though the ostensible processes are those of community-service groups, fraternal associations, or church affairs.

This, then, is a brief inventory of the range of problems embraced by the study of political socialization. Applied to an inquiry about the American Negro, it is, perhaps, a useful approach. But certain risks should be pointed out. First, learning what is expected and how to perform in either basic or specialized roles is an undertaking that seems to imply a rather homogeneous political culture, housed in monolithic institutions and with standardized induction norms. Second, it is likely to suggest that the things to be learned are, on the surface, straightforward, manifest political events and governmental patterns. Third, these, in turn, imply that learning depends upon the initiative of each student; some will get *A*'s and others *F*'s. Fourth, it conveys a rather static picture. Allowing for variations in milieu, the old textbook should continue to apply; if one is not politically inducted into the same culture, at least it is into a progressively unfolding political culture. These are all comfortable illusions.

In any extensive society there is a plurality of political milieus into which a person coming to adulthood passes. They are not equally challenging, nor easy, nor stable. In the South, a Negro "knew where he stood" and what to expect—or he used to. In the North, impersonal treatment is functional on the surface. It means access to public accommodations, a chance to vote, due process of law, and so forth. It also means isolation, exclusion, hypocrisy, and ambiguity about where the Negro stands socially.

Change does not necessarily mean revolutionary change. The actions of those in a political culture *are* largely what reaffirm or modify its norms and practices, and incidentally serve to integrate or disjoin it from other political cultures. The accretion of small changes in political practice, moreover, includes not only innovations made on purpose and by forceful leaders, but the modifications as well that result from improvisation, from fumbling, from short-sighted maneuvers, from unwillingness to continue in familiar roles, and so forth.

To learn the political game only once is not enough, whether one treats it as a spectator sport, a hobby, or a vocation. Change is too basic; resocialization is too necessary. Especially is this so in the rapidly changing areas of America's racial politics. Recent collective efforts at direct action have multiplied Negro opportunities for political experience; the organizational scaffolding of leadership and cadre roles has vastly increased the list of political tasks to be done at the same time that it has made those roles more desirable and more differentiated. New organizing skills, analytical abilities, and communication talents are being found and encouraged in the distinctive circumstances of "protest politics." Yet, in looking at the changing patterns of Negro role-playing and Negro skill-acquisition, it is still difficult to gauge the changes in Negro attitudes and motivations. It is necessary to remember the backlog of frustration, self-doubt, and anger which the neophyte must somehow control if he is to learn anything effectively. That he often fails, and in the process learns other lessons about himself and the political system, are other aspects of the problem.

This inquiry, then, becomes a case study in the use of a new conceptual paraphernalia—that of "political socialization"—applied to the complexity and recalcitrance of actual politicizing situations, as reported by Negro informants. Analyzing some of the available data in these terms is at least a way of highlighting the flimsiness of our theoretical apparatus in this area. And because it is impossible to consider the acquisition of political capacities, skills, and beliefs by a sizable segment of the population without asking what difference it is likely to make to the political system in which they will be used and are being used, this inquiry also links interpretation of Negro potentialities to the developmental prospects for the American polity. Let us turn then to a consideration of the resources and difficulties of Negro Americans in coming to terms with the political worlds that surround them.

The Noncompatibility of Negro and White Circumstances

In special ways as well as common ones, American Negroes occupy inferior statuses. Almost from birth they are discriminated against and made to feel inadequate, useless, and undesirable by the dominant white community. As a group also they tend to be poor, marginally educated, and maladapted economically.

In these latter respects, many whites living in the same localities are in similarly depressed circumstances. Some of the apathy and skepticism about American political life which we expect to find among Negroes is probably due to these socioeconomic disabilities. At the same time, the political viewpoints and roles of typical Negro citizens must substantially be seen as a response to the animosities and prejudices they experience because of their ethnic distinctiveness.

Within the Negro community as elsewhere, there is a spectrum of affluence and poverty, prominence, and ordinariness. It is increasingly hard to find a "typical" Negro. How old should he be? Does he live in a Northern city? Does he work at a menial job? Does he earn less than $5,000 a year? For every such Negro, an equal number can be found in contrasting circumstances.

Only a composite picture begins to convey at once the "central tendencies" and the "scatter" in Negro characteristics. Sample surveys, by interviewing representative cross-sections of the citizenry, secure just this kind of composite picture for the nation as a whole. Complications arise, however, when a segregated and disadvantaged subgroup like the Negroes in such a sample are compared with the larger majority-status sample of whites.

In the spring of 1960, the National Opinion Research Center (NORC) undertook a national survey of the United States, as part of a five-nation study of contemporary patterns of political socialization. Reported elsewhere, that project has disclosed many fascinating parallels and contrasts between American, British, German, Italian, and Mexican publics.[1] Many subsidiary problems were scarcely touched upon in their transnational study, although their data are directly relevant. One such problem area concerns the American Negro's past and potential induction into politics.

To investigate carefully those aspects of Negro political socialization that seem distinctive for the ethnic group, and at the same time identify attitudes and beliefs about political matters that equally characterize a set of whites in comparable socioeconomic circumstances, a matching procedure was followed. One hundred interviews had been taken with Negro respondents, as part of the NORC survey. These were now classified by region (South or North), by urban or rural residence, by age (over and under forty), by income levels (over and under $5,000 a year for family units), and by sex. Invoking all five points of distinction as either-or dichotomies produced thirty-two exclusive categories, each with two to five Negro respondents. The 870 white respondents in the national sample were then divided into the same thirty-two subsets. Random selection methods were used to choose as many white counterparts in each subset as there were Negro cases. Thus a composite group of one hundred whites

---

[1]Gabriel Almond and Sidney Verba, *The Civic Culture* (Princeton, N.J.: Princeton University Press, 1963).

was defined, deliberately matched with the Negro group on five dimensions.

TABLE 1

Composition of Negro and White Counterpart Samples
and National White Cross-Section (1960 Survey)[a]

(Cases)	Matched Subsamples		National White Cross-Section (870) %
	Negro (100) %	White (100) %	
1. Sex: Male	49	49	47
2. Age: Under forty	47	47	40
3. Residence: Big-city dwellers	53	53	42
4. Region: Southern	55	55	30
5. Income: Less than $5,000 a year	57	56	24
6. Rearing place: Rural or small town	50	55	54
7. Married	67	67	73
8. Dependents: Three + children	38	38	35
9. Intend to stay in current locale	76	78	83
10. Birth region: South	89	50	27
11. Lived in current locale "always"	36	46	47
12. Occupation:			
Unskilled workers	37	30	20
Operatives and service workers	39	28	20
Craft and white collar workers	19	28	41
Business and professional	6	13	19
13. Education:			
Only some grammar	37	25	16
Full grammar (8 grades)	19	19	16
Only some high school	22	15	18
Full high school	16	24	29
Some college	6	17	21
14. Group membership:			
Belong to no organizations	41	57	43
Belong to one organization	36	23	24
Belong to several organizations	23	20	33
15. Interviewer SES Rating: Low	48	37	15

[a]Data from NORC survey of American electorate in the spring of 1960 for Almond-Verba five-nation project.

In each component, hereafter called the Negro and the Counterpart groups, approximately half were male, under forty, big-city dwellers, Northerners, and earning over $5,000 a year. The other half were not. So far as the national white cross-section was concerned, proportions quite different from fifty-fifty were found on most of these same counts (Table 1).

A few other points of comparability deserve mention. In both Negro and Counterpart samples, approximately half grew up in rural, small-town, or farm environments. In both samples, two-thirds were married, and just under two-fifths had large families—three or more children. In both groups, also, at least three-fourths intended to stay in their current locality of residence.

On all of these points, moreover, the national white cross-section registered quite similar levels. Once having come to terms with a community, a young adult marries, raises a family, and intends to stay there. In all these respects, both the Negro and Counterpart groups are typically American.

Looked at from another vantage point, what sociologists call status-crystallization operates in ways that are dysfunctional to the Negro's most elementary solution—to move. This is illustrated by the impossibility—using the kinds of matching procedures noted—of securing a good match between Negroes and their Counterparts on either occupational or educational counts; there were simply not enough whites in menial job categories or with limited educational backgrounds, once age, sex, region, income, and residence area dimensions were stipulated.

Cumulative social constraints box in an American Negro. Unskilled or semi-skilled (76 per cent) and poorly educated (56 per cent), his problem is further exacerbated by the region and locality in which he lives and *wants to remain living*. Of the Counterpart group, only 58 per cent hold similarly low-status jobs, and only 44 per cent had comparable educational handicaps. For the larger white cross-section, these percentages dropped to 40 per cent and 32 per cent, respectively. The Counterparts are considerably closer to the Negroes on these counts than are most white Americans. Their disadvantages, nevertheless, are not so cumulative; they are not so "locked in."

The "first solution"—migration—is, of course, widely used by Negroes. In our sample, only half now live in the South, but nine-tenths were born there. Nearly half the Counterparts but only 36 per cent of the Negroes reported that they had always lived in their current locality.

The underlying point, however, relates to the generational aspect of the socialization phenomenon. For many Negroes, although not for all, "coming to terms" with a political world is almost irreversible. Basic life premises are involved. Some kinds of adult activity are so difficult, once foresworn, as to be impossible to undertake later in life. Some sets of events are so remote that they do not really touch one's daily life, however relevant, as news developments about public policy or group demonstrations, they may seem to the observer. Politics is the "art of the possible." And in school, on the job, in dealings with police or government officials, learning the art of the possible is not an abstract problem. Instead, it is a practical question of getting along with a specific teacher, a particular foreman, a well-known sheriff, a certain postal clerk or building inspector.

Consider the evidence in Table 2. Asked in 1960 whether government officials were likely to give them "equal treatment" in matters like housing regulations or taxes, 49 per cent of the Negro sample and 90 per cent of the white Counterpart group said yes. On a parallel question, asking about encounters with the police over traffic violations or similar minor offenses, a slightly reduced margin was found, with 60 per cent of the Negroes and 85 per cent of the Counterparts expecting "equal treatment."

Probing to learn what kind of treatment was expected, that is, how considerate and reasonable, the same patterns were found. Among both Negro and Counterpart groups, substantially fewer persons expected either bureaucrats or policemen to "give serious consideration" to their explanations. Counterparts are close to the scores registered on these counts by the larger white cross-section; the Negroes are about half again as likely to be pessimistic. This is a level of caution and distrust among Negro Americans toward representatives of the law with whom they have dealings which may well be substantially realistic.

It is when North-South contrasts and younger-older comparisons are made that the dynamics of Negro resocialization are suggested. While 60 per cent of the Northern Negroes expected equal treatment from officials in government agencies, only 40 per cent of the Southern Negroes were so optimistic. And, however equal the treatment might be, only 44 per cent of the Northern group and 18 per cent of the Southern expected agency officials to take their viewpoint seriously. Not only has the trek north to the metropolitan slums been accompanied by a measurable growth in confidence of equal official treatment, but also it represents a heightened feeling that the character of official treatment is not deaf or insensitive to their points of view.

Northern Counterpart whites, to be sure, are more confident (93 per cent) than Northern Negroes (60 per cent) of equal treatment. When the quality of that treatment is brought into question, however,

TABLE 2

Expected Treatment by Officialdom: Comparisons of Negro and White Counterparts, with Regional and Generational Breakdowns

	National White Cross-Section %	Matched Subsamples		Regional Breakdown[a]				Generational Breakdown[b]			
				Negro		White		Negro		White	
		Negro %	White %	N %	S %	N %	S %	Y %	O %	Y %	O %
1. Government officials would give equal treatment	87	49	90	60	40	93	87	57	42	89	91
2. Police would give equal treatment	88	60	85	47	76	84	87	77	47	87	83
3. Official would listen and take views seriously	50	30	45	44	18	49	42	36	25	43	47
4. Police would listen and take views seriously	58	36	48	29	44	51	44	45	28	55	42

a N = North,
S = South,
b Y = Younger (under forty),
O = Older.

118

they register only 49 per cent confidence of being listened to. The 44 per cent level on this point among Northern Negroes thus approaches parity.

If we look next at the parallel question of police treatment, the direction of change is just opposite. While only 47 per cent of the Northern Negroes expected equal handling by the police, 76 per cent of the Southern Negroes did. Moreover, this latter figure approaches parity with the level of confidence scored by the white Counterpart— and even the white cross-section.

Only 29 per cent of the Northern Negroes expected the police to listen to their story. Here again the level of confidence registered by Southern Negroes (44 per cent) matches that found among the Southern Counterpart. In sum, in the South of 1960 a random sample, economically and socially, of Negroes and their white counterparts reported roughly equal treatment by the police in their home communities. Equally, too, they reported that treatment to be reasonable and considerate.

A glance at the generational breakdown on these points is useful. It is younger Negroes, not those over forty, whose confidence in the police had risen to a near parity with that registered by their white Counterparts. It is younger Negroes, too, whose expectations of considerate attention from officials—although not equal treatment—had risen to a parity level.

The Negro Migration into American Urban Life

By 1960 half of America's Negro population lived outside the states of the old Confederacy, and nearly a third lived in the twelve largest metropolitan centers. More than half of the residents of Washington, more than a third of those in Detroit, Baltimore, and Cleveland, and easily a quarter in Chicago and Philadelphia were Negroes. In a ten-year period, a million and a half Negroes had left the South. No immigrant wave in American history was ever so large or came so quickly into the urban centers of the nation. In 1930, half of the Negro population lived in rural Southern areas and another quarter in the towns and cities of the South. By 1940, the ratio was one Northern to every two Southern Negroes. And while the proportion living in Northern localities went, decade by decade, from a quarter to a third to half, the size of the Negro population in absolute numbers had nearly doubled.

This massive influx of Negro citizens flooded the metropolitan slums with newcomers who, by reason of their opportunity-deprived upbringing, often lacked the incentives and goads to get ahead found among previous immigrant groups. Earlier ethnic minorities had come from culturally intact backgrounds in Europe which provided them with distinctive but, usually, well-defined standards of conduct for political life. The slave-period traditions for Negroes who had been field hands in the Delta, members of a domestic class in a plantation system, or personal servants for white masters in the urban South were quite disparate, but in all cases were heavily weighted in terms of imitating white patterns.

While this long spiral of migration continued, other trends were also at work. Techonological advances in industry and commerce were displacing unskilled and semiskilled labor—Negro labor—at an accelerating pace. Metropolitan programs for meeting transportation, education, recreation, and housing demands were inevitably displacing families—both long-established and newly come—from blighted neighborhoods.

Table 3 provides some glimpse of the magnitudes involved in the attitudinal reorientation of Negroes toward local government. In 1960, asked how important was its impact on their daily lives, nearly the same proportion—one-third—of Negroes and whites felt that the answer was "great impact." Among Northerners, whites (41 per cent) were somewhat more inclined to this view than Negroes (29 per cent).

Asked to evaluate the contribution of local government, only 50 per cent of the Negroes, compared with 72 per cent of their Counterparts, felt it had generally been helpful in their lives. In the North, however, the 60 per cent scored by Negroes was rather close to the Counterpart figure of 69 per cent. On the other hand, only 42 per cent of the Southern Negroes made this evaluation, while 75 per cent of their white Counterparts did so. When generations are compared, the margin by which whites make more favorable evaluation is similar for younger and older sets.

Those interviewed were asked to consider what could be done to prevent the village or city council from adopting a regulation which "you considered very unjust or harmful." For the national white cross-section, only 24 per cent felt it was almost impossible for them to change a bad local ordinance. Somewhat more (31 per cent) of the Counterpart whites and fully 38 per cent of the Negroes felt this way. Asked whether they had, in fact, ever tried, 70 per cent of the national cross-section of whites and 73 per cent of the Counterpart whites admitted never having done so, but 86 per cent of the Negroes had never tried.

TABLE 3

Expectations about Local Government: Comparisons of Negro and White Counterparts, with Regional and Generational Breakdowns

	National White Cross-Section %	Matched Subsamples		Regional Breakdown[a]				Generational Breakdown[b]			
		Negro %	White %	Negro		White		Negro		White	
				N %	S %	N %	S %	Y %	O %	Y %	O %
1. Local government has "great impact" on daily lives	35	31	37	29	33	40	35	36	26	38	36
2. Local-government actions are usually helpful	71	50	72	60	42	69	75	55	45	77	68
3. It is almost impossible to change a bad local regulation by own efforts	24	38	31	20	53	36	27	28	47	26	36
4. Very unlikely to try to change bad local regulation	26	43	38	31	53	50	27	34	51	26	49
5. Never have tried to influence local policy decision	70	86	73	76	95	76	71	89	83	68	77

[a] N = North, S = South.
[b] Y = Younger (under forty), O = Older.

When attention is given to the regional and age breakdowns, again the attitudinal transformation can begin to be seen. Not alienation, but heightened involvement and substantial realism in the choice of methods and targets seem to be disclosed. While fully 53 per cent of the Southern Negroes felt that changing a bad local law was virtually impossible, only 20 per cent of the Northern Negroes did so—a figure rather similar to that of Counterpart whites. The contrast in optimism was correspondingly great also between younger and older Negroes, with "virtually impossible" being the reaction of 28 per cent and 47 per cent, respectively, a substantially greater age difference than registered by whie Counterparts.

As to whether they, personally, would actively try to change a bad local law if the occasion arose, sharp contrasts are found between North and South. More than half of the Southern Negroes felt it was unlikely they would ever try; only 27 per cent of Southern Counterparts were so passive. Conversely, only 31 per cent of the Northern Negroes felt they would never try to influence such a matter, but 50 per cent of the Northern Counterparts admitted their probable inaction. For both Negroes and Counterpart whites, the younger age groups showed markedly greater propensities toward local political agitation. And when the question was posed, had any actual attempt to influence a local ordinance issue ever been made, 95 per cent of the Southern Negroes said "never." On the same question, only 76 per cent of the Northern Negroes had never tried, the same proportion as for Northern Counterparts.

The Locally Circumscribed Political World of American Negroes

In the study of American race relations today, intellectuals tend to assume that Negroes all along have felt oppressed and constrained at the mold of second-class citizenship, in 1895 as much as 1935 or 1965. Yet, little is known about their political socialization patterns, and a few cautionary points are pertinent. Ordinary Negroes lived mostly in the South. About 1890, open efforts began to disfranchise Negro voters and to impose Jim Crow circumscriptions with the force of law on Negro use of public facilities. By 1910 the political rules had been reformulated; the Supreme Court's "separate but equal" doctrine helped to quiet public concern about what was happening, while political realities ensured a steady deterioration in the public services and accommodations available in their home communities to Negroes·

Incidental to this triumph of nasty-mindedness, much race hatred was preached and countenanced, apparently in part to reassure the poor whites that they were not the next target.

Frederick Douglass, the most militant national Negro leader, fought in vain after 1880 against the trend to disengage all national machinery capable of aiding the Negro. After his death in 1894, others founded the NAACP and the Urban League, conceived as instruments for rallying the racial elite, of training the "Talented Tenth" as race spokesmen and cadres for future struggles, of pursuing political goals not in political arenas but in academic, philanthropic, religious, and journalistic modes. Themselves the products of a selective social mobility process within the Negro world, most of the Negro publicists, lawyers, academics, and others on the national scene struggled to get and to keep open elite communication lines. Their efforts reflected a middle-class presumption that the Negro masses, when mobilized, would accept their lead. There is dignity and restraint, rather than anger and impatience, in the formulation of tasks confronting the NAACP by the militant leader, W. E. B. DuBois: "By every civilized and peaceful method, we must strive for the rights which the world accords to men."[2]

Nationally, the "accommodationist" style of Negro leadership was set by Booker T. Washington. The head of Tuskegee was a man of humble origins, a self-made man who had met the world on its own terms. He was realistic. Negroes lacked the skills and knowledge to succeed economically; education was the crucial resource needed, and education was provided by local governing bodies; Southern whites would only provide that crucial resource if the "products" were reliably docile.

Just when the use of governmental machinery to enforce disadvantages on the Negro was at its peak, Washington counselled submission. Work hard, in the service of the community, and you will become accepted in proper time. His advice and example were for Negroes to give up their interest in political power as a way of securing their rights. Industrial education and an appropriate station in the emerging industrial work of twentieth-century America, were the objectives he used.

De facto segregation in the North was not implemented by state laws and local ordinances as in the South; nor were prejudices so

---

[2]Quoted in Charles E. Silberman, *Crisis in Black and White* (New York: Random House, 1964), p. 129.

openly proclaimed by militant whites. But the Northern reception system has been a pale facsimile of its Southern prototype in many ways, and especially at the local community level.

Until the postwar years it can be argued that, North and South alike, Negro adults became politically socialized almost exclusively to the circumscriptions and indirect channels of the localities in which they lived. It was irrelevant to speak of national or even state-bestowed citizen status for Negro Americans. In the outlook of edu-cated Negro elite figures, no doubt, an awareness of the life in the national and state superstructure of American politics existed. At the same time, it is quite understandable that most events occurring in the central institutional complex of American democracy would not touch the ordinary Negro American emotionally, nor arouse desires to participate. And for the Negro poor, during this whole century of segregation and lower-caste treatment, politics was white man's busi-ness; even in the local arenas of political life Negroes often could secure no electoral footing. The ambit of Negro influence was thus severely limited; it took only a primer to learn the rules of how to behave. Compliance with imposed norms was rudimentary but neces-sary, even when fellow-Negroes called it "Toming."

Myrdal's massive codification in 1942 of the circumstances of Negro life informs us about the extent to which Negroes of that and previous generations were a minority harder than Italians, Poles, or Jews to assimilate.[3] His study stressed themes that continue to preoccupy discussion today. Myrdal believed that Negroes were "exaggerated Americans," who believed in the American Creed more passionately than whites, and who should exploit their common bonds of belief with white Americans more effectively. It would not be possible for white Americans to sustain their corporate belief system unless those who asked their due were granted it, once heard. Negroes had not strenuously asked their due; avoiding scenes and temporizing had been the style.

The Negro community was dependent on the white community; whites were committed to their egalitarian, optimistic, democratic creed, as were the Negroes; by playing upon the beliefs of whites, Negroes could gain their objectives.

Did Negroes consciously or persistently aspire to full citizenship? Had they been politically socialized to want citizen status, but some-

---

[3]Gunnar Myrdal, *An American Dilemma* (New York: Harper & Brothers, 1944).

how left untutored in how to manipulate and persuade whites to grant them what was due?

Or had they undergone a harsher socialization process, one which left them not prepared to believe that the American political system, for all its protestations, would support them in their aspirations?

The argument here is *not* that Negroes were passive, apathetic, and for generations unable to protest effectively because they had become disenchanted with the American Creed—alienated from American society. Probably more commonly, Negro adults had never allowed themselves to become enchanted with "democracy" in the first place, so far as their own community and private lives went. Traditionally, Negro civic leaders occupying symbolic positions of respect were "tapped" by leaders in the white community as contact points. The influence of such "anointed" figures often depended more on their near-monopoly over liaison channels to the all-important white community's decision-makers than on any spontaneous following within the Negro community which they might have generated. Undertakers, insurance men, bankers, teachers, a few professional men—above all, ministers of Negro churches: these were the men who traditionally were treated as spokesmen for their local Negro communities. Accommodationist, conservative, dignified, personally successful men: they have been for more than half a century the prime models for Negro children asking to be shown *local* "men of influence."[4]

With the mobilization of electoral strength, the decline of Negro ministers and leaders of fraternal organizations as sources for community leadership—whether in the liaison or symbolic sense—has steadily been taking place in Southern localities. "Street lights, sidewalks, and paved streets are more common in communities where Negroes vote in substantial numbers. Such things as Negro civic centers, bandshells, playgrounds, libraries, hospital annexes, and even swimming pools are found in increasing numbers."[5]

The dynamics of political *rapprochement* in Louisiana communities, according to Fenton and Vines, have occasionally involved an alliance of "shady white and underdog Negro" elements. Local politics centers

---

[4]See Silberman, *op. cit.,* chap. vii. Also M. Elaine Burgess, *Negro Leadership in a Southern City* (Chapel Hill: University of North Carolina Press, 1962); E. F. Frazier, *The Negro in the United States* (New York: The Macmillan Company, 1949), and G. Franklin Edwards, *The Negro Professional Class* (Glencoe, Ill.: Free Press, 1959).

[5]H. D. Price, "The Negro and Florida Politics, 1944–1954," *Journal of Politics* (May 1955).

around the sheriff's office. If a sheriff permits gambling, he is charged with corruption by middle-class residents of the community; to offset their electoral threat, the sheriff in such instances has catered to the marginal Negro vote for support. "The reward . . . is respect from the politicians and attendance at Negro political meetings, cessation of police brutality, and promises made and often kept regarding such matters as street improvements and better school facilities."[6]

Thus, in Southern communities where voter registration has progressed to a point sufficient to create a substantial potential bloc, a new, self-taught, and white-tutored breed of professional Negro politicians has begun to emerge. Specifically equipped with the organizing and campaigning skills appropriate to electoral politics, these new political journeymen bargain with some effectiveness among the rival white politicians anxious for their vote.

In Northern metropolitan centers, too, professional Negro politicians have emerged, men who work inside the party machine dominating their city, men who accept the terms of political life laid down by white counterparts who are scarcely less ethnic-minded—Irish, Italian, Polish, Jewish, and Puerto Rican "spokesmen" also judged by their readiness and reasonableness in making bargains, and by their ability to deliver votes as promised. Considerable variations remain, of course, in style, in methods used, and in results obtained.[7] In Chicago, Dawson's political strength within the Democratic machine, like that of the other ethnic politicians, has depended on the historical "fit" between ward boundaries and Negro ghetto limits. Working in a solidly Negro area, he deals in tangible and divisible benefits, few of which pose clear moral questions. In New York City, on the other hand, Powell's role is also system-specific, but here a much weaker and less unified alliance of politicians runs the dominant party apparatus. There is therefore scope for Powell's agitational style. He deals in moral questions, in intangible ideals and indivisible causes which must not be compromised. His dramatic skills link these to his personal leadership. Dr. Kenneth B. Clark, himself an occasional rival of Powell in Harlem, has this to say:

> In his flamboyant personal behavior, Powell has been to the Negroes a symbol of all that life has denied them. . . . The Negro masses do not see Powell as amoral but as defiantly honest in his protest against

---

[6]J. H. Fenton and K. N. Vines, "Negro Registration in Louisiana," *American Political Science Review* (September 1957).

[7]See James Q. Wilson, *Negro Politics* (Glencoe, Ill.: Free Press, 1960) for a comparative inquiry which develops these points systematically.

the myths and hypocrisies of racism. . . . He is important precisely because he is himself a caricature, a burlesque of the personal exploitation of power.[8]

The growth of militancy among Negroes—with the decline of "accommodation"—in the modal leadership style is a double-edged blade. On the one hand, it reflects a shift away from the habit of evaluating their social position primarily within the nonpolitical, "intramural" range of Negro rivals, and a shift toward evaluating it instead by explicit comparison to a counterpart group—their opposite numbers in the white middle class.[9] On the other hand, it is a behavior pattern which, once initiated, generates its own reputation. It is far more conspicuous than the older pattern of accommodationist leadership, and it is reinforced powerfully by the way in which other Negroes, both peers and elders, respond by endorsing and accepting it. The "accommodating" style is established by a sequence of occasions when aggressive confrontations were avoided; the "militant" style is more rhetorical, and tends to be *predicted* on the basis of even a very small set of occasions when aggressive leadership options are used. Negro leaders drift into the former; they assert the latter kind of role.[10]

The Skills and Habits of Citizenship

Learning about political life, then, is not a simple, static, or finished process. Instead, it is highly complex; it is dynamic and changing; and at best, it is imperfectly realized. Many Negro adults never become very effective at organizing and improving their daily lives. How much less likely that the methods used to socialize them to onerous predetermined political rules and arrangements should regularly be effective! Indeed, if Negroes had internalized the American dream and seriously wanted it for themselves, it is hard to believe they would not long since have been radically disenchanted and militantly alienated. Instead, it is only in recent years that a new generation of Negro youths begins to think seriously about claiming their birthrights.

In 1910, for a young Negro to study the program of the then-fledgling NAACP was not to review an impressive sequence of judi-

---

[8]K. B. Clark, *Dark Ghetto* (New York: Harper & Row, 1965), p. 210.

[9]Ruth Searles and J. A. Williams, Jr., "Negro College Students' Participation in Sit-Ins," *Social Forces*, 40 (1962), pp. 215-220.

[10]See the insightful participant-observer case study by Allan P. Sindler, "Youth and the American Negro Protest Movement," prepared for the 1964 International Political Science Association Meetings in Geneva, Switzerland.

cial victories, as the task is for his 1965 counterpart. The 1910 program was a recital of watered-down hopes and carefully worded aims. Even so, Booker T. Washington and William E. B. DuBois debated the proper goals and strategy for Negroes in polemical terms that made the former's call for self-improvement seem at odds with the latter's demand for Negro civil rights at once.

Today, also, there are rivalries and polemics among Negro leaders on the national scene, conflicts brought home to Negro citizens by television and radio rather than in exclusively Negro news media. But perhaps there is now a stronger sense of the need for a division of labor: the need for militant direct action protests, to arouse the Negro poor from apathy and self-hate, and the simultaneous need for persistent integrative efforts—through the courts, in union-management bargaining and in government personnel practices, in community service organizations, and through partisan political activities. Not only the symbolic struggles that eventuate in decisions to desegregate a school, permit voter registration, make public accommodations equally accessible, or create job opportunities, but also the practical tasks of implementing and consolidating each such victory are coming to be seen by the young Negro of 1965 as part of the political world with which he must come to terms.[11]

But what does it mean to "come to terms"? One view expects each generation to produce a distinctive style, seizing new opportunities which older generations have yielded or neglected. Another view, not necessarily incompatible with the first, expects realism. Systematic adjustment to changing circumstances seems mostly to come from the older people, while youth refuse to come to terms and instead appear idealistic and unreasonable.

Not many studies of political socialization have yet been made, of Negroes or any other grouping. We have examined some systematic evidence about the attitudes and self-conceptions held by adult Negroes and their white Counterparts concerning American politics. But we know little of how those notions were first acquired, when today's adults were growing up and were gradually coming to understand their place in a white democracy. Neither for Negroes nor for other categories do we know much about the differentiation and attenuation of childhood attitudes and beliefs. Yet adults have to behave in response to situational insights, and adults have to acquire the experi-

---

[11]See the sympathetic sketches by Howard Zinn, SNCC: The New Abolitionists (Boston: Beacon Press, 1964) and the careful case study of biracial co-operation and protest activities in a Southern community by Lewis Killian and Charles Gregg, Racial Crisis in America (Englewood Cliffs, N.J.: Prentice-Hall, 1964).

ence and skills as well as the nerve and desire to mount fresh assaults on complacency and indifference.

Memorable experiences, for example, whether they arise in the midst of electoral campaigns, in moments of public crisis, or in the workaday context of civic co-operation, are hard to plan ahead of time. They tend to be memorable because of accidental and unexpected developments. The Montgomery bus boycott of 1965 began spontaneously when a weary Negro seamstress refused to yield her seat to a white. For more than a year, 17,000 Negroes refused to ride, cutting the bus line's patronage to a fourth of normal. From such unplanned rejection of roles and defiance of norms, in the ten subsequent years, boycotting has become a formidable political weapon for American Negroes. With notice spread by word of mouth or from the pulpits of Negro churches, the boycott has provided a community-level focus and has helped to create leadership-communication networks that are transforming Northern metropolitan slum areas as well as Southern colored quarters. In 1963, a third of a national cross-section of Negroes and more than two-thirds of a panel of Negro leaders reported that they had boycotted certain stores in their local communities.[12]

The syndrome of dejection, self-contempt, a sense of worthlessness, and hopelessness is what Kardiner and Ovesey called the Negro's "mark of oppression." It has been repeatedly noted in studies since their work dealing with Negro psychological adjustment problems.[13] The problems of Negro personality formation are often traced to the "identity crises" through which Negro children perforce must pass: the color-bias they develop even in pre-school play, often linked with a tense reluctance to acknowledge that they are Negro; the post-puberty estrangement of Negro youths from their white playmates, enforced by white parental racist fears of miscegenation; in young adulthood, too, after the relatively sheltered years of school and familiar neighborhood, "the full awareness of his social devaluation in the larger society" can cause severe emotional distress.[14]

Little is known about how the emotional wellsprings of love and hate, hunger and vitality are linked persistently to a set of socially "given" goals and goads. The levels of need achievement among

---

[12]William Brink and Louis Harris, *The Negro Revolution in America* (New York: Simon & Schuster, 1964), p. 203.

[13]A. Kardiner and L. Ovesey, *The Mark of Oppression* (1951); see also the comprehensive survey by Thomas F. Pettigrew, *A Profile of the Negro American* (Princeton, N.J.: D. Van Nostrand, 1964).

[14]*Op. cit.*, p. 8.

Negroes vary substantially, perhaps as much as among whites, although the standards of behavior, life-plans, and career objectives are
manifestly different in the ghetto subculture into which most Negroes
are born and in the American society which isolates them from
awareness of those norms and denies them the rewards of compliance
with those norms.

It is in interracial dyadic relationships that Negroes have usually
learned manipulative strategies, situational tactics, and bargaining
ploys. It has been in response to the emotional strain of interracial
contacts that Negroes have generated double standards of fair play,
humor, and even relaxation.

Almost every Negro adult—not only his organizational leaders—has
been schooled in ways to get along in superior-subordinate relationships. Moreover, the picture he has acquired very commonly puts him
in the latter role. The extent to which the mental outlook of oppressed
people tends toward fantasies, childlike incompetence, and passive
dependence is hard to measure; available evidence suggests that a
pervasive pattern of such behavior has historically laid its imprint on
Negro America.

But when people acquire skills and sensitivities in how to sense the
mood of superiors, how to parlay advantages, how to conceal their
emotions, how to accomplish a thousand political artifices, they often
find such assets portable to new circumstances and applicable in quite
unexpected situations. American Negroes learned these skills under
persistent conditions of duress. Perhaps many never have mastered
techniques that could be used on anyone but a white superior; many
have probably repressed all sensitivities to similar opportunities in
intraracial organizational relations. Even so, given this kind of
schooling, American Negroes must often make very acute political
followers, able to appreciate very well the difference between a
leader's pretensions and his actual performances.

The Negro revolution in America has been manifest in headlines
and news bulletins for more than ten years. It is tempting to speculate
about the ways in which scenes of militant direct action, showing
parental courage and group discipline in the face of mindless hatred,
affect young Negro children today—in the choice of their ego ideals,
in the games they play, the stories they read, the fantasies they have,
the careers they want, the nightmares they endure, and in their
heightened awareness of political rules and possibilities, now that such
awareness carries an instrumental rather than an academic tag.

There is perhaps no single event that marks the watershed in
American race relations better than the 1954 Supreme Court decision

calling for "all deliberate speed" in desegregating the nation's schools. Yet it was ten years later, in the Birmingham riots of 1964, before the Negro poor entered the protest movement:

> The riots . . . were waged not by the disciplined cadres of relatively well-educated "middle-class" Negroes but by the apathetic poor who had previously remained completely on the outside, and whose potential for violence frightened Rev. Martin Luther King's lieutenants as much as the whites.[15]

Moreover, the nonviolent direct action methods of the new protest groups—CORE, SCLC, SNCC—represent also only part of a ten-year prelude to the far more fundamental revolution that is coming in the politics of neighborhoods and communities, of school districts and residential blocks, a revolution that began in scattered localities during the 1950's and received large financial and directional support from the 1964 Civil Rights Act and the resultant antipoverty program of the Office of Economic Opportunity. In states of the South as well as of the North, and at county and municipal levels, biracial area human resources councils are being formed, to co-ordinate and sponsor programs for community action, establish and run youth job corps and urban centers, and encourage private nonprofit groups and universities to contribute to neighborhood improvement and adult education projects.

The importance of these experiences, both to acquire new skills and play new roles in civic affairs, can scarcely be overestimated. The full, genuine, and mundane "political resocialization" of American Negro citizens awaits the proliferation of such institutional scaffolding for public-spirited action.

---

[15]Silberman, *op. cit.*, p. 143.

American Jews and the Presidential Vote*

Lawrence H. Fuchs

It has been generally agreed since the publication of Professor Holcombe's *The New Party Politics*[1] that the urbanization of American society has tended to produce class differences in our politics. The sectional alignments of the 19th century gave way to class and urban-rural politics in considerable measure as Americans continued to move to the cities. By the 1932 and 1936 elections there was a marked tendency for wealth and high prestige to be associated with Republican choice.[2]

Reprinted from the *American Political Science Review*, Vol. XLIX (June 1955), 385-401 with permission of the publisher and author. Copyright 1955 by the American Political Science Association.

*Some of the research on which this paper is based was made possible by a grant from the Sigmund Livingston Fund of the Anti-Defamation League. The substance of this paper was read at the fiftieth annual meeting of the American Political Science Association in Chicago, September 10, 1954.

[1]Arthur N. Holcombe, *The New Party Politics* (New York, 1933). See also Professor Holcombe's *The Middle Class in American Politics* (Cambridge, Mass., 1940).

[2]W. F. Ogburn and Estelle Hill, "Income Classes and the Roosevelt Vote in 1932," *Political Science Quarterly*, Vol. 50, pp. 186-93 (June, 1935). See also W. F. Ogburn and L. C. Coombs, "The Economic Factor in the Roosevelt Election," this REVIEW, Vol. 34, pp. 719-27 (Aug., 1940).

Paradoxically, the most urban of all our citizens, American Jews, have not divided their presidential vote along class lines. As a group they rapidly improved their jobs, extended their incomes, and became highly educated during the 1930's and 1940's. At the same time, they drastically switched their predominant major party choice from the Republican party to the Democrats. And within the group itself differences in income or occupational prestige appear to have been of practically no significance in the formulation of presidential vote preference since 1936.

The purpose of this article is threefold: first, to trace briefly the shifts in Jewish vote preference in recent decades through the use of aggregate election statistics,[3] second, to probe the significant motivations of Jewish voters in 1952, primarily by analyzing the results of a sample survey conducted after the 1952 election in the city of Boston; and third, to suggest some of the basic reasons for Jewish resistance to class influences at the polls.

Between the election of William McKinley in 1896 and the beginning of the World War in 1914, more than two million Jewish immigrants came to the United States. Most of them were refugees from the anti-semitism and poverty of Eastern Europe. They crowded into the tenements in the slums of New York and, to a lesser extent, those of Boston, Chicago, and Philadelphia. A large majority became laborers and peddlers or worked as cutters and tailors in the needle-trades.

While to an extraordinary number of these Russian and Polish Jews the parties of the radical left (particularly the Socialists) provided the only political answers,[4] the majority chose between the major parties. Of these politically orthodox Jews, more voted for Republicans than Democrats in every presidential election from 1900 to 1928, with the possible exceptions of 1900 and 1916.

Republicans were preferred for a wide variety of reasons. Among the most important were hostility towards the Irish; gratitude to the philo-semitic Theodore Roosevelt and William Howard Taft; and advice from established coreligionists.

The radical shift from Republican allegiance in the 1920's to the current predominantly Democratic loyalties of American Jews is dra-

---

[3]Nearly all of these data are based upon original research.

[4]The literature on this subject is rich. See Morris Hillquit, *Loose Leaves from a Busy Life* (New York, 1934); Harry Rogoff, *An East Side Epic: The Life and Work of Meyer London* (New York, 1930); and Louis Waldman, *Labor Lawyer* (New York, 1944).

matically expressed in the party enrollment figures for Ward 14 in the city of Boston, a consistently heavy Jewish area from 1924 until this day. In 1928, 78 per cent of the enrolled voters there were Republicans. By 1952, only 14 per cent of the enrolled electors in Ward 14 called themselves Republican.

American Jews have spurned Republican candidates in every presidential election since 1936. In 1936, Ward 24 in Chicago was probably the most Jewish ward in the nation. There Roosevelt received 96 per cent of the vote. Elsewhere Jews were not as solidly Democratic. Four years later, Jewish wards in Boston and assembly districts in New York showed an appreciable increase in Democratic strength. Over 90 per cent of the Jews in New York County's 17th Assembly District cast ballots for F.D.R. In 1944, Jewish Democratic strength increased still further. In Boston's Jewish Ward 14, more than 95 per cent of the Jewish votes cast went to Roosevelt.

The results of national sample surveys conducted by the American Institute of Public Opinion and by the National Opinion Research Center show that more than 90 out of every 100 Jews voted Democratic in 1940 and 1944.[5]

The results of these surveys also revealed that American Jews had considerably improved their relative economic position since the twenties. By 1944 they were among the best paid and best educated of all denominational groups. On occupational prestige scales the Jews were consistently rated higher than the most Republican denominational groups—the Congregationalists, Presbyterians, and Episcopalians.[6]

Results from surveys also showed that the Jews constituted the only ethno-religious group in which differences in Democratic-Republican

---

[5]The Denver results are analyzed by Samuel J. Korchin, "Psychological Variables in the Behavior of Voting," unpub. diss. (Harvard University, 1946). The Gallup results are presented and analyzed by Wesley and Beverly Allinsmith, "Religious Affiliation and Politico-Economic Attitude," *Public Opinion Quarterly*, Vol. 12, pp. 377-89 (Fall, 1948), and by Liston Pope, "Religion and Class Structure," *The Annals of the American Academy of Political and Social Science*, Vol. 256, pp. 84-92 (March, 1948). See also an unpublished study by Robert T. Bower, "Voting Behavior of American Ethnic Groups," New York: Bureau of Applied Social Research, Columbia University (Sept. 1944).

[6]Allinsmith, "Religious Affiliation and Politico-Economic Attitude," p. 385. Jews were first in occupational status, third in educational status, and fourth in economic status. Pope, "Religion and Class Structure," pp. 84-91, lists Jews as first in occupational status and fourth on his income and education indices. "Distribution (by classes) of the Jewish group is very much like that of Episcopalians; a majority of the members of both still come from the middle and upper classes . . ." (p. 86).

strength could not be correlated with differences in occupational prestige, amount of income, or education.[7]

Jewish Democratic strength diminished in 1948, but the combined Truman-Wallace vote was almost as high in Jewish wards and assembly districts as it had been for F.D.R. in 1944. The Wallace vote was essentially Democratic. In Ward 14 the Progressive candidate received over 12 per cent of the vote. In the heavily Jewish Bronx 7th Assembly District he won 27 per cent of the vote. In the not-quite-as-Jewish Bronx 2nd Assembly District he received 21 per cent. The combined Truman-Wallace vote in both districts reached almost 90 per cent. In Hartford, Wallace ran strong only in predominantly Jewish Wards 4 and 12. In Los Angeles all five precincts which Wallace carried comprised Jewish neighborhoods. Even in suburban Brookline, Massachusetts over nine per cent of the votes in its most Jewish precinct were counted for Wallace.

Although 1948 was a year when most Democrats could be sharply separated from Republicans by status characteristics, Jewish voters could not be so simply divided. The most radical candidate, Wallace, won the votes of many well educated upper-middle class Jews who had hertofore voted for Franklin Roosevelt, but the Republicans gained very little over 1944.

In 1952 all segments of Truman-Wallace strength except Negroes shifted somewhat to Eisenhower.[8] But analysis of aggregate returns from Jewish areas and the results of national surveys show that the Jewish defection was slight indeed.[9] In Jewish Assembly Districts in New York City, in Boston's Ward 14, in Hartford's Wards 2 and 4, in Cleveland's Ward 27, in Pittsburgh's Ward 14, and in Cincinnati's Ward 13, Stevenson appears to have matched or increased the Truman percentage of the *two-party* vote.

---

[7]Bower, "Voting Behavior of American Ethnic Groups," p. 16; Korchin, "Psychological Variables in the Behavior of Voting," p. 93 and pp. 184 ff. See also Ernest Havemen and Patricia S. West, *They Went to College* (New York, 1952), an analysis of a *Time* magazine survey of 9,483 college graduates. The Jewish graduates, though earning more money in better jobs than the Gentiles, were far less Republican. Only six per cent of the Jews called themselves Republicans (pp. 187-88).

[8]Angus Campbell, Gerald Gurin, and Warren E. Miller, *The Voter Decides* (Evanston, Ill., 1954), pp. 70-73. See also Louis Harris, *Is There a Republican Majority?* (New York, 1954), p. 161. As Mr. Harris reports, the Democratic loss was a Progressive and not a Republican gain.

[9]Harris, *Is There a Republican Majority?*, pp. 160-63. The Roper organization reports that 74 per cent of the Jewish vote went to the Governor. There were 52 Jews in the Survey Research Center sample, 73 per cent of whom preferred Stevenson.

It was primarily in the suburbs that inroads were made on the Jewish Democratic vote—in such places as Westchester, New York; Newton, Massachusetts; and West Hartford, Connecticut.

I. Results of a Post-Election Survey in Boston's Most Jewish Ward

In the big cities the Jews were loyal to the Democratic party; according to the results of a "quasi-random" sample survey[10] of eligible voters conducted in Ward 14 in the city of Boston following the 1952 election, differences in Stevenson strength in the urban Jewish population cannot be accounted for by differences in income, occupational, or educational levels.

The total number of Jews in any national sample is invariably too small to permit the sub-division of the sample into meaningful sub-groups. Thus a quasi-random or "systematic" sample of 351 names was

TABLE 1

Democratic Vote of Jews and Gentiles in Boston's Ward 14
by Occupational-Income Status

Occupational-Income Group	Jews		Gentiles*	
	Number	Voted Democratic %	Number	Voted Democratic %
Low SES	36	64	15	60
Middle SES	101	66.3	12	41.7
High SES	53	72	10	30

* The distribution of Gentiles is like that found in the Roper national survey for three income groups of Irish descent: upper income 15%, lower-middle income 45%, and low income 75% Democratic. See Louis Harris, *Is There a Republican Majority?*, p. 222.

---

[10]Mildred Parten, *Surveys, Polls, and Samples: Practical Procedures* (New York, 1950), pp. 266-67. The procedure described in these pages under the heading "Sampling at Regular Intervals from a List" was the one followed in the Ward 14 survey. Miss Parten calls this type of sampling "Quasi-random" (p. 303) and suggests that the method, if executed carefully, "seems close enough to random sampling" to permit the use of confidence limits which can be estimated for pure random samples.

drawn from the 1952 Boston police list for Ward 14. Of these, 276 were finally interviewed.

The main purpose of the survey was to discover what the salient motivations of Jewish voters were in 1952. Questions were designed to produce responses which could be scaled by indices for socio-economic status, political liberalism, and ethno-religious involvement. Other census-type questions were asked on age, sex, education, nationality background, and other matters. One question called for an explanation of the vote. All questions were pre-tested on Brandeis University students; some were also pre-tested in a pilot mail questionnaire sent to the parents of students.

Nearly 84 per cent of the voters in the sample were Jewish. Of the 37 voting non-Jews, 28 were Catholic (nearly all Irish). The Jews in the sample lived in better homes, held better jobs, and made more money than the Christians; nonetheless, the Israelites gave Stevenson 70 per cent of their vote while their Gentile neighbors voted only 46 per cent Democratic.

Socio-Economic Status and the Jewish Vote

A total SES score was computed by combining income and occupational prestige scores, giving a double weight to occupation. Non-Jews in the sample, as in all national surveys, displayed much greater Republican strength in the high SES groups than they did in the low groups. However, differences in Stevenson strength among Jews in Boston cannot be accounted for by differences in socio-economic status.

Education and the Jewish Vote

There was a slight tendency for better-educated Jews to prefer Eisenhower in 1952, but the pattern is hardly significant. In fact, the percentage of Jewish college graduates in Ward 14 voting for Stevenson was almost as high as that for all Jews in the sample. The results for Gentile voters support the accepted view that Republican choice is associated with high education among non-Jews.

Age and the Jewish Vote

The results of surveys in which a breakdown of ethno-religious groups by age is made reveal that when any group—Irish Catholics, Italians, Negroes—shift from their expected political pre-disposition, it is the younger voters who swing the most. Since the Jews did not

TABLE 2

Democratic Vote of Jews and Gentiles in Boston's Ward 14
by Educational Groups

	Jews*		Gentiles*	
Educational Group	Number	Voted Democrat %	Number	Voted Democrat %
Some elementary school or less	39	79.5	1	100
Elementary school graduate	21	71.5	4	75
Some high school	24	73.9	9	66.6
High school graduate	62	64.4	9	33.3
High school plus vocational or business school	15	53.4	4	0
Some college	14	64.3	5	20
College graduate	22	68.3	5	60

* There appears to be a slight inverse correlation between SES and education among Jews because so many successful Jewish businessmen have little or no formal education, while some of the college graduates are young men and women not yet established in whatever they do.

shift their loyalties appreciably in 1952, there was little difference in the Democratic vote among age groups in Ward 14, while the pronounced defection of Irish Catholic voters to Eisenhower was most noticeable among the younger voters.

Thus, in Ward 14 the presidential choice of non-Jews in 1952 was oriented along class lines. High education, high SES, and youth all disposed Gentiles favorably toward Eisenhower. On the other hand, Jewish voters for Stevenson could not be distinguished from the Eisenhower electors by any of the usual separators. It is not clear from the demography of the Jewish vote in Ward 14 just what it was that made one in every four Jewish voters choose the General while the large majority preferred the Governor.

Ethno-Religious Involvement and the Jewish Vote

Questions were designed to test the depth of Jewish involvement felt by the respondents. Separate questions were used to measure the depth

TABLE 3

Democratic Vote of Jews and Gentiles in Boston's Ward 14
by Age Groups

Age Group	Jews*		Gentiles*	
	Number	Voted Democratic %	Number	Voted Democratic %
21–34	53	70	12	25
34–54	86	63	20	50
54 plus	54	76	5	80

of cultural, religious, and social Jewishness. When added together, the scores of all three yielded a total ethno-religious involvement score which could be scaled.

It was recognized that voters might have commitments to Judaism which ran deep but which were psychological or intellectual and could not be measured by the EI scale. For that reason all Jewish respondents were also asked to pick three statements from a list (made originally by respondents in the pilot survey in answer to an open-end question) which best expressed what their religion meant to them.

Results show that Stevenson voters scored slightly higher EI scores on the cultural and social Judaism tests, while Eisenhower voters scored slightly higher on the religious Judaism scale. The overall means of each group were quite close, only one-tenth of a point separating them on a five-point scale.

From the results given in Table 4, it is not likely that differences in the vote could be attributed to differences in ethno-religious involvement, at least as measured by these scales.[11] Moreover, Eisenhower

---

[11]It is always possible that the scales, which were elaborately worked out and pretested, are something less than a perfect measure of Jewishness. Eighteen questions in all were asked. For example, respondents were asked to rate the importance of such religious practices as saying prayers for dead parents. They were also asked to rate their approval or disapproval of such things as intermarriage and to state whether or not they regularly read a Yiddish newspaper, kept a Kosher home, etc. While the results here show that Democratic Jews are just about as Jewish as Republican Jews, the findings of Bernard R. Berelson, Paul F. Lazarsfeld, and William N. McPhee, Voting (Chicago, 1954), p. 72, are somewhat different. The authors found that in Elmira, New York those Jews expressing

TABLE 4

Democratic Vote of Jews in Boston's Ward 14
by Ethnic-Involvement Groups

Ethnic-Involvement Group	Number	Voted Democratic %
High EI	13	46.2
High-medium EL	47	72.4
Medium EI	72	69.5
Low-medium EI	43	60.5
Low EI	20	80.1

and Stevenson voters chose approximately the same kinds of statements in about the same distribution to express best what their religion meant to them.

As with the results from the SES, EI, education, and age questions, the breakdown of the Jewish vote by nationality background and generations offered no clue to explain continued Jewish Democratic strength in the face of the Eisenhower landslide. Nor do any of the results reported so far suggest what it was that prompted a minority of the Jewish voters to vote for Eisenhower.

The Jewish Response to Stevenson

What did the Jews perceive in Stevenson and the Democratic party in 1952 that made them so preponderantly Democratic, almost without regard to socio-economic and religious characteristics?

---

a strong commitment to Judaism were more Democratic than those Jews with low EI. The number of Jews involved was 108, less than half the number in the Boston survey, but sizable. However, certain sub-groups are quite small. Those Jews who neither attended services nor favored orthodox customs numbered only 12. Still the results may be quite sound. In Elmira, Jewish involvement may have correlated significantly with Democratic choice in 1948, while in Ward 14 no such correlation was forthcoming for 1952. However, even in Elmira, Republican choice among Jews may be less a function of low EI than a function of primary group contact with non-Jews. Probably both factors go somewhat together. Those Jews with low EI probably go to non-Jewish neighborhoods and participate in non-Jewish groups more than those with high EI. Those Jews who for one reason or another have frequent contact with non-Jews probably become less orthodox as a result. If both results are correct, Elmira Jews must be different from Ward 14 Jews in some important respect. It is likely that the difference lies in the sheer concentration of Ward 14 Jews. Even the low EI Jews in Ward 14 live in an intensely Jewish community. Outside of such sociological enclaves, it might well be that the EI scale used here would be a significant separator of Republicans and Democrats.

It was hoped that the answer to that question would be forthcoming in the replies to three questions placed in the interview schedule. One question was designed to test the political liberalism of respondents. This particular test was aimed at discovering the basic attitudes of respondents toward the use of power. Because of this and because the liberalism index was also used for purposes not discussed in this paper, the criteria for defining liberalism on which the question was based were: (1) a disposition to share power with out-groups, and (2) a disposition to respect those who are different.[12]

It may be said that these criteria actually define political altruism and not liberalism at all as it is commonly understood. Whether the question yields an altruism index or a liberalism index is not crucial. The results show that there was considerable difference in the Jewish and Gentile response to the question in Ward 14. After the answers were scaled, respondents were divided into six categories ranging from 'very strong liberals' to 'very strong illiberals.' While 40 per cent of the Jews qualified as liberals or altruists, only 26 per cent of the Gentiles did so.

The results were not surprising in the light of reports on other liberalism-conservatism or egalitarian-authoritarian tests.[13] No matter what criteria have been used to define liberalism and conservatism, Jews invariably have been rated overwhelmingly more liberal than Christians.

Did Jews perceive liberalism in Stevenson and the Democratic party? All Stevenson voters were asked to pick three statements from a list (all statements were originally made by respondents in answer to an open-end question in a pilot survey) which best expressed why they preferred Stevenson. They were also asked to choose two statements from another list which best expressed what they liked least about Eisenhower.

The results are instructive. To a much greater extent than the Christians the Jews in the sample emphasized the personal qualifica-

---

[12]It is recognized that the word "liberalism," like the word "class," is bound to be controversial when injected into any discussion of American politics. I am not at all certain that the definition of liberalism used in this survey is a useful one. Criteria which measure altruism in politics do not measure those elements of political ideology which have relevance in shaping the electoral choices of most voters. Later the liberalism of the Jews will be discussed in terms of specific issues.

[13]Gordon W. Allport, "The Composition of Political Attitudes," *American Journal of Sociology*, Vol. 25, pp. 220-38 (Sept., 1939). See also Allinsmith, "Religious Affiliation and Politico-Economic Attitudes," pp. 379-80; Haveman and West, *They Went to College*, pp. 98-101. All studies emphasize the egalitarianism or liberalism of the Jews.

TABLE 5

Democratic Vote of Jews and Gentiles in Boston's Ward 14
by Liberalism Groups

Liberalism Group	Jews		Gentiles	
	Number	Voted Democrat %	Number	Voted Democrat %
Liberals (Altruists)	25	87.5	4	50
Moderates	124	67	24	52.3
Illiberals	43	64.5	9	38.5

tions and liberalism of Stevenson and/or the Democratic party.
Christians tended to stress the fact that the Democrats and/or Ste-
venson favored their own economic group while Eisenhower and the
Republicans did not.

The results from these questions do not prove that it was the
political liberalism of the Jews which kept them Democratic in 1952,
but this evidence, taken together with the findings of Mr. Louis Harris
of the Elmo Roper organization, at least suggests that the Jews did
tend to think of Stevenson as the more "liberal" candidate and the
Democratic party as the more "liberal" party.[14]

Liberalism and the Stevenson-Eisenhower Choice

If, as suggested, it was the "liberalism" of the Jews which oriented
them toward a Democratic choice, it might be supposed that those Jews
who were least liberal were the Eisenhower voters. Although it is true
that a higher proportion of liberal or politically altruistic Jews voted
for Stevenson than voted for him in the moderate or illiberal groups,
the total number of liberals is quite small, and the differences between groups are not large.

It is entirely possible that the overwhelming disposition of the Jews
to vote Democratic in recent decades is a function of their liberalism,
but it is also possible that Jewish votes for Eisenhower were something other than a manifestation of illiberalism. Literally dozens of
Jewish voters indicated in their replies to open-end questions that they
thought Eisenhower was a liberal himself.

---

[14]Harris, *Is there a Republican Majority?*, pp. 161-63.

II. Interpretation

Primary Group Influences and the Jewish Eisenhower Vote

For a satisfactory explanation of the slight Jewish Democratic defection in 1952, it would be well to start with the proposition that a certain proportion of Jews were bound to be affected by the factors which caused an Eisenhower landslide in the nation at large. But which Jews were influenced and which Jews were not? It was not necessarily the rich Jews, or the well educated Jews, or the third generation Jews, or the less ethnically involved Jews, or the young Jews who showed disproportionate Republican strength in 1952.

Such evidence as is available strongly suggests that the Republican vote went up among those Jews who had the most frequent and extensive contact with non-Jews in primary groups.

While it is not possible to prove this hypothesis quantitatively with the results of the Ward 14 survey (the appropriate questions were not asked), inferences can be drawn from some of those results and from a further discussion of aggregate returns.

Three sets of data tend to support this hypothesis: first, the difference in the Stevenson vote between the men and women in Ward 14; second, the results of election surveys in predominantly Jewish colleges; third, the election results from Jewish suburban areas compared with those for metropolitan centers.

Jewish Men and Women Voters in the 1952 Election

Although the Survey Research Center reported[15] that males and females in the nation as a whole voted for Eisenhower in about the same proportion, the results of the survey in Ward 14 show that 83.3 per cent of the Jewish women voters preferred Stevenson as compared with only 59.4 per cent of the men, while there was no difference in the Stevenson vote between Gentile males and females. To be sure, the results of national surveys in the past have shown Jewish women to be somewhat more Democratic than Jewish men,[16] but the percentage difference between them was three or four and not 24.

Keeping in mind the possibility of sampling and reporting bias, the results still appear to defy explanation until consideration is given to

---

[15]Campbell, Gurin, and Miller, *The Voter Decides*, p. 70. The Roper organization found that women were generally more attracted to Eisenhower than men. Harris, *Is There a Republican Majority?*, Ch. 7.

[16]Bower, "Voting Behavior of American Ethnic Groups," p. 11 and Korchin, "Psychological Variables in the Behavior of Voting," p. 97.

the importance of primary group contacts in the formulation of electoral decision.

It is now well established that face-to-face contacts are of major importance in the shaping of vote choice.[17] And there is evidence from the results of the Ward 14 survey to suggest that differences in the male-female vote can be largely explained by the fact that Jewish women in Ward 14 have little contact with primary groups which include non-Jews, while their husbands, fathers, and brothers are thrust into such groups quite often.

Most of the women rarely leave the Ward itself. Their contacts are almost exclusively neighborhood and family contacts, nearly all of which are Jewish. One young woman reported that she had never met a Protestant in her life until she went to college. On the other hand, the men from Ward 14 often work outside of the area, and are thereby exposed, in Lazarsfeld's phrase, to "cross pressures" in mixed work and friendship groups.

In 1952 the Jewish group held fast to its Democratic moorings while the nation, for many reasons, swung to Eisenhower. While Jewish men were exposed to the opinions of non-Jewish friends at the work bench, of customers in the store, or of clients in the office, Jewish women were insulated from those cross-pressures to a considerable extent.

But, it will be asked, were not those pressures to which men were subjected filtered to most wives through their husbands? Yes, but they were diluted. It is apparent that in many cases male Eisenhower voters were either unsuccessful in attempting to dissuade their wives from a Democratic choice, or failed to make the attempt at all.[18] In at least two cases in Ward 14 such efforts were rewarded.

One young housewife, whose husband was an electrical appliance salesman for a non-Jewish firm, volunteered at the end of her interview: "I was for Stevenson until the last minute when my husband

---

[17]As Campbell, Gurin, and Miller, *The Voter Decides*, p. 207, point out, even in Lazarsfeld's "explanation of the influence of the demographic characteristics (of voters) these are primary group influences . . ." See Paul Lazarsfeld, Bernard Berelson, and Hazel Gaudet, *The People's Choice* (New York, 1948), Ch. 16.

[18]In the Ward 14 survey respondents were not asked for the votes of their spouses, but in a pilot survey of the parents of Brandeis College students which preceded the Ward 14 survey, many of the respondents were married. The results of that survey are as incredible as those for Ward 14. Of the 33 men who voted, only 23 said they chose Stevenson (69.8 pre cent). Of the 26 women voting from the Brandeis parents' sample 24 voted for Stevenson (92.3 per cent). Of course, confidence limits cannot be applied to the results of such a survey, but the respondents constituted a cross-section of American upper-middle class Jewry. The average family income of respondents was over $6,500.

made me change my mind. He felt it was time for a change, and then I thought maybe Eisenhower would end the Korean war." Another middle-aged woman was married to a sales executive at Jordan Marsh department store, "the only Jew in his department," she volunteered. Throughout the campaign he tried to persuade her to switch to Eisenhower without success. She changed to Eisenhower after she entered the voting booth. As she recalled: "I told him that morning that I would vote for Stevenson. But then I changed. I don't know why."

In both cases the husbands for Eisenhower were in frequent and sustained contact with non-Jews in their primary work groups. Both families were well educated, the kind in which the political opinions of wives and husbands are likely to be exchanged. Both wives vicariously experienced the cross pressures their husbands felt first hand. It is probable that most other housewives in the sample were less exposed to non-Jewish and Republican influences than these two.

There is one additional check on this primary group explanation for the disparity in the male-female vote. Some of the women were working women. Presumably they would be in greater contact with non-Jews and Republican cross pressures. Such contact should be reflected in their vote, and it was. While only 70 per cent of the working and single women in the Ward 14 sample voted for Stevenson, 84 per cent of the housewives chose the Governor.

There may be other reasons for the stronger female response to Stevenson. There is some evidence from the survey results that the women were slightly more disturbed than the men because Eisenhower was a military man and that Stevenson's urbane and learned manner was more pleasing to the Jewish women than to the men, but the evidence available is shadowy at best.

Jewish College Communities and the 1952 Election

At least suggestive of the importance of immediate group contacts for the Jewish vote in 1952 are the results of polls taken at Yeshiva college and Brandeis University. At Yeshiva, a school which is 100 per cent Jewish, Eisenhower received a mere four per cent of the vote. Brandeis is a non-sectarian Jewish-sponsored school. Probably as much as 10 per cent of the student body there is not Jewish.[19] In the Brandeis poll Stevenson received 88 per cent of the vote.

---

[19]Of course, it is impossible to know just how many non-Jews there are at Brandeis. While the number is growing all the time, the percentage quoted here is probably correct within five per cent for 1952.

The Jewish Brandeis students represent a cross-section of American Jewry—religious, irreligious, urban, small town, suburban, poor, well-to-do. Yet the Brandeis vote for Stevenson, including the vote of the non-Jewish students, was 14 per cent higher than that reported for the national Jewish population by survey organizations and 10 per cent higher than that reported for the sample of 59 of their own parents and relatives questioned in a pilot survey.

Jewish students came to Brandeis and Yeshiva with strong Democratic leanings. Finding their own opinions almost unanimously reinforced in student face-to-face groups, there were few defections. At home their parents were exposed to more frequent contacts with non-Jews in Republican-oriented groups.

Suburban Jewry and the 1952 Election

It has already been shown that returns from Jewish wards and assembly districts in the large cities revealed little Democratic loss from 1948. It is reasonable to conclude that what Democratic losses there were (national surveys show some overall loss) occurred among those Jews who are dispersed in Gentile areas or who live in the suburbs. The votes of the former group cannot be reported, since, as in San Francisco, they are buried in the aggregate returns for non-Jewish wards. But simple arithmetic suggests that defections took place in just such cases.

Moreover, the returns from suburban Jewish areas support the hypothesis of the importance of primary group contacts for Jewish voting choice in 1952. Reports from Westchester and Long Island in New York, and from Brookline and Newton, near Boston, indicate that Jews in the suburbs were primarily responsible for the Jewish defections which did take place.

Although Jews may cluster together in tree-lined neighborhoods and country clubs in the suburbs, they are exposed to much greater contact with Gentiles in primary groups than are the Jews of Ward 14 or the Bronx. Jewish families in the suburbs participate in community affairs. Both men and women meet their non-Jewish neighbors in primary groups. They discover a common interest in the tax rate or the problems of the high school. Their interest in the local Synagogue may be more lively than it ever was back in Brooklyn, but their associations are no longer so preponderantly Jewish.

In 1944, suburban Jewry was hardly less Democratic than coreligionists in the city, because Jewish group involvement in the outcome of the election was so high. Even in Precinct 8 in suburban Brookline,

F.D.R. received 79 per cent of the vote. In 1952 the vote there slipped to 52 per cent of the total. Brookline is a bedroom area for Boston. Its voters were subjected to cross pressures in primary groups which even many of the well-to-do in Dorchester and Mattapan (Ward 14) did not experience, and in 1952 those pressures were strongest in the suburbs where the Eisenhower plurality was the greatest.

The Democrats and the Jews

More important than the reasons for Democratic defection in 1952 are the causes of persistent Democratic attachment over the last three decades. In order to understand the fidelity of Jewish voters to the Democrats in 1948 and 1952, it is necessary to go back to Franklin Roosevelt and the almost solid Jewish vote for Roosevelt in his last three contests.

Roosevelt had the overwhelming support of Jews in his quest for a "New Deal" and his efforts at intervention in behalf of the Allies against the Fascists and Nazis. As interventionists the Jews were "internationalists," in the political parlance of the 1930's, and as New Dealers they were "liberals." The internationalism and liberalism of Roosevelt were both congenial to the interests of the Jews.

Jewish Internationalism

During the late 1930's there was no stronger interventionist group in the United States than the Jews. The survival of world Jewry itself made such a course mandatory in the 1930's and 1940's. Roosevelt, of course, had begun in 1935 a series of private and public protests against anti-semitism in Germany and was the political leader of the interventionist forces in the country. Jews could not help but be drawn to the one man who could lead Americans to a more active role in European affairs.

Recent studies show that Jewish support for internationalism persisted long after the defeat of Hitler. Survey results for 1948 and 1952 reveal that Jews support, much more strongly than Gentiles, the United Nations, Point Four, aid to Europe, liberal immigration policies, and world government plans. According to one survey of college graduates in 1948, almost twice the proportion of Jews as Catholics and Protestants were classified as internationalists, i.e., displayed stronger enthusiasm for the United Nations, liberal immigration, lower tariffs, helping other nations, and the reconciliation of international conflict.

Did Jews think that internationalism would be best served by the election of Truman or Wallace rather than Dewey in 1948? Presumably the answer is yes, otherwise it would be impossible to explain the extraordinary Jewish vote for Wallace. The Progressive candidate based much of his campaign on the failure of Truman to carry on the internationalism of Roosevelt (negotiation with Russia) while the Republicans, when they debated foreign policy at all, chided Truman for being too internationalist.[20]

What of 1952? Did Jewish internationalism manifest itself then? In the Ward 14 sample, a much higher proportion of Jews than Gentiles supported the United Nations and the extension of aid to Africa and Asia. Elmo Roper found that Jews were much more for the United Nations and world government plans than non-Jews.[21] According to Louis Harris, one of the chief attachments of Jews to Adlai Stevenson was the compatibility of the Jewish and the Democratic positions on foreign policy.

Jewish Liberalism

Other than foreign policy issues, the questions which have divided Americans in recent years have dealt with the distribution of economic power, Negro rights, and freedom of the mind. On each of these questions the Jews have taken what in everyday parlance has been called the "liberal" position. In each case Jewish opinions have been closer to the position of the Democratic candidates for President than to the one held by their Republican adversaries.

The results of surveys show that Jews have been strong supporters of the "New Deal" and the "Fair Deal." In 1932 and 1936 such views made economic sense to the Jews themselves. Like other Americans of recent immigrant stock, they felt the cruel blows of the depression and were no doubt grateful to Roosevelt for his efforts to lessen the effect of those blows. However, even though the Jews began to climb the economic class ladder in the late 1930's and 1940's, they persisted in their adherence to "New Deal" and "Fair Deal" ideas.

According to the results of American Institute of Public Opinion surveys in 1944, the Jews were the only high economic status group to

---

[20]It ought to be pointed out that the Wallace stand on Zionism was unequivocal, while some Jews were unconvinced that Truman was a firm Zionist.

[21]Elmo Roper, "American Attitudes on International Organization," *Public Opinion Quarterly*, Vol. 7, pp. 405-35, at p. 410 (Winter, 1953).

look with favor on governmental guarantees against economic insecurity. The results show that 53.8 per cent of the Jewish business and professional men were for such government guarantees, as compared to an average of about 20 per cent for non-Jews in these same occupations.

Other survey evidence showed that, even though there were proportionately fewer Jewish manual laborers than in any other religious denomination, a higher proportion of Jews than of any other group wanted to give more power and influence to working people. While 58.8 per cent of the Jews wanted to give more power to working people, only 31.1 per cent of the Congregationalists, 37.1 per cent of the Presbyterians, and 34.7 per cent of the Episcopalians—the other high occupational status groups—agreed.[22]

In 1948 Jewish college graduates were less hostile to socialism and government planning than non-Jewish college graduates. Sixty-six per cent of the Jews were indexed as pro-New Deal compared to 39 per cent of the Catholics and 34 per cent of the Protestants, in one study.[23]

In the survey of Ward 14, respondents were asked one question on the role of the national government in aiding economically underprivileged groups. Proportionately three times as many Jews as Gentiles were in strong agreement with such action.

The results of all studies show American Jews to be economic "liberals," in the sense of looking with approval upon the growth of governmental and labor power in economic affairs—even though they themselves are a favored economic group. Such economic views were crucial in the shaping of Jewish vote choice in the 1932 and 1936 elections. They were unimportant in 1940 and 1944, when Jewish interest in interventionism-internationalism was sufficient to unite them behind Roosevelt. In 1948 and 1952 the economic liberalism of the Jews again played a contributing role in sustaining their Democratic attachment.

On the issues of civil rights (in particular, Negro rights) and civil liberties (freedom of the mind) Jews have tended strongly to favor what is usually called the "liberal" position. The Jews were solid in their backing of President Truman in his quest for a Federal FEPC. Samuel Lubell reported that no white group was stronger in 1948 for FEPC measures than the Jews.[24] Again in 1952, the results of

---

[22]Allinsmith, "Religious Affiliation and Politico-Economic Attitudes," p. 379.
[23]Haveman and West, *They Went to College*, pp. 98-99.
[24]Samuel Lubell, *The Future of American Politics* (New York, 1952), pp. 96-97.

surveys on Negro rights questions showed that Jews were zealous in
their quest for legislation protecting those rights. And in 1952, as in
1948, Jews thought that the Democrats could do much more about
accomplishing such legislation than the Republicans.[25]

What is here labeled the "freedom of the mind" issue is really made
up of a number of different issues, including communism in government, the rights and wrongs of congressional investigating committees, the Federal security program, and the use of high position to
make reckless and unsubstantiated charges. According to 1952 surveys
on these issues, the opinions of Jews were at variance with those of
the rest of the population. Gallup and Roper public opinion polls
found the Jews more hostile to McCarthy, less disturbed by charges of
Democratic tolerance of communism in government, and more zealous
in defending non-conformity than Catholics and Protestants. While
these issues played little or no part in the 1948 campaign, the Jewish
view of them no doubt fortified their Democratic leanings in 1952,
and perhaps even played a vital role in bolstering Democratic loyalties.

Economic hardship may have made the Jews Democrats in 1932
and 1936; concern for the fate of coreligionists abroad may have made
them Democrats in 1940 and 1944. But by 1948 and 1952 Jews were
perched on the economic status ladder, and the Nazis had been
beaten, yet they continued to be "liberals" on economic issues, on civil
rights, and on civil liberties. They continued to be internationalists in
matters of foreign policy. And they continued to vote for Democratic
candidates for President.

Sources of Jewish Internationalism and Liberalism

It must be clear that Jewish support for internationalism and liberal
government is no transitory thing. Both are deeply rooted in the history
and character of the Jewish people. It is no surprise that Jews support
internationalist policies. They have dispersed over the face of the globe
for over 2,000 years, never long in one homeland and often in contact with co-religionists abroad. Jewish culture, language, folklore, and
religion are truly international. Moreover, the experience of the last
three decades has convinced American Jews that their own security
lies in international guarantees (United Nations world government,
genocide convention, international bill of human rights) and in the
playing of a strong international role by the United States, whose

[25]Harris, *Is There a Republican Majority?*, p. 162.

beneficence in international affairs in behalf of Jews has been well demonstrated.

There are two primary sources of Jewish political liberalism. One is the basic insecurity of the group. The other lies in Jewish group values. Of the first, it may be said that Jews are engaged in a continuing quest for security even in free and pluralistic America. No matter how high they are placed on socio-economic scales, Jews are considered by non-Jews to be an out-group, and more often than not an undesirable one.[26] There are few Jews who do not feel this in their bones. And there are few indeed who do not sense that the security of the Jewish group depends in great measure upon the largess of liberal government. Those who had doubts of this had them smashed for our time by the forces of anti-semitism unleashed by Adolph Hitler and now so strong in Soviet Russia. Thus, while American Jews may be members of high income and occupational status groups, there are other reference groups in which their involvement, even when vicarious, runs deeper—those of the underprivileged and oppressed.

The second primary source of Jewish liberalism, probably less obvious and less understood than group insecurity, is in the ethno-religious values of the Jewish group. According to a vast impressionistic literature and growing systematic study of Jewish culture, those elements of culture most valued by Jews (including American Jews) are: Learning (*Torah*), Charity (*Zedakeh*), and, for want of a better word or phrase, Non-asceticism.

In probably no other American sub-culture is so high a value placed upon learning and intellectuality, or upon the helping of the poor by the rich and the weak by the strong, or upon living a good life upon earth in full use of one's body.

American Jews are practically unaffected by the bleak influence of Calvinism or by the harsh political implications of Social Darwinism. Nor are the American Jews as yet more than touched by the American pragmatic tradition disparaging learning for its own "impractical" sake.

These Jewish values have had special relevance to some of the major issues and candidates of our time.[27] *Zedakeh,* which is the

---

[26]For a discussion of prestige and social-distance scales, see Muzafer Sherif and Carolyn W. Sherif, *Groups in Harmony and Tension* (New York, 1953), pp. 78-79. Bogardus and others have consistently shown since 1926 that Jews are thought of by all other ethnic groups as an undesirable group to live with, to marry, or to work with.

[27]A more complete discussion of the relevance of Jewish group values to political behavior will be forthcoming in the author's book on the subject.

word for charity used in the Old Testament and the Talmud, and which is one of the few Hebrew words carried over into the Yiddish idiom, actually means "righteousness" or "justice"—"social justice" would be more accurate. Even though most American Jews may be unfamiliar with the word itself, the concept of *Zedakeh* is still highly prized in Jewish community life. To give is still a *mitzvah* (blessing). Within the framework of the Jewish cultural tradition, wealth, learning, and other tangible possessions are channeled from the strong to the weak and from the rich to the poor *as a matter of right*. It is easy to see the relevance of *Zedakeh* to politics, for both deal with the distribution of power. *Zedakeh*, as well as Jewish insecurity, would help promote Jewish sympathy for the Negro, and help induce a favorable attitude toward progressive taxation, Roosevelt's war on economic royalism, social security, and most of the programs which constituted the New Deal. It would also explain the favorable attitude of Jewish business and professional men toward an extension of power to labor, as long as they thought of laborers as being relatively weak or underprivileged. It would also explain the results of the liberalism or altruism test given to the voters of Ward 14 in 1953, the much greater willingness of the Jewish voters to be taxed to aid the less fortunate in Kentucky, or even in Africa and Asia.[28] *Zedakeh* would also help explain why the results of referenda studied by the writer show that Jewish wards and precincts are more favorable to such things as pensions for the aged, raising the minimum wage, and aiding the disabled than are non-Jewish voters.

The Jewish reverence for learning has also played a role in making the Jews political liberals in recent decades. It has influenced the Jewish response to individual candidates as well as to specific issues. The positive Jewish response to Wilson and to Stevenson was in part a function of Jewish respect for learning. Twenty-two and one half per cent of the reasons given by Jewish Stevenson voters in Ward 14 for preferring the Governor concerned his personality and intelligence, compared to only 13.8 per cent of the reasons given by non-Jewish Stevenson voters. It was partly the Jewish love of learning that assured their positive response to the Roosevelt brain trust. The idea of professors in government did not seem incongruous to them, as it did to many Gentiles. For centuries Jews have been taught that the

---

[28]When asked whether they ought to help pay for the roads and education of the people in Kentucky, 56.9 per cent of the Jews and 39.8 per cent of the Christians agreed that they should. When asked whether they ought to be taxed to help raise standards of living in Asia and Africa, 44.5 per cent of the Jews and 28.9 per cent of the Christians agreed that they should.

most learned men ought to run the affairs of the community. They were not repulsed by the notion of planning in government as were many of their fellow Americans. Charity (welfare) requires planning. That is a Jewish tradition. If the state is to take an active role in assuring the welfare of its citizens, it ought to put its best brains to work to plan how this will be done.

The respect of Jews for learning has also helped to make them fierce defenders of intellectual independence in connection with civil liberties issues. While almost 12 per cent of the Jewish voters in the Ward 14 sample were in strong agreement that even Nazis and Communists ought to have free speech, not a single Gentile respondent was in agreement with that position. To be sure, the insecurity of the Jews prompts their anxiety about civil liberties, but the value which Jews place on knowledge plays a role as well.

The influence of Jewish non-asceticism on the political behavior of American Jews has been subtle, but probably no less important than the influence of *Zedakeh* and *Torah*. On such questions as the liquor or birth control issue it is easy to see how the non-asceticism or this-worldliness of the Jews influenced their position. But how has the non-asceticism of the Jews helped to make them political liberals as that term has been used in recent decades? The answer is that by Jewish emphasis on this-worldliness and the enjoyment of life here and now, Jews have been made more receptive to plans for a better life, for reconstructing society, for remaking man's environment, for socialism, and for millennialism.

Zedakeh, Torah, and this-worldliness have, along with the insecurity of the group, all promoted political liberalism among Jews in our time. Their liberalism and internationalism have favorably disposed them to a Democratic choice in recent presidential elections and largely explain the resistance of Jews to class politics.

The Negro Voter in
Northern Industrial Cities

Oscar Glantz

The political role of Negro citizens in northern industrial cities has been described and discussed in numerous reports and commentaries on Negro political behavior, particularly in reference to presidential and gubernatorial elections.[1] In presidential elections, for example, the best available data indicate that Negro voters have been supporting the Democratic party since 1936, by contrast to a history of strong

Reprinted from *Western Political Quarterly*, Vol. XIII (December 1960), 999-1010 by permission of the University of Utah, copyright owners.

[1]See, for example, Ernest M. Collins, "Cincinnati Negroes and Presidential Politics," *Journal of Negro History*, XLI (1956), 131-37; Oscar Glantz, "Recent Negro Ballots in Philadelphia, *Journal of Negro Education*, XXVIII (1959), 430-38; Harold F. Gosnell, "The Negro Voter in Northern Cities," *National Municipal Review*, XXX (1941), 264-67 and 278; Edward H. Litchfield, "A Case Study of Negro Political Behavior in Detroit," *Public Opinion Quarterly*, V (1941), 267-74; Robert E. Martin, "The Relative Political Status of the Negro in the United States, *Journal of Negro Education*, XXII (1953), 363-79; J. Erroll Miller, "The Negro in Present Day Politics, *Journal of Negro History*, XXXIII (1948), 303-43; and Henry Lee Moon, "The Negro Voter in the Presidential Election of 1956," *Journal of Negro Education*, XXVI (1957), 219-30. For representative articles in the popular literature, see Robert Bendiner, "The Negro Vote and the Democrats," *Reporter*, May 31, 1956, pp. 8-12; R. H. Brisbane, "The Negro's Growing Political Power," *Nation*, September 27, 1952, pp. 248-49; Carl Rowan, "Who Gets the Negro Vote?" *Look*, November 13, 1956, pp. 37-39; and Walter White, "Win Our Vote or Lose," *Look*, October 7, 1952, pp. 18-19 and 21-22.

allegiance to the Republican party in the seventeen elections from Reconstruction through 1932.[2] Moreover, it is evident that the northward migration of southern Negroes, plus the accelerated migration to California,[3] has served to enlarge the numerical force of the Negro body politic. In the single decade from 1940 to 1950, for example, Negro migrants accounted for more than 50 per cent of the increase in potential Negro voters in various northern cities (Table 1). In several outstanding cases, Negro migrants accounted for no less than 80 per cent of the increment.[4]

As a consequence of such increments, Negro voters in northern and western industrial cities have achieved a balance-of-power position in local, state and national elections.[5] On the national level, this position was notably effective in contributing to Mr. Truman's dramatic victory in the presidential election of 1948. When one recalls that his victory would not have been possible without the electoral votes of California, Illinois, and Ohio, and that he managed to carry those states by narrow margins of 17,000, 33,000, and 7,000 votes respectively, it is readily apparent that the overwhelming pro-Truman preference of Negro voters was indispensable in placing the three states in the Democratic column.[6] One political commentator has suggested that "less than fifteen per cent switch in the Negro vote would have

---

[2]In 1932, Mr. Roosevelt received only 23 per cent of the Negro vote in Chicago and 29 per cent in Cincinnati. Gosnell, *op. cit.*, and Collins, *op. cit.*

[3]For a discussion on the Negro voter in California and other western states, see Loren Miller, "The Negro Voter in the Far West," *Journal of Negro Education*, XXVI (1957), 262-72.

[4]A rough indication of demographic developments during the decade from 1950 to 1960 can be obtained from John M. Maclachan, "Recent Population Trends in the Southeast," *Social Forces*, XXXV (1956), 147-54. He has calculated the possible net loss of migrants from the southeastern region (eleven states) and has concluded that "the projected loss of 2,950,000 would be comprised of about 980,000 white and 1,970,000 nonwhite net migrants" (p. 150). For critical comments on Maclachan's data, see Homer L. Hitt, "Migration Between the South and Other Regions." *Social Forces*, XXXVI (1957), 9-16.

[5]The leading treatise on this subject can be found in Henry Lee Moon, *Balance of Power: The Negro Vote* (Garden City: Doubleday, 1949). For several early comments on the relationship between Negro migration and political power, see Emmett J. Scott, *Negro Migration During the War* (New York: Oxford University Press, 1920), especially the optimistic editorial from the *Philadelphia Christian Recorder* (February 1, 1917) which is reproduced on pp. 164-65.

[6]"The records show," according to R. H. Brisbane, "(1) that of the 100,000 Negroes who went to the polls in California, 70,000 voted for Truman . . . (2) that of the 119,000 votes cast in three Negro wards in Chicago, 85,000 went to Truman . . . [and] (3) that in Ohio 130,000 of 200,000 Negroes voted for Truman." *Op. cit.*, p. 249. Indeed, data in the current study suggest that Mr. Truman received a percentage of Negro ballots in Ohio which exceeds the percentage suggested by Brisbane.

delivered all three of those states to Dewey, enough to have slipped him into the White House and made Korea a 'Republican war.' "[7]

TABLE 1

Contribution of Net Negro Migration, 1940–1950,
to the Increase in Potential Negro Voters, 1940–1950

| | Number of potential voters, 1950* | Increase in potential voters, 1940–1950 | Net Migrants, 21+, 1940–1950 | |
			Number†	As percentage of increase in potential voters, 1940–1950
Chicago	331,825	140,107	110,500	78.9
Cincinnati	52,491	15,235	13,100	86.3
Cleveland	97,757	41,811	24,500	58.7
Detroit	202,101	102,231	89,700	87.8
Kansas City	39,722	9,062	4,200	46.9
New York City	511,538	194,183	160,700	82.8
Pittsburgh	53,508	12,842	9,200	71.9
St. Louis	101,911	26,761	10,900	40.9

* With the exception of New York City, the number of Negroes in the non-citizen category is a fraction of one per cent. In New York, it is approximately two or three per cent. No adjustment was made for this factor.

† To estimate the net intercensal migration of Negroes in the eight cities, the writer utilized statewide data available in Everett S. Lee, *et al*, *Population Redistribution and Economic Growth* (Philadelphia: The American Philosophical Society, 1957), Vol. I, Table 1.14, pp. 87-90. For the task at hand, the "census survival" estimate for a given state (e.g., Illinois: 215,-300) was divided proportionately according to the percentage of Negroes in the state who were resident in the city under review (e.g., Chicago: 215,300 × 76.2 = 164,058). The number allocated to the given city was then multiplied by an age standard for that city (percentage of Negroes in the 21+ age-group in 1950) in order to estimate the number of potential voters gained through net migration (e.g., Chicago: 164,058 × 67.4 = 110,575). Some refinement in this procedure was possible, of course, but the purpose of the current study did not warrant it.

---

[7]Bendiner, *op. cit.*, p. 8. To show that the Truman-Dewey contest was extremely close, it should also be noted that Dewey carried New York State, Michigan, and Indiana by 60,000, 35,000, and 13,000 votes respectively.

This is not to say that the Negro vote is sufficient in itself to assure political success to this or that candidate in any given election. For example, various cursory estimates of the Negro vote in 1952 and 1956 indicate that northern Negroes continued to return varying majorities to the Democratic party, thereby playing a negative role in the two elections. In the event of a close election, however, it is evident that a large turnout of Negro voters and a substantial proportion of ballots for one of the candidates can lead to the margin of victory in at least nine important states.[8] It must be said, of course, that such margins are meaningful only when one compares the Negro vote with the white vote taken collectively. Obviously, certain sub-groups within the white group (e.g., organized labor) are capable of contributing heavily to one particular candidate or the other, but when the white group is treated as a single group, these sub-group contributions may be counterbalancing, an effect which creates a close election.

Yet it should be noted that a close election is not an *automatic* condition whereby Negro voters gain the balance of power.

In addition to a close election, this would require the overwhelming majority of all potential Negro voters to be registered, highly organized and flexible. This is a large order, requiring most sharply drawn issues. Cohesiveness of the Negro vote increases greatly where his rights and aspirations are at issue. However, even though there is an unusually high feeling of group identity among Negroes, there are strong class differentiations and complete political solidarity is quite unlikely where both parties make any real effort to secure their support.[9]

Purpose of the Current Study

In view of the possibility of an exceedingly close presidential election in 1960, and in view of the increasingly important role of Negro voters in such elections, it was the purpose of the current study to gain a precise measure of developments in Negro political participation and preference in eight industrial cities, namely the ones which are listed in Table 1.[10] Stated as questions which can be answered on the level of empirical observation: (1) to what extent, if any, has the Negro body politic altered its pattern of political participation in the last three presidential elections, and (2) to what extent, if any,

---

[8]The nine states and their current electoral votes are as follows: California, 32; Illinois, 27; Indiana, 13; Michigan, 20; Missouri, 13; New Jersey, 16; New York, 45; Ohio, 25; and Pennsylvania, 32.

[9]Martin, *op. cit.*, p. 378.

[10]The study was supported, in part, by a grant from the All-University Research Fund, Michigan State University.

has the Negro body politic altered its pattern of political preference in the last three presidential elections?[11]

The data on political participation will refer to the percentage of registrants who exercised their political franchise by voting for a presidential candidate. The data on political preference will refer to the percentage of voters who voted for the candidate of the Democratic party. To sharpen the focus of the report, the participation and preference data for Negroes will be compared to similar data for the total population of each city. Unfortunately, it was impossible to distinguish between the total population and the white population within it. Thus, in examining the comparative data in Tables 4 and 5, one should recall that the differences would always be larger if Negro and white behavior had been compared directly.[12] Nonetheless, by placing the trends of Negro participation and preference within the context of general trends, it will be possible to draw additional inferences from the data.

Procedures

The measurement of Negro political behavior was accomplished by utilizing official data for rigorously selected sample areas in each city. On the basis of a severe "90 plus" criterion, these areas were located according to the following procedures:

1. (a) For Chicago, Cleveland, Detroit, Kansas City, Pittsburgh, and St. Louis, the writer selected all census tracts in which the Negro population exceeded 90 per cent of the total population in 1950. This approach yielded a total of 134 tracts for the six cities, ranging from 4 tracts in Kansas City to 77 in Chicago.[13]

---

[11]Evidence on the second question is also available in Moon's study of "The Negro Voter in the Presidential Election of 1956," op. cit., Tables I, II, and III. Moon presents estimates which compare the vote in 1952 to the vote in 1956 in 39 northern and 23 southern cities. Many of his figures for northern cities are related to ecological areas which are relatively heterogeneous in population composition, thereby providing us with estimates which are too imprecise for the historical record. From the vantage point of the current study, Moon's data tend to underestimate the amount of pro-Democratic preference on the part of northern Negroes.

[12]See Glantz, op. cit., for an example of a direct comparison between Negro and white political behavior in Philadelphia. Needless to say, direct comparisons add a certain amount of depth to the analysis.

[13]In five of these cities, the selection included one or two tracts in which the Negro population was somewhat less than 90 per cent of the total population in 1950. In order to enlarge the samples in Kansas City and Pittsburgh, one tract in each city which fell below the "90 plus" criterion (85.5% in Kansas City and 84.3% in Pittsburgh) was added to the tracts which met the "90 plus" criterion. Two tracts were added in Chicago (89.8% and 87.3%), in Cleveland (89.9% and 89.2%), and in St. Louis (88.1% and 86.9%) in order to establish contiguous areas and thereby to facilitate the collection of political data.

1. (b) In the case of New York City, the selection was limited to Manhattan (New York County) so as to reduce the burden of collecting the necessary political data. Moreover, the selection was limited to all census tracts in which the Negro population exceeded 90 per cent of the total population in 1940 as well as in 1950. Nonetheless, there were 14 tracts which met the double "90 plus" criterion, with approximately 157,000 Negroes in 1950.

1. (c) In Cincinnati, the sample was limited to the 16th Ward, where the Negro proportion of the total population was 92.1 per cent in 1940 and 94.5 per cent in 1950.[14]

2. (a) For the seven cities other than Cincinnati, the census tracts were plotted on maps containing political subdivisions. All precincts which fell within the census tracts *at the time of each election* were taken as the basic political units for the study. Inasmuch as precinct boundaries are changed from time to time, it should be noted that the number of precincts in each sample area varied from one election to the next.

2. (b) The same procedure was not necessary for Cincinnati, where the sample area and the basic political unit were coterminous.

One last note concerns the procedure which was employed to collect the necessary political data. They were assembled from official records in the offices of registration and election commissioners in each city.[15]

Adequacy and Representativeness of the Sample Areas

In Table 2, it can be observed that the number of Negroes in each sample area accounted for an adequate proportion of the total Negro population. The lowest figures are for New York City (21.1 per cent) and Cincinnati (23.7 per cent). The remaining percentages vary from 31.3 in Pittsburgh to 67.7 in Chicago.

To test the representativeness of each sample area, the non-white labor force, by sex, in the non-white population of each sample area was compared to the non-white labor force, by sex, in the city-wide non-white population. It was impossible to make a comparison of this sort for the Cincinnati sample, but in the other seven cities the sample areas appear to be representative (Table 3). In 10 of the 14 available comparisons, it can be seen that the difference is one per cent or less. The other four comparisons point to differences of −2.2 per cent for

---

[14]In selecting the sample for Cincinnati, the writer followed the procedure marked out by Collins, *op. cit.*

[15]The writer gratefully acknowledges his indebtedness to numerous persons in the various registration and election offices. Without their co-operation, it would have been impossible to assemble the data.

TABLE 2

Population Composition of Sample Areas, 1950*

	Sample Area			Negroes in S.A. as percentage of Negroes in city
	Total	Negro	Per cent Negro	
Chicago	339,854	333,488	98.1	67.7
Cincinnati†	19,625	18,547	94.5	23.7
Cleveland	76,355	73,135	95.8	49.5
Detroit	110,267	106,013	96.1	35.3
Kansas City	21,259	20,028	94.2	36.0
New York City	159,311	157,828	99.1	21.1
Pittsburgh	27,866	25,841	92.7	31.3
St. Louis	85,693	80,202	93.6	52.2

* Source: U.S. Bureau of the Census, *Seventeenth Census of the United States*, 1950, Volume III, Census Tract Statistics, Table 1, P-D Bulletins 10, 12, 17, 27, 37, 43 and 47; selected tracts.

† Collins, *op. cit.*, Table 2, p. 133.

males in the Cleveland sample, −3.2 per cent for males and −4.0 per cent for females in the Detroit sample, and +4.7 per cent for females in the New York sample. The minus signs indicate underrepresentation of male workers in the Cleveland sample and both male and female workers in the Detroit sample, while the plus sign indicates overrepresentation of female workers in the New York sample. To the extent that workers and non-workers differ in political behavior, the accuracy of the political data for Cleveland, Detroit, and New York may be slightly impaired.

Political Participation in 1948, 1952, and 1956

Although presidential elections fail to involve large percentages of the adult population in any region of the United States,[16] they tend

[16]In 1948, for example, the participation rates for the adult population (presidential ballots) were as follows: 60.2 per cent in the northeastern states, 61.3 per cent in the north-central states, 56.9 per cent in the western states and 30.0 per cent in the southern states. U.S. Bureau of the Census, *Current Population Reports*, Series P-25, Population Estimates, No. 63, August 31, 1952, Table 2. The reader may compare these percentages with the ones in Table 4 (current paper) on the turnout of the registered population in the cities under review.

TABLE 3

Representativeness of Sample Areas*
Non-white persons in the labor force, 14 years old and over,
as percentage of all non-white persons 14 years old and over

	Males		Females	
	City	Sample Area	City	Sample Area
Chicago	79.1	78.7	40.6	39.9
Cincinnati†	—	—	—	—
Cleveland	80.2	78.0	37.0	36.6
Detroit	81.9	78.7	29.4	25.4
Kansas City	76.2	75.4	42.7	42.8
New York City	76.6	77.0	47.6	52.3
Pittsburgh	75.4	74.4	28.7	28.5
St. Louis	72.5	73.2	37.7	37.7

* Source: U.S. Bureau of the Census, *Seventeenth Census of the United States*, 1950, Volume II, Characteristics of the Population, Chapter C, Parts 13, 22, 25, 32, 35 and 38 (city-wide data) and Volume III, Census Tract Statistics, Table 4, P-D Bulletins 10, 12, 17, 27, 37, 43 and 47 (S.A. data, selected tracts).

† Sample area is 16th Ward. Labor force data unavailable.

to attract relatively large percentages of the registered population, particularly in urban places. The latter point is evident from the data in the three columns on the left-hand side of Table 4, where the reader may note that the turnout of all registrants was typically in the range from 75 to 85 per cent in 1948 and from 80 to 90 per cent in 1952 and 1956. Thus, an individual's intention to vote in a presidential election is initially a function of his earlier motivation to get on or remain on the registration roster. In the registration-to-participation nexus, however, it is obvious that the first event is a necessary legal antecedent to the second event, so that the question of final motivation for the turnout of registrants still goes unanswered in the current study. Fortunately, several interview-studies have provided reasonable answers to the latter question by utilizing the panel technique, i.e., by conducting pre- and post-election interviews. One writer, for example, has reported recently that "the greater the feeling of in-

TABLE 4

Percentage of Registrants Who Voted for a Presidential Candidate

	Of All Registrants*			Of Negro Registrants†		
	1948	1952	1956	1948	1952	1956
Chicago	84.6	84.8	83.3	72.8	71.5	72.5
Cincinnati	77.9	82.9	83.6	61.4	66.4	63.1
Cleveland	70.9	83.2	85.0	66.0	71.0	77.5
Detroit	76.7	82.3	81.7	68.7	73.4	78.2
Kansas City	87.2	93.5	87.4	81.7	83.5	78.2
New York City‡	—	—	—	—	—	—
Pittsburgh	78.7	85.7	83.3	71.3	80.4	73.7
St. Louis	84.4	89.8	83.8	73.7	80.9	78.3

* City-wide data.
† Based on data for sample areas.
‡ Registration data unavailable for New York City.

volvement in the election campaign, the more likely the voter will fulfill a positive intention to vote."[17]

It would be injudicious to assume that a given turnout rate is likewise a measure of group-wide psychological involvement in a given election campaign, inasmuch as numerous uninvolved persons manage nonetheless to vote on election day.[18] However, to the extent that *differential turnout* is a reflection of *differential involvement*, comparative turnout rates can be taken as rough measures of group-wide *differences* in psychological involvement. Indeed, differential turnout can be attributed to differences in various psychological factors which are related presumably to political participation, e.g., the "interest complex"[19] and the "sense of political efficacy"[20] and that

---

[17]William A. Glaser, "Intention and Voting Turnout," *American Political Science Review*, LII (1958), 1032. The relation between involvement and turnout is further elaborated by Glaser in his analysis of the sociological and psychological conditions under which differential involvement leads to differential turnout (pp. 1033-40).

[18]*Ibid.*, Table IV, p. 1037. It should be added that some persons who are highly involved in the election campaign nonetheless fail to vote on election day.

[19]See Paul F. Lazarsfeld, *et al*, *The People's Choice* (New York: Duell, Sloan and Pearce, 1944), pp. 40-45. For example, "as the level of interest decreases . . . the lower the index of participation and activity in the campaign."

[20]See Angus Campbell, *et al*, *The Voter Decides* (Evanston: Row, Peterson, 1954), pp. 187-94. For example, "the higher one's sense of political efficacy, the higher the level of his participation in the 1952 election." Parenthetically, it can be noted that Campbell and associates, in examining the relationship between

old-fashioned tag known as "political apathy."[21] In these terms, differential turnout rates for two cities, e.g., 84.6 per cent for all registrants
in Chicago (1948) and 77.9 per cent for all registrants in Cincinnati
(1948), or differential turnout rates for two population groups, e.g.,
84.6 per cent for all registrants in Chicago (1948) and 72.8 per cent
for Negro registrants in Chicago (1948), or differential turnout rates
for a single population group in two elections, e.g., 72.8 per cent for
Negro registrants in Chicago (1948) and 71.5 per cent for Negro
registrants in Chicago (1952), can be taken as indications of a higher
feeling of involvement, higher interest, a higher sense of political
efficacy, less political apathy, and so on. In the current study, the
writer will exercise the option of favoring the concept of political
efficacy.

Along this line, a consistently lower group-wide sense of political
efficacy on the part of Negro registrants, by contrast with the registered population in general, can be inferred from the comparative
data in Table 4. Although the level of Negro participation varied
from city to city and from one election to the next, it never matched
the level of total participation in any of the city-by-city comparisons
in any of the three presidential elections under review. On a more
generalized basis, it can be noted that the turnout of Negro registrants
was typically in the range of 65 to 75 per cent in 1948 and from 70 to
80 per cent in 1952 and 1956. When one recalls that the turnout of all
registrants was typically in the range from 75 to 85 per cent in 1948
and from 80 to 90 per cent in 1952 and 1956, a continuous discrepancy
of approximately ten percentage points is evident. Thus, by failing to
match the turnout of the total population, Negro registrants fail to
enhance their position as a balance of power.

In connection with the 1952 election, however, it is appropriate to
emphasize the upward trend in the level of Negro participation at the
ballot box. With the exception of the turnout in Chicago (where there
was a small decrease of 1.3 percentage points), the activity of Negro
registrants increased by approximately two points in Kansas City
(where the rate was relatively high in 1948), five points in three
additional cities (Cincinnati, Cleveland, and Detroit), seven points in
St. Louis and nine points in Pittsburgh. The upturn continued into the

---

demographic components and political efficacy, reached the conclusion that "Negroes feel more politically impotent than the rest of the population."

[21]See Morris Rosenberg, "Some determinants of Political Apathy," *Public
Opinion Quarterly*, XVIII (1954), 349-66. For example, "the individual may be
a member of a group in which political apathy is a positive group norm—a group
which would discourage political action."

1956 election in Cleveland and Detroit,[22] but it was not sustained in the other cities. Nonetheless, there is some suggestion in the data for 1952 that Negro registrants are approaching a new level of political consciousness, and in these terms, a new sense of political efficacy. Under certain circumstances, of course, there is always the possibility that a significant portion of the Negro body politic may decide to boycott both parties in a given presidential election, but it is much more plausible to suggest that the concomitants of urbanization, such as educational and re-educational opportunities, intensified communications, machine politics and convenient polling places, will tend eventually to maximize political participation on the part of the Negro people. This is not to say that the aforementioned discrepancy between the total body politic and the Negro body politic will be narrowed in the immediate future. As it happens, there were parallel increments in political acitivity on the part of the total registered population in each of the cities which have been examined here.

Political Preference in 1948, 1952 and 1956

It is not uncommon, particularly in the popular literature, for publicists and political analysts to describe the Negro vote in terms which imply racial solidarity, e.g., "en masse voting" and "en bloc voting." In such terms, various writers have claimed that "Negroes must be appealed to en masse,"[23] that "Negroes, on the sole issue of civil rights, voted almost en masse [in 1948],"[24] and that "Negroes have in fact tended to vote en bloc, as a few simple statistics will testify."[25] It is not the purpose here to question these claims, but it should be said that there are some logical objections concerning the applicability and utility of this notion of bloc voting as a means of characterizing the Negro vote or the vote of any other single group. For example, in a specific reference to the Negro vote, one commentator posed the issue as follows: "In what degree ... [is it] a function not of racial-bloc voting but of socio-economic status?"[26]

---

[22]To give the reader some idea of differential estimates, it is interesting to note that Henry Lee Moon, in his study of the 1956 election, *op. cit.*, points to a *decrease* of 6.4 percentage points in Cleveland (p. 228), whereas the current study points to an *increase* of 6.5 percentage points. Additional disparities are evident when Moon's data are compared with the current data for Chicago (−12.0 vs. +1.0) and Pittsburgh (−15.4 vs. −6.7).

[23]Brisbane, *op. cit.*, p. 249.

[24]White, *op. cit.*, p. 17.

[25]Bendiner, *op. cit.*, p. 17.

[26]Comment by Professor David B. Carpenter in his discussion of my paper at the 1958 Meeting of the Population Association of America. See Oscar Glantz, "Political Implications of Negro Migration: Summary and Discussion," *Population Index*, XXIV (1958), 222.

Moreover, in a generalized reference to the voting behavior of any group, a leading pollster suggested recently that "there is no such thing as bloc voting," a term which is "too often used to describe what is just a tendency on the part of a particular group to vote more unilaterally than does the general public."[27]

With these objections in mind, the analysis of Negro voting behavior in the current study will be phrased in terms of voting strength rather than racial solidarity. From the balance-of-power standpoint, such strength can be measured in terms of two calculations, the first of which is based on four factors which determine the size of a given candidate's margin of victory among Negro voters. These factors are (1) the number of potential Negro voters in a given city or state; (2) the level of registration; (3) the level of participation at the polls; and (4) the level of support for the candidate in question. The second calculation is simply the size of the candidate's margin of victory among all voters. If the first figure is larger than the second, it can be said that the Negro body politic had sufficient strength to play a decisive role in the election.

To use the Negro vote in Chicago as an example (1948), the first calculation can be obtained on the assumption that the number of potential Negro voters was approximately 303,000 in 1948 (note in Table 1 that the number was 331,000 in 1950, with an average increase of 14,000 each year from 1940 to 1950), that the level of registration was approximately 70 per cent,[28] that the level of participation at the polls was 73 per cent (see Table 4), and that the level of support for Mr. Truman was 70 per cent (see Table 5). Thus, the number of registrants was 303,000 × .70 = 212,000; the number of voters was 212,000 × .73 = 154,833 [say 154,000); the number of votes for Truman was 154,000 × .70 = 107,800 (say 107,000); the number of votes for Dewey was 154,000 − 107,000 = 47,000; and the margin of victory for Truman was 107,000 − 47,000 = 60,000. In the entire state of Illinois, Mr. Truman's margin among all voters was 33,000, indicating clearly that the Negro vote in Chicago (to say nothing of the Negro vote in other districts of Illinois) was responsible for the statewide victory, at least when the white vote is viewed collectively. An

---

[27]Comment by Elmo Roper at the 1957 Meeting of the American Association for Public Opinion Research. See Richard S. Halpern's report in "Interpretations of the 1956 Election," *Public Opinion Quarterly*, XXI (1957), 448.

[28]With a few exceptions, registration offices in northern industrial cities do not compile registration data on the basis of race. One of these exceptions is the office in Philadelphia, where the record indicates that 69.8 per cent of the potential Negro voters (all Negroes 21 years old and over) were registered for the gubernatorial election in 1950. A reliable estimate indicates that 70.3 per cent were registered for the presidential election in 1948.

additional example of decisive voting strength in 1948 is provided by the data for two cities in Ohio, a state where Mr. Truman's margin among all voters was only 7,000. Among Negro voters, however, his margin was approximately 10,000 in Cincinnati and 18,000 in Cleveland, more than enough in either city to change the statewide decision in an election which was otherwise closely contested.

This is not to say that Mr. Truman received his strongest support from Negro voters in Chicago (70 per cent) Cincinnati (75 per cent) and Cleveland (71 per cent), but rather to indicate that these levels were crucial in the sense that they served to tip the balance in favor of a given candidate. As the reader may observe in Table 5, the level of pro-Truman support among Negro voters in the other cities under review was roughly as high in St. Louis (68 per cent) and New York (72 per cent) and higher in Kansas City (77 per cent) Pittsburgh (77 per cent) and Detroit (84 per cent). Insofar as political cohesiveness influences the general drift of social and economic decisions in various branches of government, each of these levels was significant. However, they were not crucial from the balance-of-power standpoint.[29]

On the assumption that the 1960 presidential election will be closely contested, thereby providing the Negro body politic with another opportunity to exercise the balance of power in a number of states, it is the further task of this paper to examine the extent to which Negro voters have altered their pattern of political preference since 1948. Specifically, to what extent did Negro voters endorse Mr. Stevenson's candidacy in 1952? To what extent was this endorsement withdrawn in 1956? And of greatest importance, to what extent and in which direction did the pattern in 1956 differ from the pattern in 1948?

From the data in Table 5, it can be seen that the peak of Negro allegiance to the Democratic party was reached in 1952, which is to say that Mr. Stevenson polled a larger percentage of Negro ballots in 1952 than Mr. Truman had polled in 1948, and probably a larger percentage than Mr. Roosevelt had polled in any of the previous four elections. The level of support for Mr. Stevenson was 75 per cent in Chicago, from 78 to 83 per cent in six additional cities, and one-tenth of one percentage-point short of 90 per cent in Detroit. In a year which marked the end of the New and Fair Deals for thousands of white voters, this pro-Democratic increment on the part of the Negro body politic can be taken as an outstanding example of political

---

[29]In view of Mr. Truman's margin of 262,000 among all voters in his home state of Missouri, the Negro vote in Kansas City and St. Louis was not crucial in the sense that it was not decisive. In 1952, however, the Negro vote was responsible for Mr. Stevenson's slim margin of 30,000.

TABLE 5

Percentage of Voters Who Voted for the Presidential Candidate
of the Democratic Party

	Of All Voters*			Of Negro Voters†		
	1948	1952	1956	1948	1952	1956
Chicago	58.2	54.2	48.6	70.4	74.7	62.6
Cincinnati	48.3	43.4	37.5	75.0	81.2	72.2
Cleveland	64.5	59.9	54.6	71.3	78.8	62.7
Detroit	59.3	60.2	61.7	83.9	89.9	84.4
Kansas City	61.1	51.6	53.1	77.3	81.8	70.0
New York City‡	51.5	58.4	55.7	71.8	83.2	68.9
Pittsburgh	59.6	55.7	52.2	77.6	82.0	76.9
St. Louis	64.2	62.1	61.1	68.4	79.6	74.8

* City-wide data.
† Based on data for sample areas.
‡ Limited to Manhattan (New York County). Data include Liberal vote
for Democratic candidate.

fidelity. As a consequence, the pro-Democratic gap between the Negro vote and the general vote ranged from 17 percentage points in St. Louis to 38 in Cincinnati.

However, when Mr. Stevenson altered his political posture in 1956, he lost some of the ardent support which had developed among Negro voters in his first campaign. Although there was less alienation than one might have expected in three of the cities [a decrease of approximately five percentage points in Detroit, Pittsburgh, and St. Louis), the downturn was significant in a majority of cases.[30] There was a loss of 9 points in Cincinnati, 12 points in Chicago and Kansas City, 14 points in New York, and 16 points in Cleveland. Moreover, when the data for 1956 are compared with the data for 1948, it can be seen in Table 5 that Negro voters in six of the eight cities gave Mr. Stevenson less support in 1956 than they had given Mr. Truman in 1948. The largest downturns are evident in the comparative data for

---

[30]It can be noted that Negro voters in the South, by contrast with their compatriots in the North, defected from the Democratic party to a much greater extent. In Henry Lee Moon's article on "The Negro Voter in the Presidential Election of 1956," *op. cit.*, Table III, p. 224, estimates for 23 southern cities suggest that Mr. Eisenhower received a majority of Negro ballots in 13 of them. In some of these places, the Democratic loss was greater than 50 percentage points.

Chicago (−7.8) Cleveland (−8.6) and Kansas City, (−7.3), while downturns of less significance are recorded for Cincinnati (−2.8) New York (−2.9) and Pittsburgh (−0.7).

From the balance-of-power standpoint, these developments suggest that the Democratic candidate in 1960 will have only a slim chance of gaining the electoral votes of Illinois and Ohio if the current level of Negro support in Chicago, Cleveland, and Cincinnati remains unaltered or continues downward, assuming of course that the next election will be as closely contested as was the one in 1948. With the exception of Michigan, where the current level of Democratic preference on the part of Negro voters in Detroit is extremely high, a similar conclusion can be reached for Missouri (given contradictory trends in St. Louis and Kansas City) and possibly New York and Pennsylvania. It should be noted, however, that this conclusion presupposes a relatively static situation from 1948 to 1960. In the event that the Negro body politic in these places has been augmented considerably by continuing in-migration, and in the event that this body politic manages to raise its level of participation at the polls, the current pro-Democratic level, even if it continues downward to a small extent, may be sufficient nonetheless to tip the balance in favor of the Democratic candidate. By way of illustration, if it is necessary to obtain 70 per cent of the ballots of 150,000 Negro voters in order to overcome a lead of 59,000 votes among all other voters, the same lead of 59,000 can be overcome by 60 per cent of 300,000 Negro ballots.

In summary, the leading observations and inferences from the current study are as follows: (1) There was a consistently lower groupwide sense of political efficacy on the part of Negro registrants, by contrast with the registered population in general. Although the level of Negro participation at the polls varied from city to city and from one election to the next, it never matched the level of total participation in any of the city-by-city comparisons in any of the three presidential elections under review. (2) At the same time, the participation data for 1952 indicate that there was an increase in Negro activity at the polls in seven of the eight cities examined here. These increments suggest that Negro registrants are approaching a new level of political consciousness, and in these terms, a new sense of political efficacy. (3) From the balance-of-power standpoint, Negro voters in Illinois [represented here by Chicago) and Ohio (Cleveland and Cincinnati) played a decisive role in tipping the balance in favor of Mr. Truman in 1948. (4) The peak of Negro allegiance to the Democratic party in each of the eight cities was reached in 1952, when Mr. Stevenson polled a larger percentage of Negro ballots than

Mr. Truman had polled in 1948. In a year which marked the end of the New and Fair Deals for thousands of white voters, such allegiance on the part of the Negro body politic serves as an outstanding example of political fidelity, comparable perhaps to the high level of Negro allegiance to Mr. Hoover in 1932. (5) When Mr. Stevenson posed as a moderate in 1956, he lost varying amounts of support among Negro voters in each of the eight cities. These losses were within a range from five percentage points in three of the cities to 16 points in Cleveland. (6) Moreover, Negro voters in six of the eight cities gave Mr. Stevenson less support in 1956 than they had given Mr. Truman in 1948. The largest downturns occurred in Chicago, Cleveland, and Kansas City. (7) From the balance-of-power standpoint, these downturns suggest that the Democratic candidate in 1960 will have only a slim chance of gaining the electoral votes of Illinois, Ohio and Missouri (and possibly New York and Pennsylvania) if the current level of Democratic preference remains unaltered or continues downward, assuming of course that the next election is closely contested. (8) However, to the extent that the Negro body politic has been augmented to any substantial degree by continuing northward migration, and to the extent that Negro registrants participate in greater force in the next election, the current level of Democratic preference, even if it turns downward slightly, may be sufficient to change the verdict of a closely contested election. In any event, neither party can afford to ignore the numerical weight of the Negro vote. In the next campaign, the Democratic candidate will have the responsibility of reversing the changing-image of the Democratic party,[31] while the Republican candidate will have the responsibility of enlarging the social and economic appeal of the Republican party.

---

[31]For example, Mr. Roy Wilkins, executive secretary of the NAACP, told a Chicago audience in 1956 that "we Negroes have got to consider whether we want to swap the known devil for the suspected witch." Reported by Rowan, *op. cit.*, p. 39.

Catholic Voters and the Democratic Party*

Scott Greer

Much of the recent political history of the United States has been interpreted as a consequence of the ethnic composition of the major metropolitan areas. The base of the Democratic Party outside the South has been, according to Samuel Lubell, among the immigrants and their children (particularly the latter) in the big urban centers. In his words, the basis of the New Deal was in "the revolt of the underdog, urban immigrant against the top dog of 'old American' stock." Furthermore, Lubell believes, "[the immigrant's] Catholicism was an essential element in that revolt."[1] This thesis is similar to that of sociologists, who emphasize the low social rank typical of Catholics and the importance of the differential association among Catholics as a conserving mechanism for the original pro-Democratic

Reprinted from *Public Opinion Quarterly*, Vol. 25 (Winter 1961), 611-625 with permission of the publisher and author. Copyright 1961 by Princeton University Press.

*This is a revised version of a paper presented at the meetings of the American Catholic Sociological Society in Chicago, Ill., September 1959. The research was conducted as part of the Metropolitan St. Louis Survey, a study of local government sponsored by the Public Affairs Branch of the Ford Foundation, the McDonnell Aircraft Company Charitable Trust, and St. Louis and Washington Universities.

[1]Samuel Lubell, *The Future of American Politics*, 2d ed. rev., New York, Doubleday, 1956, p. 41.

orientation, but in essentials tend to agree with the primitive theory as outlined by Lubell. Political scientists make similar assumptions, with more emphasis upon the place of the ethnic, working-class, Catholic urban population in the functioning of the old-style political machine.

However, the economic trends of the last thirty years have tended to change radically the social rank and the style of life of urban second-generation ethnics, Catholic and non-Catholic alike. The changes in job distribution, in general levels of living, and in educational norms have resulted in a strong upward drift in social rank throughout society. The urban centers have been expanding rapidly at the peripheries and declining in population at the center; millions of descendants of the immigrants have moved to the suburbs, at the same time that they have moved into skilled jobs or white-collar jobs, have completed high school or college, and have moved into the higher income brackets.

Thus the situation in which urban Catholics find themselves has changed radically, and, to the degree that this situation was determinant, the basis for the old relationship between the Democratic Party and the Catholic electorate has suffered attrition. Acculturation, vertical mobility, and suburbanization are seen as the death knells of machine dominance in the metropolitan electorate and, consequently, the end of the "Roosevelt coalition." Lubell has said as much in his later volume, *The Revolt of the Moderates.*

This paper presents some evidence bearing upon these hypotheses from the study of the metropolitan St. Louis electorate. It describes the Catholic population in the suburbs, as compared with that in the central city, and at the same time notes the differences between Catholics and others. These four populations are then compared with respect to political preference and voting in the 1956 presidential election. Finally, the political differences associated with variations in the Catholic electorate in nationality background, generation since migration, and social rank are investigated.

The data, which I collected while I was chief sociologist of the Metropolitan St. Louis Survey, derive from a survey of a systematic random sample of the residents of St. Louis City and suburban St. Louis County. The sampling intensity was 1 in 100 households in the suburbs and 1 in 400 households in the city, yielding a sample of 1,800 in all—1,285 in the suburbs, 515 in the city. The over-all response rate was 86 per cent, and the data was collected in the winter and early spring of 1956-1957.

Findings

Catholics in central city and suburb

There is strong evidence that suburban residence is related to acculturation and upward mobility. As Table 1 shows, suburban Catholics
are more likely to be from the "old migrations" (northern and western
Europe, Ireland, Germany) and to be third generation or later. Eighty-
two per cent of the suburban Catholics are from the "old migration,"
compared with 70 per cent in the central city; 64 per cent are the
second generation or later, compared with 59 per cent in the city. For
social rank we have used education as an index: only 25 per cent of the
suburban Catholics have had an eighth-grade education or less, compared with 42 per cent of those in the city, and 26 per cent have had
some college or more, as against 14 per cent in the city. Forty-nine per
cent in the suburbs have had some high school, compared with 44 per
cent in the city. Thus, of the differences between suburban and central-
city Catholics, that of education stands out clearly as the most striking,
followed by country of origin and migration date.

Nationality of origin and generation of migration are, as might be
expected, closely interlinked. Very nearly all those Catholics who are
the third generation or later since migration are from the "old mi-

TABLE 1

Country of Origin, Generation since Migration, and Education,
for Catholics and Non-Catholics in the Central City and
Suburbs of St. Louis

	Catholics Per Cent	(N)	Non-Catholics Per Cent	(N)
Central city:				
Country of origin:				
Southern and eastern Europe	24	(42)	2	(7)
Irish	14	(24)	11	(36)
German	30	(52)	21	(72)
"Old American"	26	(45)	28	(95)
Negro and other	5	(9)	32	(110)
Don't know	2	(3)	6	(20)
Total	101	(175)	100	(340)

Generation since migration:				
Migrant or first	35	(55)	26	(58)
Second	31	(49)	25	(57)
Third or later	34	(54)	49	(109)
Total	100	(158)*	100	(224)*
Education:				
0–8 years	42	(73)	49	(168)
9–12 years	44	(77)	35	(119)
Over 12 years	14	(25)	16	(53)
Total	100	(175)	100	(340)
Suburbs:				
Country of origin:				
Southern and eastern Europe	16	(65)	9	(82)
Irish	22	(90)	8	(74)
German	32	(133)	33	(292)
"Old American"	28	(114)	40	(348)
Negro and other	2	(7)	5	(46)
Don't know	†	(2)	4	(32)
Total	100	(411)	99	(874)
Generation since migration:				
Migrant or first	32	(123)	22	(175)
Second	31	(121)	30	(243)
Third or later	37	(145)	48	(392)
Total	100	(389)*	100	(810)*
Education:				
0–8 years	25	(102)	25	(223)
9–12 years	49	(201)	43	(375)
Over 12 years	26	(108)	31	(276)
Total	100	(411)	99	(874)

* These total N's are smaller because respondents not relevant to this aspect of the analysis (i.e. Negroes and those few respondents who did not know their migratory status) have been deleted. For the central-city sample these amounted to 17, or 10 per cent, of the Catholics and 116, or 34 per cent, of the non-Catholics. For the suburban sample the comparable figures are 22, or 5 per cent, of the Catholics and 64, or 7 per cent, of the non-Catholics.

† Less than 1 per cent.

gration" (98 per cent in the city, 95 per cent in the suburbs), while, of those who are foreign-born or first generation since migration, a very large proportion are from the "new migration"—from Italy and southern and eastern Europe. Sixty per cent of these Catholics in the city are from the new migration, compared with 44 per cent of the suburbs. This indicates a point of some importance, however. Of those foreign-born and first-generation Catholics who live in the suburbs, a disproportionate number are from the countries of the "old migration." A majority of the foreign-born and first generation from northern and western Europe live in the suburbs; a majority of those with similar generational "age" from eastern and southern Europe live in the central city. A similar difference holds, by nationality of origin, for those who are the second generation since migration, but it is not as striking. Thus we may say that generation since migration is closely linked to suburban versus central-city residence, but that within each generation the migrants and their descendants from northern and western Europe have the best chance of being suburbanites until we reach those who are three generations or more removed from migration, and these show no difference; practically all are from northern and western Europe.

Using these same background characteristics to compare Catholics and non-Catholics in each residential area, we find that in the suburbs Catholics are much less apt to be "old American" (northwestern Europe and the British Isles, with the exception of Germany and Ireland) in nationality background, more likely to be Irish or from southern and eastern Europe, but about equally likely to be German in nationality origin. In the central city, however, while the proportion "old American" is similar for Catholics and others, the Catholics are disproportionately from Germany or southern and eastern Europe, and the non-Catholics are one-third Negro. Thus Catholics and non-Catholics alike are preponderantly ethnic in the central city, but the flavor of that ethnic background differs sharply between the two populations.

In the suburbs Catholics are disproportionately migrants or the first generation since migration (32 per cent, compared with 22 per cent of the other suburbanites), and less frequently third generation or later (37 per cent, compared with 48 per cent). Immigrants and their children who live in suburbia are more likely than other suburbanites to be Catholic by faith. Sixty-eight per cent of the suburban Catholics are second generation or later, as against 78 per cent of the non-Catholics. In the central city 65 per cent of Catholics are second generation or older compared with 74 per cent of the non-Catholics.[2] These percentages are practically identical with the proportions in the suburbs.

With respect to education, the differences between Catholics and non-Catholics are not nearly so striking as are those between the central city and the suburban populations in each category. Catholics and non-Catholics in the suburbs have the same percentage with an eighth-grade education or less (25 per cent), although non-Catholics are slightly more apt to have college educations (31 versus 26 per cent). In the city however, these differences are exaggerated, probably because the city houses the Negro population and is the port of entry for the poorer white migrants. While 42 per cent of the city Catholics have eighth-grade educations or less, 49 per cent of the non-Catholics are so educated; 16 per cent of the non-Catholics have some college, compared with 14 per cent of the Catholics. Forty-four per cent of the Catholics have been to high school, compared with 35 per cent of the non-Catholics. Catholics are thus somewhat more likely to have a high school education in both city and suburbs, and less likely to be college-educated in the suburbs. This latter probably reflects, again, their relatively later start up the ladders of social rank.

In sum, Catholics in both the central city and the suburbs are more likely than their neighbors to be from countries of the new migration, to be migrants or the first generation since migration, and to have a high school education. Catholics differ most from non-Catholics in generation since migration and nationality of origin, when residence is controlled, and differ least in education.

Political preference and voting of Catholics in 1956

The weakening of the Catholic-Democratic Party tie in St. Louis is not apparent where political preference is concerned. When asked, "What is your usual party preference?" 62 per cent of the city Catholics and 62 per cent of the suburban Catholics answered "Democratic." It is true, however, that a larger proportion in the county preferred the Republican Party (21 per cent compared with 13 per cent in the city), but this is compensated for by the decline in those who said they were Independents or had no preference (25 per cent in the city, 17 in the county).

---

[2]Negroes and those few respondents who did not know their generational status were not included in the bases for these percentages.

This usual party preference may indicate that many county Catholics pay lip service to the Democratic Party while in process of change in political preference, or it may indicate unusual circumstances in 1956 (such as candidate charisma)—at any rate, the difference in Democratic voting between city and suburbs is marked: 53 per cent of the city Catholics voted Democratic, compared with 46 per cent in the suburbs. At the same time, the Catholic Republican vote was higher in the suburbs—38 per cent compared with 26 per cent in the city. There is little difference in the proportion not voting.

Those who have a definite party preference may be divided into the "party loyalists," the "switchers," and the nonvoters. When this is done, as in Table 2, Democratic Catholics are more apt to be party loyalists if they live in the city (70 per cent compared with 63 per cent in the suburbs), and Republican Catholics are more apt to be party loyalists if they are suburbanites (83 versus 78 per cent). Among Catholics of Democratic preference who are not party loyalists in the city, the great majority simply do not vote (only 7 per cent switched to the Republican candidate). In the county, however, Catholics who did not vote Democratic switched, overwhelmingly, to Eisenhower: 23 per cent of the county Catholics with Democratic preference voted Republican in the 1956 election. This is the largest proportion of any of our analytical categories—city or suburb, Catholic or non-Catholic—who switched parties. Thus the Catholic defection from the Democratic Party is concentrated in the suburbs and largely composed of those who still claim the Democratic Party as their party of usual preference.

Those who have no party preference are about one-fourth of Catholics and non-Catholics alike in the city, and 27 per cent of the non-Catholics in the suburbs. Suburban Catholics, however, are Independents in only 17 per cent of the cases. But when they do so define themselves, they are slightly more apt to vote Democratic than are central city Catholics, and less apt to vote Republican.

When Catholics are compared with non-Catholics, they are much more likely to have a Democratic Party preference (26 per cent difference in the suburbs, 10 per cent difference in the city) and more apt to vote Democratic (by 19 per cent in both city and county). They are less apt to prefer the Republican Party and to vote Republican (each by 8 per cent in the city, 11 per cent in the suburbs). Finally, Catholics are much more likely to have voted; the difference is 9 per cent in the city and 8 per cent in the county.

Thus the suburban Catholic electorate manifests an attrition of

TABLE 2

Party Preference and Voting in the 1956 Presidential Election
for Catholics and Non-Catholics in the Central City
and Suburbs of St. Louis
(in per cent)

| | Usual Party Preference of Catholics | | | Usual Party Preference of Non-Catholics | | |
	Democrat	Republican	None	Democrat	Republican	None
Central city:						
Voted for						
Stevenson	70	4	34	59	*	17
Voted for						
Eisenhower	7	78	45	8	77	46
Didn't vote	22	17	20	33	23	37
Total	99	99	99	100	100	100
	(108)	(23)	(44)	(177)	(87)	(76)
Suburbs:						
Voted for						
Stevenson	63	*	42	65	1	15
Voted for						
Eisenhower	23	83	34	10	85	50
Didn't vote	14	17	29	25	14	35
Total	100	100	100	100	100	100
	(253)	(88)	(70)	(311)	(330)	(233)

* Less than 1 per cent.

Democratic voting and an increase in Republican voting (or did so in 1956), but the difference between Catholics and non-Catholics in preference and in voting is as strong in the suburban county as in the central city. In both areas, a substantial plurality of the Catholic vote went to the Democratic Party. Among non-Catholics, the Republicans broke even in the city and had a handsome plurality (49 per cent compared with 27 per cent for the Democrats) among those who voted in the suburbs. Among the Independents, the Republicans had a plurality in all categories except among the county Catholics: the latter had a slight majority who voted Democratic.

The differentiation of the Catholic electorate

As noted earlier, the greater Republican and lesser Democratic vote among suburban Catholics has been conventionally explained as the result of higher social rank and acculturation. If this explanation holds, we should expect the suburban Catholics to be internally differentiated, with the persons from the "old migration" (those who have been in the country longer) and those of higher education more likely to vote Republican. If the explanation is adequate, differences between Catholics and others should begin to disappear. We shall examine the effects of these differentiators one at a time, for suburban and city Catholics and for Catholics as compared to non-Catholics.

Country of origin: In the 1956 elections Catholics of all nationality origins gave a much more impressive Democratic plurality, that is, the percentage difference in vote of winner and loser, in the central city. The range is from 26 to 48 percentage points, with the mean at 35. In the county the range is from 2 percentage points plurality for the Republican candidate to 22 for the Democratic, with a mean of 12 percentage points plurality for the Democratic candidate for all four major categories (Old Americans, Germans, Irish, and southern and eastern Europe). In general, Old Americans (or those with origins in northern and western Europe) and Germans behave in a similar fashion, while the Irish are more Democratic and those from the "new migration" more Democratic still in voting and in preference (Tables 3 and 4).

In each country-of-origin category the county Catholics are much more apt to be "switchers," but this varies by origin: of those with a "usual preference" for the Democratic Party, 30 per cent of the Old Americans, 24 per cent of the Germans, 17 per cent of the Irish, and 18 per cent of southern and eastern European origin switched their votes to the Republican candidate. In the city, in comparison, the switchers were a negligible fraction and varied little by nationality of origin (the total was less than 8 per cent of the Democratic Party membership when averaged).

Generation since migration: When generation since migration is controlled, there is very little difference between city and county Catholics who are migrants or first generation—both are overwhelmingly Democratic in their political preferences and in their voting. The big differences are between city and county Catholics of the second and later generations since migration: 49 per cent of the second-generation Catholics in the county voted Republican, compared with

24 per cent in the city, while 32 per cent of those who are third generation or more voted Republican in the county and only 20 per cent did so in the city.

In the city there is little variation in the Democratic vote by generation, but there is a decrease in the Republican vote and an increase in nonvoting with increasing generations of residence. Something similar occurs in the suburbs: while the second generation is much more likely to be Republican (as noted above), those third generation and older are *less apt to vote at all*. Nonvoting among Catholics increases with generations since migration, reaching, in the third generation, proportions comparable to those of the non-Catholics. One suspects that this reflects acculturation to the American level of political interest—or disinterest.

In general, Catholic–non-Catholic differences are greater than city-suburban differences within each religious category. It is worth noting, however, that, in St. Louis and its suburbs at least, the big central city–suburban difference in Catholic voting is *not* brought about by the "children of the immigrants": their vote varies little by residence. It is those who are two generations or more removed from foreign birth—those of Old American and German origins—who account for most of the decreasing Democratic vote in the suburbs.

Education: The higher social rank of suburbanites is frequently used as an explanation for their weaker support of the Democratic Party; this is usually combined with the acculturation argument to explain the Catholic defections in the national elections. Measured by educational level of the respondent, social rank is related to Republican versus Democratic voting: however, it is not a clear-cut and simple relationship. In the central city there is *no* variation in party of vote by education—those with an eighth-grade education or less are no more apt to vote Democratic than those with high school or college. In the suburbs, however, as Table 4 shows, the relationship is clear indeed: suburban Catholics with an eighth-grade education or less vote Democratic in 48 per cent of the cases; those with college educations do so in 39 per cent of the cases; on the other hand, the percentage Republican increases from 31 for eighth grade or less and 37 for high school to 45 for college-educated Catholics. (It should be noted, however, that the only Catholic category giving the Republican candidate a plurality was that of the college-educated suburban Catholics).

Among the non-Catholics, the Republican vote increases with education in each area, from 31 to 57 per cent in the city, from 38 to 64

TABLE 3

Usual Party Preference for Catholics and Non-Catholics in the Central City and Suburbs of St. Louis, by Country of Origin, Generation since Migration, and Education

	Per Cent of Catholics Who Prefer				Per Cent of Non-Catholics Who Prefer			
	Demo-crats	Repub-licans	None	(N)	Demo-crats	Repub-licans	None	(N)
Central city:								
Country of origin:								
Southern and eastern Europe	63	9	28	(42)	†	†	†	(7)
Irish	67*	8	25	(24)	64	14	22	(36)
German	60	8	33	(52)	26	42	32	(72)
"Old American"	62*	24	13	(45)	57	20	23	(95)
Negro and other	†	†	†	(9)	60	23	17	(110)
Don't know	†	†	†	(3)	55	35	10	(20)
Generation since migration:								
Migrant or first	60*	15	25	(55)	43	29	29	(58)
Second	61	8	31	(49)	40	30	30	(57)
Third or later	63*	17	20	(54)	53	24	23	(109)
Negro or don't know	59*	12	29	(17)	60	23	16	(116)
Education:								
0–8 years	63*	15	22	(73)	54	30	17	(168)
9–12 years	61*	10	29	(77)	55	17	29	(119)
Over 12 years	56*	16	28	(25)	38	30	32	(53)

Suburbs:

Country of origin:							
Southern and eastern Europe	60	20	20	(65)	41	28	30	(82)
Irish	64*	20	16	(90)	51	26	23	(74)
German	59	26	15	(133)	25	47	29	(292)
"Old American"	61	20	19	(114)	37	37	26	(348)
Negro and other	†	†	†	(7)	46	35	20	(46)
Don't know	†	†	†	(2)	44	22	34	(32)
Generation since migration:							
Migrant or first	67	19	15	(123)	33	39	28	(175)
Second	60	21	18	(121)	31	41	28	(243)
Third or later	62	21	17	(145)	38	35	27	(392)
Negro or don't know	32*	41	27	(22)	42	34	23	(64)
Education:							
0–8 years	59	26	15	(102)	41	36	22	(223)
9–12 years	66	16	18	(201)	41	30	29	(375)
Over 12 years	56	27	18	(108)	23	48	29	(276)

* Catholic–non-Catholic differences marked * are *not* statistically significant at the .05 level; all others are.
† Number too small for percentages to be meaningful.

TABLE 4

Presidential Voting for Catholics and Non-Catholics in the Central City and Suburbs of St. Louis, by Country of Origin, Generation since Migration, and Education, 1956

	Per Cent of Catholics Who Voted				Per Cent of Non-Catholics Who Voted			
	Democratic	Republican	Didn't	(N)	Democratic	Republican	Didn't	(N)
Central city:								
Country of origin:								
Southern and eastern Europe	58	26	16	(42)	†	†	†	(7)
Irish	58	21	21	(24)	33	19	47	(36)
German	46	27	27	(52)	28	56	17	(72)
"Old American"	51*	29	20	(45)	37	27	36	(95)
Negro and other	†	†	†	(9)	39	31	30	(110)
Don't know	†	†	†	(3)	25	20	55	(20)
Generation since migration:								
Migrant or first	51*	36	13	(55)	41	34	24	(58)
Second	53	24	22	(49)	30	40	30	(57)
Third or later	50	20	30	(54)	28	32	39	(109)
Negro or don't know	65	12	23	(17)	39	32	29	(116)
Education:								
0–8 years	53	26	21	(73)	33	31	36	(168)
9–12 years	52*	25	23	(77)	42	27	31	(119)
Over 12 years	52	28	20	(25)	23	57	21	(53)

Suburbs:

Country of origin:							
Southern and eastern Europe	49	32	19	(65)	49	27	24	(82)
Irish	51	33	16	(90)	32	38	30	(74)
German	44	41	16	(133)	18	62	20	(292)
"Old American"	40	41	19	(114)	28	50	22	(348)
Negro and other	†	†	†	(7)	30	33	37	(46)
Don't know	†	†	†	(2)	28	28	44	(32)
Generation since migration:							
Migrant or first	54	30	15	(123)	26	49	25	(175)
Second	39	49	12	(121)	28	54	18	(243)
Third or later	44	32	23	(145)	26	48	25	(392)
Negro or don't know	32*	54	14	(22)	36	34	30	(64)
Education:							
0–8 years	48	31	21	(102)	29	38	33	(223)
9–12 years	47	37	16	(201)	30	45	26	(375)
Over 12 years	39	45	16	(108)	22	64	13	(276)

* Catholic–non-Catholic differences marked * are *not* statistically significant at the .05 level; all others are.
† Number too small for percentages to be meaningful.

per cent in the suburbs. The Democratic vote does not decrease so consistently, however: the explanation is that nonvoting decreases with increasing education.

At each educational level in city and suburbs, then, Catholics are much more apt to vote Democratic and less apt to vote Republican than are others, and at each of the two lower educational levels, Catholics are less apt to be nonvoters than are non-Catholics. At the college-educated level, however, there is no Catholic–non-Catholic difference in nonvoting.

Interpretation

The most striking finding from these analyses is, simply, the continuing strength of the tie between the Democratic Party and the Catholic electorate in the St. Louis metropolitan area. Suburbanization has had an effect, and yet we find little difference in party *preference* between city and suburban Catholics and great differences in each category between Catholics and non-Catholics with respect to Republican preference. In voting, both central-city and suburban Catholics remain heavily Democratic. When we control country of origin, generation since migration, and education, only in the suburbs and in the most extreme classes do we find small Republican pluralities among Catholics—those with northern and western European backgrounds, those who are third generation, those with college educations. And these are far less Republican than their counterparts among the non-Catholics.

Thus religion seems to have independent discriminating power; when variables which are supposed to explain Catholic preference for the Democratic Party are controlled, it still makes an important difference. At the same time, within the Catholic electorate (and chiefly in the suburbs), country of origin, generation since migration, and education differentiate those more likely to vote Republican than Democratic. Thus suburban versus central-city residence also has independent discriminating power. Suburban Catholics at each level of education and acculturation are, in fact, more different from their non-Catholic neighbors in their political *preferences* than is true of city Catholics—but this is because *non-Catholics* in the suburbs are much more Republican in their preference.

To recapitulate, three great trends affecting contemporary American social structure are: a steady upward movement in social rank, a decrease in ethnic variation as the foreign-born die and their children approximate the standard American culture, and an increasing amount of variance in life style, leading many to the family-centered suburbs and the barbecue pits, while others remain in the apartment-house districts of the city. At the moment, Catholics are becoming more middle-class, less ethnic in culture, and more suburban in residence. Social rank and suburbanization work against ethnicity, for with increasing social rank people move out of the occupational and economic worlds of kin and friends; with suburbanization they move out of the nieghborhoods where they were segregated among others of "their kind." The suburbs would seem to work against preserving the ethnic subculture, for they throw the new suburbanites into relationships with neighbors of varying origins—rather than with friends, kin, *paisani* of the city block. In shorthand we might say that the central city encourages political alignment by social class and ethnic background—providing the situation for the political machine—while the suburb tends to produce political processes based in the local area as a community, one in which class and nationality differences are blurred.

Yet the staying force of the ethnic community must not be underestimated. This paper might have been called "unto the fourth generation and later." How shall we explain this persistent Democratic inclination of the Catholic electorate in St. Louis city and county? Our hypotheses, which we are now in process of investigating, are as follows:

1. Differential association among Catholics (as compared with Catholic–non-Catholic association) continues to be very important (a) because the Church is itself an organizational and associational matrix, providing a framework for social life which includes religiously segregated schools, religious endogamy, and a wealth of organized activities—thus the good Catholic can live most of his life, aside from work, within a Catholic environment; (b) because residential concentration of Catholics probably continues to be important in the city and even in the suburbs, owing to common ethnic origins, common social rank, and common need to live in the vicinity of a Church center; (c) because the network of kin tends to keep the Catholic interacting with other Catholics as a consequence of religious endogamy.

2. Differential association reinforces the shared norms among the Catholic portion of the electorate. These include norms based upon nationality of origin (which perhaps are divisive in the short run) and norms based upon commitment to a Catholic way of life. The consequences are: to emphasize normative differences between Catholics

and others, to conserve the "ethnic position" of the Catholics as a "minority," and to continue the mystique of the underdog as a norm.[3]

In summary, then, this paper has uncovered evidence in support of the hypotheses stated at the beginning. However, the findings so complicate these as to direct attention toward a much more complex theory and more precise data on the associational structure of the Catholic electorate.

In closing, a word of caution: no matter how large the metropolitan area or the sample, a study of a single city is a case study. St. Louis has its own ethnic fabric, quite different from that of Los Angeles, say. It is remarkable for the age of its Catholic establishment and the nationalities which have made up its Catholic electorate. It is also a border city in a border state. Finally, it is in the only state which went Democratic in 1956 for "non-Southern" reasons.

---

[3]For a useful discussion, see John J. Kane, "Protestant-Catholic Tensions," *American Sociological Review*, Vol. 16, 1951, pp. 663-672.

Part 3

Ethnic Groups and Urban Politics

Ethnic politics and urban politics are almost synonymous terms. Indeed, it is in the great cities of the Northeast that ethnic politics has great strength and significance. In almost every aspect of urban politics, the factor of ethnicity has great relevance. Whether it is the balanced ticket, the distribution of patronage, the parcelling out of social services, or political campaigning, few big city politicians can afford to neglect the ethnic heterogeneity of their electorates.

To a very great extent, the history of urban politics is the history of succeeding immigrant waves of Irish, Italians, Eastern European Jews, Negroes and Puerto Ricans who settled in the large cities on the East coast and elsewhere in the United States. The problem of integrating these groups into the political process became, to a large degree, the function of the political party. This is not to say that the political party altruistically took on this function; rather it served its own purposes. Thus, Elmer E. Cornwell maintains that the political party "traded" access to political power-jobs, appointment to decision-making structures, etc., in return for votes, the one great political resource that immigrants had.[1] This model, however, seems to over-simplify ethnic movement into the political system.

First of all, it was the minority party—usually the Democrats in the North—who first accepted immigrants into the organization.[2] Thus the minority party expanded the arena of political conflict by appealing to and organizing these potential voters to itself gain power.[3] For example, in Boston, the minority Democrat party solicited the votes of the Irish immigrants during the 1880's and '90's to gain power, and later the Republicans attempted the same strategy among the Italian immigrants to try to oust the Democrats.[4]

Secondly, it is fallacious to credit all of the initiative for organizing the immigrant voters to the existing party organization. Denied access to normal channels of social mobility, many immigrants turned to politics as a means to improve their social status. To a great extent, the immigrants themselves took the initiative for political organization and thus "forced" their way into the political party. Using their ethnic identity as a power resource, immigrant leaders catered to the symbolic and actual needs of their ethnic group and built up a power base independent of the local political party organization. Thus, it may be said that local party organizations did not recognize the immigrants' demands for political power until after ethnic leaders had become powerful enough to challenge local party influence. As James Q. Wilson points out, the actual pattern of influence varied from city to city.[5] William Dawson of Chicago gained political power through the party organization while Adam Clayton Powell of New York "forced" his way into Democratic politics by organizing his constituency independently of the local party.

Finally, it has been argued that traditional Protestant political elites simply abandoned electoral politics as immigrants entered into the political arena.[6] As local politics became infused with elements of

[1]Elmer E. Cornwell, "Bosses, Machines and Ethnic Groups," *Annals of the American Academy of Political and Social Sciences*, 353 (May 1964), 27-39.

[2]For an elaboration of this point see the history and analysis of Boston politics, and New England politics generally, in Duane Lockard, *New England State Politics* (Princeton: Princeton University Press, 1959).

[3]For a theoretical and historical analysis of the "expanding the arena of conflict" concept, see E. E. Schattschneider, *The Semisovereign People* (New York: Holt, Rinehart & Winston, Inc., 1960), pp. 47-96.

[4]Lockard, *op. cit.*

[5]James Q. Wilson, "Two Negro Politicians: An Interpretation," *Midwest Journal of Political Science*, 4 (November 1960), 346-369.

[6]See Peter H. Rossi and Alice S. Rossi, "An Historical Perspective on Local Politics," (Unpublished paper delivered at the 1956 meeting of the American Sociological Association).

ward and machine politics, traditional elites lost interest in electoral politics and left the way open for the new political bosses with their different political style. Immigrants were neither welcomed into local politics by the established elites, nor did they force their way into local politics by creating independent organizations. Rather they merely replaced the old leaders as the latter moved into more "respectable" forms of civic activity.[7]

The readings presented in this section are concerned with three different aspects of urban-ethnic politics. The reading by Cornwell is a general statement of the relationship of local party organizations and ethnic groups. Basically, Cornwell argues that each was dependent on the other for its survival. James Q. Wilson, in the second reading, points out that diverse relationships between political parties and ethnic groups are possible. He concludes that the relationship between ethnic leaders and party organizations will, to a great extent, be a function of the recruitment pattern of the ethnic leader. Differences in recruitment patterns can themselves be explained in terms of both the governmental and political structure of the community. Finally, Robert A. Dahl presents an explicit framework for the analysis of ethnic groups and urban politics and carefully documents the rise of various ethnic groups to positions of political power.

---

[7] See E. Digby Baltzell, *The Protestant Establishment: Aristocracy and Caste in America* (New York: Random House, Inc., 1954).

Bosses, Machines and Ethnic Politics

Elmer E. Cornwell, Jr.

Though the direction of the causal relationship may be difficult to establish, the classic urban machine and the century of immigration which ended in the 1920's were intimately intertwined phenomena. This fact is not always recognized as fully as it should be. Much of the literature on bosses and machines, beginning with the muck-rakers, but not excluding more recent studies with less overt moralistic flavor, carries the implication that such factors as the dispersal of power in urban government—under weak mayor charters and through rivalries among state, county, city and special district authorities, all plowing the same field but none with full responsibility for its cultivation— invited the machine's extralegal reconcentration of power. It is also true that attitudes engendered by a business society whose prime movers characteristically had their eye on the "main chance"—and specifically on traction franchises and the like—also fostered the growth of the essentially entrepreneurial role and amoral attitude of the boss.

Relation of Machine to Immigration

When all this has been said, however, the fact still remains that the classic machine would probably not have been possible, and certainly

Reprinted from the *Annals*, 353 (May 1964), 28-39, by permission of the author and publisher. Copyright 1964 by the American Academy of Political and Social Science.

would not have been so prominent a feature of the American political landscape, without the immigrant. Essentially, any disciplined grass-roots political organization rests upon a docile mass base which has in some manner been rendered dependable, predictable, and manipulable. The rank and file of the Soviet Communist party is disciplined by a combination of ideological allegiance, fear and hope of reward. The average party supporter in a liberal-democratic society cannot be so disciplined under ordinary circumstances, at least not for long. The newly arrived immigrant was a special case, however. He was characteristically insecure, culturally and often linguistically alien, confused, and often in actual want. Thus, even if he had valued the franchise thrust upon him by his new political mentors, its careful exercise would have taken a low priority in his daily struggle for existence. In most cases, he did not value or even understand the political role into which he was being pushed.

Thus, it was the succeeding waves of immigrants that gave the urban political organizations the manipulable mass bases without which they could not have functioned as they did. And, until immigration dried up to a trickle in the 1920's, as one generation of newcomers began to espouse traditional American values of political independence, there was always a new group, often from a different country of origin, to which the machine could turn. As long as this continued to be possible, machines persisted, and once the immigrant base finally began to disappear, so did most of the bosses of the classic model. In a very real sense, then, the one phenomenon was dependent on the other.

The argument can be made that there were other machines that clearly were not immigrant-based in this sense. All generalizations, especially those in the social sciences, are but proximate truths. At the same time, machines based on white, Protestant, "old stock" clienteles were not wholly unrelated in their motivation and operation to the factor of immigration. Platt's smooth-functioning organization in New York State[1] and Blind Boss Brayton's contemporary operation in Rhode Island[2] were both based, in the immediate sense, on what Lincoln Steffens called "the good old American stock out in the country."[3] And yet recall that both of these states were highly urbanized even in the 1890's and early 1900's when these two worthies flourished and had

---

[1]See Harold F. Gosnell, *Boss Platt and His New York Machine* (Chicago: University of Chicago Press, 1924).

[2]See Lincoln Steffens, "Rhode Island: A State for Sale," *McClure's Magazine,* Vol. 24 (February 1905), pp. 337-353.

[3]Lincoln Steffens, *Autobiography* (New York: Literary Guild, 1931), p. 367.

ingested disproportionate numbers of immigrants. As of 1920, when 38 per cent of the total United States population was foreign born or of foreign parentage, the corresponding percentages for New York and Rhode Island were 64 and 71.[4] These facts alone suggest what the political history of both makes clear: these rural "old stock" machines existed largely as means of political defense against the newcomers and doubtless would not have existed had there been no immigrants.

The point, then, is that, whereas in the cities the immigrants sold their political independence for the familiar currency of favors and aid, their rural native cousins were sometimes prompted to do the same, in part out of desire for cultural-religious as well as political, and perhaps at times economic, self-protection. Recollection of the Know-Nothing era of militant nativist activity a half-century earlier suggests that this kind of cultural-religious antagonism can be a very potent political force indeed. An analogous explanation could even be offered for the existence of machines in the South like that of Harry Byrd in Virginia, by simply substituting the perceived Negro threat for the danger of engulfment by foreigners in the North. And, curiously enough, the two examples of reasonably thoroughgoing machine-like organizations that flourished in the otherwise inhospitable English soil—Joseph Chamberlain's Birmingham caucus[5] and Archibald Salvidge's "machine" in Liverpool[6]—also were at least indirectly related to the problem of Irish home rule, and, in Liverpool, to actual rivalry with Irish immigrants over religion and jobs.

In short, whatever else may be said about the conditions and forces that spawned the classic machine, this kind of disciplined political entity must rest at bottom on a clientele which has felt it necessary to exchange political independence—its votes, in a word—for something seen as more essential to its well-being and security. In general, such a group will be the product of some kind of socioeconomic disequilibrium or cultural tension which finds its members in an insecure or seriously disadvantaged situation. Thus, the immigrant was willing to submit to the boss in exchange for aid—real or imagined—in gaining his foothold in the new environment, and the old-stock machine supporters, North or South, submitted in part for protection against swarming aliens or a potential Negro threat to white dominance.

---

[4] E. P. Hutchinson, *Immigrants and their Children* (New York: John Wiley, 1956), p. 27.

[5] See J. L. Garvin, *The Life of Joseph Chamberlain* (3 vols.; London: Macmillan, 1932-34).

[6] Stanley Salvidge, *Salvidge of Liverpool* (London: Hodder and Stoughton, 1934).

The Classic Machine in Operation

It cannot be assumed that the process of machine exploitation of succeeding groups of newcomers was a smooth and simple operation. Any formal organization, political or otherwise must maintain a continuing balance among a series of often contradictory forces.[7] Its very existence rests on the success with which it achieves its objective—in the case of a political party, the winning of elections and, thus, power. In the long run, this success depends on the organization's continuing ability to tap fresh sources of support as time goes on and old reliances dwindle and may at times depend on keeping newly available resources away from its rival or rivals. For the machine, this has meant wooing each new ethnic contingent. Yet this process of growth and renewal will inevitably threaten the very position of many of the proprietors of the organization itself by recruiting rivals for their roles. Any organizational entity must not only achieve its corporate goals but, to survive, it must also satisfy the needs and desires of its members as individuals. If it fails in this, its supporters will vanish and its own objectives remain unattainable. Specifically, for the machine, this fact of organizational life often tempered missionary zeal and tempted its members to protect even an eroding *status quo.*

Usually the machine did yield in the long run to the political imperative that all groups of potential supporters must be wooed, if for no other reason than to keep them from the enemy. The short-term risk to the present leadership often must have appeared minimal. The plight of the newcomers was so pitiful, their needs so elemental, and their prospects of achieving security and independence so problematical in the foreseeable future that they must have appeared like a windfall to the machine proprietors. Thus, after initial hesitancy, the Irish were taken into Tammany and found their way into the ranks of the clientele of other big city party organizations.

The ways in which immigrant political support was purchased are familiar and need no elaborate review here. They had at least three kinds of needs which the ward heeler could fill on behalf of the party leadership. Above all, they needed the means of physical existence: jobs, loans, rent money, contributions of food or fuel to tide them over, and the like. Secondly, they needed a buffer against an unfamiliar state and its legal minions: help when they or their offspring got in

---

[7]For an elaboration of this approach to the internal dynamics of the machine, see James Q. Wilson, "The Economy of Patronage," *Journal of Political Economy,* Vol. 69, pp. 369-380.

trouble with the police, help in dealing with inspectors, in seeking pushcart licenses, or in other relations with the public bureaucracy. Finally, they needed the intangibles of friendship, sympathy, and social intercourse. These were available, variously, through contact with the precinct captain, the hospitality of the political clubhouse, the attendance of the neighborhood boss at wakes and weddings, and the annual ward outing.[8]

As has often been noted, these kinds of services were not available, as they are today, at the hands of "United Fund" agencies, city welfare departments with their platoons of social workers, or through federal social security legislation. The sporadic and quite inadequate aid rendered by the boss and his lieutenants thus filled a vacuum. Their only rivals were the self-help associations which did spring up within each ethnic group as soon as available resources allowed a meager surplus to support burial societies and the like. The fact that the politicians acted from self-serving motives in distributing their largess, expecting and receiving a *quid pro quo,* is obvious but not wholly relevant. At least it was not relevant in judging the social importance of the services rendered. It was highly relevant, of course, in terms of the political power base thus acquired.

Some of the later arrivals following the pioneering Irish were in at least as great need of aid. The Irish did speak English and had had some experience with political action and representative institutions at home. This, plus the fact that they got here first, doubtless accounts for their rapid rise in their chosen party, the Democracy. The groups that followed, however, usually did not know English and bore the additional burden of a cultural heritage that had less in common with the American patterns they encountered than had been the case with the Irish. And, too, almost all groups, the Sons of Erin included, differed religiously from the basic Protestant consensus of their Anglo-Saxon predecessors.

As group followed group—not only into the country but into the rickety tenements and "river wards" reserved, as it were, for the latest arrivals—the processes of absorption became more complex. The Irish ward politicians doubtless had, if anything, more difficulty bridging the cultural and language gap to meet the newcomers than the "Yankees" had had in dealing with themselves some decades earlier. Also, while it may well be that the Yankees gave up their party committee posts fairly willingly to the Irish, because politics was not

---

[8]One of the most readable depictions of these machine functions is to be found in Edwin O'Connor's novel *The Last Hurrah* (Boston: Little, Brown, 1956).

essential to their well-being either economically or psychologically, the Irish were in a rather different position when their turn came to move over and make room.[9] They had not fully outgrown their dependence on politics for financial and psychic security. Thus, the conflicting demands of the machine for new sources of support versus the reluctance of the incumbents to encourage rivalry for their own positions, produced tension. In the long run, however, most of the new ethnic groups found their place in the party system. In some cases, as with the Italians, the Republicans, generally less skillful in these arts, won support by default when the Irish were especially inhospitable.

The Machine as Social Integrator

There is another side to the coin of machine dependence on the continuing flow of immigrants. The "invisible hand"—to use an analogy with Adam Smith's economics—which operated to produce social benefits out of the *quid pro quo* which the ward heelers exchanged for votes was at work in other ways, too. Henry Jones Ford noted in the 1890's, while discussing the role of party:[10]

> This nationalizing influence continues to produce results of the greatest social value, for in co-ordinating the various elements of the population for political purposes, party organization at the same time tends to fuse them into one mass of citizenship, pervaded by a common order of ideas and sentiments, and actuated by the same class of motives. This is probably the secret of the powerful solvent influence which American civilization exerts upon the enormous deposits of alien population thrown upon this country by the torrent of emigration.

Again, in other words, the selfish quest by the politician for electoral support and power was transmuted by the "invisible hand" into the major force integrating the immigrant into the community.

This process has had several facets. In the first place, the mere seeking out of the immigrants in quest of their support, the assistance rendered in getting them naturalized (when it was necessary to observe these legal niceties), and so forth were of considerable importance in laying the foundation for their more meaningful political participation later. In addition, the parties have progressively drawn

---

[9]See the author's "Some Occupational Patterns in Party Committee Membership," *Rhode Island History*, Vol. 20 (July 1961), pp. 87-96.

[10]*The Rise and Growth of American Politics* (New York: Macmillan, 1911), p. 306.

into their own hierarchies and committee offices representatives of the various ethnic groups. The mechanics of this process were varied. In some cases, there doubtless emerged leaders of a particular group in one ward or neighborhood who, if given official party status, would automatically bring their followings along with them.[11] On other occasions, new ethnic enclaves may have sought or even demanded representation in exchange for support. Perhaps prior to either of these, the machine sought to co-opt individuals who could speak the language and act as a cultural bridge between the party and the newcomers. Depending on the situation, it probably was essential to do this and impossible for precinct captains of a different background to develop adequate rapport. It is at this point that ethnic group rivalry in the organization becomes difficult. Gratitude to the boss for initial admission into the lower ranks of the hierarchy would be bound to change in time into demands, of growing insistence, for further recognition of the individual and his group.

These general patterns can to some extent be documented, at least illustratively. The tendency for the urban machines to reap the Irish vote and later much of the vote of more recent arrivals is well known. The process of infiltration by group representatives into party structure is harder to identify precisely. With this in mind, the author did a study of the members of party ward committees in Providence, Rhode Island, the findings of which may reflect trends elsewhere.[12] Analysis of committee membership lists or their equivalent going back to the 1860's and 1870's showed initial overwhelming Anglo-Saxon majorities. For the Democrats, however, this majority gave way, between the 1880's and 1900, to a roughly 75 per cent Irish preponderance, while the Republican committees stayed "Yankee" until after the First World War. Then, in the 1920's, both parties simultaneously recruited Italian committeemen to replace some of the Irish and white Protestants, respectively. Today, both have varied, and roughly similar, proportions of all major groups in the city population. In other cities, the timing of shifts and the ethnic groups involved will have differed, but the general process and its relation to local patterns of immigration were doubtless similar.

It is incredible, viewed now with hindsight, how reckless the American republic was in its unpremeditated policy of the open door and the implied assumption that somehow, without any governmental or

---

[11]*Ibid.*, p. 307.
[12]"Party Absorption of Ethnic Groups," *Social Forces*, Vol. 38 (March 1960), pp. 205-210.

even organized private assistance, hundreds of thousands of immigrants from dozens of diverse cultures would fit themselves smoothly and automatically into a native culture which had its own share of ethnocentrism. The fact of the matter was that the process did not operate smoothly or particularly effectively. There were tensions and incidents which accentuated cultural differences and engendered bitterness. These ranged, chronologically, all the way from the abuses of the more militant Know-Nothings to the Ku Klux Klan activity of the 1920's.

Economically, most occupational doors that did not lead to manual labor jobs were closed to the Irish and later arrivals and were only gradually pried open after much time had passed and many lasting intergroup enmities had been engendered. Here again, the party organizations represented one of the few mechanisms, public or private, that lubricated a process of integration which, in its very nature, was bound to generate enormous amounts of friction. Besides drawing group representatives into its councils, party work also was one of the few career ladders available to the immigrant and his ambitious sons. Here, status could be achieved, as well as a comfortable income, one way or another, when few other routes were open. This became not just status for the individual but a measure of recognition and acceptance for the group as a whole through the individual's success. In fact, not only did the newcomer use this alternative career ladder, but he carried over into the political sphere some of the "Horatio Alger" quest for success and other aspects of an essentially pragmatic, materialistic American culture as well.

Politics for the machine politician never was an ideological enterprise or a matter of beliefs and principles. As someone once said, the boss had only seven principles, five loaves and two fishes. Rather, politics was an entrepreneurial vocation like any other business. Banfield and Wilson have written: "A political machine is a business organization in a particular field of business—getting votes and winning elections. As a Chicago machine boss once said . . . it is 'just like any sales organization trying to sell its product.' "[13] The politician's aim was and is so to invest his supply of capital—jobs, favors, and the like—as to earn a profit, some of which he will take as "income" and the rest reinvest in quest of larger returns. In other words, the immigrant political leader took the one vocation open to him, politics, and made it into as close an approximation as he could of the more

---

[13] Edward Banfield and James Q. Wilson, *City Politics* (Cambridge: Harvard and M.I.T. Presses, 1963), p. 115.

valued business callings in the society, from which he was effectively barred. He acted out the American success story in the only way open to him.

Obviously, the foregoing is not designed to portray the machine as a knight-errant rescuing American society from its willful folly. In the first place, the folly was not willful, and perhaps not folly. In the second, the boss's contribution toward making the melting pot melt should not be overrated. At the same time, many have testified—as does the record itself—to the almost unique ability of party as organization to bring people together across cultural and similar barriers. As Glazer and Moynihan have written of New York City:[14]

> . . . political life itself emphasizes the ethnic character of the city, with its balanced tickets and its special appeals. . . . For those in the field itself, there is more contact across the ethnic lines, and the ethnic lines themselves mean less, than in other areas of the city's life.

Ticket-balancing, or United Nations politics, as it is sometimes called, is perhaps symbolic of the ultimate step in the process of granting group recognition and confirming the fact that something approaching intergroup equality has been achieved. Either, as with the Manhattan Borough presidency and the Negro group, certain prescriptive rights become established to a particular office or to one place on a city-wide ticket or ethnic allocation is made using the background of the head of the ticket as point of departure.

In short, the classic urban machine rested upon the immigrants, while at the same time it fostered their integration into American life. It also made, in the process, a major contribution to the over-all American political style. It is true that politics as a pragmatic entrepreneurial vocation owes much in America to the contributions of Burr, Van Buren, Weed, Marcy (to the victor belong the spoils), and, in a sense, to Andrew Jackson himself. Thus, Richard Hofstadter's attribution of one of the two central systems of political ethnics in America to the immigrants is only partially valid.[15] He is clearly correct, however, in suggesting that a political style which stressed "personal obligations, and placed strong personal loyalties above allegiance to abstract codes of law or morals"[16] was congenial to the machine politicians and their followers, and they made it their own,

---

[14]Nathan Glazer and Daniel Patrick Moynihan, *Beyond the Melting Pot* (Cambridge: Harvard and M.I.T. Presses, 1963), p. 20.

[15]Richard Hofstadter, *The Age of Reform* (New York: Knopf, 1955), pp. 8 ff.

[16]*Ibid.*, p. 9.

developing its full implications in the process. At the same time, the immigrant versus old stock cultural cleavage prompted the latter to espouse the more vigorously the typically middle-class, reformist style which stresses honesty, impartiality, and efficiency. These two styles or ethnics, since the late nineteenth century, have, by their interaction, shaped both the evolution of urban politics and the machinery of urban government.

The Decline of the Machine

The decline and fall of the boss as a political phenomenon has often been chronicled and explained. It is argued, *inter alia*, that reforms like the direct primary, nonpartisan systems of election, voting machines and tightened registration requirements, and city-manager schemes often dealt crippling blows. In the aggregate, they doubtless did, though many exceptions can be found to prove the rule. One particular contribution of the reformers which has had unquestioned importance—though circumvention has not proven impossible—was the elimination of patronage with the installation of civil service based on the merit principle. And, generally, educational levels have risen, and occupational levels and incomes have risen as well. Even where patronage remains available, the latter development has rendered it less attractive, and to fewer people. Finally, and most often cited, there was the impact of the New Deal. Its installation of publicly sponsored welfare programs eliminated many of the rough-and-ready welfare functions of the precinct captain, though the more imaginative recouped part of their loss by helping to steer constituents through the bureaucratic maze, claiming credit for the benefits thus obtained.

Granting the importance of all of these developments, in the long run, the decline of immigration doubtless proved the most important blow to the traditional machine operation. New arrivals had been entering the country at a rate in excess of four million each half decade up to the First World War. The rate averaged barely more than one third of that between 1915 and 1930 and dropped to a mere trickle for most of the period down to the present. Sharply restrictive legislation passed in 1921 and 1924 was responsible. Obviously, the impact on the machines came in the form of a delayed reaction, but most of them gradually withered. The few that survived did so through shrewd adaptation to changed conditions, specifically through judicious self-administered doses of reformism, as, for example, with the Daley organization in Chicago.

Thus ended an era. Immigration may not have called the boss into being, but the two in most cases were closely linked. Two questions remain to be dealt with. What contemporary counterparts are there, if any, of the immigrant influx of yesteryear and how are the parties dealing with them? And what can be said of the current political behavior of the children and grandchildren of the former immigrants?

The Parties and the New Immigration

There are, of course, two major groups that do represent close parallels with the earlier influx and at the same time carry important differences. These are the Negroes who have been migrating in increasing numbers from the South to northern urban centers since the First World War and the Puerto Ricans who began coming to New York City, for the most part, after the Second World War.[17] Both resemble their alien predecessors in the magnitude of their numbers, their basic and important cultural differences from the population into whose midst they are moving, an almost invariable need of assistance in adjusting to a new environment, and their potential impact on the political balance of forces.

The major points of difference are also worth noting. Both come bearing the credentials of American citizenship, which was not the case with the earlier groups. Though this factor should make for easier adjustment, other group characteristics operate to make acceptance more difficult. For the Negro, there is the fundamental problem of color, coupled with cultural characteristics which, though acquired ostensibly in the American environment, operate to make assimilation more difficult. These include all the long deposit of servitude and enforced inferior status: loose marital ties and correspondingly weak family ties generally, a poverty of leadership potential, low literacy and skill levels, and the like. For the Puerto Ricans, there is language, plus differences of culture, and a partial color barrier which operates to cause at least some Spanish Americans to be classified—against their will—as Negroes. On balance, it is probably true that, so far as these two groups are concerned as groups, they face higher barriers to integration into American life than almost any earlier group save, possibly, the orientals.

But the society itself has changed enormously from the society to which the Irish, Italians, and Jews sought entrance. Urban areas are

---

[17]Two recent books are especially useful discussions of these groups: Glazer and Moynihan, *op. cit.;* and Oscar Handlin, *The Newcomers: Negroes and Puerto Ricans in a Changing Metropolis* (Cambridge: Harvard Press, 1959).

now equipped with facilities to which the newcomer can turn for aid that counterbalance to some degree the particular hostilities which members of these two groups arouse. There are now elaborate public welfare programs, there is Aid to Dependent Children for the many fatherless families, there are numerous private agencies and charities which stand ready to help, and, in the case of the Puerto Ricans, their land of origin has taken a unique interest in the welfare of its emigrants. There have even been legislative efforts to ban the discrimination in housing or employment which they encounter.

Though these facilities stand ready to ease aspects of the economic and social integration of these latest immigrants, there still remains the question of political absorption. Here, too, the situation today sharply differs from the past. The political parties now have neither the incentive nor the means with which to perform the functions they performed for the earlier immigrants. The machine in most affected areas is gone beyond recall, and there remain in its place party organizations that are hollow shells of their former strength and vigor. Party in general, given the proliferation of both public bureaucracies and the mass entertainment industry, has been pushed to the fringes of the average citizen's attention span and often to the fringes of the governing process itself. The debilitating impact of reform legislation contributed to the same end, needless to say. Thus, in general, the new immigrants can look to the parties for little of the former assistance they once provided in gaining entrance and leverage in the political processes of their new homes.

There are partial exceptions here, as there are to all the foregoing generalizations. Mayor Daley's modern Chicago version of the old-style machine has been mentioned earlier. Within his over-all Cook County Democratic organization, there is the "sub-machine" comprising the Negro followers of Representative William E. Dawson.[18] Dawson, a former maverick Republican, shifted parties in 1939 and joined forces with Mayor-boss Kelly. Some twenty years later, he had put together a combination, under his leadership, of five or six Negro wards. This "organization within an organization" appears to bargain as a unit through Dawson and his lieutenants for patronage and other kinds of preferment in the gift of Mayor Daley and in turn tends to exert a moderating influence on the more aggressive elements in the Negro community. Trends suggest that this is not destined to be a permanent arrangement. The population of the Dawson-controlled

---

[18]This discussion of the Dawson organization draws particularly on James Q. Wilson, *Negro Politics* (Glencoe, Ill.: Free Press, 1960), pp. 50 ff. and *passim*.

wards has been declining as the more prosperous Negroes manage to settle in more desirable locations, and, as Dawson and his associates grow older, they become more conservative. Whether or not this latter is partly an illusion produced by the rapid rise in Negro militancy since 1954 would be hard to say. It is probably true that leaders of the Dawson type will get more "out of phase" with the civil rights movement as that movement gains further momentum.

New York City, almost by traditional right, is *the* locale for the study of the behavior of American parties in relation to the immigrant. The 1960 census reported just over a million Negroes in New York City and somewhat more than 600,000 Puerto Ricans. In broad terms, it can be said that, since the days of Al Smith and Boss Murphy, New York politics have been long on confusion and fragmentation and short on centralized, disciplined organization. There was, therefore, little possibility that a relationship such as Representative Dawson worked out with his Negro clientele on the one hand and the leaders of the Cook County Democracy on the other could be developed in New York. Especially in Manhattan—which we shall take for analysis—one finds exemplified the more typical contemporary party situation: no dominating borough-wide authority save that in the hands of the mayor himself, hence a series of local feudal chiefs who are rarely willing to exchange their relative independence for the rather meager supplies of patronage available, and the whole system wracked periodically by factional feuding.

The Negro in New York, in apparent contrast to the Chicago situation, has been more fragmented in his political organization, has found little borough-wide structure with which to associate, but has made more spectacular symbolic gains in the party and city government. Representative Adam Clayton Powell, the rather erratic champion of the city's nonwhites, reaps vastly more national publicity for his espoused cause than the publicity-shy Congressman Dawson.[19] How much this means in concrete benefits would be hard to determine. More significant is the fact that in 1953 a Negro, Hulan Jack, was elected for the first time to a major office in the city, that of Borough President of Manhattan. Powell had a major role in this, though he later broke with Jack. Since then, this position has become an accepted Negro prerogative. Other high positions have been filled by Negroes in the city administration in recent years.

---

[19]A useful source on Powell is David Hapgood, *The Purge that Failed: Tammany v. Powell* (New York: Holt, 1959).

Representation on Party Committees

A somewhat more useful basis for judging the reality of ethnic or racial group political absorption and power position than possession of some of these "commanding heights" (in Lenin's phrase) would be an analysis of the extent to which they had gained footholds in the lower and intermediate levels of the party organization. The ethnic proportions among Providence ward committee members cited above are a relatively accurate reflection of the nationality power relationships in city politics. For example, the fact that the Irish Democrats have held onto about half of the ward committee seats after yielding some places to Italians reflects the fact that they still have the dominant voice in the party. The rise of the Italians on the Republican side to the status of the largest single ethnic group also reflects their growing power.[20]

Table 1 shows the approximate percentages of ethnic/racial representation in the total New York City population and, in the second column, the background of the Manhattan Democratic Assembly district leaders and coleaders insofar as these could be determined.[21] There are sixteen Assembly districts, but most are divided into two or three parts with a leader and coleader for each. There were some vacancies at the time the data were obtained. It can be seen that the Negro has done quite well by this measure of political integration in that the group has considerably more than the share of district leadership positions it would be entitled to on a strict population basis. The bulk of these Negroes preside over districts in or around Harlem, as might be expected—the 11th, 12th, 13th, 14th, and 16th Assembly districts. Of the eighteen occupied positions in these five Assembly districts, they hold twelve. There are two Negroes, one each in the 5th and 10th, to the west and east of Central Park, respectively, but none to the south of the Park at all.

In passing it might be noted that the other groups on the Table each have something approximating their proportionate share of the leaderships. The Jewish contingent is disproportionately large, due in considerable measure to the fact that three-fifths of all the anti-Tammany "reform" leaders come from that part of the city population. True to what one knows about their situation in other cities, the Italians appear to be underrepresented. The Irish, however, even in

---

[20]"Partly Absorption of Ethnic Groups," *op. cit.*

[21]Thanks are due the author's former student, Edwin Cohen, now active in Manhattan politics, and to George Osborne, himself a district leader, for tracking down the leadership data used.

TABLE 1

Comparison of Ethnic Proportions in Population with
Democratic District Leaders in Manhattan

	Approximate Percentage of New York City 1960 Population[a]	Percentage of Democratic Assembly District Leaders (N = 66)
Negroes	14	21
Puerto Ricans	8	6
Jews	25±	38
Italians	17±	11
Irish	10±	9
Others	26±	15[b]
	100	100

[a] Population percentage estimates are from Nathan Glazer and D. P. Moynihan, *Beyond the Melting Pot* (Cambridge: Massachusetts Institute of Technology and Harvard Press, 1963). Only figures for Negroes and Puerto Ricans were given in the 1960 census. It was impossible to get ethnic group percentages for Manhattan alone.

[b] Includes Anglo-Saxon Protestants and others of unidentified background.

view of the extreme difficulty in guessing their share of the city population, have far fewer positions than the prevailing myth of continuing Irish dominance of urban Democratic politics would suggest.

Turning now to the Puerto Ricans, they offer the best opportunity for assessing the ability of at least the Manhattan Democratic organization to absorb a genuinely new ethnic group. In Table 2, the backgrounds of the district leaders in the areas of heaviest Puerto Rican population are tabulated. Also included, in the last two columns, are figures on the personnel of the lowest level of "grass-roots" party organization, the election district captains. Out of the twelve district leader positions occupied at the time the data were obtained, four were held by Puerto Ricans, giving that group representation in three of the six most heavily Puerto Rican districts. Though only firsthand knowledge would indicate how effective these individuals are in representing their ethnic group and bargaining on its behalf, there is indication here of rather significant infiltration into the party structure. The figures for election district captains, where

TABLE 2

Areas of Heavy Puerto Rican Population[a]

			Election District Captains	
Area	Assembly District	District Leaders	Total	Puerto Ricans
Lower East Side	4th, South	2 Jewish	29	7
East Harlem	10th, North	1 Puerto Rican and 1 Negro	16	9
	14th, South	2 Puerto Ricans	17	8
	14th, North	2 Negroes	__[b]	__[b]
	16th, South	1 Italian and 1 Puerto Rican	__[b]	__[b]
Upper West Side	13th, South	1 Italian and 1 Negro	52	23

[a] Puerto Rican population location was determined by plotting location of census tracts with at least 15 per cent Puerto Ricans and coloring these in according to density. There are scatterings in a few other parts of Manhattan as well.

[b] Data could not be obtained.

these could be obtained, point to the same conclusion. Except for the lower east side, where the proportion is smaller, roughly half of these captains are also Puerto Rican, casting further doubt on common assumptions that the party in Manhattan is lagging seriously in making room for this latest group to arrive.

In general, both Table 1 and Table 2 suggest that the Puerto Ricans have secured, in the relatively short time since their arrival in large numbers, party offices roughly commensurate with their share of the population overall and in areas of high concentration. In addition, there are three state assemblymen from this group (two from East Harlem and one from the Bronx) and four or five with high positions in the city administration.[22]

These achievements, obviously, as well as the district leaderships themselves and election district captaincies, can only be taken as rough indicators of the political progress of the group as a whole and are doubtless far less significant than they could have been viewed in

[22]Layhmond Robinson, "Voting Gain Made by Puerto Ricans," *New York Times*, November 23, 1963.

the political setting of forty or fifty years ago when parties were central to the governing process and urban life generally. At the same time, they must be evaluated in light of the fact that New York State will not accept literacy in a language other than English (such as Spanish) as qualification to vote, and, thus, only some 150,000 to 175,000 of the total Puerto Rican group are on the rolls.

Returning for a moment to the current status of descendents of earlier immigrants, the assumption that significant cultural distinctions and tendencies toward common political attitude and behavior would disappear in two or three generations has proven erroneous. Ticket-balancing, for example, in ethnic or religious terms is as prevalent, perhaps, as it ever was and shows few signs of disappearing in the immediate future. The election of an Irish Catholic President in 1960, if anything, enhanced the importance of such balancing tactics, as the discussion in early 1964 of Democratic vice-presidential candidates indicated. In psychoanalysis, it is well recognized that problems have to be clearly recognized and frankly made explicit before they can be eliminated. The same may in a sense be true of ethnic factors in American politics. Only the frank recognition of the once-potent barrier to a Catholic in the White House paved the way for the Kennedy election. At the state and local level, it is probably also true that only after various groups have achieved and enjoyed the recognition they feel they are entitled to and have done so for a long enough period to transform a privilege into a quasi right will it become possible, gradually, to choose candidates without these criteria in mind. The unfortunate thing is that American parties have decayed as organizations to the point that they can make far less contribution to this process of adjustment than they could and did in the past.

Two Negro Politicians:
An Interpretation

James Q. Wilson

This is an attempt to describe, and in part to account for, the differences between two powerful political leaders, whose constituencies are roughly similar. Although the two congressmen in question are well-known Negroes—Adam Clayton Powell, Jr. of New York and William L. Dawson of Chicago—the analysis of the character of their political life is not meant to explain their idiosyncratic features. It is hoped, rather, that these remarks will illuminate some of the central features of the role of any congressman. By choosing for study two men who, in many ways, are polar opposites but who at the same time share many of the same problems and resources, the contrasts between them can be made more vivid and the argument employed can be sketched in bold strokes.[1]

Powell and Dawson are the most famous Negro Democratic congressmen. The former was first elected in 1944, the latter in 1942. Both represent districts that are almost entirely Negro in composition, and which have within them both appalling slums and expensive homes and apartments. Both are relatively senior members of the

Reprinted from *Midwest Journal of Political Science*, Vol. 4, No. 4 (November 1960), 346-369 by permission of the Wayne State University Press and the author. Copyright 1960 by the Wayne State University Press.

[1]This article is based on interview research conducted in Chicago, New York, and Washington, D.C., on Negro politics. For my larger findings, plus much of the detail which is omitted from this interpretative article, see my book, *Negro Politics* (Glencoe: The Free Press, 1960).

House of Representatives. Dawson is the chairman of the House Government Operations Committee; Powell is the second-ranking Democrat on the Education and Labor Committee and is a sub-committee
chairman on the Interior Committee. Both have received national
publicity, Powell more than Dawson, and both are well-known to
their colleagues. Both tend to support the Democratic leadership of
the House fairly consistently. On "party votes" (i.e., votes which pit a
majority of one party against a majority of the other party), neither
Dawson nor Powell will as a rule vote against his party in more than
two or three per cent of the cases. Neither Dawson nor Powell has an
especially good record of voting participation in House roll calls.
Although Dawson is better than Powell in most sessions, both are well
below the average for the House as a whole. Powell has on occasion
been among the very lowest—sometimes *the* lowest—in voting participation, and rarely averages higher than 50 per cent. Dawson has
steadily increased his voting participation, rising from 38 per cent in
1947-48 to 83 per cent in 1958.[2]

The similarities between the two men are, however, superficial. The
differences are profound. Each has a unique political style which
transcends issues, roll calls, or personal fortunes. The one is an orator,
the other an organizer; one is flamboyant, the other is conservative;
one is militant on the race question, the other is moderate.[3] One
seeks publicity and speaks almost always "on the record"; the other
shuns publicity and speaks to interviewers only off the record. One is
considered by most of his House colleagues to be demagogic and
unreliable; the other has the confidence and respect of many influential congressmen. One raises the race issue on every occasion; the
other goes out of his way to avoid discussing race or race questions.
One is light-skinned, handsome, boyish, gregarious, fun-loving; the
other is brown-skinned, aged, reserved, quiet. One spends his free
time (of which he has a great deal) in world travel, entertaining, and
night life; the other rarely travels, devotes himself completely to
politics, and leads a home life carefully screened by privacy and
silence. The two most prominent Negro politicians are radically dissimilar, avoid each other's company, speak disparagingly of one anoth-

---

[2] See *Congressional Quarterly Almanac*, 1950 through 1958.

[3] On Powell, see Roi Ottley, *New World A'Coming* (Boston: Houghton Mifflin
Co., 1943); David Hapgood, *The Purge That Failed: Tammany v. Powell* ("Case
Studies in Practical Politics"; New York: Henry Holt & Co., 1959); Will Chasan,
"Congressman Powell's Downhill Fight in Harlem," *Reporter*, 20 (July 10,
1958), 24. On Dawson, see John Madigan, "The Durable Mr. Dawson of Cook
County, Illinois," *Reporter*, 18 (August 9, 1956), 9; Fletcher Martin and John
Madigan, "The Boss of Bronzeville," *Chicago Magazine*, 1 (July, 1955), 22.

er, and elicit the most violent attitudes of love and hate from their many friends and enemies.

An explanation can be offered that will both account for many of these differences and suggest something of interest about the relationship of any political leader to his organization and his constituents. This explanation will endeavor to show that Powell and Dawson are not simply two interesting and perhaps unique men, but that they are also political leaders who have created and who seek to maintain two important kinds of political organizations. The creation and maintenance of these organizations places certain constraints on the actions of the leaders. The leaders' political styles reflect these constraints. It will be necessary, to make this argument plausible, to describe how these organizations were built, the nature of the political systems of which they are part, the maintenance needs these organizations have, and the implications these needs have for the political style of the leader.

We will argue, first, that the most important single factor in creating or modifying the political style of each leader is the character of the organization which supports the leader and the nature of the incentives which he must distribute to sustain it.[4] Each political leader acts so as to maintain the strength of his organization. The strength of the organization is measured in terms of the number and size of the contributions to it, the extent to which a single undisputed leadership can control it, and the extent to which it can attain its collective goal (in this case, the retention of political office). To maintain the flow of contributions (the time, money, and energies of organization workers and the votes of the electorate), incentives must be distributed by the leader. In the case of Powell, these are largely intangible (non-material or "ideal") incentives; in the case of Dawson, these are largely tangible or material.

The second argument will be that the character of the organization which the leader must maintain is largely determined by the nature of the local political system. The aspects of that system most relevant here include the size and composition of the political districts and the

---

[4]Cf., Chester Barnard, *The Functions of the Executive* (Cambridge: Harvard University Press, 1938). I adopt here the standard methodological dodge of arguing, not that each leader in every case acts so as to sustain his organization, but that he acts *as if* this were his rule. My argument is an assumption, not a law; it is used to order data and give them meaning. The limitations of this assumption will be discussed at a later point. See also Max Weber on "ideal" and "material" benefits in *The Theory of Social and Economic Organization,* trans. A. H. Henderson and Talcott Parsons (Glencoe: The Free Press, 1947), pp. 407-12.

relative strength and unity of the city-wide political organization. The maintenance of a Negro political organization is intimately bound up with the maintenance of the political system of the community as a whole.

Powell

Adam Clayton Powell, Jr., was not, until the summer of 1959, a member of the regular party organization in New York City. When Powell sought to enter Congress in 1944, Tammany was a weakened machine. Eleven years of rule by LaGuardia, the adoption of a new city charter, and the extension of civil service had left the Tiger in a state of chronic malnutrition. The organization was shot through with factions and internecine warfare, both in Harlem and elsewhere. Rival leaders made competing alliances, broke them, and made new ones. The strength of the Manhattan organization declined, and other forces —such as the Bronx organization of Edward Flynn—rose to power. Few, inside or outside the organization, could depend on machine discipline or machine voting strength. Other bases of political power had to be found by those who sought a permanent and rising career in politics. Powell found his in the pulpit. He built his organization and his political following from outside the city machine. Although he received the endorsement of Tammany when he first ran for Congress in 1944, and subsequently until 1958, he felt he could not rely on either that endorsement or the efforts of the workers in the regular organization. The base of support for Powell was and is the Abyssinian Baptist Church, a church of perhaps 10,000 members that has existed since 1808. It was the church of his father, who retired in 1937. It is independent of any larger organization, and financially self-sustaining. In addition to the church, Powell was co-editor of a Harlem weekly, the *People's Voice*. In the stormy Harlem of the 1930's, Powell was a familiar and dramatic figure in and around the various Negro boycott movements, strikes, and protest demonstrations. He was opposed for the Democratic nomination for Congress in 1944 by the Negro who was then the most important Harlem district leader, but Tammany—either unsure of its ability to elect an alternative candidate, receptive to suggestions from other forces, or desirous of rebuking a rebellious district leader—chose to ignore the leader's protest and endorse Powell.

Powell created a personal organization. In part it was formed because Powell began his career from outside of the established organization, and in part it was necessary because even a position inside the Tammany machine was fraught with dangers and uncertainties. Whether outside or inside the organization, independent political strength was at least an advantage and probably a necessity. A church can be an ideal source of such strength. It directly recruits and organizes the masses, it can be financially independent, it has a variety of channels of communication throughout the community, and it has the luster of an indisputably good institution. In recent elections, Powell has been able to call upon as many as one thousand church workers for his campaigns, mostly volunteers. They are already organized through the elaborate committee structure and social service system of the church, and many of them hear Powell speak every Sunday. The church, in addition, has a paid bureaucracy of workers to provide the necessary staff. The appeals to these supporters are almost entirely intangible. The appeals are even larger than simply the exploitation of established race issues. They are centered around Powell as the personal embodiment, the projective personality, of the Negroes in his congregation. He is the vivid and colorful manifestation of their collective aspirations and expectations.

The use of intangible appeals in political organizations creates a set of constraints upon the user. When appeals are to principle, to lofty moral and racial goals, to the deepest wishes and fears of the listener, they enforce a logic upon the user which is compelling. Three important consequences of this kind of appeal can be mentioned.

First, these appeals tend to be "indivisible"; that is, they cannot easily be reduced to discrete units, given relative priorities, and dealt with apart from other aspects of the leader's career. Rather, they tend to function as a whole, a montage of interrelated ends and means, to which all phases of a leader's life must respond. Powell, for example, does not and probably could not divorce his career in Washington from his career in New York. His role as a congressman is inseparable from his role as a Harlem politician, Negro minister, and colorful personality. Politics for him is not a specific, but a general role, and the appeals upon which it is based are ramified and indivisible. Politics is "functionally diffuse."[5] Powell's position as a congressman is an extension of his position as a Harlem leader. The two offices, in Washington and New York, are systematically related. Both receive a relatively large number of constituents. In Washington, four staff

---

[5]Cf., the treatment by Parsons and Shils of the pattern variables of "specificity" and "diffuseness" as aspects of the role-expectations governing the relevance of social objects. Talcott Parsons and Edward A. Shils, *Toward a General Theory of Action* (Cambridge: Harvard University Press, 1954), pp. 83-84.

workers are in Powell's office; in New York, three. In Washington, Powell receives as many as five to eight hundred letters a week, perhaps 250 of which state personal problems or requests for information and services. In New York, his congressional office is almost indistinguishable from his church organization, both of which deal with a wide range of the needs and requests of his followers. The church has in its congregation an estimated ten percent of the registered voters in the Sixteenth Congressional District.[6] Powell speaks to some four thousand people every Sunday, and upwards of one thousand persons come to the church or its community house every day of the week. There is little difference between voter and parishioner, between constituency and congregation.

The generality of Powell's political role is further suggested by the extent to which he intervenes in New York City political affairs in the same manner in which he intervenes in national affairs. Powell frequently makes public charges of race discrimination and injustice in Manhattan and he is not slow to attack the Mayor, the Police Commissioner, Carmine De Sapio, and other officials. Harlem is not simply a constituency which elects Powell to Congress; it is also a source of political issues. Powell's political style in part depends on the existence of an "enemy"—a source of alleged injustice against which Powell can direct his fire. Since his power has not been received from the political organization of the city, the organization is not immune from that fire.

On the other hand, Powell is usually not readily available in his district for receiving constituents. Although he maintains a congressional staff in Harlem which is closely linked with his church staff, he does not personally perform the services usual for a local political leader—hear complaints, requests, and demands from the voters who seek out their politicians directly. These services are provided by lieutenants.

The mingling of political, religious, and civic roles is seen in the organization of his headquarters. The secretary of the church's Board of Trustees acts as financial secretary of Powell's political club (the "Alfred Isaacs Democratic Club"). His congressional administrative assistant, charged with handling local political affairs, has an office adjacent to that of the church's full-time social worker, and the two share the task of dealing with voters-parishioners. The church, a $100,000-a-year enterprise, provided 600 to 1200 political vounteers at various stages of Powell's 1959 campaign for district leader and helped to raise the $30,000 necessary for the 1958 congressional campaign.

---

[6]Hapgood, *op. cit.*, p. 3.

Second, intangible appeals tend to be endowed with a sacrosanct quality which renders them difficult to manipulate. This would be true whether the appeal is that of a charismatic leader with the "gift of grace" or of political principles which are invested with a sacred quality. There are undoubtedly elements of both charisma and ideology in Powell's appeal to his followers; how much of each would be difficult to assess. Although there would be important differences in detail, the general effect of either a charismatic or ideological appeal is that the leader becomes ill-suited for a bargaining role. As the manifestation of the private aspirations of individual Negroes, as the assertion of the great public ends of the race, or as the revelation of a prophetic, heroic, or exemplary personality, these appeals are endowed with a sacrosanct quality which makes both the leader and the ends he may represent superior to the leaders and goals of others. To compromise either the position of the leader or the essence of these goals would be to give way to morally inferior persons or demands; in short, it would be to corrupt them. To oppose Powell in an election is to take the side of evil, to be an "Uncle Tom," and to be a "field hand" on the "white man's plantation."

Paradoxically, this does not mean that Powell cannot escape his position on issues affecting the race which come before the local or national government. He can, and has, advanced and then dropped causes which involved race ends. Powell has frequently announced a dramatic move in local or national politics, but often little or nothing is in fact done. This was the case with his promised "boycott" of the 1952 presidential election and the independent political organization he promised in 1958. Few followers seem disturbed by this. Powell's own explanation is that such moves, even if only threats, serve to keep Tammany and others "off balance."

It may even be that Powell could reverse himself on some important issue, relying on his personal standing with his followers to justify the move. Charisma would compensate for ideology where the latter had to be sacrificed.[7] Such may have been the case, for example,

---

[7] It will be interesting to discover to what extent Powell's charisma can become "routinized." (Cf., Weber, *op. cit.,* pp. 363 ff.) The accession of Powell to the chairmanship of the House Committee on Education and Labor, predicted for the 87th Congress in 1961, will bring him under a new set of constraints which he may in part accept in hope of enjoying certain of the rewards of chairmanship. At the local level, Powell—by entering Tammany as a district leader—will have a limited amount of patronage and the necessity for creating something more in the way of a specifically political administrative apparatus. These constraints need not be too severe, for Tammany undoubtedly needs Powell more than he needs it. Clearly, Powell is unlikely to trade his non-material appeals for the scanty material ones at the disposal of DeSapio. But marginal adjustments might be expected, all in the direction of routinizing what has been a strictly personal and irregular position.

when he joined with the other three Negro congressmen in voting against a Republican-sponsored civil rights amendment to the 1959 Housing Act on the grounds that it intended to defeat the bill by making it unacceptable to Southerners. Previously, he had sponsored and fought for a civil rights amendment to the federal education bill which, when adopted by the House, was followed by the defeat of the bill as a whole.[8] But considered as a set of appeals, Powell's identification with race issues and aspirations leads to further and further commitments and reduces the opportunity for compromise or the deliberate choice of means. Means, in the words of another student of race and nationalism, always have an "end-component."[9] Means cannot be selected simply on the basis of whether they are efficiently adapted to the attainment of given ends. Means are not valued merely on the basis of utility. Almost all means which might be used toward given ends have a value in and of themselves. Ends react on means, imbue them with value, and render it difficult for a leader to be selective. The means Powell employs are precisely of this character. They involve defying the white man, asserting loudly the rights of Negroes, pressing for liberalizing legislation regardless of the costs to other values held by the society, and keeping the issues alive and hot.

Powell's political appeals lend themselves to campaigns based on the Negro ministry. The church is a vital part of Powell's base of support and, even though some ministers individually do not like Powell, most of them can be counted on to campaign in his behalf. It is principally through the mobilized resources of the Harlem ministry that Powell speaks to the people, addressing them from the pulpits of dozens of churches.

Third, Powell indulges his personal wants to an extraordinary extent. Powell stated in 1956 that his income was an estimated $115,000 a year—$40,000 a year earned by him as congressman and minister, and $75,000 earned by his wife (the noted jazz pianist, Hazel Scott).[10] He owns fancy sports cars, several homes, and two boats. Since Powell does not hold his followers and workers by material benefits, they rarely feel cheated by his obvious material success. In part, the lack of resentment is probably due to the feelings of gratification less fortunate Negroes derive from the sight of Powell in

---

[8]See *Congresional Record*, 84th Cong., 2d Sess., 1956, CII, Part 9, 11773-883.

[9]See David E. Apter, "Political Modernization in Ghana and Uganda—An Essay in Political Anthropology," 1959 (mimeo).

[10]Hapgood, *op. cit.*, p. 3. Powell and his wife are now officially separated, and his worldly possessions may have decreased as a result.

expensive restaurants and night clubs. He is doing what many of them understandably would like to do. But in addition, his money and material benefits are not the basis of his political power. Since his organization is not built through the distribution of tangible rewards, Powell can possess an abnormally large share of such rewards without depriving his followers of what they feel ought to be theirs. They support him for other reasons and derive other rewards from his success.[11]

Dawson

William L. Dawson was at one time an expert and frequent user of many of the same kinds of appeals that now characterize Powell. As an insurgent Republican, seeking to force an entry into the regular organization in Chicago, Dawson was a well-known street-corner speaker with a magnetic personality. He built a personal following outside the machine, in part by holding out to them the hope of eventual material reward, and in part by arousing their interest in the race issues of the day and by appealing to their aspirations. After some success within the Republican Party (he served as an alderman from 1935 to 1939), Dawson joined the Democrats then under the leadership of Edward Kelly and Pat Nash. His entry into the party was the beginning of his first real career as a regular organization man, and it was the beginning of the end of his career as a purveyor of race rhetoric.

Kelly became mayor of Chicago, at about the same time that LaGuardia became mayor of New York. The implications of this

---

[11]Weber (op. cit., pp. 360-3) comments on various kinds of charismatic leaders who were themselves well rewarded (Germanic kings, Chinese monarchs, etc.) with benefits the followers did not share. The recruiting and paying of workers is part of the process (and problem) of routinization. This may become evident with control, in Powell's case, of a congressional committee and a district organization. Since it would be almost impossible to remove him from the committee chairmanship, and very difficult to attack him as district leader, he may be able to sustain both his personal appeal and his administrative structure. The interesting point thus far is that, contrary to Weber's view, Powell has not had to "deliver" beyond winning successive challenges to his position. (See Weber, op. cit., p. 360: "If he is for long unsuccessful, above all if his leadership fails to benefit his followers, it is likely that his charismatic authority will disappear.") The explanation in Powell's case seems to be that the need for "delivering" in terms of substantive ends and benefits has been in great part obviated by his success in finding and defeating political enemies. This would mean that the existence of an enemy is of crucial significance in permitting intangible, charismatic-ideological politics to function. One "delivers" in a purely formal sense by crushing the opposition.

difference are far-reaching. LaGuardia took over a city administration under heavy attack from the reformers, and proceeded to hasten the rate of reform and further weaken the political machine that he had defeated. Kelly inherited a city administration and a political machine which were intact and in reasonably good health, and he proceeded to strengthen both. At the very time when Tammany was being starved, the Cook County Democracy was being feasted. In New York, the path to political power and success was becoming uncertain and strewn with traps; in Chicago, the same path was more clearly than ever becoming a private road belonging to the Democratic machine. Once inside such an organization, Dawson discovered that rhetorical or other intangible appeals were not only no longer useful, they could be a positive embarrassment. The stock of material incentives which the machine held—patronage and favors—was enormous and growing. Power came to him who could distribute them, and the right to distribute them was reserved to those in good standing with the organization. Remaining in such good standing means, among other things, not dividing or weakening the organization by raising issues which split the machine or which require it to act against its own best interests.

Dawson created an organization in his ward, and extended it to other Negro wards, which attracted and held its workers mostly through the opportunity for jobs. In turn, the organization began the slow and laborious task of altering the voting habits of a Negro population which had been firmly committed to the Republican party. In part the switch of allegiance was accomplished simply by exploiting the national trend among Negroes to the Democratic party, in part it was done by providing services and favors to voters, and in part it was done by bringing them into a complex and thorough set of organizations which clustered about the political machine—women's auxiliaries, youth groups, building and block organizations, and so on. By 1942 the organization was able to send Dawson to Congress by a slim majority (in fact, Dawson was unable to carry his own ward at the time), and then to control an aldermanic election by delivering a winning majority to an organization Democrat who was being challenged by a popular, non-organization Democrat. From that time on, the size of the organization's majorities grew steadily until they reached a stable level of about three-to-one, where they have remained ever since. In the process, Dawson acquired influence over four other Negro ward leaders.

Several consequences flow in part from the character of the organization of which Dawson is a leader and the nature of the rewards which must be distributed to sustain it.

First, tangible rewards tend to be divisible in a sense in which intangible ones are not. The distribution of material rewards can be kept separate from other aspects of the leader's position. His role as a local politician can become a fairly specific one, permitting him to play other roles without creating conflicts. There need be no inevitable connection between local political leadership in Chicago and congressional political acitvity in Washington, D.C. Few expectations about Dawson's performance and style as a congressman are created among his constituents or his workers. Indeed, Dawson has gone to considerable lengths to divorce his Chicago base of support from his Washington field of action. There is little contact between the Washington and the Chicago office. The staffs are separately recruited and separately organized. The flow of communications between the two centers is relatively small.

The ward headquarters in Chicago performs most of the services to constituents which are necessary; relatively few demands reach Washington. Dawson is to a greater extent than most other congressmen freed from constituency pressures, and he deliberately cultivates this situation. Dawson attends to his constituency assiduously, but in a manner entirely different from Powell. Dawson's Chicago headquarters are located in the very heart of the most depressed Negro area in a modest building. It is drab on the outside and plain on the inside, and deliberately so. It is accessible to the least advantaged constituent and nothing about the office is allowed to make the constituent feel he is out of his element or in unfamiliar surroundings. Dawson, when in Chicago (and he is there frequently), spends almost all his time in his ward office. No appointment is necessary to see him, and the visitor need not state his business to the receptionist. On the bench outside his office on a typical day might be found a police captain, a couple on relief, a young Negro lawyer, an unemployed man, a politician, and a university professor. When Dawson is not in the city, his place is taken by lieutenants who function in the same fashion. His Washington office and its work load are markedly smaller than Powell's, or indeed of other congressmen generally. Where Powell has four staff workers in his Washington office, Dawson has one; where Powell receives five to eight hundred letters a week, Dawson receives one hundred; where Powell replies to 250 "case letters" (requesting information or services) per week, Dawson receives one-third as many. Where Powell mails out large numbers of *Record* reprints and other items, Dawson mails almost none.

Dawson cherishes his reputation as a congressman. He is the chairman of the House Government Operations Committee, one of the three or four largest and most powerful committees in the House. He is

highly esteemed by almost all his colleagues, who go out of their way
to compliment him and his committee. He enjoys the respect of many
southerners as well as large numbers of liberal northern Democrats. He
has built his committee since 1949 (when he became its chairman),
and his success is measured by the most important yardstick used in
government—the size of its budget. In the 81st Congress, it received
$300,000; in the 85th, $1,175,000. Its staff is competent and largely
free of purely patronage appointments; the proceedings of the committee reflect an attention to business and an aversion to simple
publicity that is unusual.

Dawson conceives of his Chicago organization as a base of support
which produces, without commitment to issues or similar appeals,
automatic majorities for him and his slate. For his role as Chicago
ward leader, Dawson has one set of attitudes and action. He is strong,
sometimes ruthless; he brooks no rivals; he crushes opposition and the
ambitions of men who would challenge him; and he insists on organizational loyalty. In Washington, he plays an entirely different role.
There, he is a leader interested in good government and liberal
measures. He presides over the committee with authority, but not
harshly. He encourages junior colleagues to take on new responsibilities and rise in committee work. He does not feel that he has rivals or
opponents, and is friendly with everyone. Although he has considerable power as a congressman, he rarely uses that power for political
ends in Chicago. By and large, the political power he has assembled
in Washington is used for national goals, and only rarely for Chicago
goals. Issues in Chicago affairs have arisen which were in some
measure vulnerable to congressional intervention. He did not inter-
vene.

One of the few themes common to both his local and national roles
is the avoidance of race as a public issue. As in Chicago, so in
Washington, Dawson rarely engages in a *public* discussion of race
goals. He has not used his committee staff as a source of "race patronage." Only two of the fifty staff members are Negroes. It is explained
that this reflects the shortage of qualified Negro personnel. The committee has wide jurisdiction, but rarely is its investigative power
turned toward explicitly racial issues. Some members of the staff
regret this. Many were unhappy about his opposition to the Powell
Amendment in 1956. On that occasion he ignored the requests of the
NAACP and the numerous representations made to him from people
in his district and not only voted but spoke out against the civil rights
amendment on the grounds that if it were adopted it would mean
southern opposition would be aroused and there would be no federal
education bill at all. Dawson, although on friendly terms with two of

the three other Negro congressmen, does not confine his association to them. He seems to prefer his wide range of contacts with many congressmen, particularly the House leadership. Although he is not a militant advocate of race ends in Congress. since 1956 he has not voted against such matters on the floor. Dawson, personally, feels that his political power can best be used for the advancement of Negroes in ways other than pressing for legislative correction of racial abuses. He sees himself as promoting Negro interests by intervening on their behalf with the authorities, placing more Negroes in government, and demonstrating the achievements possible for a Negro leader.[12]

The most important single source of controversy about Dawson is whether his political influence and position—which admittedly are rarely used publicly for race ends—are used in a private, unpublicized manner. Dawson and his supporters point to his intervention in many issues involving Negro rights. He has conferred with southern political leaders about Negro registration and segregation in party meetings and functions in the South. He intervened in the Emmet Till lynch case and moved to cut off the hostile, southern-led congressional investigation of school integration in Washington, D.C. All of these facts are difficult to document, given the secrecy which has surrounded them. The truth probably is that Dawson has had more effect than his critics allege and less than his most ardent supporters claim.

The other theme common to both Chicago and Washington is the extent to which Dawson shuns publicity. When Powell grants an interview, it is usually understood to be on the record; when Dawson does, it is almost always specified as off the record. Dawson's aversion to publicity is legendary, and goes far beyond that which is called for simply by prudence. He feels that he has been mistreated by an essentially hostile press, mostly in Chicago, that even friendly reporters are not allowed to print stories favorable to him, and that publicity invariably ends by embarrassing him or his political allies.

The *second* consequence of Dawson's position in an organization is the high degree of discretion he has on legislative matters. Dawson shuns race issues. His local organization meets weekly to hear Dawson and others speak; rarely is race a theme of their remarks. Dawson's attitude is that race progress must be made from within the party. If

---

[12]On this score, Dawson has had a series of conflicts with the executive branch on the distribution of patronage among Negroes. When the Democrats controlled the White House under Truman, Dawson saw himself in competition with the NAACP and similar groups for the right to make decisive endorsements. On occasion he intervened directly with the President on these matters after feeling slighted by presidential assistants who were in charge of patronage. NAACP leaders usually deny that they were attempting to undercut Dawson or that they were involved in patronage matters at all.

the organization can be persuaded to espouse race causes, well and good; if it cannot, then one must accept that fact as the inevitable cost of belonging. Dawson's view of appropriate race ends is largely confined to what has been termed elsewhere "welfare" ends—i.e., ends which are specific, direct, and tangible and which tend to improve the lot of the Negro without necessarily attaining some true measure of integration.[13] Party, not racial, unity is stressed.

Dawson has been challenged by individuals and voluntary associations such as the local NAACP for not taking more vigorous *public* stands on race issues such as lynching, the Democratic Party's platform on civil rights, and other matters. Dawson has been criticized in the Negro press. The important fact is that such challenges and criticisms account for little; his electoral strength is barely affected. Dawson, like Powell, is stronger than any single issue which might be used against him. He can survive almost any position he takes on any single issue. But unlike Powell, he need not devote himself to issues and aspirations. His freedom of choice in this matter is much wider. He can be far more deliberate in his choice of ends and means. He can devote himself almost entirely to the pursuit of other, non-racial goals without being penalized. His range of discretion regarding means to any important political ends is broad. This is true in part because he can afford the luxury of little or no publicity, and in part because he need not consider the extent to which the means he uses are endowed with value significance. Means, to Dawson, can be more completely instrumental than to Powell.

Nowhere is the contrast between the Dawson and Powell organizations more striking or important than in the differing roles of the Negro ministry. The ministry is politically significant only in those Negro communities where no independent base of political power exists—i. e., where there is no strong, patronage-oriented machine. Dawson has deliberately worked for twenty years to reduce or eliminate the role of the Negro minister as a political influence in Chicago, and he has in great part succeeded. A fundamental distinction between Negro political systems is whether they must work through existing mass organizations (churches and labor unions) or whether it is possible to organize the community *directly* for political ends.[14] Dawson, to be sure, has ministerial allies, but he discourages the participation of ministers in politics for the most part. Nor is Powell

---

[13]See my *Negro Politics*, Chap. VI.

[14]Cf., Hugh Douglas Price, "The Negro and Florida Politics, 1944-1954" *Journal of Politics*, XVII (May, 1955), 198-220. Price notes the decline in the political importance of Negro ministers and social organizations with the rise in Negro registration and the emergence of specific Negro political roles.

"dependent" on the ministers. The relationship is symbiotic; each needs the other. The distinction is between one system in which the ends and basis of influence of the politician are relatively *independent* of other ends and bases of influence in the community (as in Chicago) and the alternative system in which political ends and influences are *implicated* in the community (as in New York).

Third, Dawson stands in an entirely different relationship to his followers and workers than does Powell. Because of the character of the incentives used by Dawson to hold their allegiance and maintain discipline, he is subject to a set of constraints from which Powell is largely exempt. The "status gap" between Powell and his supporters is manifestly greater than the disparity between Dawson and his followers. Powell, since he embodies the racial goals and private aspirations of many of his followers, can enrich his own position without weakening his stature—indeed, he may enhance it. Dawson leads a group of men who fundamentally, although not exclusively, are in politics for more tangible rewards. Dawson weakens his position by the extent to which he appears to gain at the expense of his followers. His supporters must be convinced that they can gain in proportion to the gains of Dawson. If Dawson gains disproportionately to his followers, he causes resentment, jealousy, and antagonisms.

This speaks to the question of the nature of Dawson's political skills. In part, of course, they are the skills of any leader of men—the ability to move other men to act in accordance with one's intentions. This requires arranging the situation so that the wants of individuals lead them to act toward the ends of the leader. A typical, but short-sighted, view as to the basis of a machine leader's power is that he "controls patronage." This is an insufficient and in part a misleading explanation. In reality, it says little more than that a man is powerful because he is powerful. The question remains, *why* has *he* been able to grasp and retain control of patronage for the purpose of sustaining his organization? If control of patronage were the only variable, then Negro politics in Chicago might be in a state of constant factional rivalry. The essential element in the use of tangible incentives to sustain political organizations is that the followers must never be allowed to feel that the gains of breaking with the leader outweigh the costs of such a break. The leader ought to create a pattern of expectations among his followers which he appears willing to satisfy even at his own expense.

This is made possible when the leader, such as Dawson, derives intangible rewards from a political system that produces tangible rewards for the followers. Dawson's gratifications are not in money and material perquisites, but in prestige, the sense of power, and the fun of the game. He lives austerely, drives second-hand cars, avoids ostentation, spends money freely on others, and generally minimizes the outward or material rewards of his position. He does not appear to be competing with his followers for the scarce material rewards of politics. Perhaps he could afford greater outward display than he does, but it seems clear that the lack of such display enhances his position.[15]

Chicago and New York

These differences between the two organizations can be accounted for largely by the differences in the political systems of which they are parts. In New York, the steady weakening of the Tammany organization which has gone on since 1933 has made it difficult for it to enforce its will on its members and impossible for it to turn back the challenge of a man like Powell. Further, Tammany attempted, during the LaGuardia-Fusion period, to govern Harlem from outside the district, through "absentee" leaders whose influence rested in part on keeping Negro political leadership divided and off balance.[16] Tammany failed—in part through unwillingness and in part through lack of resources—to build a strong, centralized Negro leadership in Harlem. Powell now seeks to fill that void. After his election as a district leader (together with three other leaders allied with him) he sought to create a unified "Leadership Team" for Harlem. In January,

---

[15]Cf., Max Weber's description of the creative entrepreneur and his willingness to forgo immediate gain for the sake of investment and ultimate returns which may be only the sense of achievement and power. This can be contrasted to his subordinates or successors who have lost the ethic of work and sense of calling, occupy a bureaucratized position, and derive more material rewards. *The Protestant Ethic and the Spirit of Capitalism,* trans. R. H. Tawney (London: G. Allen and Unwin, 1930). Dawson is not alone in seeking intangible rewards for his political work. Many contemporary leaders such as Richard Daley of Chicago and David Lawrence of Pittsburg are men for whom politics is not a path to wealth. It would be interesting to analyze past "bosses" to see what rewards attracted the most successful of them, and how the shift in those rewards—in part resulting from closer public scrutiny—from tangible to intangible has altered recruitment patterns and leadership styles. It is likely that even many of the "old line" bosses—like Charles F. Murphy of New York—got less in a material sense out of politics than is commonly believed. Some of the bosses who failed to hold their power were conspicuously men who "took" out of proportion to the gains of their followers.

[16]Cf., *New York Times,* January 10, 1960, p. 1.

1960, Powell's group received control of the Tammany patronage in Harlem. Although he has now entered the regular organization, Powell's independent base of support and the paucity of the rewards Tammany can offer his followers means that Tammany needs Powell more than he needs it. All doubt on this matter was quickly dispelled when Powell made public attacks on New York political leaders for failing to give Negroes more representation in government, for denying Negroes patronage, for persecuting Borough President Hulan Jack (Powell's erstwhile political scapegoat), and for allowing police to drive out Negro numbers racketeers in favor of Italians.

Dawson's organization is a strong portion of a powerful city machine. The possibility of a Powell arising on Chicago's South Side is substantially reduced by this fact. In 1947-1955, an effort was made by a popular minister to become an independent political force in the community. He managed to serve two terms in the City Council as alderman of the Third Ward. But the Dawson organization defeated him in 1955 for several reasons—all of which are indicative of the differences in politics between Chicago and New York. The Dawson organization has available to it perhaps three times the amount of patronage available to comparable districts in Harlem. The independent had to fight, not a group of quarreling factions, but a single, organized opponent who was well-staffed with workers. The independent could gain relatively few civic allies; most were already committed to the strongest force in the community—the Dawson group. Although the independent was a minister, other ministers could not be mobilized as a solid group behind him. Finally, it was necessary in a city where the Democratic primary was invariably dominated by the regular organization for the independent to run as a Republican (where his sympathies happened to lie anyway) and this was a grave weakness in a community overwhelmingly Democratic. (Chicago's aldermanic elections are only nominally nonpartisan.) When the independent attempted to emulate Powell by moving from the city council to Congress, he had again to run as a Republican, and this was fatal.

Thus, the character of the political system into which Powell and Dawson moved in their formative years (the late 1930's and early 1940's) was of decisive importance in molding the kind of organization each created. Dawson found a strong, active apparatus in which he had to create a place for himself. Powell encountered a weak, divided organization which it was necessary neither to join nor to defeat.

Some Conclusions

Two important congressmen with roughly comparable constituencies have been compared. Both men, it has been argued, act as if the maintenance of their organizations were their goal. Since the organizations and the incentives necessary to maintain them differ, the political styles of the two men differ.

One organization was created and is sustained by a system of ideal or non-material benefits. This has certain consequences. (1) The benefits are indivisible, and the role of the leader who dispenses them tends to become diffuse and general. All aspects of his career are treated as part of a whole, and all choices relate to a single set of values. (2) The benefits have a sacred component, and thus are difficult to compromise. Means used to attain them share in the moral or sancrosanct quality of the ends themselves; means can only with difficulty be regarded as purely instrumental. (3) The ideal benefits which followers share permit the leader to indulge himself in outward display without alienating them—indeed, he may enhance his position with them. The other organization was created and is sustained by a system of tangible rewards. Among the consequences of this are: (1) The rewards are divisible and may be isolated to the local organization. The role of the leader can be specific and compartmentalized. He may separate his base of support from his national field of action. (2) The absence of race or ideological appeals gives the leader a greater discretion as to the choice of ends to pursue. Means tend to be more thoroughly instrumental. Few of his actions are deliberately imbued with moral significance. (3) The power of the leader in part depends on his ability to satisfy his followers that they gain in proportion to him—that he does not gain at their expense. The "status-gap" between the leader and the led is relatively small.

Further, it has been argued that the character of the two organizations, and hence the nature of their maintenance needs, can be traced to the political systems of which they are parts. One political system (Chicago) has a single leadership which disposes of a large amount of patronage, is unified, and can control its own primaries with ease. The other (New York) has a leadership which constantly must meet challenges, has a short supply of patronage, and cannot invariably control its own primaries. In the latter Powell succeeded; in the former, a Powell-like leader tried and failed.

This mode of analysis has an obvious shortcoming. A political style which may have been, at some early point, functional in terms of the needs of the situation, later tends to become temperamental. Political style tends to become the independent variable, *creating* in part the situation it had formerly served; that is, the image a leader creates of himself inevitably tends to react back on him and modify his behavior apart from what might be considered as the "objective" needs of the situation. Both Dawson and Powell undoubtedly carry many of their attributes to an unusual extreme, and settled habits have now replaced earlier experiments. But we need not linger too long on the problem of untangling the man from the situation, for however subtle a pattern of interaction exists between the two levels, the burden of the analysis remains this: the political style of the two leaders is functional to the organization they must maintain and the position they hold within the larger political system of which they are part.

It is interesting to note the opinion of these men held by prominent Negroes in New York and Chicago. Publicly, both have been criticized and even attacked. The *Chicago Defender* was critical of Dawson in 1956; the New York *Amsterdam News* supported Powell's opponent in 1958. But public criticism is far rarer and much more gentle than the private criticism which can be found directed at both men. The followers are aligned in two intent and mutually exclusive camps. Neither man has anything like universal admiration from the Negro middle class or from Negro intellectuals. Both are criticized by many thoughtful Negroes: Dawson for doing nothing, Powell for being irresponsible. At the same time, both get grudging respect from most Negro civic leaders—Dawson because of his personal position, his stature, and his power; Powell because he is "not afraid of the white man" and because he "stirs things up" and thus makes it easier for civic organizations to gain leverage against influential whites. The important aspect of the private praise and blame heaped on these men is that in the last analysis it is not concerned with ends or accomplishments. Neither leader has "accomplished" much in the way of legislation directed at race goals. Although Powell supporters criticize Dawson for "doing nothing," in fact, of course, Powell has no greater a list of accomplishments. And when pressed, many Negroes will concede this.

This means that most criticism of the two leaders centers on the nature of their political styles. In a situation in which *ends* are largely unattainable (at least by Negro action alone), *means* become all-important. On the basis of the means employed—the political style used—men make judgments as to the worth of the leader and his reputation. Means, in short, tend to become ends in themselves; what is important is not what you do, but how you do it. As pointed out earlier in another context, means acquire an "end-component" either because (a) ends are unattainable or (b) ends are morally endowed.

The relationship of leader to organization in these two cases raises interesting questions concerning the role of congressmen. It has often been assumed that one mark of the statesman is an interest in issues, rather than patronage, as the currency of politics. Schattschneider, for example, censures the "local bosses" because they are irresponsible and because they interfere in national politics to its detriment.[17] The thrust of this paper is that, for a variety of reasons, a "boss" may deliberately separate his local and national roles. Further, he may use his local machine (a) to filter out constituency demands by satisfying them at the local level and (b) to sustain himself in office without extensive or irrevocable commitments on policy matters and without accepting the support of organized pressure groups. The very position of a person such as Dawson enables him, if he chooses, to disregard both the localistic demands of constituents and the demands of local or national pressure groups. The needs of the constituents can be met largely on an issue-free basis; the demands of the pressure groups can be ignored, as they can do little either to help or harm the leader. In theory, this leaves the congressman free to pursue the public interest, however he chooses to define it. Rather than constraining him and rendering him irresponsible, the existence of the local machine may liberate him and permit him to vote as his conscience dictates. Congressmen without such a powerful and non-ideological base of support may have much less discretion in such matters.[18]

Aside from the theoretical advantages of such a position, there of course remains the empirical question whether a political leader who has risen through the ranks of a local machine would have any elevated view of the public interest. The way of life a machine creates for its members is such that it might render even its best

---

[17]E. E. Schattschneider, *Party Government* (New York: Farrar and Rinehart, Inc., 1942), esp. chap. vii. A valuable but neglected challenge to this view is A. L. Lowell, *The Government of England* (3rd ed.; New York: Macmillan Co., 1926), II, 91-5. Lowell presents an analysis of voting in the U.S. Congress among representatives from "machine" constituencies as well as in state legislatures. He concludes that there are few party votes in part because "the machine meddles little with general legislation" (p. 94).

[18]In fact, both Powell and Dawson can ignore most pressure groups nationally. Neither requires the support of organized labor, and they have frequently made labor lobbyists unhappy by their actions. Powell undoubtedly finds it in his interest to yield to the NAACP on most matters, although he probably could defy it on any single issue. But Powell cannot yield to any temptation to ignore the demands of his constituents for issue agitation on race matters.

leaders incapable of taking a broad and enlightened view of public affairs even though the organization enforces no constraints that would objectively prevent acting on the basis of such a view. In the psychological dimension of representation, there is a great variation in the roles played. Of all the Democrats in Congress supported by the Cook County organization, some take a narrow and routine view of their functions whereas others (such as Dawson) deliberately endeavor to act on the basis of an enlarged view of the functions of a congressman. No categorical judgments can be made on this point, but the interpretations presented in this study may suggest an approach to the re-examination of the impact of the constituency on the function of representation and a re-evaluation of the role of the local machine in contemporary politics.

The Ex-Plebes

Robert A. Dahl

Galpin, the Pecks, Brewster, Jerome, English, Welch, Sargent, and the other entrepreneurs transformed the political, social, and economic life of New Haven: they created a proletariat, and the proletariat—the "ex-plebes"—ultimately displaced them in public office and leadership of the political parties.

Coming of the Immigrants

Throughout the period of patrician rule, the artisan class had been of the same ethnic stock as the patricians themselves. In the 1820's, an Irishman was still a rarity in Connecticut. The number of immigrants entering the port of New Haven between 1820 and 1845 varied each year from six to less than a hundred.[1] But the new industries required workers; the era of the industrial entrepreneur was also the era of immigration. The Irish came first, starting at mid-century, with a small sprinkling of Germans, followed by the Italians and East Europeans in the 1880's. By 1870, 28 per cent of the people in New Haven were foreign-born, a proportion that remained almost exactly the same for the next three decades. By 1900, however, in four of the city's fifteen wards, two persons out of every three were immigrants. By 1910, one-third of New Haven's population was foreign-born and

Reprinted with permission of the publisher from Robert A. Dahl, *Who Governs? Democracy and Power in an American City*, pp. 32–51. Copyright 1961 by the Yale University Press.
[1]Morse, *A Neglected Period*, pp. 23, 286.

another third had at least one immigrant parent. In every ward in the city except the First Ward, first- and second-generation Americans made up more than half the population; and even in the First, where Yale and a few elegant residential areas still held the middle and upper classes, 46 per cent of the population were either immigrants or second generation. In four wards, nearly nine out of every ten residents were immigrants or had at least one foreign-born parent.

"Ethnics" and Politics

In New Haven as in many other cities, the "ethnic"—the immigrant, the Catholic, the Jew, the Negro—found that his ethnic identification colored his life, his relations with others, his attitudes toward himself and the world.[2] Ideas of equality and unlimited opportunity, stressed in the American ideology taught in schools and used on ceremonial occasions, often gave rise to expectations among immigrants and Negroes that were frustrated by the actual conditions in which they found themselves. Frequently, too, the ethnic felt a sharp conflict between normal needs for self-respect and the actual treatment he received. Many of his problems arose, of course, not merely because he was of foreign stock but because of all the factors associated with his immigrant origins: his education, speech, dress, demeanor, skills, income, neighborhood, ignorance of American institutions and folkways, and lack of self-confidence. In a nation where some citizens had great power, high prestige, and enormous income, the ethnic was often at the bottom of the pile. And when he looked about him, often the only citizens as badly off in power, prestige, and income were other ethnics; like as not, even some ethnic groups were already higher up the socioeconomic ladder than his own.

Any political leader who could help members of an ethnic group to overcome the handicaps and humiliations associated with their identity, who could increase the power, prestige, and income of an ethnic or religious out-group, automatically had an effective strategy for earning support and loyalty. Politicians themselves, in fact, were often ethnics who knew from personal experience the problems of an out-group. Probably no other political strategy held quite so much promise of capturing the loyalties of citizens for party coalitions. Hence the pol-

---

[2]The best examination of this question is in Irvin Child's study of second-generation Italians in New Haven, *Italian or American?* (New Haven, Yale University Press, 1943). For an historical treatment of another ethnic group in New Haven, see Robert Warner, *New Haven Negroes—A Social History* (New Haven, Yale University Press, 1940).

itics of New Haven became a kind of ethnic politics; it was a politics of assimilation rather than a politics of reform, a politics that simultaneously emphasized the divisive rather than the unifying characteristics of voters and yet played upon the yearnings for assimilation and acceptance.

But neither the strategies of politicians nor the yearnings of the ethnics entailed a root-and-branch attack on socioeconomic inequalities. On the contrary, the object was simply to enlarge the opportunities for ethnics to rise without undue discrimination in a system that contained built-in inequalities in the distribution of resources. Political leaders and their ethnic followings combined to use the political system in order to eliminate the handicaps associated with ethnic identity rather than to reduce disadvantages stemming from the distribution of resources by the existing socioeconomic order itself. The socioeconomic order was not considered illegitimate; discrimination *was*. Local politics—and for that matter state and national politics—was like a rope dangling down the formidable slope of the socioeconomic system. If the ethnic pulled himself up a bit with the help of the rope, he could often gain a toe hold in the system; the higher he climbed, the higher he could reach for another pull upward. He was not greatly interested in leveling the mountain itself.

Yet in spite of this fact, a paradoxical and highly important long-run consequence was to accelerate the transformation of a system of cumulative inequality of political resources into a system of dispersed inequalities.

Since political leaders hoped to expand their own influence with the votes of ethnic groups, they helped the immigrant overcome his initial political powerlessness by engaging him in politics. Whatever else the ethnics lacked, they had numbers. Hence politicians took the initiative; they made it easy for immigrants to become citizens, encouraged ethnics to register, put them on the party rolls, and aided them in meeting the innumerable specific problems resulting from their poverty, strangeness, and lowly position. To obtain and hold the votes, the political leaders rewarded them with city jobs. They also appealed to their desire for ethnic prestige and self-respect by running members of the ethnic group as candidates for elective offices.

Yet ethnic politics, like the politics of the patrician oligarchy and the entrepreneurs, is clearly a transitional phenomenon. The very success of politicians who use the ethnic approach leads to the obsolescence of their strategy. As assimilation progresses, new unities and cleavages supersede the old, and the politician whose only skill is ethnic politics becomes as obsolete as the patrician who responded to nineteenth-century democratic impulses with eighteenth-century techniques of oligarchy. In order to retain their positions, politicians are forced to search for new issues, new strategies, new coalitions.

It will help us to place ethnic politics in perspective if we hypothesize that an ethnic group passes through three stages on the way to political assimilation.

First stage: Members of an ethnic group in this stage are almost exclusively proletarian. They work with their hands, for wages, in shops and factories. In some socioeconomic characteristics, they are highly homogeneous. They are low in status, income, and influence. For leadership, they depend on influential politicians who have come from previously assimilated ethnic groups. Members of the new group serve sometimes as intermediaries between the group and the older leaders, acquiring in the process moderate influence and experience as subleaders. Some of these ethnic subleaders eventually receive nominations for minor offices, such as alderman, where the constituency is drawn predominantly from the subleaders ethnic group. In this stage, the group ordinarily has a high degree of political homogeneity; ethnic similarity is associated with similarity in political attitude, and there is a pronounced tendency toward voting alike. Ethnic ties are partly responsible, but in addition all aspects of life tend to converge and thus to create similar interests and political attitudes. Political homogeneity, then, is a function of socioeconomic homogeneity. Policies that will help an individual to cope with the problems created by his status as a first- or second-generation immigrant are not much different from policies that appeal to him as a wage-earner, a resident of a tenement in a ghetto, a member of a family with a low and uncertain income, a victim of unemployment, a person of little social prestige, or an object of discrimination by middle-class citizens of Anglo-Saxon stock.

Second stage: Socioeconomically, the group has become more heterogeneous. It is no longer predominantly proletarian. An increasing and by now significant proportion of the group have white-collar jobs and other social characteristics of the middling strata. Higher status, income, and self-confidence allow some to gain considerable political influence. They begin to challenge and overthrow the incumbent leaders on whom they hitherto have been dependent; amid charges of betrayal and ingratitude they now move into positions of leadership. Depending on the size of his ethnic group and local attitudes, an ethnic leader may even receive a major party nomination for a leading city-wide office, such as the mayoralty, that cannot be won simply by the votes of his own ethnic group. Although the political homogeneity of the group declines in this stage because of the increasing differentiation of the middling segments from the working-class strata, even the middling segments retain a high sensitivity to their ethnic origins. Consequently, an ethnic candidate who can avoid divisive socioeconomic issues is still able to activate strong sentiments of ethnic solidarity in all strata of his ethnic group; he can command a significantly higher proportion of the votes of his group than can a candidate without the ethnic tie.

Third stage: Socioeconomically, the group is now highly heterogeneous. Large segments are assimilated into the middling and upper strata; they have middle-class jobs, accept middle-class ideas, adopt a middle-class style of life, live in middle-class neighborhoods, and look to others in the middling strata for friends, associates, and marriage partners. To these people, ethnic politics is often embarrassing or meaningless. Political attitudes and loyalties have become a function of socioeconomic characteristics. Members of the group display little political homogeneity. Although sentimental and traditional attachments to a particular party may persist, they are easily ruptured. The political effectiveness of a purely ethnic appeal is now negligible among the middling and upper strata. A middle-class or upper-class candidate who happens to be drawn from an ethnic group may use this tie to awaken sentiments of pride; he may win votes, but to do so he must also emphasize socioeconomic issues, even though stressing such issues may split his ethnic group wide open.

In New Haven different ethnic groups have been passing through these stages at different times in the course of the last century. One stage merges so imperceptibly into the next that it would be foolish to attribute much significance to precise dates; but something like the following is perhaps useful as an impressionistic summary of assorted evidence on occupations, residence, and voting patterns.

	First Stage	Second Stage	Third Stage
Germans	1840-1880	1880-1920	1920-
Irish	1840-1890	1890-1930	1930-
"Russians"	1880-1920	1920-1940	1940-
Italians	1880-1930	1930-1950	1950-
Negroes[3]	1784-1950	1950-	

[3]In 1791, there were 207 Negroes in New Haven, of whom 78 were slaves; Negroes then comprised 4.5% of the population. In 1830, there were 941 free Negroes and 43 slaves. The proportion of slaves to free Negroes continued to decline until 1848, when slavery was abolished in Connecticut. See Warner, *New Haven Negroes,* p. 300.

Rise of the Ex-plebes

Long before the last industrialist was elected mayor, the immigrants had secured representation on the Board of Aldermen. As late as 1855 the mayor, the aldermen, the treasurer, the clerk, the collector of taxes, and the members of the Committee on Finance (later called Board of Finance) were all business or professional men of New England stock. But in 1853 the city had been divided into four wards; in 1857 the four wards became six; later they grew to ten, twelve, and by 1909 they numbered fifteen. Once aldermen began to be elected from wards, the immigrants were bound to elect some of their own people.

The first man with a distinctly Irish name appeared on the Board in 1857 as the alderman from the Third Ward; since that time (despite changes in ward boundaries) the Third invariably has elected at least one Irishman[4] as alderman or councilman. In 1900, when 69 per cent of the people in the Third were foreign-born, its two aldermen were a plumber named Corcoran and a painter named McGill. Six of the then twelve wards in the city were evidently electing Irishmen as early as about 1880. The Germans, a smaller group who seem to have moved more rapidly out of the working class than the Irish, began appearing on the Board of Aldermen in 1886; at least four men from well-known German-Jewish business families served on the Board at various times between 1866 and 1884.

By 1900, the Boards of Aldermen and Finance had been transformed not only in ethnic but also in occupational composition. The proportion of businessmen had declined drastically (Figure 1) as men with clerical and laboring jobs assumed their places. (Figure 2) Of the thirty aldermen in 1900 (two from each ward), the majority were neither patricians nor leading businessmen. In addition to the plumber and the painter, there were three saloon keepers, three foremen, three factory employees, two bill collectors, two druggists, two salesmen, a grocer, a shipping clerk, a florist, and a linotype operator. One of the two aldermen from the Fifth Ward was unemployed (the other was one of the three saloon keepers). The rest included three lawyers, a doctor, an assistant superintendent at Winchester's, and three

---

[4]To avoid cumbersome phrases, I refer throughout this book to Americans of Irish stock as Irishmen, to Americans of Italian stock as Italians, to Americans of English or Scotch-Irish stock long in New England as Yankees, etc. I hope the sensibilities of my readers will not be offended by usages that in other contexts are sometimes meant or felt to be invidious. Here the terms are intended only as convenient, succinct, descriptive, neutral, and widely understood labels.

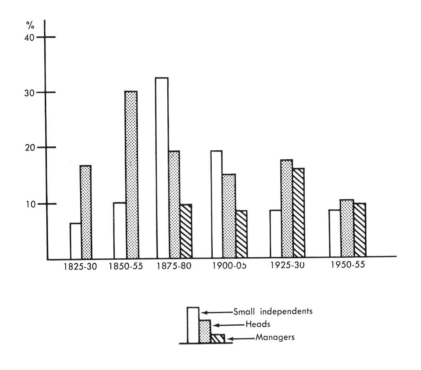

Figure 1

Business on the Boards of Aldermen and Finance as percentage of total membership during five-year periods, 1825–1955

people who ran their own small businesses. The president of the Board was the alderman from the Twelfth Ward, a druggist named Cornelius H. Conway.

In the city elections of 1897, the Democrats had lost when they split their votes between a Gold Democrat and a Silver Democrat. Two years later they united around Cornelius R. Driscoll, a lawyer living on Wooster Street in the heart of the old Fifth Ward (the present Tenth Ward), which had been densely populated by the Irish and was then receiving vast numbers of Italian immigrants, Driscoll, an Irishman from County Cork and a Roman Catholic, had helped to found the Knights of Columbus in 1882. He had been sent from the Fifth Ward to the City Council and to the Board of Aldermen. In 1899, with the Democrats behind him, he defeated the Republican incumbent (who was the president and treasurer of a foundry) and thereby became the first immigrant to be elected mayor of New

Haven. Since Driscoll's time every victorious Democratic candidate for mayor has been an Irish Catholic.

If the Republicans had not had the foresight to see that in order to survive they would have to break the hold of the Democrats on the recent Americans, doubtless New Haven would soon have become a predominantly one-party community like so many other American cities. But about the time of Driscoll's election, two brothers of German extraction and Jewish faith, Isaac and Louis Ullman, began moving into undisputed control over the New Haven Republican party. In many ways, they were replicas of the Yankee businessmen of the preceding period. Their father, an immigrant coachman, died when they were young; their mother, also an immigrant from Germany, took in washing; the boys themselves began peddling newspapers in their early teens. Later they both went to work for the Strouse-Adler Corset Company, then the largest corset manufacturing concern in the

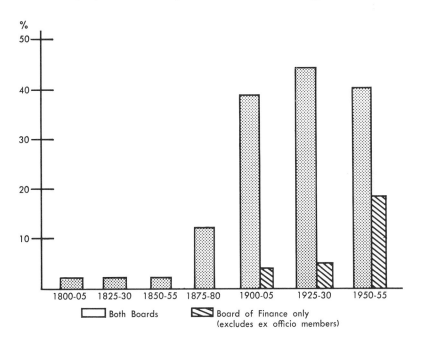

Figure 2

*Clerical and working-class occupations on the Boards of Aldermen
and Finance as percentage of total membership during
five-year periods, 1800–1955*

United States and with its 3,000 employees one of the biggest firms in New Haven. Its president, Max Adler, was a leading figure in the business and civic life of New Haven. Isaac Ullman soon became a foreman; Louis was his assistant. Later Isaac married Max Adler's daughter and, with the support of his father-in-law, quickly became president of the firm. Louis married the young widow of Edwin Strouse, a son of the principle owner, and his father-in-law, a pioneer New Haven cigar manufacturer named Lewis Osterweis, bought him a one-third interest in the corset company; Louis too, became a leading official in the company.

What distinguished the Ullmans from the earlier entrepreneurs, however, was not simply their German-Jewish background but their passion for politics. Indeed, unlike the Yankee businessmen who preceded them in politics, they seem to have preferred political entrepreneurship to business; in fact, when the fortunes of the corset company declined badly after the First World War, critics of their business conduct said that the Ullman brothers had been more interested in winning votes for the Republican party than winning customers for their corsets. However that may be, the Ullmans gained control of the Republican party in the first decade of this century and pretty much ran it for a generation.

They were shrewd enough to know that Republicans could not win against Irish-Catholic Democrats by running wealthy Yankee manufacturers for office and appealing only to Yankee voters. They therefore went into the Italian wards, which had been neglected by the Irish ward leaders in the Democratic party, and helped to pull some of the Italians into the Republican ward organizations. In 1909, the Republicans won the mayoralty election with Frank J. Rice, who was almost the last Yankee to be elected mayor of New Haven. Rice was, however, no great entrepreneur; he had been a trolley conductor, a manager of properties for a real estate firm, and president of the Young Men's Republican Club.[5] On his death in office after his fourth election in 1915, he was succeeded by Samuel Campner, president of the Board of Aldermen. Campner, a Jew, had been born in Russia and brought to New Haven as an infant; he went to Yale College and the Yale Law School and became a properous lawyer and distinguished member of the New Haven Jewish community.[6]

---

[5]N. G. Osborn, ed., *Men of Mark in Connecticut*, 5 (Hartford, William R. Goodspeed, 1910), 377.

[6]M. H. Mitchell, ed., *History of New Haven County* (Chicago and Boston, Pioneer Historical Publishing Co., 1930), 2, 378-81.

The election of 1917 saw Samuel Campner, a Russian Jew, running against David Fitzgerald, an Irish Catholic. Though his parents were Irish immigrants, Fitzgerald himself had been born in New Haven; like Campner he had gone to Yale College and to the Yale Law School, and had become a prosperous lawyer.[7] Both were members of the Racebrook Country Club, a suburban club deliberately organized by a group of Protestants, Catholics, and Jews as an alternative to the New Haven Country Club, which then closed its doors to both Jews and Catholics. In the election Campner carried only five wards out of fifteen, and Fitzgerald won hands down.

From that time on, both parties usually nominated candidates who did not suffer from the handicap of being Yankee. Since Fitzgerald's time, the Democratic party leader has invariably been a Roman Catholic; by the mid-thirties, after the Ullmans had passed from the scene, the acknowledged Republican leader was also an Irish Catholic. In 1939, however, the Republican nominee for mayor was an undertaker of Italian parentage; although this time he lost, he finally won in his second try in 1945. His election marked the growing influence of the Italians, who by that time outnumbered the Irish. In 1959, the Republican town chairman was also of Italian origin; he ran the party in an uneasy coalition with the old Irish-Catholic boss, whose power had waned. The Democratic party was dominated by a triumvirate consisting of the mayor, a Roman Catholic of mixed Irish, English, and Scottish antecedents; the national committeeman, an Irish insurance broker prominent in Catholic lay activities; and the town chairman, a man of Italian ancestry.

Meanwhile equally significant changes were occurring in the occupations of political leaders. Not a single manufacturer or executive of a large corporation has been elected mayor in the twentieth century. Of the eleven mayors in this period, five have been lawyers (though none of these were with the leading law firms of New Haven); the rest include a real estate operator, a garage owner, an official of a printing firm, a business agent for a union, an undertaker, and a director of publicity for Yale.

Nothing less is revealed than a massive invasion of the political system by the ethnics. City jobs, minor offices, major elective and appointive offices—all fell before the irresistible tide of the plebes and ex-plebes of immigrant stock. With respect to city jobs, a survey

---

[7]Osborn, *Men of Mark*, 5, 511, and Charles W. Burpee, *Burpee's The Story of Connecticut* (New York, American Historical Co., 1939), 4, 848-49.

of 1,600 New Haven families made in 1933 by the Yale Institute of Human Relations furnishes an interesting snapshot of the state of affairs at that time. (Figure 3) By 1933, the Irish had become by far the most numerous in holding city jobs; politics was evidently one of the main routes the Irish took to climb out of the wage-earning class. Although the Irish comprised only 13 per cent of the families in the sample, they held almost half the jobs in city government. Not all city positions were, to be sure, white-collar jobs; but as school teachers, clerks, aldermen, commissioners, and even mayors, the Irish had gained a place for themselves in the middling strata of New Haven. By this time they were evidently also receiving a fair share of white-collar jobs in private industry. They had not yet won their way into business and the professions, where their connections were still weak, though some of the business and professional people of American-born parents, who made up 60 per cent of the total, were no doubt of Irish extraction. With a foothold in the middle classes gained through politics and city jobs, in the next two decades the Irish moved rapidly into

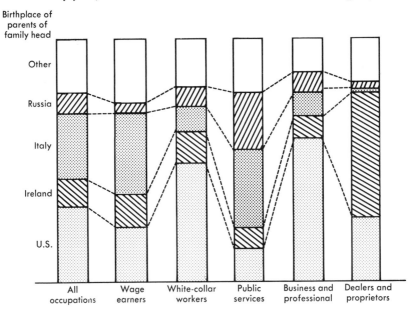

Source: John W. McConnell, *The Evolution of Social Classes* (Washington, D.C., American Council on Public Affairs, 1942) Table I, p. 214.

Figure 3

Occupations of family heads in New Haven, 1933

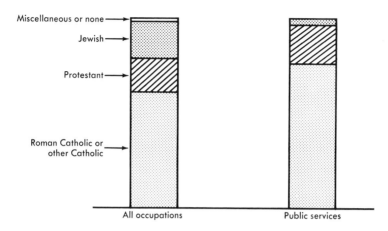

Source: McConnell, *Evolution of Social Classes.*

Figure 4

Religious affiliations of family heads in New Haven, 1933

business and professional life. Due largely to the Irish, three out of four family heads in public service in New Haven in 1933 were Catholic, though Catholics comprised only 56 per cent of the sample.

Irish domination of government jobs made it more difficult of course for later immigrants, particularly Italians and East Europeans, to climb the socioeconomic ladder by pulling themselves up with the help of white-collar patronage. In addition to this, however, distinctive cultural backgrounds probably promoted a stronger tendency among Jews and Italians to go into small business. The Irish had brought with them no tradition of business enterprise or the learned professions. By contrast, immigrants of Russian origin were mainly Jews whose exodus followed a series of pogroms beginning in 1881;[8] they were more accustomed to the world of business, particularly as small shop-owners, and they also brought with them a traditional respect for learning and the professions. The Italians, too, were evidently more inclined than the Irish to become peddlers and shopkeepers. In fact, the Russians and the Italians together made up almost two-thirds of the shopkeepers in the 1933 family survey. Where the Irish used politics to surmount obstacles to their advance in the

---

[8]Osterweis, *Three Centuries of New Haven,* pp. 372 ff.

socioeconomic world, Italians and Jews more frequently used gains in the socioeconomic world to attain elective positions in politics.

Myers has traced the movement of Italians to jobs in the city government from 1890 to 1940.[9] They first began receiving jobs as city employees between 1900 and 1910, probably as a result of the efforts of the Ullman brothers; after 1910 their share of patronage grew rapidly. However, by 1940, a year after William Celentano was defeated in the first bid of an Italian for mayor, they held only about half their "quota"[10] of the lowest jobs in city government—janitors and laborers—and only a third of their "quota" of the top appointive positions. (Table 1)

Even though the Italians were to some extent blocked by the Irish and the Yankees from city jobs, the professionals nonetheless found it advantageous to appeal to Italian voters by including Italian candidates for elective office on the party ticket; ever since 1890 Italians

TABLE 1
Italians in city jobs, 1890–1940

Group	Percentage of Italian "quota" fulfilled in:					
	1890	1900	1910	1920	1930	1940
Appointive boards and commissions	0	0	0	24	13	34
Department heads, city executives	0	0	0	0	0	33
Teachers, professional workers	0	0	3	9	14	22
Clerical workers, firemen, policemen	0	0	2	6	16	21
Janitors, custodians, laborers	0	0	0	15	27	56

Source: Myers, "Assimilation in the Political Community," Tables 2 and 3. Myers made his estimates from names in city directories and manuals. For an explanation of "quota," see footnote 10.

[9]Jerome K. Myers, "Assimilation in the Political Community," Sociology and Social Research, 35 (1951), 175-82. See also his "Assimilation to the Ecological and Social Systems of a Community," American Sociological Review, 15 (1950), 367-72.

[10]By "quota," I mean that if the proportion of Italians in city jobs were the same as the proportion of Italians in the population, the "quota" would be fulfilled 100%. Half the quota means that Italians had half as many city jobs as they would if jobs were distributed according to the size of the Italian group in the city population.

have been nominated in considerable numbers. By 1940 leaders of Italian stock were moving into positions of key influence in the Republican party. In the minor elective offices, as Myers shows, the Italians were receiving their fair share by 1940, though they still ran a little behind in the more important elective plums. (Figure 5)

In 1945, an Italian Republican candidate for mayor was elected, and the Italians were at last at the top in local politics. After winning the mayoralty election in 1953, the Democrats made vigorous efforts to overcome the historical alienation of Italians from the Irish-dominated Democratic party; among other things the new mayor appointed a man of Italian stock to the politically important post of director of public works. By 1959, the Italians were winning their full share of both major and minor elective offices. In fact, the three largest ethnic groups—Irish Catholics, Italian Catholics, and Jews—were, if anything, all over-represented in elective posts.[11] (Table 2)

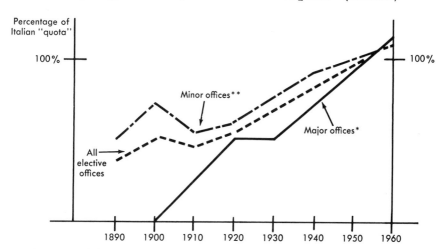

*Mayor, city clerk, treasurer, collector of taxes, sheriff, town clerk, registrar of vital statistics, registrar of voters, aldermen.

**Selectmen, constables, grand jurors, justices of the peace.

Source: For 1890-1940 figures, see Myers, "Assimilation in the Political Community," Table 1 and p. 178. For source of 1959 figures, see Table

Figure 5

Italians in elective offices, 1890–1959

[11]Because fourth-generation Americans of Irish or Italian stock would not meet the criteria of Table 2, there is undoubtedly some underestimate of those who might identify themselves as Irish or Italian. The Irish in particular are probably significantly underestimated.

TABLE 2

Ethnics in Elective Offices, 1959

	Registered voters %	Major offices held %	Minor offices held %
Ethnic group			
Italian	31	34	33
Irish	11	29	11
Jewish	15	19	24
Other	43	17	31
Total	100	99	99
N	525	41	96

Source: Figures for registered voters are from our survey in 1959. Respondent was identified as Italian or Irish only if a parent or grandparent was born there, with father's birthplace determining in case of conflict. "Jewish" represents stated religious preference. Breakdown of major and minor offices follows Myers, "Assimilation in the Political Community." Ethnic affiliation of office holders determined by name or direct information.

Ethnic Politics, 1900-1950

From about 1900 on, political leaders in both parties played the game of ethnic politics. The Democrats were more successful at it, probably because they started first. The Democratic party was overwhelmingly the party of the immigrants by 1900 and remained so until about 1940, when the Republicans began to make new inroads on the loyalties of the ethnics.

In the presidential election of 1904, the proportion of foreign-born residents in a ward was closely related to the percentage of the total two-party vote from that ward that went to the Democratic candidate. (Figure 6) In the next two elections, this relationship was weaker, probably because some Italians defected to the Republican party with the encouragement of the Ullmans. The correlation then remained moderately close and steady until 1928, when support from the immigrant wards for Democratic presidential candidates rose to a high level that was sustained until 1940. In that year a decline in the correlation commenced that was only temporarily interrupted by the 1948 election.[12] The story has been much the same in elections for

---

[12]The significance of the figures rests partly on the assumption that the proportion of foreign-born in a ward is highly correlated with the proportion of persons of recent immigrant background whether or not they were born abroad. A similar assumption is made in identifying Italian, Russian, or Irish wards.

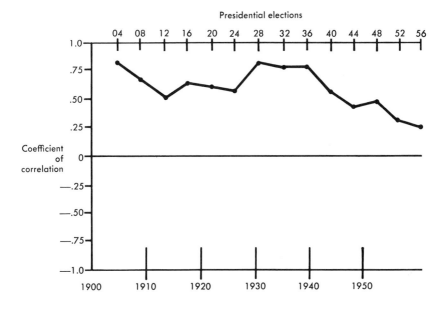

Figure 6

*Relation between percentage of foreign-born residents in New Haven
wards and percentage of two-party vote cast for Democratic
candidates for president, 1904–1956*

mayor (Figure 7), except that the breakdown in the relationship
since 1939 is more obvious.

After the split in the mayoralty election in 1897 between Gold
Democrats and Silver Democrats, some of the conservative Democrats—business and professional men horrified by William Jennings
Bryan,—evidently began to find the Republican party more to their
liking. Thus Yankees deserted the Democrats as Irishmen like Cornelius Driscoll moved to the top. By the end of the first decade, a
pattern was well-established that held for half a century; in local
elections the Irish were mostly in one party, the Yankees in the other.
Figure 8 shows how the ward with the fewest foreign-born—and
presumably the largest number of Yankees—was consistently Republican in every mayoralty election in this century until 1953. By contrast,
the ward with the greatest percentage of Irish foreign-born, and
probably the heaviest concentration of Irish stock, voted Democratic
by a large margin in every election except two throughout the entire
six decades.

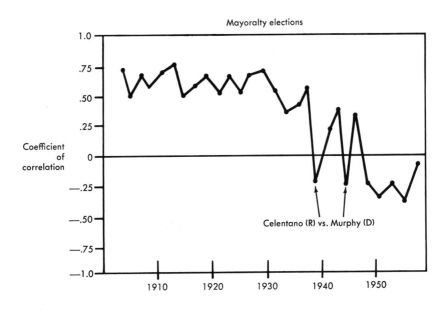

Figure 7

*Relation between percentage of foreign-born residents in New Haven
wards and percentage of two-party vote cast for
Democratic candidates for mayor, 1903–1959*

Obviously the middle-class Yankees were too greatly outnumbered
by the proletarian immigrants and their children to retain much voice
in a political system that was sharply split on precisely these lines. It
was a brilliant strategy, then, when the Ullmans, whose own origins
doubtless gave them a much better understanding of the desires of
immigrants than the Yankees possessed, set out to lure the Italian
proletariat into a coalition with the Yankee middle classes. They had a
good deal to work with, including the prestige and wealth of the
Yankees, resentments between the Irish and the Italians, and patronage. Although the Ullmans did not succeed in welding the Italians
into a solid bloc of Republican votes, their strategy did preserve
effective two-party competition in New Haven by providing the Republican party with a base of support among an important immigrant
group.

In the three wards with the greatest number of Italians, the greater
the proportion of Italians the smaller the Democratic vote has been in

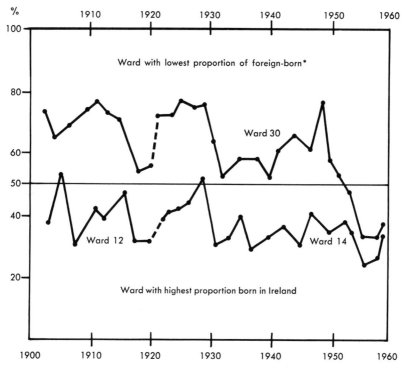

*The Nineteenth Ward, which was 72% Negro in 1950, and the First
Ward, heavily populated by Yale students, were excluded.

Figure 8

*Republican vote, as percentage of two-party vote, in ward with
highest proportion of Irish residents and ward with lowest proportion
of foreign-born residents—mayoralty elections, 1901–1959*

mayoralty elections over the past sixty years. (Figure 9) In the Tenth
Ward, in 1910, half the population was foreign-born; four out of five
of these were Italian; in fact, until the census of 1940, when it was
passed by two other wards, the Tenth had the largest proportion of
Italian-born residents. Throughout the century, the Tenth has given
more support to Republican candidates for mayor than the Eleventh,
which is the next most densely Italian-populated. The Eleventh, in
turn, has regularly voted more heavily Republican than the ward with
the next highest density of Italian residents.[13] Except for the elec-

---

[13]To avoid confusion I have used present ward numbers.

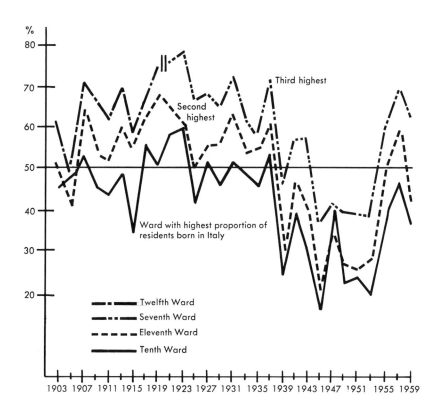

Figure 9

*Democratic vote, as percentage of two-party vote, in three wards
with highest proportion of residents born in Italy—
mayoralty elections, 1903–1959*

tion of 1948, the same pattern has held in presidential elections.
(Figure 10)

Yet despite the fact that the Republicans made inroads in the old
Democratic monopoly among the ethnics, even among the Italians
support for Democratic candidates was high. The densely Italian
Tenth Ward, which gave greater support to the Republicans than any
other immigrant ward, voted more strongly Democratic than the rest
of the city in about two out of three elections for president or mayor
up to 1939. (Figure 11) In the same period the next two most densely
Italian wards cast majorities for Democratic mayoralty candidates in

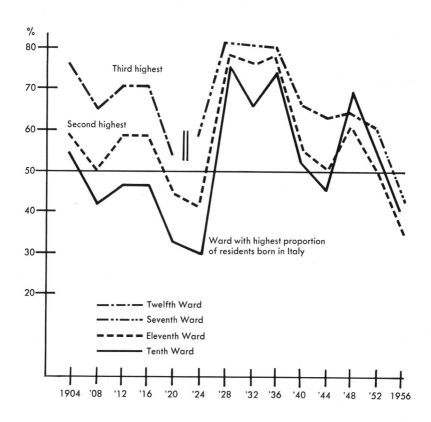

%

Third highest

Second highest

Ward with highest proportion
of residents born in Italy

— · — · — Twelfth Ward
— · · — · · Seventh Ward
— — — — Eleventh Ward
———— Tenth Ward

1904 '08 '12 '16 '20 '24 '28 '32 '36 '40 '44 '48 '52 1956

Figure 10

*Democratic vote, as percentage of two-party vote, in three wards
with highest proportion of residents born in Italy—
presidential elections, 1904–1956*

every election except one and generally exceeded the Democratic
vote of the city as a whole by a substantial margin; in every presidential election from 1904 through 1936 these two wards voted more
heavily Democratic than the city as a whole by margins never less
than 8 per cent and sometimes over 20 per cent.

The fact is that throughout most of this period the Italians of New
Haven were in their first stage of political, social, and economic
assimilation. They were predominantly workers, near the lower end of
the socioeconomic scale. Like other immigrants, they felt the pull of

the Democratic party. Normally, the Republican fraction of the Italian voting population should have continued to expand as the middle class grew. But Alfred E. Smith and the Great Depression reversed this trend.

The presidential candidacy of Smith in 1928 gave the Democrats an enormously powerful appeal to all ethnic groups in New Haven, not only because of Smith's Catholicism, which generated sympathy among the Irish and Italians, but also because of his stress on the familiar problems of urban wage earners. The effect of his candidacy on the ethnics of New Haven was electrifying. (Figure 6) Smith attracted the Irish, already a dwindling minority in New Haven, but as Figure 10 reveals he also won the Italians. In the three main Italian wards the vote for Smith ran 18-25 per cent higher than in the city as a whole. The Depression, extensive unemployment among the Italian working classes, and the New Deal continued the process that Smith had begun. The three most densely Italian wards supported Roosevelt in 1932 and 1936 as heavily as they had Smith in 1928.

As jobs became available and war neared, ethnic factors reasserted themselves locally and nationally among the Italians, who had by this time reached the second stage of assimilation in New Haven. As we have seen, William Celentano was nominated for mayor by the Republicans in 1939; no person of Italian origin had ever before been nominated for such a high post. The policies of strict economy pursued by the incumbent Democratic mayor and the prescriptive right of the Irish to city jobs weakened any economic or social appeal a Democratic mayor might have had for Italians. In 1937 the three most densely Italian wards had gone Democratic. In 1939 there was a net shift in the city of 10 per cent to the Republicans, but in the three Italian wards, the net shift was about 30 per cent. Celentano lost that election by a small margin, but in the Tenth and Eleventh Wards he carried more than seven voters out of every ten.

As a burgeoning defense economy soaked up the unemployed and President Roosevelt revealed with increasing frankness his sympathy for the Allies, Italian support for the Democrats also declined at the national level. In 1940, Roosevelt accused Mussolini of delivering a cowardly "stab in the back" to France as she sought vainly to defend herself against the Nazis. War with Italy grew imminent. In the presidential election of 1940, Roosevelt's vote declined sharply in the three Italian wards (as it did in Italian areas elsewhere in the United States); it remained low in 1944. (Figure 10) In 1945, Celentano ran again for mayor on the Republican ticket. This time, the disaffection of school teachers and parents added a large bloc of hitherto Dem-

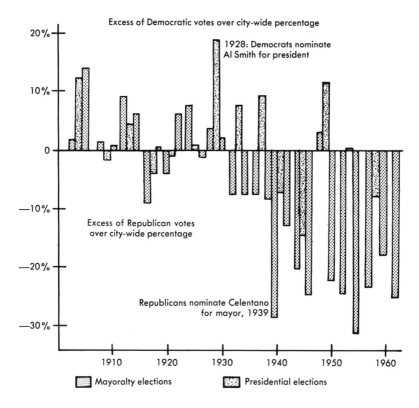

Excess of Democratic votes over city-wide percentage

1928: Democrats nominate
Al Smith for president

Excess of Republican votes
over city-wide percentage

Republicans nominate Celentano
for mayor, 1939

▦ Mayoralty elections   ▨ Presidential elections

Figure 11

*The Tenth Ward: extent to which percentages of Democratic
or Republican votes have exceeded city-wide percentages
in elections for president and mayor, 1903–1959*

ocratic voters—many of them Irish—to the Yankee-Italian coalition
that had narrowly lost in 1939, and this time Celentano won. In the
Italian wards, Celentano's support was even greater than it had been
in 1939. (Figure 9) Two years later the Democrats managed to split
the Italian community by running a dentist of Italian origin for
mayor. But they lost so disastrously in the rest of the city that they
made no further attempt to repeat the strategy. As a strategy for the
Democrats, old-fashioned ethnic politics had obviously become a losing game. After a brief period of success the same thing was destined
to happen to the Republicans. By the end of the 1950's, ethnic politics

was on the decline in New Haven. And the ex-plebes who knew nothing but the skills of ethnic politics were—like the patricians and the entrepreneurs before them—gradually giving way to new leaders.

What the immigrants and the ex-plebes had accomplished, however, was a further split in political resources. Popularity had been split off from both wealth and social standing. Popularity meant votes; votes meant office; office meant influence. Thus the ex-plebes completed the transition from the old pattern of oligarchy based upon cumulative inequalities to new patterns of leadership based upon dispersed inequalities.

Part 4

The Persistence of Ethnic Group Politics

Is there a role for ethnic groups in future American politics? Two quite different concepts have dominated the consideration of this problem: that of Americanization or acculturation and that of the melting pot or assimilation. The extraordinary degree to which many ethnics have adopted the life styles of the majority is undeniable; yet many maintain their ethnic identification. As Theodore Lowi cogently put it: "Dual loyalties are nothing new to the United States."[1] Under such circumstances it is not easy to determine the future role of ethnic groups in the American political system. It is possible, however, on the basis of present evidence, to hazard some guesses about the probabilities of the persistence of ethnic group politics.

Some scholars see the decline of ethnic minorities in politics as indicative of their assimilation into American society.[2] Others such

---

[1]Theodore J. Lowi, *At the Pleasure of the Mayor* (New York: The Free Press of Glencoe, 1964), p. 44.

[2]Duane Lockard, *New England State Politics* (Princeton, N.J.: Princeton University Press, 1959), p. 308.

251

as Robert Dahl argue that ethnic minorities are of increasing importance in politics but that contrariwise this is a mark of their assimilation into the American mainstream. In the first article, using the case of New Haven, Dahl documents the extent to which he sees this assimilation coming about. He argues, essentially, that class politics will not necessarily replace ethnic politics but that, except among Negroes, ethnicity as a factor must certainly recede since the strategies of both class and ethnic politics have been unsuitable for dealing with the burning issues of the last decade.

Many scholars do not see ethnic politics declining in significance despite the increasing assimilation of ethnic minorities in the American mainstream. Raymond Wolfinger, for example, argues that although many ethnic group members have acquired middle class status and identify more with the majority society, parties continue to compete for the support of ethnics by parcelling out rewards in an "ethnic way"—balancing tickets, making ethnic appointments, etc. Ethnic group identification is thus heightened and politics continues to be structured as ethnic conflict.[3]

Michael Parenti, however, questions the assimilationist theory of Dahl and the alternate explanations of Wolfinger in the second article. He argues that "the question why do ethnics continue to vote as ethnics despite increasing assimilation" is the wrong one to ask, "because the answer may simply be that minorities are not assimilating."[4] Parenti suggests that the failure to perceive what is happening to ethnic politics lies in the failure to make a conceptual distinction between acculturation and assimilation.

Acculturation, Parenti says, has to do with the accommodation to American life styles and customs; assimilation with one's incorporation into the structural-identificational group relations of the dominant society. Acculturation, then, is the ethnic group's acceptance of the beliefs, styles, approaches and modes of adjustment to the environment. When this is accomplished within the context of our society one is said to have become "Americanized." Assimilation involves the ethnic group's relations with the host society. Assimilation into the larger society assumes primary and secondary group relations which extend beyond one's fellow ethnics. When such relations exist on a large scale, ethnic consciousness is reduced. Utilizing this distinction, Parenti concludes that acculturation, not assimilation, is taking place

[3]Raymond E. Wolfinger, "The Development and Persistence of Ethnic Voting," *American Political Science Review,* LIX (December 1965) 899.

[4]Michael Parenti, "Ethnic Politics and the Persistence of Ethnic Identification," *American Political Science Review,* LXI (September 1967), 718.

and that ethnics will continue to behave as ethnics politically (lack of assimilation), while becoming even more firmly American in their life styles (evidence of acculturation).

Accepting the validity of the Parenti distinction between acculturation and assimilation, it becomes clear that ethnicity as a factor in politics with regard to Negroes will have a long life. Because of the generally poor economic condition of Negroes, full acculturation is yet to be achieved as well as the more difficult process of assimilation.

In the third article, Essien-Udom discusses why the rise of black nationalism has occurred in the United States and where the movement may lead. He argues that black nationalism has grown because the realities of the Negro's social situation, especially those of the lower class, do not support an assimilationist mentality. This argument appears to be one of mistaken emphasis. Ethnics may become acculturated without becoming assimilated. This being so, the Negro's problem lies not in his fear of assimilation (loss of racial identity, etc.) and hence an acceptance of black nationalism, but in his overwhelmingly inferior economic condition which precludes his adoption of mainstream American life styles (acculturation).

In any event, Essien-Udom's study makes it clear that the Negro's economic situation may isolate him even further from the American mainstream. Under such circumstances it is hardly likely that Negro ethnicity will soon decline as a factor in American politics.

In fact, some black leaders would make use of the Negro's isolation from the American mainstream to develop group solidarity and build a political and economic force based upon racial identity. In the fourth selection, two leading exponents of black power, one an academician, the other an activist, spell out what this means and how it is to be accomplished. Whether or not the advocates will be successful in developing black power, and whether or not this will aid the long run goals of the Negro, remain to be seen. In any event, black power and racial pride are extremely important variables in contemporary ethnic group politics.

In the final article, Glazer and Moynihan argue that the melting pot has not happened. The group characteristics of ethnic social life have remained, especially with regard to religion and race. Only with respect to nationality groups has ethnicity as a factor in American politics notably declined. All of the evidence, say Glazer and Moynihan, points to religion and race defining the next stages of the politics of the American people. The great issues of the 1950's and 60's lend credence to this view.

The New Men

Robert A. Dahl

In the 1950s, politics in New Haven underwent certain rapid and dramatic transformations. Because the changes are so recent it is probably too much to expect to distinguish correctly between ephemeral alterations that now loom large and durable changes that may now seem minor. However, that politics in New Haven has changed in certain essential respects and that new men are playing new roles —often in coalition with older and more easily recognizable political types—is beyond doubt.

What are the new sources of leadership? How different are the new leaders from the old? What lines of cleavage and cohesion are politicians building on?

Class Interests and Ethnic Politics

To gain perspective on recent events in New Haven, it might help to consider for a moment several possible ways by which individuals or

---

groups benefit from the actions of political leaders.[1] Certain benefits are *divisible* in such a way that they can be allocated to specific individuals; jobs, contracts, and welfare payments are examples of divisible benefits. Other benefits are more nearly *indivisible;* parks, playgrounds, schools, national defense and foreign policies, for example, either cannot be or ordinarily are not allocated by dividing the benefits piecemeal and allocating various pieces to specific individuals. With indivisible benefits, if one person receives benefits many others necessarily must also, though whether or not a particular citizen is affected may depend on the criteria used in allocating the benefits or costs. For the purposes of this chapter, perhaps it is enough to distinguish criteria according to whether they primarily relate to ethnic characteristics, sources and levels of income, or other factors—age, for example, or place of residence. One might, without reading too much into the word, refer to differences in sources and levels of income as "class" characteristics. The various possibilities are brought together in Table 1. One might say that in ethnic politics politicians seek to win votes by conferring divisible benefits on individuals selected according to ethnic criteria; in class politics, politicians try to win votes by conferring mainly divisible but to some extent indivisible benefits on individuals and groups selected according to the source and size of their incomes.

TABLE 1

Criteria for allocating benefits to beneficiaries

Characteristics of the benefits:	Ethnic	Criteria: Class	Other
Divisible (individual)	(1a)	(2a)	(3a)
Indivisible (shared)	(1b)	(2b)	(3b)

---

[1]Here as elsewhere terms such as benefit and reward are intended to refer to subjective, psychological appraisals by the recipients, rather than appraisals by other observers. An action can be said to confer benefits on an individual, in this sense, if he *believes* he has benefited, even though, from the point of view of observers, his belief is false or perhaps ethically wrong. Thus the term is intended to be ethically neutral and independent of "objective" fact other than the perceptions of the recipient. Any reader who feels uncomfortable with this usage may want to read the terms as if they were placed between quotation marks: "benefits," "rewards," etc.

When an ethnic group is in its first stage, the six categories in Table 1 are not sharply distinguished. Politicians who play the game of ethnic politics confer individual benefits like jobs, nominations, bribes, gratuities, and assistance of all sorts on individuals more or less according to ethnic criteria. But ethnic characteristics serve as a kind of comprehensive symbol for class and other criteria. Moreover, benefits conferred on an individual member of an ethnic group are actually shared to some degree by the rest of the group, for every time one member makes a social or economic breakthrough, others are likely to learn of it, to take pride in his accomplishment, and to find it easier themselves to achieve the same sort of advance. The strategies of politicians are designed to confer specific benefits on particular individuals and thus to win the support of the whole group.

How different is ethnic politics from class politics? A plausible case can be made that if a large part of the electorate is divided along ethnic lines, as it has been in New Haven, the existence of ethnic identifications inhibits the development of class politics based on differences in levels of income, occupations, and other socioeconomic factors. Confronted with his perpetual need to build winning coalitions, the professional politician in New Haven quickly seized upon the most obvious way of categorizing citizens: their ethnic differences. This was by no means the only way, it might be argued, and perhaps not even the most effective way to win elections. Nonetheless, the politician devised his strategies on the assumption that whatever happened in elections could be adequately explained by shifts in ethnic blocs. Because of the uncertainty surrounding voting decisions, these explanations, which then became a part of the local political culture, were too persuasive to be rejected, even when they were incomplete or even wrong. Yet the very fact that the politician exploited ethnic unities and distinctions helped to fortify and maintain—at times perhaps even to create—feelings of ethnic difference among voters of otherwise similar social and economic circumstances. The politicians acted out a self-fulfilling prophecy; by treating ethnic distinctions as fundamental in politics, they *made* them fundamental. Had there been no ethnic distinctions to work with, class or socioeconomic differences would have been more obvious. Politicians probably would have shaped their strategies in order to appeal to socioeconomic groups or classes, and class politics probably would have developed in New Haven, just as it did in more ethnically homogeneous countries like England, Sweden, France, and Germany.

One might argue, in rejoinder, that ethnic politics was not a *sub-*

stitute for class politics; it *was* class politics in disguise, for during the first stage of assimilation, the socioeconomic homogeneity of an ethnic group determines its political homogeneity; and as the group moves through the second and third stages, political heterogeneity follows socioeconomic heterogeneity. In other words (it might be said) socioeconomic factors are always paramount; the ethnic tie is always subordinate to socioeconomic factors.

Although there is a large measure of truth in both these views, both probably underestimate the independent force of ethnic feelings. An awareness of ethnic identification is not something created by politicians; it is created by the whole social system. Ethnic similarities are a palpable reality, built into the everyday awareness of the ethnic from early childhood to old age. Nor are they always subordinate to socioeconomic factors; if they were, it would be difficult to account for certain aspects of the political behavior of the New Haven electorate.

The electoral failure of all parties that have shaped their appeals mainly in socioeconomic terms is one such aspect. If socioeconomic factors were invariably paramount, one might reasonably expect that, from about 1880 on, the Socialists, who at one time strongly emphasized the distinctive frustrations encountered by the working man in coping with life in a capitalist system, would have gained an increasing following among the working classes—as Socialist parties did in almost every other major industrial nation. Actually, however, their record in New Haven is one of total inability to win a large following. In nearly a century of effort all the minor parties together have never won more than a quarter of the votes in any election; usually they have won a good deal fewer than that. (Figures 1 and 2) In recent years, as Socialist candidates have ceased to emphasize class issues and have turned to questions of economy, efficiency, and public honesty, a Socialist vote has served largely as an expression of sporadic middle-class discontent with the candidates of the two major parties. Thus in the mayoralty election of 1947, when for the only time in the city's history both major party candidates were of Italian stock, the Socialist candidate suddenly acquired unexpected popularity (Figure 2); his support in working-class wards was much lower than in the middling and upper residential areas.

The failures of Socialist and other minor parties in the United States doubtless cannot be explained by any one factor, but the fragmentation of urban workers into a variety of ethnic groups undoubtedly created special obstacles to that rising "solidarity of the working class" for which Socialists looked in vain. The Socialist parties them-

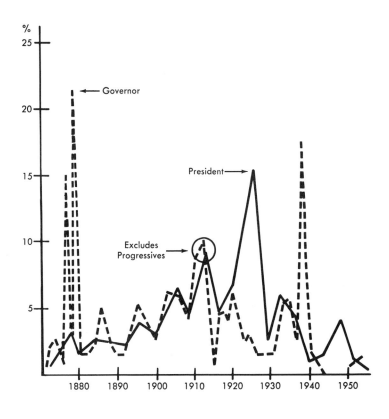

Figure 1

*Votes cast for third-party candidates for president and governor,
as percentage of total vote cast in New Haven, 1870–1956*

selves were torn by ethnic rivalries. A close student of New Haven's
working classes, who observed them in the middle of the Great Depression, wrote that even then:

> While it is true that a distinction exists between white-collar work-
> ers and wage earners in their relationships to politics, a much more
> serious type of cleavage is based on nationality groups. . . . The
> dominant political groups that are apparently arising among wage
> earners are not groups with a common economic or political philoso-
> phy embracing all wage earners, but national groups whose only tie
> is that of having come to America from the same place. . . . In New
> Haven nationality groups affiliated with the Socialist Labor Party had

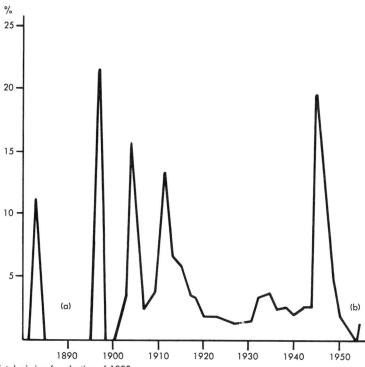

(a) Total missing for election of 1893.
(b) Vote for Malkan, Independent Democrat.

Figure 2

Votes cast for third-party candidates for mayor, as percentage of total vote cast in New Haven, 1887–1957

been meeting separately for years with much petty friction over the disposition of dues. . . . Nationality and language groups have maintained separate identities within the city central branch of the Socialist Party in New Haven.[2]

Moreover, the hypothesis that socioeconomic differences and similarities outweigh ethnic ties fails to explain the voting behavior of different ethnic groups having very similar socioeconomic characteristics. In New Haven, for example, changes in the voting patterns of

------

[2]John W. McConnell, *The Evolution of Social Classes* (Washington, D. C., American Council on Public Affairs, 1942), pp. 159 ff.

the Nineteenth Ward, the principal Negro ward in the city, have run directly counter to changes in the Eleventh Ward, as we have seen is one of the principal Italian areas. The Nineteenth and the Eleventh are hardly distinguishable in their socioeconomic characteristics. In 1950, both were low-income, working-class wards. (Table 2) Yet

TABLE 2

Socioeconomic Characteristics of Two Working-Class Wards
in New Haven, 1950

	Eleventh Ward	Rank*	Nineteenth Ward	Rank*
Median income	$2,318	26	$2,117	30
White-collar occupations	7.4%	31	7.8%	29
Families with incomes $500 or less	16.9%	27	18.8%	28
Median school years completed, 25 years old or over	8.2	32	8.8	20
Attended college	12.9%	15	5.1%	27

* Out of 33 wards.

over the past generation, the two wards have followed opposite paths. As the Italian ward has become more Republican, the Negro ward has become more Democratic. (Figure 3)

To explain this difference, one does not need to assume that socioeconomic factors are unimportant; the evidence pointing in the other direction is, as we have already seen, too persuasive. But the salience of socioeconomic factors varies just as the salience of ethnic characteristics varies. Neither ethnic nor class factors are constants; on the contrary, both are variables. When an ethnic group is in its first stage, ethnic and socioeconomic factors are *both* likely to be important in the life of the individual and in the way he responds to political appeals. But ordinarily, as we have seen, the two are not in conflict; the life of the ethnic is all of a piece.

So long as *both* sets of factors operate, politicians are likely to shape their appeals to encompass both. In some circumstances, however, the salience of ethnic identifications may decline relative to economic factors; or, conversely, economic factors may grow less salient than ethnic factors. During the Great Depression, problems of jobs, relief, wages, and economic security became paramount among wage earn-

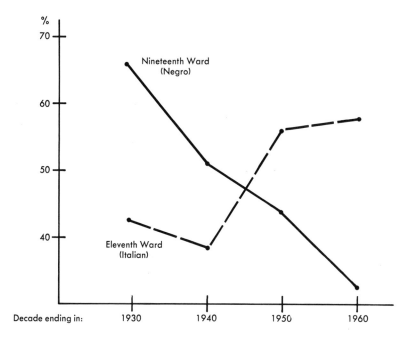

Figure 3

Percentage voting Republican in two New Haven working-class wards—
all elections for president, governor, and mayor, by decades, 1920–1960

ers; during these years, as we have noted, the Italians of New Haven
gave strong support to the Democrats. But later, with the decline in
unemployment and the development of unemployment compensation,
trade unions, and other forms of security, the pressure of economic
problems declined. Meanwhile, conflict with Italy and the nomination
of Celentano by the Republicans increased the tendency toward ethnic
identification. Hence the Italians drifted toward the Republican party,
which now offered them greater ethnic rewards than the Democratic.

At the same time, a different combination of the same factors operated among Negroes. Traditionally the Negroes of New Haven, like
Negroes elsewhere in the United States, voted Republican, largely
because of sentimental ties with the party of Lincoln, as well as patronage and other benefits. The Depression, F.D.R., and the New Deal
obliterated these old loyalties. Negroes were harder hit by unemployment than any other group in the city. In 1933 three times as many

TABLE 3

Percentage of the Two-Party Vote for Republican Candidates
in the Nineteenth Ward, 1920–1959

Decade	Nonwhite %	Elections for president %	governor %	mayor %	All elections %
1920–1929	51	69	67	64	66
1930–1939	66	47	51	55	52
1940–1949	72	34	46	49	45
1950–1959	72	38	31	31	33

Source: Percentages of nonwhites are based on figures from U.S. Census, except for 1950–59, which is based on our 1959 survey of registered voters.

families were on relief in the Nineteenth Ward as in the city as a whole. Negroes turned, like most of the unemployed, to the party of the New Deal. In the decade before 1930 the Nineteenth Ward was exceeded only by the wealthy Fifteenth in the extent of its support for Republican candidates. In the decade before 1960, by contrast, no other ward in the city cast such a small percentage of Republican votes. (Table 3)

With Negroes, the shift to the Democratic party was evidently induced primarily by salient economic needs during the Depression. But the shift entailed no undue conflict between ethnic aspirations and economic wants, for northern Democrats were fully as strong in advocating civil rights as Republicans, if not more so. In New Haven, the Democratic mayor elected in 1953 consolidated Negro support with patronage, contracts, leading appointments, and support for programs to ease some of the most critical social and economic problems faced by New Haven's Negroes.

Yet if our guiding hypothesis as to the three stages in political assimilation is correct, in the long run ethnic influences must decline and socioeconomic factors must correspondingly increase in importance. As the struggle for respect and acceptance is gradually won and professional and middle-class strata emerge, the old bonds of unity must give way to disunities. Political heterogeneity follows socioeconomic heterogeneity. When this happens, will class politics replace ethnic politics?

The Shift to Collective Benefits

Not necessarily. Indeed, judging from New Haven politics in the 1950s one should say, probably not.

By 1950 all ethnic groups in New Haven except the Negroes were rapidly approaching, if they were not already well into, the third stage of political, social, and economic assimilation. Socioeconomic differences within ethnic groups were becoming more noticeable than similarities. For two reasons, however, class politics did not replace ethnic politics. In the first place, in spite of growing assimilation, ethnic factors continued to make themselves felt with astonishing tenacity. The legacy of ethnic politics is sharply revealed in Table 4. In the center of the table, the various ethnic groups in our sample of registered voters are ranked according to the percentage that reported working-class occupations in 1959—that is, skilled, unskilled, or manual workers. The proportions range from three out of four among Negroes and six out of ten among Italian Catholics to one out of five among Irish Catholics and one out of six among European Jews. If class position were the dominant influence on party preference, Negroes and Italians would be the most strongly Democratic, and Irish Catholics and Jews would be the most strongly Republican. Yet an inspection of the right side of Table 4 shows a quite different situation. The Negroes, to be sure, are one of the most strongly Democratic groups in the city, but they are exceeded by the Irish and closely followed by

TABLE 4

Ethnic Groups in New Haven: Percentage in Working-Class
Occupations and Percentage Democratic, 1959

Number in sample		Skilled, semi-skilled, unskilled manual workers		Democratic	
		%	Rank	%	Rank
47	Negroes	76	1	57	2
157	Italian Catholics	61	2	37	5
53	European Catholics	58	3	48	4
56	European Protestants	35	4	16	6
34	American Protestants*	27	5	9	7
53	Irish Catholics	20	6	64	1
74	European Jews	15	7	52	3

* "American" in this sense means parents and grandparents born in the United States.

Source: The table is based on 474 persons (in an original sample of 525 voters) who could be definitely identified by religion and by place of birth of themselves, parents, or grandparents. The percentages Democratic are those who identified themselves as Democrats in response to the question: "Generally speaking, do you usually think of yourself as a Republican, a Democrat, or what?"

the European Jews. The Italian Catholics, on the other hand, are more strongly Republican than all others except European and American Protestants.

In the second place, there was a change in the character of the main political issues. The new issues did not so much emphasize divisible costs and benefits—either to an ethnic group or a class—as shared costs and benefits diffused across many different groups and strata. It is true that the direct effects on incomes from certain policies pursued in the 1950s were felt more strongly by some categories of citizens than others. For example, downtown property owners and construction contractors probably gained more income directly from redevelopment, at least initially, than any other groups of citizens in New Haven. Yet in its appeal, redevelopment—far from taking on a class aspect—cut across class or socioeconomic differences more than any local issue has done in decades.

What occurred in the 1950s was a change in the kinds of issues that concerned the political stratum, both nationally and locally. Attention shifted to policies that appeared to allocate shared benefits to citizens less by ethnic or class criteria than by other criteria that were sometimes sharp and sometimes vague but invariably tended to blur ethnic and class lines. It therefore became increasingly difficult to build or hold followings by means of hallowed appeals to ethnic loyalties or effects on income; new electoral coalitions superseded the old. The strategies appropriate to ethnic politics or to class politics were inappropriate to the issues of the 1950s, and the politicians who consciously or unconsciously rejected the older strategies profited most.

In some ways, the following built across the nation by a Republican president, Dwight D. Eisenhower, was remarkably similar to the following developed at the local New Haven level by Richard C. Lee, the Democratic mayor elected in 1953. Both men developed followings that bore only slight resemblance to the party coalitions of their predecessors; in both cases, the followings cut across ethnic and socioeconomic lines to an unprecedented extent; in both cases, their policies emphasized shared benefits to citizens in general rather than to specific categories.

At the national level, problems of war and cold war, defense, foreign policy, subversion, and corruption displaced the issues of the New Deal period. In New Haven, as in many other cities, the presidential election of 1952 shattered the customary patterns of ward voting. The extent of the electoral revolution wrought by Eisenhower is indicated by the remarkably low correlation between the two-party vote in the wards in 1952 and any previous election. In all presidential elections since the present wards were created in 1920, the proportion of the vote each party received in a ward has tended to be rather similar from one election to the next. For example, the correlation of the vote in the various wards for Truman in 1948 with the vote for Smith in 1928 was unbelievably high (0.91). The smallest relationship in any two presidential elections from 1924 to 1948 was between Truman's vote in 1948 and the vote for John W. Davis in 1924; even this correlation, however, was 0.77. By contrast, the correlation between Stevenson's vote in 1952 and Smith's in 1928 was only 0.29; even between Stevenson and Truman, the correlation was only 0.54.

At the local level, a similar change was taking place. Although Lee's election in 1953 rested on the kind of support that had typically served Democrats in the past, once in office he rapidly took advantage of the altered character of the electorate to build up a new following. Neither party could any longer claim to be the party of the ethnics. Perhaps the best symbol of the change is the fact that the Thirtieth Ward, which in 1950 had the highest median income, the highest median school years completed, the largest percentage of college graduates, and the third lowest percentage of foreign-born residents,[3] voted for Lee in 1955, 1957, and 1959 almost as heavily as the Fourteenth, which had the highest percentage of residents born in Ireland. In fact, in these elections the correlation between the various socioeconomic characteristics of the wards and the vote for Lee was, for all practical purposes, zero.

Although Lee did not neglect ethnic issues, particularly with Negroes and Italians, or individual benefits to specific socioeconomic groups, his appeal evidently rested in considerable part on his emphasis on the collective benefits to be gained from redevelopment, neighborhood renewal, the attempt to rescue the downtown business area from economic decline, the need for new schools, the possibilities of better parking and more playgrounds, and so on. In 1959, our sample of registered voters was asked, "In your opinion what are the most important problems in New Haven?" Far and away the most commonly mentioned problems were redevelopment, traffic, and parking—the very problems Lee emphasized most heavily. When voters were asked, "Are there things Mayor Lee has done that you particularly like?" far more (46 per cent) mentioned redevelopment than anything

---

[3]The ward with the fewest foreign-born was the Nineteenth, which was 72% nonwhite; next was the First, in which Yale is located.

else; and only 3 per cent mentioned redevelopment as among things Lee had done that they particularly did *not* like. The change in the nature of issues is indicated by the fact that redevelopment was cited as a problem five times more frequently than unemployment; it was mentioned first ten times more often than unemployment.[4]

Although redevelopment may decline as an important issue during the next decade, the new problems of urban life probably will not. Except among Negroes, the strength of ethnic ties as a factor in local politics surely must recede. Physical and economic deterioration in downtown areas; the flight to the suburbs; the overloading of all public facilities because of rising population, higher incomes, and more automobiles; the clamor for better schools; the intensifying competition for a place in the better colleges; the spread of middle-class tastes, wants, and demands throughout the white-collar and wage-earning strata; the ugliness, limitations, and inconveniences of the metropolitan sprawl; changes in esthetic standards; growing intolerance of civic corruption—all these and still other changes will probably give new importance in the politics and policies of city governments to technicians, planners, professional administrators, and above all to professional politicians with capacities for building durable coalitions out of traditionally noncooperative and even mutually suspicious social strata. The new men in local politics may very well prove to be the bureaucrats and experts—and politicians who know how to use them.

---

[4]In New Haven in 1959 only 8% of our sample mentioned unemployment as a problem. In Gallup polls of a nation-wide cross-section between 1935 and 1939, from 21% to 42% of the respondents mentioned unemployment as "the most vital issue before the American people today." In 1945, 53% said they thought it would be the most important problem facing this country during the next year. Hadley Cantril, ed., *Public Opinion, 1935–1946* (Princeton, Princeton University Press, 1951), pp. 680-81.

Ethnic Politics and the Persistence of Ethnic Identification

Michael Parenti

A question that has puzzled students of ethnic politics can be stated as follows: in the face of increasing assimilation why do ethnics continue to vote as ethnics with about the same frequency as in earlier decades? On the basis of his New Haven study, Robert Dahl observes that ". . . in spite of growing assimilation, ethnic factors continued to make themselves felt with astonishing tenacity."[1] Nevertheless, he asserts, "the strength of ethnic ties as a factor in local politics surely must recede."[2] Dahl sets up a "three-stage" model to describe how political assimilation will follow a more general social assimilation. However, one of his co-researchers, Raymond Wolfinger, demonstrates in a recent article[3] that ethnic voting patterns persist into the second and third generations, and that "at least in New Haven, all the social changes of the 1940's and 1950's do not seem to have reduced the political importance of national origins."[4] The same observation can be made of religious-ethnic identities, for as Wolfinger notes,

Reprinted from the *American Political Science Review*, LXI (September 1967), 717-726 with permission of the publisher and author. Copyright 1967 by the American Political Science Association.

[1] Robert Dahl, *Who Governs?* (New Haven: Yale University Press, 1961), p. 59.

[2] *Ibid.*, p. 62. See also pp. 32-62 inclusive.

[3] Raymond E. Wolfinger, "The Development and Persistence of Ethnic Voting," *American Political Science Review*, 59 (December, 1965), 896-908.

[4] *Ibid.*, p. 907.

citing data from the Elmira study, social mobility in no way diminishes the religious factor as a determinant of voting behavior; in fact, in the case of upper and middle class Catholics and Protestants, religion seems to assume a heightened importance as a voting determinant.[5] Wolfinger marshals evidence to support the arresting proposition that, melting pot or not, ethnic voting may be with us for a long time to come, a finding which craves explanation.

Part of the reason for the persistence of ethnic voting may rest in the political system itself. Rather than being a purely dependent variable, the political system, i.e., party, precinct workers, candidates, elections, patronage, etc., continues to rely upon ethnic strategies such as those extended to accommodate the claims of newly-arrived ethnic middle-class leadership; as a mediator and mobilizer of minority symbols and interests, the political system must be taken into account.[6]

Wolfinger suggests several further explanations, which may be briefly summarized as follows: (a) "Family-political identification." Voting studies show that as many as four-fifths of all voters maintain the same party identification as did their parents, a continuity which is not merely a reflection of similar life conditions but is in part ascribable to the independent influence of primary group relations.[7] (b) "Critical elections theory." The emergence of highly salient ethnic candidates and issues may cause a dramatic realignment so that a particular party becomes the repository of ethnic loyalty even after the ethnically salient candidate and issues have passed.[8] (c) "Historical after-effects." Partisan affiliations, as Key and Munger have demonstrated for Indiana, persist generations after the reasons for their emergence have ceased to be politically relevant. Thus "even when ethnic salience has faded, . . . its political effects will remain."[9] (d) "Militant core-city residue." The ethnic community may retain a group awareness despite a growing class heterogeneity because the assimi-

---

[5]*Ibid.*, see also Bernard R. Berelson *et al.*, *Voting* (Chicago: University of Chicago Press, 1954), p. 65.

[6]Besides the studies cited in Wolfinger, *op. cit.*, and his own data on New Haven, almost all the literature on the relationship between the political machine and the ethnic lends support to this proposition.

[7]Cf. Wolfinger *op. cit.*, p. 907 and the studies cited therein. Also Herbert Hyman, *Political Socialization* (New York: The Free Press of Glencoe, 1959), and much of the work done by Fred I. Greenstein.

[8]Here Wolfinger is applying Key's hypothesis. See V. O. Key, Jr. "A Theory of Critical Elections," *Journal of Politics*, 17 (February, 1955), 3-18.

[9]The quotation is from Wolfinger, *op. cit.*, p. 908. See also V. O. Key and Frank Munger, "Social Determinism and Electoral Decision: the Case of Indiana," in Eugene Burdick and Arthur J. Brodbeck (eds.), *American Voting Behavior* (Glencoe, Ill.: The Free Press, 1959), pp. 281-299.

lationist-minded will advance to the suburbs while those among the upwardly mobile who choose to stay in the ethnic city settlements are more likely to be the most strongly in-group oriented.[10]

Several comments are in order before we proceed further: of the above explanations, there seems to be some question as to whether (a), (b) and (c) are concerned with independent variables. It does seem that the Key-Munger historical after-effect idea in (c) is an extension of the "fixation" of the "crucial elections" notion in (b) and that both must rest in large part on the strong inheritance and continuity of family partisan identifications in (a). Explanation (d), while suggestive, is wanting in substantiating data. What evidence we have does not necessarily support the "militant core-city residue" idea, and certainly does not lend substance to the image of a homogenized, assimilated suburbia, as we shall see below. Nevertheless, the above hypotheses submitted by Wolfinger may serve as useful explanations for the political continuity of all social groups, ethnics included.[11]

Yet, after all is said and done, I cannot free myself from the suspicion that perhaps a false problem has been created which can best be resolved by applying certain analytic and theoretical distinctions, supported by data that extend beyond the usual voting studies. If, in fact, it can be demonstrated that assimilation is not taking place, then the assimilation theory as propounded by Dahl, along with Wolfinger's alternate explanations are somewhat beside the point. And the question, why do ethnics continue to vote as ethnics despite increasing assimilation, becomes the wrong one to ask—because the answer may simply be that minorities are not assimilating. At first glance, such an assertion seems to violate the evidence of our senses. Have not old-world immigrant cultures all but disappeared? Are not the ethnics scattering into homogeneously Americanized suburbs? Is not the educational level of the national minorities continually increasing? Are not ethnic occupational distributions changing? etc.

The confusion rests, I submit, in the failure—common to many of us political scientists, and even to some sociologists and anthropologists—to make a conceptual distinction between "acculturation" and "assimilation." The distinction is crucial in reading correct meaning into our data and in guiding us to fruitful theoretical conclusions. For

---

[10]Wolfinger, *loc. cit.*

[11]For a more extended and systematic treatment of the question of political continuities and discontinuities see Seymour M. Lipset *et al.*, "The Psychology of Voting: An Analysis of Political Behavior," in Gardner Lindzey (ed.), *Handbook of Social Psychology*, Vol. II (Cambridge, Mass.: Addison-Wesley, 1954), pp. 1124-1170.

while it is established that ethnics have accommodated themselves to American styles and customs (acculturation) by the second generation, and while perhaps they may enjoy increased occupational and geographic mobility, it is not at all clear that they are incorporating themselves into the structural-identificational-group relations of the dominant society (assimilation). On close examination we find that the term "assimilation," as commonly used, refers to a multiplicity of cultural, social and idenificational processes which need closer scrutiny.[12]

I. Acculturation and Assimilation

At the outset, it is necessary, as Talcott Parsons and others have urged, to distinguish between *cultural* and *social* systems: the cultural is the system of beliefs, values, norms, practices, symbols and ideas (science, art, artifacts, language, law and learning included); the social is the system of interrelations and associations among individuals and groups. Thus a church, family, club, informal friendship group, or formal organization, etc., composed of individuals interacting in some kind of context involving roles and statuses are part of the *social* system, or, one might say, represent particular subsocietal systems within the society; while the beliefs, symbols, and practices mediated and adhered to by members of the church, family, club, etc., are part of the *cultural* system or sub-cultural systems within the total culture. By abstracting two analytically distinct sets of components from the same concrete phenomena we are able to observe that, although there may often be an important interaction, the order of relationships and the actions and conditions within one are independent of those in the other. Attention to this independence increases analytical precision.[13]

What was considered as one general process becomes a multifaceted configuration of processes. And if it can be said that there is no inevitable one-to-one relationship between the various processes, and that imperatives operative in one system are not wholly dependent upon the other, then ethnic political behavior becomes something less of a mystery. *For ethnic social sub-systems may persist or evolve new structures independent of the host society and despite dramatic cultural transitions in the direction of the mainstream culture.*

---

[12]For instance, Wolfinger uses the term "assimilation" synonymously with "general acculturation and occupational differentiation," in the same body of propositions, *op. cit.*, p. 906.

[13]A. L. Kroeber and Talcott Parsons, "The Concepts of Culture and of Social System," *American Sociological Review,* 23 (October, 1958), 582-583; also Talcott Parsons, *The Social System* (Glencoe, Ill.: The Free Press, 1951).

Since early colonial times, nearly every group arriving in America has attempted to reconstruct communities that were replications of the old world societies from which they had emerged. With the exception of a few isolated sectarian enclaves such as the Hutterites, the Amish and the Hasidic, they failed to do so. If culture is to be represented as the accumulated beliefs, styles, solutions and practices which represent a society's total and continuing adjustment to its environment, then it would seem to follow that no specific cultural system can be transplanted from one environment to another without some measure of change. Unable to draw upon a complete cultural base of their own in the new world, and with no larger constellation of societal and institutional forces beyond the ghetto boundaries to back them, the immigrants eventually lost the battle to maintain their indigenous ways. By the second generation, attention was directed almost exclusively toward American events and standards, American language, dress, recreation, work, and mass media, while interest in old world culture became minimal or, more usually, non-existent. To one extent or another, all major historical and sociological studies of immigration and ethnicity document this cultural transition of the American-born generation.[14]

However, such acculturation was most often *not* followed by social assimilation; the group became "Americanized" in much of its *cultural* practices, but this says little about its *social* relations with the host society. In the face of widespread acculturation, the minority still maintained a social sub-structure encompassing primary and secondary group relations composed essentially of fellow ethnics. A study of a Polish-American industrial town illustrates this cultural-social distinction. The Polish children treat their immigrant parents with either patronization or contempt, speak American slang, are addicted to American popular music and popular culture, accept fully the American way of piling up money and material goods when possible. Yet they keep almost all their social contacts within the confines of the Polish-American community and have no direct exposure to, and little

---

[14]See for instance: Oscar Handlin, *Boston's Immigrants, A Study in Acculturation* (Cambridge: Harvard University Press, rev. ed. 1959); Oscar Handlin, *The Uprooted* (New York: Grosset and Dunlap, 1951); R. E. Park and H. A. Miller, *Old World Traits Transplanted* (New York: Harper, 1921); W. I. Thomas and F. Znaniecki, *The Polish Peasant in Europe and America*, 5 vols. (Boston: Badger, 1918–20); E. V. Stonequist, *The Marginal Man, A Study in Personality and Culture Conflict* (New York: Scribner, 1937); W. L. Warner and Leo Srole, *The Social Systems of American Ethnic Groups* (New Haven: Yale Univ. Press, 1945); William Foote Whyte, *Street Corner Society* (Chicago: University of Chicago Press, 1943); Herbert J. Gans, *The Urban Villagers* (New York: Free Press of Glencoe, 1962).

interest in, middle-class American society.[15] Similar findings were made by Whyte and Gans in their respective studies—done twenty years apart—of Italian-American communities in Boston. American styles, language, sports and consumption patterns predominated, but interpersonal relations and social group structures were almost exclusively Italian-American in both the North End of the 1940's and the West End of the 1960's.[16]

From birth in the sectarian hospital to childhood play-groups to cliques and fraternities in high school and college to the selection of a spouse, a church affiliation, social and service clubs, a vacation resort, and, as life nears completion, an old-age home and sectarian cemetery—the ethnic, if he so desires, may live within the confines of his sub-societal matrix—and many do.[17] Even if he should find himself in the oppressively integrated confines of prison, the ethnic discovers that Italian, Irish, Jewish, Negro and Puerto Rican inmates coalesce into distinct groups in "a complex web of prejudices and hostilities, friendships and alliances."[18]

Hollingshead, in a study of New Haven, discerned vertical social divisions based on race, religion and national origin along with the expected horizontal cleavages due to income and residence. Cutting across the class strata were the parallel dissections of the black and white worlds, with the latter further fissured into Catholic, Jewish and Protestant components which, in turn, sub-divided into Irish, Italian, Polish, etc. Within this highly compartmentalized world were to be found the ethnic associational patterns.[19]

---

[15]Arnold W. Green, "A Re-examination of the Marginal Man Concept," *Social Forces*, 26 (1947), 167-171.

[16]Whyte, *op. cit.*, and Gans, *op. cit.* A socially unassimilated pluralism is readily visible in many areas of American life. Thus, in a single weekend in New York, separate dances for persons of Hungarian, Irish, Italian, German, Greek and Polish extractions are advertised in neighborhood newspapers and the foreign language press.

[17]See Milton M. Gordon, *Assimilation in American Life* (New York: Oxford University Press, 1964), p. 34; also Erich Rosenthal, "Acculturation without Assimilation?" *American Journal of Sociology*, 66 (November, 1960), 275-288; Amitai Etzioni, "The Ghetto—a Re-evaluation," *Social Forces* (March, 1959), 255-262; J. Milton Yinger, "Social Forces Involved in Group Identification or Withdrawal," *Daedalus*, 90 (Spring, 1961), 247-262; Y. J. Chyz and R. Lewis, "Agencies Organized by Nationality Groups in the United States," *The Annals of the American Academy of Political and Social Science*, 262 (1949).

[18]M. Arc, "The Prison 'Culture' From the Inside," *New York Times Magazine*, February 28, 1965, p. 63.

[19]August B. Hollingshead, "Trends in Social Stratification: A Case Study," *American Sociological Review*, 17 (1952), 685 f; see also Gans, *op. cit.*; Warner and Srole, *op. cit.*, for further evidence of ethnic sub-societal systems.

II. Heterogeneity within the Homogeneous Society

Could not such unassimilated sub-structures be more representative of a time when urban areas were segmented into ghettos untouched by post-war affluence, upward occupational mobility and treks to the suburbs? This is the question which seems to anticipate both Dahl and Wolfinger. In actuality, while individual ethnics have entered professional and occupational roles previously beyond their reach, minority group mobility has not been as dramatic as is often supposed. A comparison of first and second generation occupational statuses as reported in the 1950 national census shows no evidence of any substantial convergence of intergroup status levels. The occupational differences among ethnic groups, with the Irish as a possible exception, remain virtually the same for both generations, leading C. B. Nam to observe that even with the absence of large-scale immigration, "the importance of nationality distinctions for the American stratification system will remain for some time to come."[20] If today's ethnics enjoy a better living standard than did their parents, it is because there has been an across-the-board rise throughout America. Fewer pick-and-shovel jobs and more white collar positions for minority members are less the result of ethnic mobility than of an over-all structural transition in our national economy and the composition of our labor force.[21]

Furthermore, despite the popular literature on the hopeless homogeneity of suburbia,[22] suburbs are not great *social* melting pots. Scott Greer, after noting the breakup of some of the central city ethnic communities, cautions: "The staying force of the ethnic community (in suburbia) must not be underestimated." The good Catholic, for instance, "can live most of his life, aside from work, within a Catholic environment,"[23] in a sub-societal network of schools, religious endogamy, family, church, social, athletic and youth organizations, and Catholic residential areas. Similarly, Robert Wood observes that suburbs tend toward ethnic clusters. In the more "mixed areas," ethnic

---

[20]C. B. Nam, "Nationality Groups and Social Stratification in America," *Social Forces*, 37 (1959), p. 333. The assumption that Negroes have been enjoying a slow but steady economic advance is laid to rest by Dale Hiestand, *Economic Growth and Employment Opportunities for Minorities* (New York: Columbia University Press, 1964).

[21]See Lewis Corey, "Problems of the Peace: IV. The Middle Class," *Antioch Review*, 5, 68-87.

[22]For instance William H. Whyte, *The Organization Man* (Garden City: Doubleday, 1957); A. C. Spectorsky, *The Ex-Urbanites* (New York: J. B. Lippincott, 1955).

[23]Scott Greer, "Catholic Voters and the Democratic Party," *Public Opinion Quarterly*, 25 (1961), p. 624.

political blocs are not unknown. As in the city, the tension between the older resident and the newcomer sometimes reinforces ethnic political alignments and ethnic social identifications.[24] Minority concentrations are less visible in suburban than in urban areas because less immigrant and second-generation persons reside there. Lieberson's study of ten major metropolitan areas shows that the groups most highly segregated from native whites in the central city are also most residentially concentrated in the suburbs, so that suburban patterns bear a strong similarity to those found in the city.[25]

Finally, residential segregation is not a necessary prerequisite for the maintenance of an ethnic sub-societal structure; *a group can maintain ethnic social cohesion and identity, while lacking an ecological basis.*[26] The Jews of Park Forest live scattered over a wide area and "participate with other Park Foresters in American middle-class culture," that is, they clearly are acculturated. Yet in one year a Jewish sub-community consisting of informal friendship groups, a women's club, a B'nai B'rith lodge and a Sunday School had emerged. Similarly distinct Lutheran and Catholic social groupings also had developed in which national origin played a large part. (Religion, according to Herbert Gans, was not the exclusive concern of any of the three groups.)[27]

The neighborhood stores, bars, coffee-shops, barber shops, and fraternal clubrooms which serve as social nerve centers in the ecologically contiguous first-settlement urban areas are difficult to reconstruct in the new topography of shopping centers and one-family homes, but they are frequently replaced by suburban-styled church, charity and social organizations, informal evening home-centered gatherings and

---

[24]Robert C. Wood, *Suburbia, Its People and Their Politics* (Boston: Houghton Mifflin Co., 1958), p. 178. As impressive as is the trek to the suburbs, more recent developments should not go unrecorded. Of great significance, and hitherto unobserved because it is of such recent occurrence, is the effect of the revised and liberalized national origins quota system of our immigration laws. Direct observation of immigration into several of the Italian and Greek communities in New York during 1965–66 leaves me with the conviction that the ethnic core-city community is far from declining. In certain urban centers, such as the Brownsville section of New York, the gradual depletion of old ethnic neighborhoods is being amply and visibly counterbalanced by new injections of Polish refugees, along with Italian, Greek and Latin American immigrants who not only reinforce the core-city neighborhoods but frequently lend them certain first-generation touches reminiscent of an earlier day.

[25]Stanley Lieberson, "Suburbs and Ethnic Residential Patterns," *American Journal of Sociology,* 67 (1962), 673-681.

[26]See Etzioni, *op. cit.,* for a discussion of this point.

[27]Herbert J. Gans, "Park Forest: Birth of a Jewish Community," *Commentary,* 7 (1951), 330-339.

extended family ties kept intact over a wide area with the technical assistance of the omnipresent automobile. The move to second and third settlement areas and the emergence of American-born generations, rather than presaging an inevitable process of disintegration has led to new adjustments in minority organization and communication. *Even when most of the life-styles assume an American middle-class stamp, these in-group social patterns reinforce ethnic identifications and seem to give them an enduring nature.* Today identifiable groups remain not as survivals from the age of immigration but with new attributes many of which were unknown to the immigrants.[28] In short, changes are taking place in ethnic social patterns, but the direction does not seem to be toward greater assimilation into the dominant Anglo-American social structure.

In addition to the movement of ethnics from first settlement areas to the surrounding suburbs there is a smaller "secondary migration" to the Far West. What little evidence we have of this phenomenon suggests that highly visible acculturation styles do not lead to the loss of ethnic consciousness. The numerous Italian, Armenian, Greek, Finnish and Jewish sub-societal organizations, to cite the West Coast groups that have come to my attention, suggest that structural assimilation into the Anglo-Protestant mainstream is far from inevitable in the "newer America." Friedman, observing how the Jews in Albuquerque are so well integrated as to be "almost indistinguishable from the community at large," then goes on to describe a Jewish network of social organizations such as Hadassah, B'nai B'rith, Shul, Temple, etc.[29] The strenuous efforts made by West Coast Greek-Americans on behalf of Mayor Christopher of San Francisco, including appeals that reached segments of the Greek community in New York, indicate that old-style political ethnic appeals are not unknown in California. The recent gubernatorial contest in Nevada, with its appeals to Mormons, Catholics and Italians, moved one observer to comment that "the Nevada campaign made it clear once again that American elections more often than not are heavily dependent on a maze of ethnic, religious and minority group voting factors that few candidates discuss in public."[30] At the same time, the emerging political articulation of

---

[28]Cf. Etzioni, *op. cit.*, p. 258; also Nathan Glazer and Daniel P. Moynihan, *Beyond the Melting Pot* (Cambridge: M.I.T. and Harvard University Press, 1963), pp. 13-16.

[29]Morris Friedman, "The Jews of Albuquerque," *Commentary*, 28 (1959), 55-62.

[30]Tom Wicker, "Hidden Issues in Nevada," *The New York Times*, July 23, 1966.

Mexican-Americans throughout the Far West should remind us that growing acculturation often leads to *more* rather than less ethnic political awareness.[31]

In general terms, the new "affluence," often cited as a conductor of greater assimilation, may actually provide minorities with the financial and psychological wherewithal for building even more elaborate parallel subsocietal structures, including those needed for political action. In prosperous suburban locales, while the oldest and most exclusive country clubs belong to old-stock Protestant families, the newer clubs are of Jewish or varying Catholic-ethnic antecedents. Among Chicago's debutantes, established "society," primarily Anglo-Protestant, holds a coming-out at the Passavant hospital ball. Debutantes of other origins make do with a Presentation Ball (Jewish), a Links Ball (Negro) and the White and Red Ball (Polish). Similar developments can be observed in numerous other urban and suburban regions.[32] Rather than the expected structural assimilation, parallel social structures flourish among the more affluent ethnics. Increasing prosperity among Catholics has been accompanied by an increase in Catholic institutional and social organizations including a vast parochial education system,[33] and the proliferation in sectarian higher education often means a heightened ethnic consciousness. Thus Lenski finds, after controlling for income and party affiliation, that parochially educated Catholics tend to be more doctrinally orthodox and politically conservative than publicly educated Catholice.[34]

If ethnic social relations show this notable viability, it might also be remembered that ethnic sub-cultures have not been totally absorbed into mainstream America. Numerous writers have observed the influence of ethnic cultural valuations on political life, causing one to conclude that not only is there slim evidence to show that assimilation is taking place, but there is even some question as to whether acculturation is anywhere complete.[35] Acculturation itself is a multifaceted

---

[31]See Joan W. Moore and Ralph Guzman, "The Mexican-Americans: New Wind from the Southwest," *The Nation*, May 30, 1966, pp. 645-648.

[32]*Cf.*, E. Digby Baltzell, *The Protestant Establishment, Aristocracy and Caste in America* (New York: Random House, 1964), p. 357; and "Life and Leisure," *Newsweek*, December 21, 1964.

[33]John Tracy Ellis, *American Catholicism* (Chicago: University of Chicago Press, 1956), *passim*; also James P. Shannon, "The Irish Catholic Immigration," in Thomas T. McAvoy (ed.), *Roman Catholicism and The American Way of Life* (Notre Dame: University of Notre Dame Press, 1960), pp. 204-210.

[34]Gerhard Lenski, *The Religious Factor* (Garden City, N.Y.: Doubleday, 1963, rev. ed.), pp. 268-270.

[35]*Cf.* Wesley and Beverly Allinsmith, "Religious Affiliation and Politico-Economic Attitude," *Public Opinion Quarterly*, 12 (1948), 377-389; Lawrence Fuchs, *The Political Behavior of the American Jews*, (Glencoe, Ill.: The Free Press, 1956).

process, and even as American styles, practices, language, and values are adopted, certain ethnic values and attitudes may persist as a vital influence; for instance, the attitude that fellow-ethnics are preferable companions in primary group relations.

That ethnic subcultures may still operate as independent variables in political life can be seen in the recent Wilson and Banfield study. In twenty referenda elections held in seven major cities between 1956 and 1963 for expenditures to pay for public services such as hospitals, schools and parks, it was found that the groups which, because of their income level, would pay little or nothing while benefitting most, were least likely to support such services, namely Poles, Czechs, Italians, Irish and other ethnics.[36] Conversely, upper-income White Protestants and Jews, the very groups that would be paying the costs while benefitting least, were the strongest supporters of these proposed expenditures. The correlations are too compelling for one to assume that the voters of all groups were acting out of ignorance of their actual material interests. More likely, the authors conclude, there is something in the White Protestant and Jewish subcultural belief systems which tends "to be more public-regarding and less private —(self or family)—regarding" than in the other ethnic subcultures.[37] In sum, *cultural belief systems or residual components of such systems may persist as cultural and political forces independently of objective and material factors.*[38]

III. Identificational Durability

From the time he is born, the individual responds to cultural cues mediated by representatives that help shape his personal character structure. As Parsons suggests, beside the distinction made between the cultural and social systems, one must take into account the personality system.[39] Insofar as the individual internalizes experiences

---

[36]James Q. Wilson and Edward C. Banfield, "Public Regardingness As a Value Premise in Voting Behavior," *American Political Science Review*, 58, (December, 1964), 876-887.

[37]*Ibid.*, pp. 882-885. Wilson and Banfield offer no delineation of these subcultural ingredients. For an attempted analysis of the components of religious belief systems which are politically salient see Michael Parenti, "Political Values and Religious Culture: Jews, Catholics and Protestants," *The Journal for the Scientific Study of Religion*, (forthcoming).

[38]For the classic statement of this proposition see Max Weber, *The Protestant Ethic and the Spirit of Capitalism* (New York: Scribner's Sons, 1958). For application of this proposition to the American scene see Seymour Martin Lipset, *The First New Nation* (New York: Basic Books, 1963), pp. 110-129.

[39]Parsons actually constructs a four-systems model which includes the social, cultural, personality and physiological systems; the fourth system is not immediately pertinent to our discussion. See Talcott Parsons, "Malinowski and the Theory of the Social System" in R. Firth (ed.), *Man and Culture* (London: Routledge and Kegan Paul, 1960).

from earlier social positions and sub-cultural matrices, his personality may act as a determinant—or character interpreter—of his present socio-cultural world. To apply that model to our present analysis: ethnic identifications are no matter of indifference even for the person who is both culturally and socially assimilated to the extent that his professional, recreational, and neighborhood relations and perhaps also his wife are of the wider White Protestant world. A holiday dinner at his parents' home may be his only active ethnic link, or it may be —as Stanley Edgar Hyman said when asked what being Jewish meant to him—nothing more than "a midnight longing for a hot pastrami sandwich;" yet it is a rare person who reaches adulthood without some internalized feeling about his ethnic identification. Just as social assimilation moves along a different and slower path than that of acculturation, so does identity assimilation, or rather non-assimilation, enjoy a pertinacity not wholly responsive to the other two processes.

There are several explanations for the persistence of individual ethnic identity in such cases. First, even if the available range of social exposure brings a man into more frequent contact with out-group members, early in-group experiences, family name and filial attachments may implant in him a natural awareness of, and perhaps a pride in, his ethnic origins. An individual who speaks and behaves like something close to the Anglo-American prototype may still prefer to identify with those of his own racial, religious or national background because it helps tell him who he is. For fear of "losing my identity" some individuals have no desire to pass completely into a "nondescript" "non-ethnic" American status. In an age of "mass society" when the "search for identity" concerns many, an identification which is larger than the self yet smaller than the nation is not without its compensations.[40]

Furthermore, the acculturated ethnic may be no more acceptable to the nativist than the unacculturated. Since the beginning of our nation, the native population has wanted minority groups to acculturate or "Americanize," a process entailing the destruction of alien customs and apearances offensive to American sensibilities. But this was not to be taken as an invitation into Anglo-American primary group relations. (It seems that nativists well understood the distinction between acculturation and assimilation.) To be sure, there is little to suggest that the host society has been a gracious host.[41] Even

---

[40]See Gordon, *op. cit.*; also Gans, "Park Forest," *op. cit.*
[41]See Baltzell, *op. cit.*, for a study of White Protestant exclusiveness; also Gordon, *op. cit.*, pp. 111-12.

if full social acceptance is won without serious encounters with bigotry, it is unlikely that from childhood to adulthood one will have
escaped a realization that some kind of stigma is attached to one's
minority identity, that one is in some way "marginal."[42] Ethnic identifications are, after all, rarely neutral. Few things so effectively assure
the persistence of in-group awareness as out-group rejection, and much
of the ethnic cradle-to-grave social structure, often considered "clan-
nish," is really defensive.[43] The greater the animosity, exclusion and
disadvantage, generally the more will ethnic self-awareness permeate
the individual's feelings and evaluations. For groups enjoying some
measure of acceptance ethnicity plays an intermittent rather than constant role in self-identity, whereas for those groups which have experienced maximum hostility and oppression—for instance, the Negro
American—the question of ethnic identification takes on a ubiquitous
quality, there being few instances when, for real or imagined reasons,
race does not define, shape or intrude upon both the ordinary business
of living and the extraordinary business of politics.[44]

As long as distinctions obtain in the dominant society, and the foreseeable future seems to promise no revolutionary flowering of brotherly love, and as long as the family and early group attachments hold
some carry-over meaning for the individual, ethnic identifications and
ethnic-oriented responses will still be found among those who have
made a "secure" professional and social position for themselves in the
dominant Anglo-Protestant world.

---

[42]For supporting data see Michael Parenti, *Ethnic and Political Attitudes: Three
Generations of Italian Americans,* (unpublished Ph.D. dissertation, Yale Univer-
sity, 1962); also Gordon W. Allport, *The Nature of Prejudice* (Garden City,
N.Y.: Doubleday, 1958).

[43]Hansen observes: "When the natives combined to crush what they considered
the undue influence of alien groups they committed a tactical error, for the
newcomers, far from being crushed were prompted to consolidate their hitherto
scattered forces:" Marcus Lee Hansen, *The Immigrant in American History* (New
York: Harper and Row, 1960 ed.), p. 136.

[44]Race consciousness is, James Q. Wilson notes, "an ever-present factor in the
thought and action of Negroes of all strata of society," and is "the single most
consistent theme in Negro discussion of civic issues." *Negro Politics: The Search
for Leadership* (Glencoe: The Free Press, 1960), p. 170. It is true, however, that
members of any one group, because of individual experiences and personalities,
may vary as to the amount of emphasis they place upon their ethnic status: see
Aaron Antonovsky, "Toward a Refinement of the 'Marginal Man' Concept,"
Social Forces, 35 (1956), 57-62, for a study of in-group attitudes among Jewish
males; also Irwin Child, *Italian or American? The Second Generation in Conflict*
(New Haven: Yale University Press, 1943). To my knowledge there exists no
quantifiable cross-group comparative study of in-group awareness. The impression
one draws from non-comparative studies as implied above is that the groups most
disliked by the wider society harbor the greatest number of individuals of militant ethnic self-awareness.

IV. Conclusion

By way of concluding I may summarize my major propositions and discuss their broader political and theoretical applications.

1. If the wrong question is asked, then the answers are irrelevant. If our conceptual and analytic tools are insufficient, then we fail to do justice to our data. The question of why ethnics continue to vote as ethnics despite increasing assimilation focuses on a false problem because minority groups are not assimilating. Using an admittedly simplified application of Parson's model, we arrive at the hypothesis that the cultural, social and personality systems may operate with complex independent imperatives to maintain ethnic consciousness. *Assimilation involves much more than occupational, educational and geographic mobility.* From the evidence and analysis proffered in the foregoing pages, there is reason to believe that despite a wide degree of second and third generation acculturation: (1) residual ethnic cultural valuations and attitudes persist; acculturation is far from complete; (2) the vast pluralistic parallel systems of ethnic social and institutional life show impressive viability; structural assimilation seems neither inevitable nor imminent; (3) psychological feelings of minority group identity, both of the positive-enjoyment and negative-defensive varieties, are still deeply internalized. In sum, ethnic distinctiveness can still be treated as a factor in social and political pluralism.

Dahl's assertion that the Germans, Irish, Jews and Italians of New Haven are entering into the "third stage of assimilation" in which middle-class jobs, neighborhoods, ideas, associates and styles of life make ethnicity a negligible factor, and Wolfinger's assertions that "ethnic consciousness is fading; it is already faint in some parts of the country and for some ethnic groups," and that "continuing increases in education, geographic dispersion, intermarriage and inter-group contacts are all likely to reduce ethnic consciousness,"[45] should be scrutinized carefully. We can see that (a) increases in education have not necessarily led to a diminished ethnic consciousness; indeed, the increase in sectarian education often brings a heightened ethnic consciousness.[46] (b) Increases in income and adaptation to middle-class

---

[45]Dahl, *op. cit.*, pp. 35-6; Wolfinger *op. cit.*, p. 908.

[46]Lenski, *loc. cit.* Lenski's entire study points to the persistence of sub-cultural religio-ethnic variables in political and economic life. The transition away from the Democratic Party by Catholics is not, as Wolfinger seems to suggest, a symptom of assimilation; in fact, by Lenski's data, it is a manifestation of a growing commitment to religious conservatism.

styles have not noticeably diminished the viability and frequency of ethnic formal and informal structural associations. Such stylistic changes as have occurred may just as easily evolve *within* the confines of the ethnically stratified social systems, thereby leading to a proliferation of parallel structures rather than absorption into Anglo-Protestant social systems. (c) Geographical dispersion, like occupational and class mobility has been greatly over-estimated. Movement from the first settlement area actually may represent a transplanting of the ethnic community to suburbia. Furthermore, as we have seen, even without the usual *geographic* contiguity, *socially* and *psychologically* contiguous ethnic communities persist. (d) Inter-group contacts, such as may occur, do not necessarily lead to a lessened ethnic awareness; they may serve to activate a new and positive appreciation of personal ethnic identity. Or intergroup contacts may often be abrasive and therefore conducive to ethnic defensiveness and compensatory in-group militancy. Perhaps intermarriage, as a genetic integration (for the offspring) will hasten assimilation; where hate has failed, love may succeed in obliterating the ethnic. But intermarriage remains the exception to the rule, and in the foreseeable future does not promise a large-scale structural group assimilation. Furthermore, in the absence of pertinent data, we need not assume that the offspring of mixed marriages are devoid of ethnic identifications of one kind or another.

2. While not denying what was granted earlier, namely that the political system itself may be an instigator and fabricator of ethnic appeals, we would do well to avoid common overstatements along these lines. It is quite true that politicians are capable of amazing alertness to ethnic sensibilities even in instances where such sensibilities fail to materialize.[47] Yet in the light of the above discussion it would be unduly hasty to conclude that politicians betray a "cultural lag" or perceptual laziness by their continued attention to ethnic groups. The political organization attempting to mobilize support faces the problem of having to construct definitions of its constituency which will reduce the undifferentiated whole into more accessible, manageable, and hopefully more responsive components. The politician, then, is not completely unlike the scientific investigator—if we may allow ourselves an extended analogy—who in dealing with a mass of data must find some means of ordering it into meaningful and more manipulatable categories. More specifically, he must find means of making his constituency accessible to him in the most economical way. Given

---

[47]See, for instance, the study of balanced ticket calculations in a New York state-wide campaign in the concluding chapter of Glazer and Moynihan, *op. cit.*

the limited availability of campaign resources and the potentially limitless demands for expenditure, the candidate is in need of a ready-made formal and informal network of relational substructures within his constituency. He discovers that "reaching the people" is often a matter of reaching particular people who themselves can reach, or help him reach, still other people.

A growing acculturation may have diminished the salience of the more blatant ethnic appeals, and the candidate knows that a nostalgic reference to the old country no longer strikes the resonant note it did thirty years ago; indeed, it may elicit a self-consciously negative response from the American-born generations. But he also should know that social assimilation (whether he calls it that or not) is far from an accomplished reality, as he finds himself confronted with leaders and members from a wide melange of ethnic associations, be they professional, business, labor, veteran, neighborhood, educational, church, charitable, recreational or fraternal. Unhampered by any premature anticipations of assimilation, the politician can work with what is at hand. Even if "ethnic issues," as such, do not emerge in a campaign, ethnic social life provides him with ready-made avenues to constituent audiences, audiences which—no matter how well acculturated—are not noted for their indifference to being courted by public figures.

That many urban and suburban politicians persist in giving attentive consideration to minority social groupings in American-born constituencies, then, may be due less to their inveterate stupidity than to the fact that ethnic substructures and identifications are still extant, highly visible and, if handled carefully, highly accessible and responsive. The political practitioner who chooses to ignore the web of formal and informal ethnic substructures on the presumption that such groupings are a thing of the past does so at his own risk.

3. Historically, the theoretical choice posed for the ethnic has been either isolated existence in autonomous cultural enclaves or total identificational immersion into the American society. We have seen that neither of these "either-or" conditions have evolved. In 1915, Woodrow Wilson observed: "America does not consist of groups. A man who thinks of himself as belonging to a particular national group in America has not yet become an American."[48] As was so often the case when he addressed himself to the problem of national minorities, Wilson took the simple view. His was the commonly accepted assumption

---

[48]Quoted in Oscar Handlin, *The American People in the Twentieth Century* (Boston: Beacon Press, 1963, rev. ed.), p. 121.

that a person's identity or position in the social system were indivisible qualities; therefore, identity choices were mutually exclusive. But in reality a person experiences cumulative and usually complementary identifications, and his life experiences may expose him to some of the social relations and cultural cues of the dominant society while yet placing him predominantly within the confines of a particular minority substructure. For the ethnic, a minority group identity is no more incompatible with life in America and with loyalty to the nation than is any regional, class, or other particular group attachment. A pluralistic society, after all, could not really exist without pluralistic substructures and identities. Ethnics can thus sometimes behave politically as ethnics while remaining firmly American. It may be said that minorities have injected a new meaning into a national motto originally addressed to the fusion of thirteen separate states: *e pluribus unum*, a supreme allegiance to, and political participation in, the commonality of the Union, with the reserved right to remain distinct unassimilated entities in certain limited cultural, social and identificational respects.

The disappearance of ethnicity as a factor in political behavior waits in large part upon total ethnic structural-identificational assimilation into the host society. Perhaps even in that far-off future "when national origins are forgotten, the political allegiances formed in the old days of ethnic salience will be reflected in the partisan choices of totally assimilated descendants of the old immigrants."[49] If so, then the forces of political continuity will once more have proven themselves, and ethnicity will join long-past regional ties, wars, depressions, defunct political machines, deceased charismatic leaders and a host of other half-forgotten forces whose effects are transmitted down through the generations to shape the political continuities and allegiances of all social groups. But before relegating them to the history of tomorrow, the unassimilated ethnics should be seen as very much alive and with us today.

---

[49]Wolfinger, *loc. cit.*

Black Nationalism:
Conclusions and Trends

E. U. Essien-Udom

Broadly, the study of black nationalism is a case study of the social and psychological consequences of what Gunnar Myrdal aptly summed up as "An American Dilemma" on the personal and group life of American Negroes. The sum total of these consequences—psychological constraints, institutional weaknesses, contradictory "value systems" of the subculture, and the absence of an ethos—is what we described as the Negro dilemma, dramatized in the doctrines of black nationalism. These constraints are deeply rooted in the subculture although they depend on and are supported by the white society. The Negro dilemma, in a subtle and profound way, exercises a constraint, which is by no means easy to specify, on the social advancement of the masses of Negroes, especially in northern United States. Although the study points to a possible relationship between these constraints and the obstacles imposed on Negroes by the white society, it does not, however, tell us much about the relative weight to be attached to one or the other on the advancement of the masses of Negroes. Common sense suggests, however, that the attitudes and actions of the white society are more decisive. Nevertheless, both are inextricably interwoven, and analytically, they are difficult to disentangle. The uneasy co-existence between them is not adequately understood or appreciated. Black nationalism, especially the Muslim movement, is an attempt to "break through" the vicious circle which emerges from this relationship.

Furthermore, the study underscores the Negroes' ambivalence toward assimilation, i.e., the loss of their identity, cultural traits, and history. Black nationalism, the Muslim movement in particular, raises such questions: Can the majority of Negroes be assimilated into American society? Do they really want to be assimilated? What "price" will they have to pay for assimilation or non-assimilation? If they want to be assimilated, what are they themselves doing to facilitate this process? If not, are there discernible attitudes among Negroes which impede this process? Were there a rational choice, can the Negro subculture successfully resist the pressure for conformity exerted upon it by the dominant culture? Can they (Negroes) revitalize and regenerate the subculture?

Negroes will argue, and often glibly, that they are not concerned with assimilation but with integration (i.e., total acceptance without discrimination) and that the prospects for the former are very remote. Hence, they dismiss the question as academic. Although the probability of assimilation is remote, the question is not psychologically insignificant for the Negroes. It is significant, in part, because one's attitude toward assimilation may or may not foster the feeling of separateness and will determine the intensity of one's effort to merge into the larger culture and society. However, the question is particularly important during this period of rapid improvement in the Negro's status and the trend toward integration. These changes, in themselves, are sources of anxiety to many Negroes.[1] Although Negroes do not express their concern publicly, the writer found that it was widely, but privately, voiced in and outside the Muslim movement. This concern and their ambivalent attitudes—be it at the level of conscious or unconscious awareness—explain, in part, why so many Negroes pay attention to black nationalism but do not actively support the Muslim movement, which is only a specific manifestation

---

[1] It is interesting to note that a report of a two-year study of Negro and white attitudes toward integration, prepared for the State Commission on Civil Rights in Connecticut by Elmo Roper, revealed that although 90 per cent of Negroes questioned hoped for integration and favored it (in most phases of activities), 37 per cent voiced some misgivings for racial mixing in purely social affairs, especially "parties", 46 per cent whites questioned objected to racial mixing in purely social affairs. "Connecticut Ends Study of Integration" by David Anderson, *New York Times*, April 14, 1961, p. 21.

of their uncertainties. This question involves the "destiny" of the Negro people in America. We should seek to understand it; we should not explain it away. The price for assimilation is clear; the price for non-assimilation is not obvious. If, however, the sense of separateness and ethnic consciousness now developing were to dominate, society at large will have to pay a price for minority exclusiveness, especially for the kind now fostered by the Muslim movement.

Ideologically and culturally, however, the assimilationist strand has been stronger among Negroes. The dominance of this strand is already discernible and much stronger among the middle- and upper-class Negroes and intellectuals.[2] But this strand is somewhat weaker among the lower classes because the realities of their social situation do not support their assimilationist mentality. Consequently, the sense of separateness and ethnic consciousness actually dominate their lives. This feeling has always been present but they lacked positive articulation. The intensification of these feelings is one of the most important developments in the contemporary social situation of American Negroes.

Perhaps, the black nationalists' agitation is the loudest expression of a "manifesto of identity"—the Negroes' conscious, though slow, awakening to their heritage of abuse and degradation, and especially, to their possible destiny as human beings. It may well signal the beginning of the end of the Negroes' aimless and vain desire to hide their dark skins behind a white mask. The manifesto of identity is a subjectivity: its voice reflects the past and the present and perhaps the future as well. It requires no real objects and relationships for its expression; yet in a significant way, the manifesto brings to public attention "voices from within the veil" and subtle and imperceptible changes which are occurring among the black masses. They are voices heralding perhaps the psychological and spiritual liberation of the black masses from the shackles of a past that still haunts the present. The manifesto announces their "presence" in America and their impatience and disaffection with the limitations imposed upon their "equality in opportunity." Their impatience and disaffection cannot be disassociated from the important changes (most contributing significantly to the general improvement of the Negroes) in the United States as a whole and in the Negro community or from the rising

---

[2]Elmo Roper, the chairman of the Connecticut Civil Rights Commission report, referred to previously, explains that Negroes harboring racial prejudice against white people are either well-educated Negroes who have come up from the South and are resentful of their treatment there, or else are northern Negroes of poor education. *Christian Science Monitor*, April 14, 1961, p. 6.

protest of millions in the non-white world against discrimination and exploitation based solely on racial or religious distinctions.

The "voices from within the veil" and the manifesto of identity do not deny the Negro's Americanism. Indeed, they affirm what is commonly known: that the Negro is American in heart, loyalties, and in everything else. In its mild forms the manifesto of identity is best expressed in the "Negro History Week" and by such organizations as the American Society of African Culture or the Afro-American Heritage Association. Its voice is a reaffirmation of the Negroes' faith in the possibilities offered by the pluralistic character of American society for their cultural, intellectual, and spiritual development. In its extreme form, the Muslim movement is the best example; it reveals how deeply the cancer of American racism has infected all its parts, making the oppressed and the oppressor mutually depraved.

The study of black nationalism illustrates the desperate character of the social situation of the lower-class Negroes in the large northern cities and the tensions which arise from this situation. We tried to show that their life is devoid of meaning and purpose. They are estranged from the larger society which they seek to enter, but which rejects them. Similarly, they are estranged from their own group which they despise. The result of this feeling of dual alienation is apathy, futility, and emptiness of purpose. In a psychological sense, many are lonesome within and outside their own group. They are rootless and restless. They are without an identity, i.e., a sense of belonging and membership in society. In this situation, there is neither hope nor optimism. In fact, most lower-class Negroes in these large cities see little or no "future" for themselves and posterity. This is partly because they have no faith in themselves or in their potential as black men in America and especially because important decisions which shape their lives appear entirely beyond their control. We should stress, however, that the sense of social estrangement and alienation is not limited to the Negroes. In fact, it is a problem common to urban dwellers. The consequence for a meaningful life is, in varying degrees, the same for Negroes as well as others in comparable social situations. The point, however, is that the impact of contemporary urban tensions and anxieties on an already marginal and despised group is dramatic and paralyzing. It corrupts the personality of its victims, depriving them of any sense of human worth and dignity.

Three more factors in the contemporary social situation of Negroes help to explain the growing sense of separateness and ethnic consciousness among the Negro masses: the bifurcation of the Negro caste, i.e., the emergence of a real Negro middle class and the Negro's re-definition of himself not only in terms of the whites but in relation to this "new" class; his re-definition of himself in relation to Africa; and his reactions to the traditional Negro institutions and leadership groups in terms of these new definitions.

The bifurcation of the caste, especially in the North, is an important development of which the implications are not generally recognized. Nevertheless, the emergence of a Negro middle-class may have serious consequences for the Negro masses, creating an "imbalance" within the Negro community. One obvious consequence is that lower class Negroes are beginning to re-define themselves not only in relations to the white society but also to the Negro middle- and upper-class "society." For this reason, they resent middle-class Negroes whose social situation is incomparably better than theirs. This situation is important for understanding the character of race relations in the North. First, the position of the middle-class Negroes tends to obscure the problems of the lower-class Negroes, in part because Negro "progress" (with some justification) is defined largely in middle-class terms; it is measured by the conspicuous consumption of the middle- and upper-class Negroes, who, in fact, have found their identity with the white middle-class. As individuals, they can escape the open contempt which Northern whites have for the less fortunate of their race. They, too, display haughtiness toward the lower-class Negroes. The "bonds of solidarity in chains" which previously characterized the relationship between them is no longer apparent, i.e., the fact that in the past middle- and upper-class Negroes were able to identify with the struggles and aspirations of lower class Negroes. The interests of the middle class are different and, in some measure, lower-class Negroes are estranged from them. But, like middle classes everywhere, the essentially middle-class Negro leadership takes for granted that its strivings represent unquestionably the interest of the masses. This may well be, but the estrangement between the two classes is incontestable. The important point is that precisely because lower-class Negroes are beginning to define themselves in relations to the Negro "image" portrayed by the middle-class and are attracted to it, they are also repelled by it because their actual conditions do not permit genuine identification with the middle-class Negroes. As it is in their relations with the white society, lower-class Negroes tend to withdraw and disassociate themselves from the middle and upper-class Negroes. This estrangement suggests the beginning of class consciousness and conflict among the Negro masses, directed not against the whites, but against the Negro middle and upper classes. This development aggravates tensions in the Negro community and produces distrust of the middle-class leadership among the lower-class Negroes.

These Negroes feel powerless not only in relation to the white-power complex but also to what appears to them as the monopoly of power by Negro middle-class leadership. Black nationalism, especially the Muslim movement, reflects this sense of dual marginality and impotence in both power centers. But an important distinction should be made here: although black nationalism is a general reaction against whites as "possessors" of vital social, economic, and political power, the nationalists do not question, except in utopian and religious terms, the legitimacy of the white power monopoly, nor have they sought to alter it. Instead, their sense of impotence produces a need for withdrawal and racial separation (a desire for a homeland) as the means by which Negroes might become masters of their destiny. However, the Muslim movement reflects the increasing class consciousness and conflict[3] among the lower-class Negroes and questions, specifically the legitimacy of the Negro middle-class leadership. In other words, the movement questions the "monopoly" of power by the middle-class leadership in defining both the "needs" and "destiny" of the Negro people in America. It questions the trend toward integration which its leaders see as a trend toward assimilation. Furthermore, its leaders question the "balance" between the ideal of integration and the definition of lower-class Negro "needs" in practical terms. The Muslim movement, in a real sense, is an attempt to alter the power relationship within the Negro community. The concerns now voiced by the black nationalists may well determine the character and style of future Negro leadership in their communities.

Another defect in the contemporary social situation of the urban Negro masses is the impotence of traditional Negro institutions in dealing with either the psychological or practical needs of their community. For a long time, these institutions and leadership groups have been the interpreters of the social scene for the masses of Negroes. Of these, the Negro church is the most important. There is evidence that the Negro church has lost its significance for the urban proletarian who seeks to define his situation in terms of the church. However, where its influence is still felt, the Negro church is particularly culpable for its general lack of concern for the moral and social problems of the community. Rather than face the problem of the degradation of its people and take positive action for moral, cultural, and economic

---

[3]That this conflict has not found widespread organized expression is not important for our analysis.

reconstruction, it has been accommodatory. Fostering indulgence in religious sentimentality, and riveting the attention of the masses on the bounties of a hereafter, the Negro church remains a refuge, an escape from the cruel realities of the here and now. Furthermore, evidence abounds of the misuse of the pulpit for furthering personal ambitions at the expense of the already harshly exploited masses. The grim fact is that the pulpit, with exceptions spread far and wide, has become during the present century and especially in the large cities of the North, a route to social mobility for the charlatans in the Negro community. There is some evidence, however, of growing realization of their social responsibilities among many Negro church leaders. The most important evidence is the Southern Christian Leadership Conference, led by the Rev. Dr. Martin Luther King, Jr.[4] The same concern was shown by Dr. Joseph H. Jackson, President of the five-million-member National Baptist Convention, who recently announced the purchase of 600 acres of farmland for resettlement of Negro tenant and sharecropper families dispossessed of any means of livelihood by whites in Fayette and Haywood Counties as reprisals for their attempt to exercise the right to vote.[5] In large measure, however, both the Negro Church and other traditional leadership groups do not seem to appreciate how debased the life of the urban lower-class Negro is, nor the magnitude of effort in thought and action required for the reconstruction of the "Souls of Black Folk."

Lastly, the liberation movements and the emergence of the independent African states have had a significant impact on the Negro's total redefinition of himself, in relation to both his situation in America and to Africa. These events have not only awakened an unprecedented interest in Africa but have led, in a limited way at least, to what may be called "an African orientation." This does not mean that their effort to redefine themselves in relation to Africa is an expression of their desire to emigrate there. The practical importance of their African orientation should not be exaggerated. It should be balanced against the strong integration and assimilationist trends. We may observe, however, that recent developments in Africa have led a great many Negroes to identify with the struggles and aspirations of the African people. This, together with the domestic developments and changes, appears to create a psychological situation fostering and intensifying the sense of separateness and ethnic consciousness among the masses.

---

[4]See Martin Luther King, Jr. *Stride Toward Freedom: The Montgomery Story* (New York: Harper and Brothers, 1958).

[5]*The New York Courier*, March 25, 1961, Sec. 2, p. 18. The *Courier* editorially described Dr. Jackson's action as "Statesmanship in the Pulpit."

This psychological situation fosters among Negroes a new self-image, pride, and an impatient and urgent desire for equality, personal dignity and self-assertion. In some measure, the consequences of their "new" psychology are evident in the confidence shown by southern Negro student "sit-in" demonstrations. Similarly, the emotional appeal, though otherwise limited, of black nationalism to the Northern urban Negro masses suggests the same psychological changes.[6] We might add, qualifiedly, that the Negro's need for an identity and his desire for equality and dignity lead him increasingly to merge his aspirations with those of millions throughout the non-white world who are protesting against discrimination and exploitation. They, too, are caught in the "revolution of rising expectations!"

Elijah Muhammad, then, emerges against this background of tensions, change, and of neglect by the traditional Negro institutions and leaders; the failure of the white society to extend "equality in opportunity" to the Negro people, the Negro's dual sense of alienation and marginality; and the increasing sensitivity of the masses to their lowly material fortunes and the anxieties about their "destiny" in America. Keeping this background in mind, and disregarding but not condoning the excesses of Muhammad's ideological concoctions or racial mysticism, it is clear that his is a unique effort to reconstruct the Negro soul, by providing a "world" (a *mystique*) in which one could be black and unashamed, and by regenerating the Negro's moral and social values. So far as the writer knows, no Negro has ever dared to tackle the bewildering problems of the "Negro in the mud" with equal vigor and such obdurate determination as Mr. Muhammad. Seen in this light, and in the light of the limited alternatives open to these Negroes, the Nation of Islam, with its moral and economic reforms, provides a way out for these Negroes. The ideological and racialist excesses are more symptomatic and symbolic than crucial in themselves. They reflect the harsh cruelties, discontent, and the grave social malaise which afflicts millions of Negroes in America. Stated simply, the message of the Nation of Islam is this: Despite important,

---

[6]It is interesting to note that Dr. Joseph H. Jackson announced recently that the National Baptist Convention has sent a three-man commission to Liberia with a view to arranging for purchase of 5,000 acres of land for young Negroes interested in resettling there. Although, Dr. Jackson stressed that his project was not a "back-to-Africa" movement, it is significant that this is the first commission of this nature sent to Africa since the abortive effort of Garvey in the twenties. *The Courier*, p. 18. For our analysis, what we describe as "an African Orientation" is important because for the first time in recent history, some Negroes are beginning to look to Africa as a possible alternative to the United States. Some are interested in business and cultural ties, but there are many who are interested in emigration.

though slow, changes which have occurred in the Negro's formal status as citizens, the lot of the masses of Negroes in the North has not changed in substance. Evidence of pauperization, cultural disorientation, and moral degradation persist in spite of, and perhaps because of, the facade of public progress. These, Muhammad asserts, exist in spite of the fact that inequalities between blacks and whites are not legislated in the North; that the subordination of the masses of Negroes in the North reveals a few stubborn facts of social life which no amount of declarations of good intentions or wishful optimism can obviate. The first, he says, is the unequal distribution of political and economic power between blacks and whites. The possibility of an equalization of this distribution of vital social power is too remote to warrant speculation; but for a long time, there shall exist Negro communities, and the position of Negroes is likely to remain marginal. Thus, Negro striving for advancement, Mr. Muhammad says, is fundamentally circumscribed by their awareness of this fact. Their formal freedom is concomitantly limited by the substantive limitations as well as by their perception of the limitations. Yet within these restrictions, Negroes can give meaning to their freedom.

Formal freedom, insists Muhammad, without a substantive basis is, in effect, meaningless. Substantive freedom, a people's style of life—material, cultural, moral and a sense of human dignity—cannot be bestowed upon people who do not want it, and if they do, are not prepared to help themselves and make the sacrifice necessary for its attainment; they must help create the conditions for it. Thus, if the masses of Negroes are to rise in the social scale, if they are to gain respect from others, if they are to be regarded as human beings rather than social outcasts, they must become consciously aware of their predicament, their degradation which is the bond of their common identity. They must also become conscious of their opportunities, however limited, and must take advantage of them. It is pointless to indulge in the fantasy that through some biological miracle black Americans will be transformed into white Americans or that the Negro communities will disappear in the foreseeable future.

Muhammad is convinced that the chief obstacle to be overcome is the "mentality" of the masses of Negroes. This is the true enemy of their advancement and progress. The result of centuries of oppression, it has helped to produce the moral and material conditions in which the Negro masses now find themselves. The enemy of the Negro people, he maintains, is not simply white people, but also the "value system" of the subculture.

The writer is convinced that Muhammad's ideological pronouncements, which are popularly termed "black supremacy," are aimed at purging lower-class Negroes of their inferiority complex. The "real" rather than the "ostensible" enemy of the Nation of Islam or of the Negro masses in general, is not the white people *per se*, but the Negro himself—his subculture, his image of himself and of his "place" in society, his attitude toward white people, and his idealization of all that is white. From the point of view of all black nationalists, the Negro can never be really free until he has purged from his mind all notions of white superiority and Negro inferiority and thus ceases to despise himself and his group. In doing so, he may have to shed the outward appearances of white culture and, most importantly, the "old time" religion. Indeed, they insist that Negroes should proudly accept rather than deny any contrasts between them and whites. Thus, it seems, the mission of the Nation of Islam is to reverse the process toward assimilation by means of militant separatism.

The process by which whites have been able to create and sustain the Negro's image of his own inferiority is known in common parlance as "brainwashing." In Muhammad's teaching, this process is known as "tricknowledgy." It would appear to the observer that it takes another kind of "tricknowledgy" to undo the former. This, in the writer's view, is in part the significance of the racial doctrines, especially the eschatology emphasizing the eventual "supremacy" of the Black Nation. If, indeed, Muhammad is aware that whites used "tricks" to "fool" the Negro, then it is plausible that his eschatology or other doctrines of "racial supremacy" are gimmicks meant for the consumption of his followers and for combatting the "enemy within" —the Negro's "mentality." If this is correct, the frequent comparison of the Muslim movement with the Ku Klux Klan or with the White Citizen Council misses the point and has only a superficial relevance. Although alike in the crudity of their racial diatribes, they differ significantly in their objectives—for instance, the Muslims do not seek to deprive their fellow citizens of their political rights.

The Nation of Islam represents an esoteric, in-group struggle to provide standards by which the social, cultural, and moral life of the Negro masses can be raised to a meaningful community fabric. It seeks an outlet for Negro striving and performance. The movement combines the attractions of religion, nationalism, and political "pies in the sky" with a peculiar sense of belonging and achievement, and proposes the possibility of "greater" achievement for its members. The Nation assists its members to strive for traditional American middle-class values while maintaining their identity with the Negro community.

However, these values are interpreted for the members *via* the dogma of Islam, which in a direct and uncompromising way, assists them to overcome lower-class values which are held to impede the advancement of the Negro masses. Religious and nationalistic symbols, combined with a mutilated version of western eschatology, endow the practical and moral concerns of the members with meaning and a strong sense of purpose and destiny. However, these ideological strands seem to dominate the "community" fabric and conceal the socially relevant aspects of Mr. Muhammad's teachings, the primary concern of which is the "quality" of life of the urban lower-class Negroes. Although the ideological strands give the Nation of Islam an appearance of a wholly anti-white movement, properly conceived, it is uncompromisingly anti-lower-class Negro values, anti-Negro middle-class complacency and opportunism, and anti-white paternalism and injustice. Perhaps, more than the movement has been credited, it is far more opposed to the entire "way of life" of the lower-class Negro and the "dependence" mentality of their leaders than it appears.

The Nation of Islam is important not because it tells whites how bitterly Negroes feel about their present conditions, but for showing the Negro masses "why" they feel the way they do, "how" they may get out of their degradation, and "how" they may become self-respecting citizens. The Nation sets standards of achievement and excellence for its members and interprets for them standards of morality and economic norms generally cherished by middle-class Americans. (Of course there are some deviations.) The Nation recognizes the needs of Negroes, like other human beings, for membership and identity in some community. It insists that Negroes have the capacity to redeem themselves and recover their sense of human worth; that they must take the initiative in their struggle for human dignity. The alternative to these admonitions, says Muhammad, is continued complacency, moral deterioration, cultural degradation, crime, juvenile delinquency, and social and cultural stagnation.

Negro middle-class leadership being what it is and white attitudes being essentially unchanged in the vital areas of housing, equal opportunities in employment, etc., even in the Northern cities—what logical type of leadership can one envisage emerging from the deplorable conditions of the northern ghettos? What alternatives exist for meeting the urgent needs of the Negro communities except through an appeal to Negro initiative? It seems conceivable that if the masses of Negroes were in the *mood* for the Nation of Islam or for something akin to it, under the right kind of conditions and leadership, communal initiative (call it nationalism or what you will) not chauvinism, holds some promise as a way out for them. If this should happen, then it would be tragic if the white society did not understand it. The white society may even encourage it. In fact it promises to be for the good of society. In communal oriented activities, presently woefully lacking, Negroes would discover their identity and would best reflect what is good about America through self-assertion. It might enable them to develop their potential, a greater sense of the "public interest" and to participate more constructively in the society. The Negro is unquestionably an American, "reluctantly" at times, even as the deviant doctrines of Mr. Muhammad show; yet he is a member of a group with four centuries of unique experiences and traditions that cannot be easily wished away. Besides, the Negro, though removed by centuries from Africa, has never been, and cannot now be expected to be, indifferent to the land of his forebearers. This remote heritage, no matter how insignificant its content may be, is part and parcel of the Negro's being. This too, like his Americanism, should be understood. In these circumstances, sentimentality toward assimilation or toward chauvinistic nationalism is blatantly wishful, unrealistic, and contrary to fact, in so far as the masses of Negroes are concerned.

American Negroes have contributed to American culture not by denying their identity (or contrasts) but by asserting it through music, folklore, etc., in spite of the harsh circumstances in which they found themselves. Indeed, they stand to contribute more to the culture and welfare of their society by recognizing and appreciating their own identity, rather than despising themselves. Until most have been assimilated, the desire for ethnic self-assertion will continue to manifest itself in their social and cultural life, in private as well as in public matters, though taking various forms.

The Muslim movement is a grand reaction to the American scene and especially, the Negro's position in it; yet the scenery (the stage-set) shackles and delimits the drama—the potential for meaningful political or social action. Herein lie the factors which limit its social usefulness. It is handicapped by its very "style of life"—i.e., the mentality, the social and moral values and economic habits of the group which it seeks to redeem. Its separatist ideology is irreconcilably in conflict with the dominant assimilationist thinking of the vast majority of Negroes. On the other hand, it is limited by its anti-white ideology which strikes deep at the Negroes' fears as well as those of whites—their fear of a possibility of a "Black Revenge." The stark reality is that there can be no substantial or disruptive political action by the Nation of Islam other than that akin to the campus gadfly—a nuisance, mildly frightening, but actually not as deadly as the Tse-tse fly. Yet a frightened public or civic authorities, incensed by a sensational press, may well be led in such a way as to precipitate the fulfillment of alarmist prophecies.

Black Power

Stokely Carmichael
Charles Hamilton

The adoption of the concept of Black Power is one of the most legitimate and healthy developments in American politics and race relations in our time. The concept of Black Power speaks to all the needs mentioned in this chapter. It is a call for black people in this country to unite, to recognize their heritage, to build a sense of community. It is a call for black people to begin to define their own goals, to lead their own organizations and to support those organizations. It is a call to reject the racist institutions and values of this society.

The concept of Black Power rests on a fundamental premise: *Before a group can enter the open society, it must first close ranks.* By this we mean that group solidarity is necessary before a group can operate effectively from a bargaining position of strength in a pluralistic society. Traditionally, each new ethnic group in this society has found the route to social and political viability through the organization of its own institutions with which to represent its needs within the larger society. Studies in voting behavior specifically, and political behavior generally, have made it clear that politically the American pot has not melted. Italians vote for Rubino over O'Brien; Irish for Murphy over Goldberg, etc. This phenomenon may seem distasteful to

Reprinted from *Black Power: The Politics of Liberation in America* by Stokely Carmichael and Charles V. Hamilton by permission of Random House. Copyright 1967 by Stokely Carmichael and Charles Hamilton.

some, but it has been and remains today a central fact of the American political system. There are other examples of ways in which groups in the society have remembered their roots and used this effectively in the political arena. Theodore Sorensen describes the politics of foreign aid during the Kennedy Administration in his book *Kennedy:*

> No powerful constituencies or interest groups backed foreign aid. The Marshall Plan at least had appealed to Americans who traced their roots to the Western European nations aided. But there were few voters who identified with India, Colombia or Tanganyika [p. 351].

The extent to which black Americans can and do "trace their roots" to Africa, to that extent will they be able to be more effective on the political scene.

A white reporter set forth this point in other terms when he made the following observation about white Mississippi's manipulation of the anti-poverty program:

> The war on poverty has been predicated on the notion that there is such a thing as a community which can be defined geographically and mobilized for a collective effort to help the poor. This theory has no relationship to reality in the deep South. In every Mississippi county there are two communities. Despite all the pious platitudes of the moderates on both sides, these two communities habitually see their interests in terms of conflict rather than cooperation. Only when the Negro community can muster enough political, economic and professional strength to compete on somewhat equal terms, will Negroes believe in the possibility of true cooperation and whites accept its necessity. En route to integration, the Negro community needs to develop a greater independence—a chance to run its own affairs and not cave in whenever "the man" barks—or so it seems to me, and to most of the knowledgeable people with whom I talked in Mississippi. To OEO, this judgment may sound like black nationalism. . . .[1]

The point is obvious: black people must lead and run their own organizations. Only black people can convey the revolutionary idea—and it is a revolutionary idea—that black people are able to do things themselves. Only they can help create in the community an aroused and continuing black consciousness that will provide the basis for political strength. In the past, white allies have often furthered white supremacy without the whites involved realizing it, or even wanting

---

[1]Christopher Jencks, "Accommodating Whites: A New Look at Mississippi," *The New Republic* (April 16, 1966).

to do so. Black people must come together and do things for themselves. They must achieve self-identity and self-determination in order to have their daily needs met.

Black Power means, for example, that in Lowndes County, Alabama, a black sheriff can end police brutality. A black tax assessor and tax collector and county board of revenue can lay, collect, and channel tax monies for the building of better roads and schools serving black people. In such areas as Lowndes, where black people have a majority, they will attempt to use power to exercise control. This is what they seek: control. When black people lack a majority, Black Power means proper representation and sharing of control. It means the creation of power bases, of strength, from which black people can press to change local or nation-wide patterns of oppression —instead of from weakness.

It does not mean *merely* putting black faces into office. Black visibility is not Black Power. Most of the black politicians around the country today are not examples of Black Power. The power must be that of a community, and emanate from there. The black politicians must start from there. The black politicians must stop being representatives of "downtown" machines, whatever the cost might be in terms of lost patronage and holiday handouts.

Black Power recognizes—it must recognize—the ethnic basis of American politics as well as the power-oriented nature of American politics. Black Power therefore calls for black people to consolidate behind their own, so that they can bargain from a position of strength. But while we endorse the *procedure* of group solidarity and identity for the purpose of attaining certain goals in the body politic, this does not mean that black people should strive for the same kind of rewards (i.e., end results) obtained by the white society. The ultimate values and goals are not domination or exploitation of other groups, but rather an effective share in the total power of the society.

Nevertheless, some observers have labeled those who advocate Black Power as racists; they have said that the call for self-identification and self-determination is "racism in reverse" or "black supremacy." This is a deliberate and absurd lie. There is no analogy—by any stretch of definition or imagination—between the advocates of Black Power and white racists. Racism is not merely exclusion on the basis of race but exclusion for the purpose of subjugating or maintaining subjugation. The goal of the racists is to keep black people on the bottom, arbitrarily and dictatorially, as they have done in this country for over three hundred years. The goal of black self-determination and black self-identity—Black Power—is full participation in the decision-making processes affecting the lives of black people, and recognition of the virtues in themselves as black people. The black people of this country have not lynched whites, bombed their churches, murdered their children and manipulated laws and institutions to maintain oppression. White racists have. Congressional laws, one after the other, have not been necessary to stop black people from oppressing others and denying others the full enjoyment of their rights. White racists have made such laws necessary. The goal of Black Power is positive and functional to a free and viable society. No white racist can make this claim.

A great deal of public attention and press space was devoted to the hysterical accusation of "black racism" when the call for Black Power was first sounded. A national committee of influential black churchmen affiliated with the National Council of Churches, despite their obvious respectability and responsibility, had to resort to a paid advertisement to articulate their position, while anyone yapping "black racism" made front-page news. In their statement, published in the *New York Times* of July 31, 1966, the churchmen said:

> We, an informal group of Negro churchmen in America, are deeply disturbed about the crisis brought upon our country by historic distortions of important human realities in the controversy about "black power." What we see shining through the variety of rhetoric is not anything new but the same old problem of power and race which has faced our beloved country since 1619.
>
> . . . The conscience of black men is corrupted because having no power to implement the demands of conscience, the concern for justice in the absence of justice becomes a chaotic self-surrender. Powerlessness breeds a race of beggars. We are faced with a situation where powerless conscience meets conscienceless power, threatening the very foundations of our Nation.
>
> We deplore the overt violence of riots, but we feel it is more important to focus on the real sources of these eruptions. These sources may be abetted inside the Ghetto, but their basic cause lies in the silent and covert violence which white middle class America inflicts upon the victims of the inner city.
>
> . . . In short, the failure of American leaders to use American power to creat equal opportunity *in life* as well as *law*, this is the real problem and not the anguished cry for black power.
>
> . . . Without the capacity to participate with power, i.e., to have some organized political and economic strength to really influence people with whom one interacts, integration is not meaningful.
>
> . . . America has asked its Negro citizens to fight for opportunity as *individuals*, whereas at certain points in our history what we have

needed most has been opportunity for the *whole group*, not just for selected and approved Negroes.

. . . We must not apologize for the existence of this form of group power, for we have been oppressed as a group and not as individuals. We will not find our way out of that oppression until both we and America accept the need for Negro Americans, as well as for Jews, Italians, Poles, and white Anglo-Saxon Protestants, among others, to have and to wield group power.

It is a commentary on the fundamentally racist nature of this society that the concept of group strength for black people must be articulated —not to mention defended. No other group would submit to being led by others. Italians do not run the Anti-Defamation League of B'nai B'rith. Irish do not chair Christopher Columbus Societies. Yet when black people call for black-run and all-black organizations, they are immediately classed in a category with the Ku Klux Klan. This is interesting and ironic, but by no means surprising: the society does not expect black people to be able to take care of their business, and there are many who prefer it precisely that way.

In the end, we cannot and shall not offer any guarantees that Black Power, if achieved, would be non-racist. No one can predict human behavior. Social change always has unanticipated consequences. If black racism is what the larger society fears, we cannot help them. We can only state what we hope will be the result, given the fact that the present situation is unacceptable and that we have no real alternative but to work for Black Power. The final truth is that the white society is not entitled to reassurances, even if it were possible to offer them.

We have outlined the meaning and goals of Black Power; we have also discussed one major thing which it is not. There are others of greater importance. The advocates of Black Power reject the old slogans and meaningless rhetoric of previous years in the civil rights struggle. The language of yesterday is indeed irrelevant: progress, non-violence, integration, fear of "white backlash," coalition. Let us look at the rhetoric and see why these terms must be set aside or redefined.

One of the tragedies of the struggle against racism is that up to this point there has been no national organization which could speak to the growing militancy of young black people in the urban ghettos and the black-belt South. There has been only a "civil rights" movement, whose tone of voice was adapted to an audience of middle-class whites. It served as a sort of buffer zone between that audience and angry young blacks. It claimed to speak for the needs of a community, but it did not speak in the tone of that community. None of its so-called leaders could go into a rioting community and be listened to. In a sense, the blame must be shared—along with the mass media—by those leaders for what happened in Watts, Harlem, Chicago, Cleveland and other places. Each time the black people in those cities saw Dr. Martin Luther King get slapped they became angry. When they saw little black girls bombed to death *in a church* and civil rights workers ambushed and murdered, they were angrier; and when nothing happened, they were steaming mad. We had nothing to offer that they could see, except to go out and be beaten again. We helped to build their frustration.

We had only the old language of love and suffering. And in most places—that is, from the liberals and middle class—we got back the old language of patience and progress. The civil rights leaders were saying to the country: "Look, you guys are supposed to be nice guys, and we are only going to do what we are supposed to do. Why do you beat us up? Why don't you give us what we ask? Why don't you straighten yourselves out?" For the masses of black people, this language resulted in virtually nothing. In fact, their objective day-to-day condition worsened. The unemployment rate among black people increased while that among white declined. Housing conditions in the black communities deteriorated. Schools in the black ghettos continued to plod along on outmoded techniques, inadequate curricula, and with all too many tired and indifferent teachers. Meanwhile, the President picked up the refrain of "We Shall Overcome" while the Congress passed civil rights law after civil rights law, only to have them effectively nullified by deliberately weak enforcement. "Progress is being made," we were told.

Such language, along with admonitions to remain non-violent and fear the white backlash, convinced some that that course was the *only* course to follow. It misled some into believing that a black minority could bow its head and get whipped into a meaningful position of power. The very notion is absurd. The white society devised the language, adopted the rules and had the black community narcotized into believing that that language and those rules were, in fact, relevant. The black community was told time and again how *other* immigrants finally won *acceptance:* that is, by following the Protestant Ethic of Work and Achievement. They worked hard; therefore, they achieved. We were not told that it was by building Irish Power, Italian Power, Polish Power or Jewish Power that these groups got themselves together and operated from positions of strength. We were not told that "the American dream" wasn't designed for black people. That while today, to whites, the dream may *seem* to include black people, it cannot do so by the very nature of this nation's political and economic system, which imposes institutional racism on the black masses if not upon every individual black. A notable comment on that "dream" was made by Dr. Percy Julian, the black scientist and director of the Julian Research Institute in Chicago, a man for whom the dream seems to have come true. While not subscribing to "black power" as he understood it, Dr. Julian clearly understood the basis for it: "The false concept of basic Negro inferiority is one of the curses that still lingers. It is a problem created by the white man. Our children just no longer are going to accept the patience we were taught by our generation. We were taught a pretty little lie—excel and the whole world lies open before you. *I obeyed the injunction and found it to be wishful thinking.*" (Authors' italics)[2]

A key phrase in our buffer-zone days was non-violence. For years it has been thought that black people would not literally fight for their lives. Why this has been so is not entirely clear; neither the larger society nor black people are noted for passivity. The notion apparently stems from the years of marches and demonstrations and sit-ins where black people did not strike back and the violence always came from white mobs. There are many who still sincerely believe in that approach. From our viewpoint, rampaging white mobs and white nightriders must be made to understand that their days of free head-whipping are over. Black people should and must fight back. Nothing more quickly repels someone bent on destroying you than the unequivocal message: "O.K., fool, make your move, and run the same risk I run—of dying."

When the concept of Black Power is set forth, many people immediately conjure up notions of violence. The country's reaction to the Deacons for Defense and Justice, which originated in Louisiana, is instructive. Here is a group which realized that the "law" and law enforcement agencies would not protect people, so they had to do it themselves. If a nation fails to protect its citizens, then that nation cannot condemn those who take up the task themselves. The Deacons and all other blacks who resort to self-defense represent a simple answer to a simple question: what man would not defend his family and home from attack?

But this frightened some white people, because they knew that black people would now fight back. They knew that this was precisely what *they* would have long since done if *they* were subjected to the

---

[2]*The New York Times* (April 30, 1967), p. 30.

injustices and oppression heaped on blacks. Those of us who advocate Black Power are quite clear in our own minds that a "non-violent" approach to civil rights is an approach black people cannot afford and a luxury white people do not deserve. It is crystal clear to us—and it must become so with the white society—*that there can be no social order without social justice*. White people must be made to understand that they must stop messing with black people, or the blacks *will* fight back!

Next, we must deal with the term "integration." According to its advocates, social justice will be accomplished by "integrating the Negro into the mainstream institutions of the society from which he has been traditionally excluded." This concept is based on the assumption that there is nothing of value in the black community and that little of value could be created among black people. The thing to do is siphon off the "acceptable" black people into the surrounding middle-class white community.

The goals of integrationists are middle-class goals, articulated primarily by a small group of Negroes with middle-class aspirations or status. Their kind of integration has meant that a few blacks "make it," leaving the black community, sapping it of leadership potential and know-how. As we noted . . . those token Negroes—absorbed into a white mass—are of no value to the remaining black masses. They become meaningless show-pieces for a conscience-soothed white society. Such people will state that they would prefer to be treated "only as individuals, not as Negroes"; that they "are not and should not be preoccupied with race." This is a totally unrealistic position. In the first place, black people have not suffered as individuals but as members of a group; therefore, their liberation lies in group action. This is why SNCC—and the concept of Black Power—affirms that helping *individual* black people to solve their problems on an *individual* basis does little to alleviate the mass of black people. Secondly, while color blindness *may* be a sound goal ultimately, we must realize that race is an overwhelming fact of life in this historical period. There is no black man in this country who can live "simply as a man." His blackness is an ever-present fact of this racist society, whether he recognizes it or not. It is unlikely that this or the next generation will witness the time when race will no longer be relevant in the conduct of public affairs and in public policy decision-making. To realize this and to attempt to deal with it does not make one a racist or overly preoccupied with race; it puts one in the forefront of a significant *struggle*. If there is no intense struggle today, there will be no meaningful results tomorrow.

"Integration" as a goal today speaks to the problem of blackness not only in an unrealistic way but also in a despicable way. It is based on complete acceptance of the fact that in order to have a decent house or education, black people must move into a white neighborhood or send their children to a white school. This reinforces, among both black and white, the idea that "white" is automatically superior and "black" is by definition inferior. For this reason, "integration" is a subterfuge for the maintenance of white supremacy. It allows the nation to focus on a handful of Southern black children who get into white schools at a great price, and to ignore the ninety-four percent who are left in unimproved all-black schools. Such situations will not change until black people become equal in a way that means something, and integration ceases to be a one-way street. Then integration does not mean draining skills and energies from the black ghetto into white neighborhoods. To sprinkle black children among white pupils in outlying schools is at best a stop-gap measure. The goal is not to take black children out of the black community and expose them to white middle-class values; the goal is to build and strengthen the black community.

"Integration" also means that black people must give up their identity, deny their heritage. We recall the conclusion of Killian and Grigg: "At the present time, integration as a solution to the race problem demands that the Negro foreswear his identity as a Negro." The fact is that integration, as traditionally articulated, would abolish the black community. The fact is that what must be abolished is not the black community, but the dependent colonial status that has been inflicted upon it.

The racial and cultural personality of the black community must be preserved and that community must win its freedom while preserving its cultural integrity. Integrity includes a pride—in the sense of self-acceptance, not chauvinism—in being black, in the historical attainments and contributions of black people. No person can be healthy, complete and mature if he must deny a part of himself; this is what "integration" has required thus far. This is the essential difference between integration as it is currently practiced and the concept of Black Power.

The idea of cultural integrity is so obvious that it seems almost simple-minded to spell things out at this length. Yet millions of Americans resist such truths when they are applied to black people. Again, that resistance is a comment on the fundamental racism in the society. Irish Catholics took care of their own first without a lot of apology for doing so, without any dubious language from timid leadership about guarding against "backlash." Everyone understood it to be a perfectly legitimate procedure. Of course, there would be "backlash." Organization begets counterorganization, but this was no reason to defer.

The so-called white backlash against black people is something else: the embedded traditions of institutional racism being brought into the open and calling forth overt manifestations of individual racism. In the summer of 1966, when the protest marches into Cicero, Illinois, began, the black people knew they were not allowed to live in Cicero and the white people knew it. When blacks began to demand the right to live in homes in that town, the whites simply reminded them of the status quo. Some people called this "backlash." It was, in fact, racism defending itself. In the black community, this is called "White folks showing their color." It is ludicrous to blame black people for what is simply an overt manifestation of white racism. Dr. Martin Luther King stated clearly that the protest marches were not the cause of the racism but merely exposed a long-term cancerous condition in the society.

Beyond the Melting Pot

Nathan Glazer
Daniel P. Moynihan

The idea of the melting pot is as old as the Republic. "I could point out to you a family," wrote the naturalized New Yorker, M-G. Jean de Crèvecoeur, in 1782, "whose grandfather was an Englishman, whose wife was Dutch, whose son married a French woman, and whose present four sons have now four wives of different nations. *He* is an American, who leaving behind him all his ancient prejudices and manners, receives new ones from the new mode of life he has embraced. . . . Here individuals of all nations are melted into a new race of men. . . ."[1] It was an idea close to the heart of the American self-image. But as a century passed, and the number of individuals and nations involved grew, the confidence that they could be fused together waned, and so also the conviction that it would be a good thing if they were to be. In 1882 the Chinese were excluded, and the first general immigration law was enacted. In a steady succession thereafter, new and more selective barriers were raised until, by the National Origins Act of 1924, the nation formally adopted the policy of using immigration to reinforce, rather than further dilute, the racial stock of the early America.

Reprinted with permission of the M.I.T. Press from *Beyond the Melting Pot* by Nathan Glazer and Daniel P. Moynihan. Copyright The M.I.T. Press, and the President and Fellows of Harvard, 1963.

[1] J. Hector St. John Crèvecoeur (Michel-Guillaume Jean de Crèvecoeur), *Letters from an American Farmer*, New York: Fox, Duffield & Co., 1904, pp. 54-55.

307

This latter process was well underway, had become in ways inexorable, when Israel Zangwill's play *The Melting Pot* was first performed in 1908. The play (quite a bad one) was an instant success. It ran for months on Broadway; its title was seized upon as a concise evocation of a profoundly significant American fact.

Behold David Quixano, the Russian Jewish immigrant—a "pogrom orphan"—escaped to New York City, exulting in the glory of his new country:

> . . . America is God's Crucible, the great Melting Pot where all the races of Europe are melting and reforming! Here you stand, good folk, think I, when I see them at Ellis Island, here you stand in your fifty groups with your fifty languages and histories, and your fifty blood hatreds and rivalries, but you won't be long like that brothers, for these are the fires of God you've come to—these are the fires of God. A fig for your feuds and vendettas! German and Frenchman, Irishman and Englishman, Jews and Russians—into the Crucible with you all! God is making the American.
>
> . . . .
> . . . The real American has not yet arrived. He is only in the Crucible, I tell you—he will be the fusion of all the races, the coming superman.[2]

Yet looking back, it is possible to speculate that the response to *The Melting Pot* was as much one of relief as of affirmation: more a matter of reassurance that what had already taken place would turn out all right, rather than encouragement to carry on in the same direction.

Zangwill's hero throws himself into the amalgam process with the utmost energy; by curtainfall he has written his American symphony and won his Muscovite aristocrat: almost all concerned have been reconciled to the homogeneous future. Yet the play seems but little involved with American reality. It is a drama about Jewish separatism and Russian anti-Semitism, with a German concertmaster and an Irish maid thrown in for comic relief. Both protagonists are New Model Europeans of the time. Free thinkers and revolutionaries, it was doubtless in the power of such to merge. But neither of these doctrines was dominant among the ethnic groups of New York City in the 1900's, and in significant ways this became less so as time passed. Individuals, in very considerable numbers to be sure, broke out of their mold, but the groups remained. The experience of Zangwill's

---

[2]Israel Zangwill, *The Melting Pot*, New York: Macmillan, 1909, pp. 37-38.

hero and heroine was *not* general. The point about the melting pot is that it did not happen.

Significantly, Zangwill was himself much involved in one of the more significant deterrents to the melting pot process. He was a Zionist. He gave more and more of his energy to this cause as time passed, and retreated from his earlier position on racial and religious mixture. Only eight years after the opening of *The Melting Pot* he was writing "It was vain for Paul to declare that there should be neither Jew nor Greek. Nature will return even if driven out with a pitchfork, still more if driven out with a dogma."[3]

We may argue whether it was "nature" that returned to frustrate continually the imminent creation of a single American nationality. The fact is that in every generation, throughout the history of the American republic, the merging of the varying streams of population differentiated from one another by origin, religion, outlook has seemed to lie just ahead—a generation, perhaps, in the future. This continual deferral of the final smelting of the different ingredients (or at least the different white ingredients) into a seamless national web as is to be found in the major national states of Europe suggests that we must search for some systematic and general causes for this American pattern of subnationalities; that it is not the temporary upsetting inflow of new and unassimilated immigrants that creates a pattern of ethnic groups within the nation, but rather some central tendency in the national ethos which structures people, whether those coming in afresh or the descendants of those who have been here for generations, into groups of different status and character.

It is striking that in 1963, almost forty years after mass immigration from Europe to this country ended, the ethnic pattern is still so strong in New York City. It is true we can point to specific causes that have served to maintain the pattern. But we know that it was not created by the great new migrations of Southern Negroes and Puerto Ricans into the city; nor by the "new" immigration, which added the great communities of East European Jews and Italians to the city; it was not even created by the great migration of Irish and Germans in the 1840's. Even in the 1830's, while the migration from Europe was still mild, and still consisted for the most part of English-speaking groups, one still finds in the politics of New York State, and of the city, the strong impress of group differentiation. In a fascinating study of the politics of the Jacksonian period in New York State, Lee Benson concludes: "At least since the 1820's, when manhood suffrage became

---

[3]Joseph Leftwich, *Israel Zangwill*, New York: Thomas Yoseloff, 1957, p. 255.

widespread, ethnic and religious differences have tended to be *relatively* the most widespread sources of political differences."[4]

There were ways of making distinctions among Welshmen and Englishmen, Yorkers and New Englanders, long before people speaking strange tongues and practicing strange religions came upon the scene. The group-forming characteristics of American social life—more concretely, the general expectation among those of new and old groups that group membership is significant and formative for opinion and behavior—are as old as the city. The tendency is fixed deep in American life generally; the specific pattern of ethnic differentiation, however, in every generation is created by specific events.

We can distinguish four major events or processes that have structured this pattern in New York during the past generation and whose effects will remain to maintain this pattern for some time to come—to be replaced by others we can scarcely now discern. These four formative events are the following:

First, the shaping of the Jewish community under the impact of the Nazi persecution of the Jews in Europe and the establishment of the state of Israel; second, the parallel, if less marked, shaping of a Catholic community by the reemergence of the Catholic school controversy; third, the migration of Southern Negroes to New York following World War I and continuing through the fifties; fourth, the influx of Puerto Ricans during the fifteen years following World War II.

The Jews

Developments within the Jewish community have had the most immediate significance. A fourth of the city is Jewish; very much more than a fourth of its wealth, energy, talent, and style is derived from the Jews. Over the past thirty years this community has undergone profound emotional experiences, centered almost entirely on the fact of Jewishness, has been measurably strengthened by immigration, and has become involved in vast Zionist enterprises, the rationale of which is exclusively Jewish. There are two aspects of these developments as they affect melting pot tendencies, one negative, the other positive.

The negative aspect has prevented a change that might otherwise have occurred. Prior to the 1930's Jews contributed significantly to the

---

[4]Lee Benson, *The Concept of Jacksonian Democracy*, Princeton, N.J.: Princeton University Press, 1961, p. 165.

ethnic pattern of New York politics by virtue of their radicalism. This
kept them apart from the Catholic establishment in the Democratic
party and the Protestant regime within the Republican party but did
give them a distinct role of their own. At the time of *The Melting Pot*
there were, to be sure, a great many Democratic and Republican
Jewish merchants and businessmen. Most East Side Jews probably
voted the Tammany ticket. But indigenous Jewish politics, the politics
of the *Jewish Daily Forward*, of the Workmen's Circle, and the needle-
trades unions were predominantly socialist. The Russian Revolution, in
which Russian Jews played a prominent role, had a strong attraction
for a small but important number of their kinsmen in New York. It
would appear, for example, that during the 1930's most Communist
party members in New York City were Jewish.[5] It must be stressed
that the vast majority of New York Jews had nothing whatever to do
with Communism. Some of the strongest centers of anti-Communist
activity were and are to be found within the New York Jewish community. Nonetheless there was an ethnic cast to this form of political
radicalism in New York, as there had been to the earlier Socialist
movement.

Both Socialism and Communism are now considerably diminished
and both have lost almost entirely any ethnic base. But just at the
moment when the last distinctly Jewish political activity might have
disappeared, a transcendent Jewish political interest was created by
the ghastly persecutions of the Nazis, the vast dislocations of World
War II, and the establishment of the State of Israel. These were matters that no Jew or Christian could ignore. They were equally matters
about which little could be done except through politics. From the
beginnings of the Zionist movement a certain number of New York
Jews have been involved on that account with the high politics of the
nation. Since the mid-1930's, however, this involvement has reached
deeper and deeper into the New York Jewish community. They are
the one group in the city (apart from the white Protestant financial
establishment) of which it may fairly be said that among the leadership echelons there is a lively, active, and effective interest in who
will be the next U.S. Secretary of State but one . . . or two, or three.

In a positive sense, events of the Nazi era and its aftermath have
produced an intense group consciousness among New York Jews that
binds together persons of widely disparate situations and beliefs. A
pronounced religious revival has occurred. Among those without for-

---

[5]See Nathan Glazer, *The Social Basis of American Communism*, New York:
Harcourt, Brace & World, 1961, Chap. IV.

mal religious ties there is a heightened sense of the defensive importance of organized Jewish activity. Among intellectuals, the feeling of Jewishness is never far from the surface.

Now, as in the past, the Jewish community in New York is the one most actively committed to the principles of racial integration and group tolerance. But open housing is something different from the melting pot. There is no reason to think that any considerable portion of the Jewish community of New York ever subscribed to Israel Zangwill's vision of a nonreligious, intermarried, homogeneous population, but it surely does not do so today. To the contrary, much of the visible activity of the community is aimed in directions that will intensify Jewish identity: Jewish elementary and secondary schools, Jewish colleges and universities, Jewish periodicals, Jewish investments in Israel, and the like. In the meantime, Jewish politicians make more (or at least not less) of the "Jewish" vote.

This is not to say the Jewish community of New York has been *created* or *maintained* by these events of the thirties or forties: that would be too narrow a view of Jewish history, and would ignore the group-making characteristics of American civilization. But the Jewish community was *shaped* by these events. Moving rapidly from working-class to middle-class occupations and styles of life, many alternative courses of development were possible. Within the frame set by these large social movements, the historical drama shaped a community intensely conscious of its Jewishness. Religion plays in many ways the smallest part of the story of American Jews. In New York City in particular the religious definition of the group explains least. Here the formal religious groups are weakest, the degree of affiliation to synagogues and temples smallest. In a city with 2,000,000 Jews, Jews need make no excuses to explain Jewishness and Jewish interests. On the one hand, there is the social and economic structure of the community; on the other, ideologies and emotions molded by the specific history of recent decades. Together they have shaped a community that itself shapes New York and will for generations to come.[6]

The Catholics

Outwardly, events since World War I have brought Catholics, notably the Irish Catholics, ever closer to the centers of power and doc-

---

[6]For the complex interplay of religious, ideological, and socioeconomic factors within the American Jewish community, see *American Judaism* by Nathan Glazer, Chicago: University of Chicago Press, 1957.

trine in American life. But following a pattern common in human affairs, the process of closing the gap has heightened resentment, among some at all events, that a gap should exist. Here, as in much else concerning this general subject, it is hardly possible to isolate New York events from those of the nation generally, but because New York tends to be the center of Catholic thinking and publishing, the distinction is not crucial. The great division between the Catholic Church and the leftist and liberal groups in the city during the period from the Spanish Civil War to the era of McCarthy has been narrowed, with most elements of city politics converging on center positions. However issues of church-state relations have become considerably more difficult, and the issue of government aid to Catholic schools has become acute.

Controversy over church-state relations is nothing new to the American Catholic Church. What is new, however, and what is increasingly avowed, is the extent to which the current controversy derives from Catholic-Jewish disagreements rather than from traditional Catholic-Protestant differences. Relations between the two latter groups have steadily improved: to the point that after three centuries of separation Catholics in the 1960's began increasingly to talk of the prospects of reestablishing Christian unity. In general (there are, of course, many individual exceptions) the dominant view within Protestant and Catholic circles is that the United States is and ought to be a Christian commonwealth, to the point at very least of proclaiming "In God We Trust" on the currency and celebrating Christmas in the public schools. However, as this *rapprochement* has proceeded, within the Jewish community a contrary view has arisen which asserts that the separation of church and state ought to be even more complete than it has been, and that the "Post-Protestant era" means Post-Christian as well, insofar as government relations with religion are concerned.

The most dramatic episode of this development was the decision of the United State Supreme Court on June 25, 1962, that the recitation of an official prayer in the New York school system was unconstitutional. The case was brought by five parents of children in the public schools of the New York City suburb of New Hyde Park. Two of the parents were Jewish, one a member of the Ethical Culture Society, one a Unitarian, and one a nonbeliever. Before it concluded, however, the principal protagonists of the Catholic-Jewish controversy in New York City were involved. The attorney for the Archdiocese of New York, for example, argued in the Supreme Court for a group of parents who supported the prayer. The response to the decision could hardly have been more diametrical. Cardinal Spellman declared, "I am shocked and frightened. . . ." The New York Board of Rabbis, on the other hand, hailed the decision: "The recitation of prayers in the public schools, which is tantamount to the teaching of prayer, is not in conformity with the spirit of the American concept of the separation of church and state. All the religious groups in this country will best advance their respective faiths by adherence to this principle." The American Jewish Committee, the American Jewish Congress, and the Anti-Defamation League of B'nai B'rith strongly supported the Court. Only among the Orthodox was there mild disagreement with the Supreme Court decision.

Although the argument could certainly be made that the American Catholic Church ought to be the first to object to the spectacle of civil servants composing government prayers, and although many Catholic commentators noted that the decision strengthened the case for private Church-sponsored schools, the general Catholic reaction was most hostile. The Jesuit publication *America,* in an editorial "To our Jewish Friends," declared that Jewish efforts to assert an ever more strict separation of church and state were painting the Jewish community into a corner, where it would be isolated from the rest of Americans.

Significantly, Protestant reaction to the decision was mixed. The Brooklyn *Tablet* took the cue, stating that the crucial question raised by the decision was "What are the Protestants going to do about it? For, although this is a national problem, it is particularly a Protestant problem, given the large Protestant enrollment in the public schools. Catholics have been fighting long—and sometimes alone—against the Church-State extremists. May we count on Protestants to supply more leadership in this case? If so, we pledge our support to joint efforts against the common enemy: secularism."[7]

The subject of aid to Catholic schools is only one aspect of the more general issue of church-state relations, and here again the ethnic composition of New York City tends to produce the same alignment of opposing groups. There are elements within the Jewish community, again the Orthodox, that favor public assistance for religious schools, but the dominant view is opposed. In 1961 the New York Republican party at the state level made a tentative move toward the Catholic position by proposing a Constitutional amendment that would have permitted state construction loans to private institutions of higher learning, sectarian as well as secular. Opposition from Jewish (as well as some

---

[7]Quoted in the *New York Herald Tribune,* July 2, 1962.

Protestant) groups was pronounced, and the measure was beaten at the polls.

The situation developing in this area could soberly be termed dangerous. An element of interfaith competition has entered the controversy. As the costs of education mount, it becomes increasingly difficult to maintain the quality of the education provided by private schools deprived of public assistance. It is not uncommon to hear it stated in Catholic circles that the results of national scholarship competitions already point to the weakness of Catholic education in fields such as the physical sciences. The specter is raised that a parochial education will involve sacrifice for the students as well as for their parents.

There is understandably much resentment within Catholic educational circles at the relative crudity of most such observations. At the same time this resentment is often accompanied by an unmistakable withdrawal. In a thoughtful address calling for more meticulous assessment of the qualities of Catholic education, Bishop McEntegart of the Diocese of Brooklyn went on to state that "Judgment on the effectiveness of an educational system should be something more profound and more subtle than counting heads of so-called intellectuals who happen to be named in Who's Who or the 'Social Register.'"[8]

Whether the course of the controversy will lead Catholics further into separatist views of this kind is not clear. But it is abundantly evident that so long as Catholics maintain a separate education system and the rest of the community refuses to help support it by tax funds or tax relief, a basic divisive issue will exist. This will be an ethnic issue in measure that the Catholic community continues to include the bulk of the Irish, Italian, and Polish population in the city, at least the bulk of those affiliated with organizations taking a position on the issue. If, as may very well happen, the Catholic abandon elementary and even

---

[8]*The Tablet*, February 17, 1962. In an address given in Washington on April 30, 1962, Very Reverend William F. Kelley, S.J., President of Marquette University, implicitly proposed a secondary role for Catholic education. As reported in *The Washington Post*, Father Kelley suggested that Catholic schools leave "research and the exploration for new knowledge" to "research institutes" like Hopkins, Harvard, and M.I.T., it being "perfectly respectable and professionally honorable" to concentrate on the transmission of the knowledge of the past:

It is an entirely sound plan to be trailing along at a respectable distance with a trained and educated citizenry competent to appreciate and consume the discovery of the successful investigator. Let us remember that if there are no followers, there can be no leader.

secondary education to concentrate on their colleges and universities, the larger issue of church-state relations will no doubt subside.

But it is not the single issue of school aid, no matter how important and long-lived it is, that alone shapes the polarization between the Jewish and the emerging Catholic community. There have been other issues in the past—for example, the struggle over the legitimacy of city hospitals giving advice on birth control, which put Jews and liberal Protestants on one side and Catholics on the other. There are the recurrent disputes over government censorship of books and movies and magazines that have become freer and freer in their handling of sex and sexual perversion. This again ranges Jewish and Protestant supports of the widest possible freedom of speech against Catholics who are more anxious about the impact of such material on young people and family life. One can see emerging such issues as the rigid state laws on divorce and abortion.[9]

Many of these issues involve Catholic *religious* doctrine. But there exists here a situation that is broader than a conflict over doctrines and the degree to which government should recognize them. What is involved is the emergence of two subcultures, two value systems, shaped and defined certainly in part by religious practice and experience and organization but by now supported by the existence of two communities. If the bishops and the rabbis were to disappear tomorrow, the subcultures and subcommunities would remain. One is secular in its attitudes, liberal in its outlook on sexual life and divorce, positive about science and social science. The other is religious in its outlook, resists the growing liberalization in sexual mores and its reflection in cultural and family life, feels strongly the tension between moral values and modern science and technology. The conflict may be seen in many ways—not least in the fact that the new disciplines such as psychoanalysis, particularly in New York, are so largely staffed by Jews.

Thus a Jewish ethos and a Catholic ethos emerge: they are more strongly affected by a specific religious doctrine in the Catholic case than in the Jewish, but neither is purely the expression of the spirit of a religion. Each is the result of the interplay of religion, ethnic group, American setting, and specific issues. The important fact is that the differences in values and attitudes between the two groups do not, in general, become smaller with time. On the contrary: there is prob-

---

[9]See *A Tale of Ten Cities*, Albert Vorspan and Eugene Lipman, New York: *Union of American Hebrew Congregations*, 1962, pp. 175 ff.

ably a wider gap between Jews and Catholics in New York today than in the days of Al Smith.[10]

Negroes and Puerto Ricans

A close examination of Catholic-Jewish relations will reveal some of the tendency of ethnic relations in New York to be a form of class relations as well. However, the tendency is unmistakably clear with regard to the Negroes and Puerto Ricans. Some 22 per cent of the population of the city is now Negro or Puerto Rican, and the proportion will increase. (Thirty-six per cent of the births in 1961 were Negro or Puerto Rican.) To a degree that cannot fail to startle anyone who encounters the reality for the first time, the overwhelming portion of both groups constitutes a submerged, exploited, and very possible permanent proletariat.

New York is properly regarded as the wealthiest city in the nation. Its more affluent suburbs enjoy some of the highest standards of living on earth. In the city itself white-collar wages are high, and skilled labor through aggressive trade union activity has obtained almost unprecedented standards. Bricklayers earn $5.35 an hour, plus 52¢ for pension, vacation, and insurance benefits. Electricians have a nominal twenty-five hour week and a base pay of $4.96 an hour plus fringe benefits.[11] But amidst such plenty, unbelievable squalor persists: the line of demarcation is a color line in the case of Negroes, a less definite but equally real ethnic line in the case of Puerto Ricans.

The relationships between the rise of the Negro-Puerto Rican labor supply and the decline of industrial wages is unmistakable. In 1950 there were 246,000 Puerto Ricans in the city. By 1960 this number had increased by two and one-half times to 613,000, or 8 per cent. In 1950 the average hourly earnings of manufacturing production workers in New York City ranked tenth in the nation. By 1960 they ranked thirtieth. In the same period comparable wages in Birmingham, Alabama, rose from thirty-third to tenth. In 1959 median family income for

---

[10]Gerhard Lenski, *The Religious Factor*, New York: Doubleday, 1961, gives a great deal of evidence to the effect that value differences between Catholics and white Protestants and Jews (the latter two often linked, but not always) in Detroit have increased as the groups move from working-class and immigrant generation to middle-class and later generations. Parochial schooling plays some part in these differences. For an interesting evocation of the milieu in which Jewish-Catholic political cooperation flourished, see *Al Smith*, by Oscar Handlin, Boston: Little, Brown, 1958.

[11]U. S. Bureau of Labor Statistics data for October, 1962.

Puerto Ricans was $3,811 as against $6,091 for all the city's families (and $8,052 for suburbs of Westchester). In 1962 average weekly earnings of manufacturing production workers were 19 per cent higher in Birmingham than in New York City, 15 per cent higher in New Orleans, and almost 10 per cent higher in the nation as a whole.

These economic conditions vastly reinforce the ethnic distinctions that serve to separate the Negro community and the Puerto Rican community from the rest of the city. The Negro separation is strengthened by the fact that the colored community is on the whole Protestant, and much of its leadership comes from Protestant clergy. Thus the Negroes provide the missing element of the Protestant-Catholic-Jew triad.

Housing segregation, otherwise an intolerable offense to the persons affected, serves nonetheless to ensure the Negroes a share of seats on the City Council and in the State Legislature and Congress. This power, as well as their voting power generally, has brought Negro political leaders to positions of considerable prominence. Following the 1961 mayoralty election, Mayor Wagner appointed the talented Harlem leader, J. Raymond Jones, as a political secretary through whom he would deal with all the Democratic party organizations of the city. Puerto Ricans have only begun to make their influence felt, but they are clearly on the way to doing so.

Their fate gives them an interest in the same issues: the housing of the poor in a city of perpetual housing shortage; the raising of the wages of the poorly paid service semiskilled occupations in which most of them work; the development of new approaches to raising motivation and capacity by means of education and training in the depressed areas of the city. They live adjacent to each other in vast neighborhoods. And they cooperate on many specific issues—for example, in fighting urban renewal programs that would displace them. But there are deeply felt differences between them. The more Americanized group is also more deeply marked by color. The furtive hope of the new group that it may move ahead as other immigrants have without the barrier of color, and the powerful links of language and culture that mark off the Puerto Ricans, suggest that, despite the fact that the two groups increasingly comprise the proletariat of the city, their history will be distinct.

Thus the cast of major characters for the next decades is complete: the Jews; the Catholics, subdivided at least into Irish and Italian components; the Negroes; the Puerto Ricans; and, of course, the white Anglo-Saxon Protestants. These latter, ranging from the Rockefeller brothers to reform district leaders in the Democratic party are, man for man, among the most influential and powerful persons in the city, and will continue to play a conspicuous and creative role in almost every aspect of the life of the metropolis.

The Role of Politics

The large movements of history and people which tend to reinforce the role of the ethnic groups in the city have been accompanied by new developments in political life which similarly strengthen ethnic identities. This is a complicated matter, but we can point to a number of elements. First, there is some tendency (encouraged by the development of genuine ethnic-class combinations) to substitute ethnic issues in politics for class issues. Second, there has been a decline in the vigor and creativity of politics in New York City, which seems to make New York politicians prefer to deal in terms of premelting pot verities rather than to cope with the chaotic present. Third, the development of public opinion polling would seem to have significantly strengthened the historic tendency of New York political parties to occupy the same middle ground on substantive issues, and indirectly has the effect of strengthening the ethnic component in political campaigns. As competing parties and factions use substantially the same polling techniques, they get substantially the same information about the likes and dislikes of the electorate. Hence they tend to adopt similar positions on political issues. (In much the same way, the development of marketing survey techniques in business has produced standardized commercial products such as cigarettes, automobiles, detergents, and so forth.) For the time being at least, this seems to have increased the importance of racial and ethnic distinctions that, like advertising, can still create distinctions in appearance even if little or none exist in fact. Everything we say in this field is highly speculative, but the impression that the political patterns of the city strengthen the roles of ethnic groups is overwhelming.

It is not easy to illustrate the substitution of ethnic appeals for class appeals. To the extent it occurs, those involved would hope to conceal it, always assuming the practice is deliberate. The basic fact is that for the first half of the twentieth century New York was a center of political radicalism. Faced with fierce opposition, some at least of the left wing discovered that their best tactic was to couch class appeals in ethnic terms. In such manner Vito Marcantonio, a notorious fellow traveler, flourished in the United States Congress as an Italian representative of the Italians and Puerto Ricans of East Harlem. In response to such tactics, the traditional parties have themselves employed the ethnic shorthand to deal with what are essentially class problems. Thus much was made in terms of its ethnic significance of the appointment of a Puerto Rican as a City Commissioner responsible for the relocation of families affected by urban renewal projects, but behind this significance was the more basic one that the slum-dwelling proletariat of the city was being given some control over its housing. In much the same way the balanced ticket makes it possible to offer a slate of candidates ranging across the social spectrum—rich man, poor man, beggar man, thief—but to do so in terms of the ethnic groups represented rather than the classes. In a democratic culture that has never much liked to identify individuals in terms of social classes, and does so less in the aftermath of the radical 1930's and 1940's, the ethnic shorthand is a considerable advantage.

This is of course possible only because of the splintering of traditional economic classes along ethnic lines, which tends to create class-ethnic combinations that have considerable significance at the present time in New York. The sharp division and increasing conflict between the well-paid Jewish cutters in the International Ladies' Garment Workers' Union and the low-paid Negro and Puerto Rican majority in the union have been widely publicized. One Negro cutter hailed the union before the State Commission for Human Rights and obtained a favorable decision. Similar distinctions between skilled and unskilled workers are common enough throughout the trade unions of the city. At a higher level, not dissimilar patterns can be found among the large law firms and banks, where Protestant-Catholic-Jew distinctions exist and are important, even if somewhat less so than in past times.

From time to time the most significant issues of class relations assume ethnic form. Reform movements in New York City politics have invariably been class movements as well. Citing a study of Theodore Lowi, showing that reform in New York City has always meant a change in the class and ethnic background of top city appointees, James Q. Wilson summarized the phenomenon as follows:

> The three "reform" mayors preceding Wagner favored upper-middle-class Yankee Protestants six to one over the Irish as appointees. Almost 40 per cent of the appointees of Seth Low were listed in the Social Register. Further, all four reform mayors—Low, Mitchel, La Guardia, and Wagner—have appointed a much larger percentage of Jews to their cabinets than their regular organization predecessors.
>
> In fact, of course, the problem posed by the amateur Democrats is not simply one of ethnic succession. Militant reform leaders in Manhattan get angry when they hear this "explanation" of their motives,

for they reject the idea that ethnicity or religion ought to be considered at all in politics. Although most amateur Democrats are either Jewish or Anglo-Saxon and practically none are Catholic, it is not their entry into politics so much as it is their desire to see a certain political ethic (which middle-class Jews and Yankees happen to share) implemented in local politics.[12]

The 1961 Democratic primary fight, which ended with the defeat of Carmine DeSapio and the regular Democratic organization, was a mixture of class and ethnic conflict that produced the utmost bitterness. In the mayoralty election that followed, the Democratic State Chairman, Michael H. Prendergast, in an unprecedented move, came out in support of an independent candidate, a conservative Italian Catholic, Lawrence E. Gerosa, against Mayor Wagner, who was running for reelection with the support of the middle-class reform elements within the Democratic party. In a bitter *cri de coeur*, almost inevitably his last statement as an acknowledged political leader, Prendergast lashed out at what he regarded as a leftwing conspiracy to take over the Democratic party and merge it with the Liberal party of David Dubinsky and Alex Rose, in the process excluding the traditional Catholic leadership of the city democracy. He declared:

> The New York Post lays the whole plot bare in a signed column entitled "One Big Party?" in its September 27 issue. Every Democrat should read it. "The first prerequisite of the new coalition," James A. Wechsler writes, "is that Mayor Wagner win the election." He goes on to say that the new "troops" which Messrs. Dubinsky and Rose will bring to this alliance will have to fight a "rear-guard action" on the part of "Catholics of Irish descent" who, Mr. Wechsler declares, "take their temporal guidance from Patrick Scanlan and his Brooklyn Tablet propaganda sheet.

> . . . .

> It's time to call a spade a spade. The party of Al Smith's time was big enough for Democrats of all descent. The Democratic party of today is big enough for Americans of every race, creed, color or national origin.

Although much larger issues were at stake, it was natural enough for a traditionalist in politics such as Prendergast to describe the conflict

---

[12]James Q. Wilson, *The Amateur Democrat,* Chicago: University of Chicago Press, 1962, p. 304.

in ethnic terms. And in justice it must be said that the ethnic elements of the controversy were probably much more significant than Prendergast's opponents would likely admit.

Apart from the reform movement represented by the Committee for Democratic Voters (which has yet to wield any decisive power over city—or statewide political nominations), the level of political creativity in New York politics has not been high over the past several decades. The almost pathetic tendency to follow established patterns has been reinforced by the growing practice of nominating sons and grandsons of prominent public persons. The cast of such men as Roosevelt, Rockefeller, Harriman, Wagner, and Morgenthau seems almost bent on recreating the gaslight era. In this context the balanced ticket and the balanced distribution of patronage along ethnic lines have assumed an almost fervid sanctity—to the point indeed of caricature, as in the 1961 mayoralty contest in which the Republican team of Lefkowitz, Gilhooley, and Fino faced Democrats Wagner, Screvane, and Beame, the latter victors in a primary contest with Levitt, Mackell, and Di Fede. It will be noted that each ticket consisted of a Jew, an Italian Catholic, and an Irish Catholic, or German-Irish Catholic in the case of Wagner.

The development of polling techniques has greatly facilitated the calculations—and perhaps also the illusions—that go into the construction of a balanced ticket. It should be noted that these techniques would apply equally well, or badly, to all manner of social and economic classifications, but that so far it is the ethnic information that has attracted the interest of the political leaders and persons of influence in politics. Here, for example, is the key passage of the poll on the basis of which Robert M. Morgenthau was nominated as the Democratic candidate for governor in 1962:

The optimum way to look at the anatomy of the New York State electorate is to take three symbolic races for Governor and two for the Senate and compare them group by group. The three we will select for Governor are Screvane, Morgenthau, and Burke.* We select these because each represents a different fundamental assumption. Screvane makes sense as a candidate, if the election should be cast in terms of an extension of the Wagner-Rockefeller fight. This could have the advantage of potentially firming up a strong New York City vote, where, in fact, the election must be won by the Democrats. On the other hand, a Rockefeller-Screvane battle would make it more

---

*Paul R. Screvane, President of the City Council, an Italian Catholic; Robert M. Morgenthau, United States Attorney for the Southern District of New York, a Jew; Adrian P. Burke, Judge of the Court of Appeals, an Irish Catholic.

difficult to cast the election in national terms of Rockefeller vs. Kennedy, which, as we shall also see, is a critical dimension to pursue.

A Morgenthau-Rockefeller race is run mainly because it represents meeting the Rockefeller-Javits ticket on its own grounds of maximum strength: among Jewish and liberal-minded voters, especially in New York City. Morgenthau is the kind of name that stands with Lehman, and, as we shall see, has undoubted appeal with Jewish voters. The question of running a moderately liberal Jewish candidate for Governor is whether this would in turn lose the Democrats some conservative Catholic voters who are not enchanted with Rockefeller and Javits to begin with, but who might normally vote Republican.

The third tack that might be taken on the Governorship is to put up an outstanding Irish Catholic candidate on the assumption that with liberal Republicans Rockefeller and Javits running, the Catholic vote can be moved appreciably over to the Democratic column, especially in view of Rockefeller's divorce as a silent but powerful issue. Here, Court of Appeals Judge Adrian Burke, who far outstripped the statewide ticket in 1954 might be considered typical of this type of candidate.

Let us then look at each of these alternatives and see how the pattern of the vote varies by each. For it is certain that the key Democratic decision in 1962 must be over the candidate for Governor first, and then followed by the candidate for U.S. Senate. We also include the breakdowns by key groups for Bunche and Murrow against Javits.*

Here some fascinating and revealing patterns emerge which point the way sharply toward the kind of choice the Democrats can make optimally in their selection of Gubernatorial and Senatorial candidates for 1962 in New York:

—By area, it appears that the recent Democratic gains in the suburbs are quite solid, and a range of from 40 to 43 per cent of the vote seems wholly obtainable.

—By race and religion, we find equally revealing results. The Protestant vote is as low as it was for Kennedy in 1960, when the religious issue was running strong.

—By contrast, the Catholic vote remains relatively stable, with a slight play for Burke above the rest, and with Bunche and Murrow showing some weakness here. (The relative percentages, however, for

---

*Ralph J. Bunche, United Nations official, a Negro; Edward R. Murrow, Director, United States Information Agency, a white Protestant; Jacob K. Javits, United States Senator, a Jew.

KEY GROUP BREAKDOWNS †

	Democratic Candidates for Governor Pitted Against Rockefeller			Democratic Candidates for U.S. Senate Against Javits	
	Screvane	Burke	Morgenthau	Bunche	Murrow
	%	%	%	%	%
Statewide	47	43	49	47	46
By Area					
New York City (43%)	61	54	61	57	55
Suburbs (16%)	41	41	43	42	40
Upstate (41%)	35	35	40	40	40
By Occupation					
Business and Professional (14%)	35	22	30	57	33
White Collar (19%)	36	44	51	50	44
Sales and Service (8%)	49	49	54	42	42
Labor (34%)	56	53	57	34	52
Small Business, Shopkeeper (5%)	38	41	41	42	36
Retired and other (13%)	39	30	39	52	43
By Ethnic Groups					
White USA (29%)	35	37	36	36	40
Irish (9%)	44	49	44	48	36
English-Scotch (7%)	42	26	33	34	34
German (16%)	29	34	39	42	41
Italian (13%)	59	53	53	45	55
By Religion and Race					
White Protestant (37%)	27	27	29	35	32
White Catholic (37%)	51	54	51	42	48
White Jewish (18%)	70	56	82	71	61
Negro (8%)	70	55	68	93	74
Sex by Age					
Men (49%)	47	40	48	47	43
21–34 (15%)	42	39	40	43	34
35–49 (16%)	53	39	54	43	54
50 and over (18%)	48	43	51	55	42
Women (51%)	47	48	50	47	49
21–34 (15%)	56	56	58	55	45
35–49 (18%)	50	52	59	53	58
50 and over (18%)	39	35	36	37	41

† Each figure gives the percentage of total vote that the proposed candidate received in the specified category. Thus, 35 per cent of the business and professional vote were recorded as saying they would vote for Screvane against Rockefeller.

By Union Membership

Union Member (25%)	66	61	65	49	57
Union Family (11%)	56	59	57	52	47
Nonunion (64%)	38	35	42	45	40

By Income Groups

Upper Middle (22%)	33	20	32	40	27
Lower Middle (64%)	47	47	52	45	48
Low (14%)	63	61	62	66	61

a James A. Farley* race against Javits show Farley with 30 percent Protestant, a relatively lower standing; 58 percent of the Catholics, a very good showing, but with only 36 percent of the Jewish vote, a very poor result, and 67 per cent of the Negro vote, only a fair showing).

The really volatile votes in this election clearly are going to be the Jewish and Negro votes. The Jewish vote ranges from a low of 56 percent (for Burke); 61 percent for Murrow (against Javits); 70 percent for Screvane (against Rockefeller); a very good 71 percent for Bunche (against Javits); and a thumping 82 percent for Morgenthau (against Rockefeller). Here the conclusion is perfectly obvious: by running a Lehman type of Jewish candidate against Rockefeller, the Jewish vote can be anchored well up into the high 70's and even into the 80's. By running an Irish Catholic candidate against Rockefeller, the Jewish vote comes tumbling precipitously down into the 50's. What is more, with Javits on the ticket, with strong appeal among Jews, any weakness among Jews with the Gubernatorial candidate, and the defection of the Jewish vote can be large enough to reduce the city vote to disastrously low proportions for the Democrats.

The Negro vote is only slightly less volatile. It ranges from a low of 55 percent (for Burke, again); to 68 percent for Morgenthau, not too good (an indication that Negroes will not automatically vote for a Jewish candidate, there being friction between the two groups); 70 percent for Screvane (who carried over some of the strong Wagner appeal among Negroes); 74 percent for Murrow, a good showing; and an incredibly high 93 percent for Bunche.

Observation: The conclusion for Governor seems self-evident from these results. A candidate who would run in the Wagner image, such as Screvane, would poll a powerful New York vote, but would fade more upstate and would not pull in a full measure of the Jewish swing vote. An Irish Catholic candidate would not do appreciably better than Screvane upstate (a pattern that has been repeated throughout New York's modern political history, with Kennedy the sole exception in 1960), but with good appeal in the suburbs, yet with a disastrous

---

*James A. Farley, former Postmaster General, an Irish Catholic.

showing among Jews and Negroes in New York City. A Lehman-type Jewish candidate, such as Morgenthau, by contrast, would appeal to a number of Protestants upstate (as, indeed, Lehman always did in his runs), would hold well in the suburbs, and could bring in solidly the pivotal Jewish vote in New York City.

The first choice must be a Jewish candidate for Governor of the highest caliber. (*sic.*)

There are two things to note about this poll. In the first place, the New York Jews did *not* vote solidly for Morgenthau, who lost by half a million votes. A week before the election Morgenthau headquarters received a report that a follow-up poll showed that 50 percent of New York City Jews who had voted for the Democratic candidate Averell Harriman in 1958 were undecided about voting for Morgenthau four years later. An analysis of the vote cast in predominately Jewish election districts shows that Rockefeller significantly improved his performance over 1958, when he had run against Averell Harriman, another white Protestant. In important areas such as Long Beach, Rockefeller went from 37.2 percent in 1958 to 62.7 percent in 1962, which is sufficient evidence that a Jewish name alone does not pull many votes. It could also confirm the preelection fears of the Democrats that the notoriety of their search for a "Lehman type of Jewish candidate" had produced a strong resentment within the Jewish community. The following are returns from predominantly Jewish districts:

	Rockefeller			Javits		
	1962	1958	Dif.	1962	1956	Dif.
NEW YORK CITY						
Bronx AD 2, School 90	27.2	20.5	+6.7	41.9	19.2	+22.7
3	21.6	18.7	+2.9	44.0	17.5	+26.5
5	26.4	19.8	+6.6	39.9	21.4	+18.5
Queens AD 7 School 164	43.8	36.5	+7.3	66.5	32.0	+34.5
SUBURBS						
Jericho (part)	50.7	34.4	+16.3	60.7	36.1	+24.6
Long Beach (part)	62.7	37.2	+25.5	66.2	34.3	+31.9
Harrison (part)	71.3	69.6	+1.7	71.4	64.6	+6.8
New Rochelle Ward 4	57.8	58.8	−1.0	57.1	55.8	+1.3

These returns, which are typical enough, reveal an important fact about ethnic voting. Class interests and geographical location are the dominant influences in voting behavior, whatever the ethnic group involved. In urban, Democratic Bronx, the great majority of Jews vote Democratic. In suburban, Republican Westchester, the next county, the great majority of Jews vote Republican. But within that over-all pattern a definite ethnic swing does occur. Thus Rockefeller got barely a fifth of the vote in the third Assembly district of Democratic Bronx, while he got almost three-quarters in Harrison in Republican Westchester, *but he improved his performance in both areas* despite the fact that his 1962 plurality was lower, statewide, than 1948. Similarly, Rockefeller got as little as 8.8 percent of the vote in the predominately Negro third ward of Democratic Albany, and as much as 76 percent in upper-middle-class, Republican Rye in Westchester, but generally speaking, Rockefeller appears to have lost Negro votes in 1962 over 1958.

A second point to note is that while the poll provided detailed information on the response to the various potential candidates classified by sex, occupational status, and similar characteristics of the persons interviewed, the candidates proposed were all essentially ethnic prototypes, and the responses analyzed in the commentary were those on the ethnic line. These are terms, howsoever misleading, which are familiar to New York politics, and with which New York politicians prefer to deal.

The Future

We have tried to show how deeply the pattern of ethnicity is impressed on the life of the city. Ethnicity is more than an influence on events; it is commonly the source of events. Social and political institutions do not merely respond to ethnic interests; a great number of institutions exist for the specific purpose of serving ethnic interests. This in turn tends to perpetuate them. In many ways, the atmosphere of New York City is hospitable to ethnic groupings: it recognizes them, and rewards them, and to that extent encourages them.

This is not to say that no individual group will disappear. This, on the contrary, is a recurring phenomenon. The disappearance of the Germans is a particularly revealing case.

In terms of size or the achievements of its members, the Germans ought certainly to be included among the principal ethnic groups of the city. If never quite as numerous as the Irish, they were indisputably the second largest group in the late nineteenth century, accounting

for perhaps a third of the population and enjoying the highest reputation. But today, while German influence is to be seen in virtually
every aspect of the city's life, the Germans *as a group* are vanished.
No appeals are made to the German vote, there are no German
politicians in the sense that there are Irish or Italian politicians, there
are in fact few Germans in political life and, generally speaking, no
German component in the structure of the ethnic interests of the city.

The logical explanation of this development, in terms of the
presumed course of American social evolution, is simply that the
Germans have been "assimilated" by the Anglo-Saxon center. To
some extent this has happened. The German immigrants of the nineteenth century were certainly much closer to the old Americans than
were the Irish who arrived in the same period. Many were Protestants,
many were skilled workers or even members of the professions, and
their level of education in general was high. Despite the language
difference, they did not seem nearly so alien to the New York mercan-
tile establishment as did the Irish. At the time of their arrival German
sympathies were high in New York. (George Templeton Strong was
violent in his support of doughty Prussia in its struggle with imperial,
tyrannical France.) All of this greatly facilitated German assimilation.

In any event, there were obstacles to the Germans' becoming a
distinct ethnic bloc. Each of the five groups we have discussed arrived
with a high degree of homogeneity: in matters of education, skills,
and religion the members of the group were for the most part alike.
This homogeneity, as we have tried to show, invested ethnicity with
meaning and importance that it would not otherwise have had. But
this was not so with the Germans, who were split between Catholics
and Protestants, liberals and conservatives, craftsmen and businessmen
and laborers. They reflected, as it were, an entire modern society, not
simply an element of one. The only things all had in common were
the outward manifestations of German culture: language for a generation or two, and after that a fondness for certain types of food and
drink and a consciousness of the German fatherland. This was a powerful enough bond and would very likely be visible today, except for
the impact of the World Wars. The Germanophobia of America during
the First World War is, of course, notorious. It had limits in New York
where, for instance, German was *not* driven from the public school
curriculum, but the attraction of things German was marred. This
period was followed, in hardly more than a decade, by the Nazi era,
during which German fascism made its appearance in Jewish New
York with what results one can imagine. The German American

Bund was never a major force in the city, but it did exist. The revulsion against Nazism extended indiscriminately to things German. Thereafter, German Americans, as shocked by the Nazis as any, were disinclined to make overmuch of their national origins.

Even so, it is not clear that consciousness of German nationality has entirely ceased to exist among German-Americans in the city, or elsewhere. There is evidence that for many it has simply been submerged. In New York City, which ought logically to be producing a series of Italian and Jewish mayors, the political phenomenon of the postwar period has been Robert F. Wagner.

It is even possible that the future will see a certain resurgence of German identity in New York, although we expect it will be mild. The enemy of two world wars has become an increasingly powerful and important ally in the Cold War. Berlin has become a symbol of resistance to totalitarianism; Germany has become an integral part of the New Europe. Significantly, the German Americans of the city have recently begun an annual Steuben Day Parade, adding for the politicians of the city yet another command performance at an ethnic outing.

Despite this mild German resurgence, it is a good general rule that except where color is involved as well the specifically *national* aspect of most ethnic groups rarely survives the third generation in any significant terms. The intermarriage which de Crèvecoeur described continues apace, so that even the strongest national traditions are steadily diluted. The groups do not disappear, however, because of their *religious* aspect which serves as the basis of a subcommunity, and a subculture. Doctrines and practices are modified to some extent to conform to an American norm, but a distinctive set of values is nurtured in the social groupings defined by religious affiliation. This is quite contrary to early expectations. It appeared to de Crèvecoeur, for example, that religious as well as national identity was being melted into one by the process of mixed neighborhoods and marriage:

> . . . This mixed neighborhood will exhibit a strange religious medley, that will be neither pure Catholicism nor pure Calvinism. A very perceptible indifference even in the first generation, will become apparent; and it may happen that the daughter of the Catholic will marry the son of the seceder, and settle by themselves at a distance from their parents. What religious education will they give their children? A very imperfect one. If there happens to be in the neighborhood any place of worship, we will suppose a Quaker's meeting; rather than not shew their fine clothes, they will go to it, and some of them may attach them-

selves to that society. Others will remain in a perfect state of indifference; the children of these zealous parents will not be able to tell what their religious principles are, and their grandchildren still less.

Thus all sects are mixed as well as all nations; thus religious indifference is imperceptibly disseminated from one continent to the other; which is at present one of the strongest characteristics of the Americans.[13]

If this was the case in the late eighteenth century, it is no longer. Religious identities are strongly held by New Yorkers, and Americans generally, and they are for the most part transmitted by blood line from the original immigrant group. A great deal of intermarriage occurs among nationality groups of the three great religious groups, of the kind Ruby Jo Kennedy described in New Haven, Connecticut under the general term of the Triple Melting Pot,[14] but this does not weaken religious identity. When marriages occur between different religions, often one is dominant, and the result among the children is not indifference, but an increase in the numbers of one of the groups.

Religion and race seem to define the major groups into which American society is evolving as the specifically national aspect of ethnicity declines. In our large American cities, four major groups emerge: Catholics, Jews, white Protestants, and Negroes, each making up the city in different proportions. This evolution is by no means complete. And yet we can discern that the next stage of the evolution of the immigrant groups will involve a Catholic group in which the distinctions between Irish, Italian, Polish, and German Catholic are steadily reduced by intermarriage; A Jewish group, in which the line between East European, German, and Near Eastern Jews is already weak; the Negro group; and a white Protestant group, which adds to its Anglo-Saxon and Dutch old-stock elements German and Scandinavian Protestants, as well as, more typically, the white Protestant immigrants to the city from the interior.

The white Protestants are a distinct ethnic group in New York, one that has probably passed its low point and will now begin to grow in numbers and probably also in influence. It has its special occupations, with the customary freemasonry. This involves the banks, corporation front offices, educational and philanthropic institutions, and the law offices who serve them. It has its own social world (epitomized by,

---

[13]de Crèvecoeur, *op. cit.*, pp. 65-66.

[14]Ruby Jo Reeves Kennedy, "Single or Triple Melting Pot: Intermarriage in New Haven," *American Journal of Sociology*, Vol. 58, No. 1, July, 1952, pp. 55-66.

but by no means confined to, the *Social Register*), its own churches, schools, voluntary organizations and all the varied institutions of a New York minority. These are accompanied by the characteristic styles in food, clothing, and drink, special family patterns, special psychological problems and ailments. For a long while political conservatism, as well as social aloofness, tended to keep the white Protestants out of the main stream of New York politics, much in the way that political radicalism tended to isolate the Jews in the early parts of the century. Theodore Roosevelt, when cautioned that none of his friends would touch New York politics, had a point in replying that it must follow that none of his friends were members of the governing classes.

There has been a resurgence of liberalism within the white Protestant group, in part based on its growth through vigorous young migrants from outside the city, who are conspicuous in the communications industry, law firms, and corporation offices of New York. These are the young people that supported Adlai Stevenson and helped lead and staff the Democratic reform movement. The influence of the white Protestant group on this city, it appears, must now grow as its numbers grow.

In this large array of the four major religio-racial groups, where do the Puerto Ricans stand? Ultimately perhaps they are to be absorbed into the Catholic group. But that is a long time away. The Puerto Ricans are separated from the Catholics as well as the Negroes by color and culture. One cannot even guess how this large element will ultimately relate itself to the other elements of the city; perhaps it will serve, in line with its own nature and genius, to soften the sharp lines that divide them.

Protestants will enjoy immunities in politics even in New York. When the Irish era came to an end in the Brooklyn Democratic party in 1961, Joseph T. Sharkey was succeeded by a troika (as it was called) of an Irish Catholic, a Jew, and a Negro Protestant. The last was a distinguished clergyman, who was at the same time head of the New York City Council of Protestant Churches. It would have been unlikely for a rabbi, unheard of for a priest, to hold such a position.

Religion and race define the next stage in the evolution of the American peoples. But the American nationality is still forming: its processes are mysterious, and the final form, if there is ever to be a final form, is as yet unknown.